The Secret Life of Words

Also by Henry Hitchings

Dr Johnson's Dictionary

The Secret Life of Words

How English Became English

HENRY HITCHINGS

JOHN MURRAY

First published in Great Britain in 2008 by John Murray (Publishers)
An Hachette Livre UK company

5

© Henry Hitchings 2008

The right of Henry Hitchings to be identified as the Author of the
Work has been asserted by him in accordance with the Copyright,
Designs and Patents Act 1988.

A CIP catalogue record for this title is available from the British Library

ISBN 978-0-7195-6454-3

Typeset in Bembo by Palimpsest Book Production Limited
Grangemouth, Stirlingshire

Printed and bound by Clays Ltd, St Ives plc

John Murray policy is to use papers that are natural,
renewable and recyclable products and
made from wood grown in sustainable forests.
The logging and manufacturing processes are
expected to conform to the environmental regulations
of the country of origin.

John Murray (Publishers)
338 Euston Road
London NW1 3BH

www.johnmurray.co.uk

Contents

1. Ensemble

Together, at the same time; the united performance of all voices

From the French, which derives from the late Latin *insimul*, comprising *in*, 'in', and *simul*, 'at the same time'

'All these trifling things . . . collectively form that pleasing *je ne sais quoi*, that *ensemble*' – Lord Chesterfield, 1748

On a smoky October morning in 1697, a Puritan magistrate called Samuel Sewall went to visit the Lieutenant Governor at Dorchester, which is now a suburb of Boston on the American east coast. Born in England, in a rural part of Hampshire, Sewall had arrived in America as an adolescent. He had studied at Harvard, had managed the Boston printing press, and in 1692 had been one of the nine judges appointed to hear the Salem witch trials. Not long before his trip to Dorchester he had publicly expressed shame over his role in the last of these, but that October morning this bulky, big-framed figure had more appetizing business on his mind. Dorchester seems to have been a place to go for good things to eat; Sewall had once taken his wife, Hannah, there so they could feast on cherries and raspberries. At the Lieutenant Governor's he met with his friend Samuel Torrey, a man chiefly distinguished for having declined the presidency of Harvard College, and together they breakfasted on 'Venison and Chockalatte', with Sewall amusedly reflecting that 'Massachuset and Mexico met at his Honour's Table.'[1]

Samuel Sewall's breakfast sounds a little quirky, but its two elements are richly symbolic. The venison was indeed good Massachusetts fare, even if the taste for it was one he had acquired not in New England, but in England's New Forest. The word, meanwhile, derived from the Latin *venari*, 'to hunt', and had entered English through French following the Norman Conquest – one of many culinary

1

markers of the Normans' influence. At first in English it had applied to the flesh not just of deer, but also of hare, rabbit and even boar. By the fifteenth century it seems to have been widely understood as restricted to deer's meat, and this is what Sewall's venison will almost certainly have been, although it is worth noting that John Josselyn writes in *New England's Rarities* (1672) that 'Bears are very fat in the fall of the leaf, at which time they are excellent venison.' We can be sure, regardless, that the dish Sewall ate tasted wild and gamy. But what of its accompaniment? He and Samuel Torrey consumed something we would not now recognize as chocolate. To English-speakers of the seventeenth century, *chocolate* usually denoted the drink made from the dark pods of the cacao tree or – Sewall's preferred form – a ball of paste confected out of these. Its name had been learnt from the Spanish, who had heard in Nahuatl, the ethereal language of the Aztecs, the noun *xocoatl*, meaning 'bitter water'.

That breakfast in Dorchester was a blend, then, of the old and the new, in terms of both gastronomy and vocabulary. Moreover, old and new alike were 'borrowed'. 'We . . . have been remarkable borrowers,' the philologist James Harris could opine half a century after Sewall's breakfast. By 'We' he meant speakers of English, and he cited the examples of literary terminology taken from Greek, the language of music from Italian, and terms of cookery from French. 'These many and very different Sources of our Language may be the cause, why it so deficient in *Regularity* . . . Yet we have this advantage to compensate the defect, that what we want in *Elegance*, we gain in *Copiousness*.'[2]

These many and different sources are the ingredients of this book. English was imported into Britain, as it later was into North America: the history of this hybrid tongue and above all of its vocabulary, which has proved hospitable to words from more than 350 other languages, is the history of who its speakers really are. So this is the story of the acquisitiveness of English, and of the meetings between what purists may label 'our' language and the external influences that have shaped it. At the same time, it considers the roles of individual people in this history, as agents and as barriers.

We need to communicate – that much is clear. Words bind us together, and can drive us apart. Not all communication is verbal, but language is our most dynamic instrument of communication, and words, imperfect though they often are, prove more lasting than gestures. We tend to accept unquestioningly our ability to express ourselves in language: the sources of our language and its power are rarely of concern to us. From time to time we may pause to wonder what, if anything, a *walnut* has to do with walls, or why, when it is not a kind of fish, a *crayfish* is so called. Actually, the word *walnut* is a modern form of the Old English *walhnutu*, which literally meant 'foreign nut'. The nut grew mainly in Italy, and when introduced into northern Europe it was labelled 'foreign' in order to distinguish it from the native hazelnut. For its part, *crayfish* is a corruption of the Old French name for this freshwater crustacean, *crevice*, which derived from the German *crebiz* and survives in modern French as *écrevisse*. Its *fish*-y quality is the result of a sort of creative mishearing. The important point, though, is that we seldom ask why we speak the language that we do, what we have in common with its other speakers, what its pedigree and career tell us about our ancestors, or what particular ways it has of framing our perceptions of the world. Perhaps we should.

Language is a social energy, and our capacity for articulate speech is the key factor that makes us different from other species. We are not as fast as cheetahs – or even as horses. Nor are we as strong as bulls or as adaptable as bacteria. But our brains are equipped with the facility to produce and process speech, and we are capable of abstract thought. A bee may dance to show other bees the location of a source of food, a green monkey may deliver sophisticated vocal signals, and a sparrow may manage as many as thirteen different types of song, but an animal's system of communication has a limited repertoire: ours, on the other hand, is 'open', and its mechanisms permit a potentially infinite variety of utterances.[3] For at least 80,000 years and perhaps as many as 150,000, language has enabled the sharing of ideas, communication between and within different groups, warfare (and its avoidance), courtship and mating, and the manufacture of what we may broadly label 'tools'.

Every language has a character. Our relationship with our own language can be complacent, but when we speak a foreign tongue we sense more keenly the 'characterfulness' of that language, the peculiar ways it channels history and culture, its special version of the world, its distinctive textures and codes. Different languages seem suited to different areas of experience. Tradition has it that Charles V, the Holy Roman Emperor, preferred to speak French to diplomats, Italian to ladies, German to stable boys and Spanish to God. English he seems to have used sparingly – to talk to geese. Nicholas Ostler, in his macro-history *Empires of the Word*, sketches 'some of the distinctive traits of the various traditions: Arabic's austere grandeur and egalitarianism; Chinese and Egyptian's unshakeable self-regard; Sanskrit's luxuriating classifications and hierarchies; Greek's self-confident innovation leading to self-obsession and pedantry; Latin's civic sense; Spanish rigidity, cupidity, and fidelity; French admiration for rationality; and English admiration for business acumen'.[4] This type of generalization is attractive, albeit limiting, and hints at a deeper truth: that our languages reveal the nature of our world, and the history of their development is a history of consciousness.

Studying language enables an archaeology of human experience: words contain the fossils of past dreams and traumas. If you are reading this book in its original English, you and I are sharing not only a language, but also an assortment of inherited values and cultural traditions, for our language contains traces of the histories of those who have spoken and written it before us. Even if we are at odds in many of our attitudes, we share certain modes of expression that are unique to this language – sayings, for instance, and clichés, shibboleths and slang. We share a sense of the familiar associations of words. Our language creates communities and solidarities, as well as divisions and disagreements. These are very possibly imaginary or illusory, but potent all the same.

Words are witnesses. To quote George Steiner, 'When using a word we wake into resonance . . . its entire previous history.'[5] When new territory is breached, its novelty is reflected in language. I am sure you will have had the experience of looking up a word in a dictionary and finding that it comes from somewhere else. But there are other languages whose speakers will not have shared this.

A person who speaks Arabic or, say, Hungarian will be able to trace most of the elements of his or her vocabulary back to that language's now-exhausted ancestors, rather than to other living languages. English is, to an unusual degree, a place of strange meetings.

This has prompted some to label English 'promiscuous', a whore among languages. The image is useful, but it needs tightening a little: it is a mistake to think that English is wonderfully (or shamefully) open to offers. Its adventures have been many and various, but its appetites have been confident, not insecure. In one sense, English *has* proved to be a whore among languages: in order for it to lay itself open to new intrusions or infusions, there has usually had to be a clear offer of reward. The supposed hospitality of the English language is not exactly benevolent. Sensitivity to the routes by which words have entered our language is important to our understanding of who we are, and this understanding, while often invigorating, can also be unsettling, a reminder of a turbulent, brutal or exploitative past.

Initially English was coerced into absorbing foreign terms, as Latin, Norse and French influences encroached on its territory. Since then, in the course of its travels, English has reversed the process, forcing itself on speakers of many other languages. It has done so not thanks to any special qualities it possesses, but because political events have made it so useful and necessary a language to understand. Its history is a history of encounters – profound, lucrative, violent. Yet to those who know the language intimately it has a strange power of alchemy, the capacity to transform whatever it touches.

A new word is a solution to a problem. It answers a need – intellectual, experiential. Often the need is obvious, but sometimes it is unseen or barely felt, and then it is only in finding something to plug the gap that we actually realize the gap was there in the first place. We all know the experience of coming up against a new word. I could have written 'seeing' or 'hearing', but the preposition *against* has its place here: when we encounter a word we have not seen before, the experience is a collision. What did you think the first time you chanced upon *chutzpah*, which is of Yiddish origin, or *aficionado*, which is from Spanish and originally denoted a devotee of bull-fighting? A likely reaction is bewilderment: what *is* this word? A second reaction is to ask what its existence tells us. A third is to start using it.

We relish playing with words: making them up, acquiring them, bending them to new purposes. Often this book examines writers who have used language innovatively. Some are chosen because of their enduring influence, others because they are barometers of their age's linguistic atmosphere. Imaginative writing is, to paraphrase George Orwell, a flank attack on positions inaccessible from the front; one of a writer's weapons is novelty, the potency of a new technique or term. We owe *pandemonium* to Milton's *Paradise Lost* (where it is 'the high Capital of Satan and his Peers'), *diplomacy* to Edmund Burke, and *pessimism* to Samuel Taylor Coleridge. *Picnic* was first used by the Earl of Chesterfield, the modish eighteenth-century politico and arbiter of public taste, whose letters were considered by Dr Johnson to 'teach the morals of a whore and the manners of a dancing master'. Sir Thomas Browne, an eccentric doctor and collector who lived during the seventeenth century, seems to have coined *amphibious* and *anomalous*. Among more recent innovators was the Russian-born Vladimir Nabokov, whose novel *Bend Sinister* is trophied with delightful oddities like *kwazinka* ('a slit between the folding parts of a screen') and *shchekotiki* (which is 'half-tingle, half-tickle').[6]

The American essayist Ralph Waldo Emerson argued that 'Language is the archives of history': additions to a language may signal a new political movement, a recent discovery, or a sweeping revision of attitudes. Spotting innovations in language affords us an impression of the changing practical, intellectual, social and aesthetic needs of society. Our changing pleasures and priorities, along with our dislikes and anxieties, are reflected in our vocabulary. Words become obsolete as the things they denote disappear or significantly alter; plenty of loans lapse, though some, having done so, are later renewed.

English has existed for only 1,500 years. Its history is usually divided into two periods: in the first, which lasted up until the end of the sixteenth century, the language was being formed; and since then it has been spread – or, in academic parlance, propagated – throughout the world. (This, at least, is the standard view, although a handful of mavericks have put forward a different account – suggesting, among other things, that English was being spoken in Britain before the arrival of the Romans, and that Latin is partly derived from English, rather than the other way round.[7]) Over its lifetime, English has come into contact with a vast range of other languages, at first through contact with invaders and colonists, and then through its speakers' colonial and commercial exploits, which have conveyed the language into almost every corner of the world, forever accumulating new material along the way.

A thousand years ago there were about 50,000 English words: today, according to whose estimate you accept, there are 700,000, 1 million or even double that number.

Very few 'new' words are fresh coinages. Most are borrowings, compounds, fusions of existing terms, or revivals of old ones. Prefixes and suffixes can multiply the terms that branch from a single root. Abbreviations evolve in step with our desire to speed life up. A word which has traditionally been one part of speech can become another: take for example the development of *executive*, which was an adjective for 150 years before it became also a noun. We are familiar with the way a word can extend its meaning: experience amplifies it, or hammers it down to an airy sort of thinness. Misunderstandings, be they ingenuous or wilful, are another source of new words. So is 'back-formation', in which a word is created by removing a prefix or suffix from a longer word that already exists. Examples are the verbs *to sculpt*, which first appears long after *sculptor* and *sculpture*, and *to enthuse*, which is antedated by *enthusiasm*. *Genetic* was used in its technical sense by Charles Darwin in *On The Origin of Species* (1859), but Wilhelm Johannsen's coinage *gene* is not attested till 1911. Of all these types of novelty, borrowings are the most provoking, for they testify to one culture chafing against another.

Our vocabulary is amazingly heterogeneous. Fewer than a quarter of today's English words reflect the language's Germanic origins. Mention of these Germanic origins seems an appropriate moment to speak briefly of English's place among the languages of the world. The West Germanic group to which it belongs includes not just

German, but also Dutch, Yiddish and Luxemburgish. Among its North Germanic relatives are Danish, Norwegian, Swedish, Icelandic and – most obscurely – Faroese. These two groups, along with the extinct East Germanic languages (chief among them Gothic), are parts of the much larger Indo-European family of languages. This includes the Italic group, which contains Latin and today consists principally of the Romance languages French, Spanish, Catalan, Portuguese, Romanian and Italian. The Indo-European family also encompasses Slavic languages such as Russian, Bulgarian, Polish and Czech; Baltic ones (Latvian, Lithuanian); Indo-Iranian ones, among them Persian, Gujarati, Bengali and Kurdish; together with Greek, Albanian, Armenian and the extinct Tocharian languages spoken within the ancient trade network known as the Silk Road. According to one popular hypothesis, the common ancestor of these languages, 'Proto-Indo-European', was spread by the advance of farming about 9,000 years ago.[8] Many of these languages parted company several millennia ago: a phrase in the Indo-European language Latvian, 'Patíkami ar jums iepazíties', meaning 'Pleased to meet you', may look no more familiar to us than the same phrase in (non-Indo-European) Estonian, 'Meeldiv teid kohata'.

A friend of mine, on being presented with the incomplete list above, concluded, 'It might just be quicker to say which languages aren't Indo-European.' It would not be. The languages of China and the indigenous languages of the Americas are other significant groups. The Afro-Asiatic family, which includes Arabic, is but one of several important groupings in Africa, where there are more different languages than on any other continent. Other notable families are the Dravidian, the Austro-Asiatic (such as the Khmer of Cambodia), the Indo-Pacific and Austronesian (Javanese, for instance), and the Altaic, a controversial designation which embraces among others Turkish, Azeri and Uzbek. Within Europe, the most conspicuous examples of languages outside the Indo-European family are Hungarian and Finnish, which are both, like Estonian, members of the Uralic family. Furthermore, there are 'isolates' that bear little resemblance to any other living tongue; the most celebrated example is probably Basque, known to its roughly 600,000 speakers as Euskara.

English is anything but isolated. To return to a figure from a moment ago, English has absorbed words from more than 350 other languages. Borrowings have their origins in a political or diplomatic moment, and testify at a more profound level to a social, cultural or economic motive. Languages become 'great' not because of any inherent qualities they may be deemed to have, but because of the political, military and intellectual force behind them. When colonists arrive in a country, they exchange their language with the native inhabitants, and sometimes force it down their throats. They may also try to foist their religion on them. Yet at the same time they adopt indigenous terms. An invader's vocabulary will expand to reflect the concerns of those he has invaded. In such situations, bilingualism has often been necessary and inevitable. But English-speakers without any capability in a foreign language have assimilated snippets here and there, and these new elements have assured English's opulently international character. The hybridity of the British and the Americans and other English-speaking communities (in Canada, for instance, and Australia) is registered in the hybrid languages we employ. A borrowed word is distinguished from other new terms in having already 'proved' itself: a compound or a word I make up has no pedigree, but a loanword has previously shown itself, in another language, to be viable. About half of English words have been borrowed, and many of the other half are compounds or mutations of earlier borrowings. The linguist John McWhorter comments, 'English's vocabulary is like San Francisco's architecture: thriving and beautiful but with ultimately sparse roots.'[9]

Moreover, since the time of Chaucer in the fourteenth century, its number of inflexions has dramatically decreased, and as an 'analytic' language – that is, one in which meaning is mainly shaped by word order and the use of particles such as prepositions and conjunctions – it has been able to absorb words without any concern for how to fit them into its grammar. In an English sentence, word order is paramount: change the order and you radically change the meaning ('Fred ate ostrich' is obviously different from 'Ostrich ate Fred') – something untrue of Latin or Basque or Sanskrit or the Australian Aboriginal language Dyirbal. This feature of English has allowed its writers and speakers a remarkable flexibility. A newly adopted noun can easily be turned into an adjective – once you know what a *chimera* is, you're just a whisper away from *chimerical* – and just about anything can be made into a verb. If I have accepted the Japanese words *shiatsu* and *sashimi*, I'll have no problem saying, 'I'm going to get shiatsued' or 'Let's sashimi the tuna.'

Studying a language involves an understanding of its syntax, punctuation, rhetorical nuances and patterns of formality. This book, however, is concerned with vocabulary. Except in circumstances where there is strong cultural pressure to assimilate other features of a different language, borrowing is restricted to this domain, for languages (and people) resist adopting new forms of grammar. The development of the word-stock is a measure of society's development. Words – or lexemes, as linguists call them – are 'the means by which we make direct reference to extralinguistic reality, converting our basic perception of the world around us into language', and they 'serve as labels for segments of . . . reality which a speech community finds nameworthy'.[10] In our daily lives we are continually conscious of our growing or changing personal vocabularies, and from an early age this is the domain where our increasing competence is most clear. Later – much later – this is one of the domains where our decline is first registered: we forget words, and are troubled by our doing so. We've most of us had the experience of watching an elderly relative groping for a particular noun: *voucher* or *colander* or *blanket*.

New ideas and products are named, and their names usually tell us something of where they have come from. Borrowings have a 'psychological climate'.[11] Rather than using history to explain language, we can use details of language to open up a historical vista. Before the sixteenth century there are no significant borrowings from Spanish and Portuguese; those that followed tell us about the competition between the different European seaborne empires and about the rewards of exploration. In similar vein, if we look at loans from Latin and Greek we can draw conclusions – albeit perhaps rather impressionistic ones – from the fact that *area* and *crisis* were borrowed earlier than *alibi* and *dogma*, which in turn came before *persona* and *euphoria*.

If we can quickly grasp why the words *Bolshevik* and *Soviet* first appear in the English-language press in 1917, it may be more titillating to find out that we can trace to 1966 – the year England won the football World Cup – *The Oxford English Dictionary's* first citations of *chlamydia, jacuzzi, freak-out* and *mind-fuck.* We would be surprised to find a reference to the artistic *avant-garde* in Jane Austen, but it would not seem out of place in Virginia Woolf; and when we come across the *avant-garde* in Thomas Malory's *Le Morte d'Arthur,* which was published in 1485, we recognize it must be an obsolete military term. Some borrowings are much earlier than we would tend to expect. It seems odd to find Dr Johnson mention a *duvet,* as he does in a magazine essay dating from 1758, or to find a volume from 1698 referring to a *shaman* – a word acquired from Russian, which had absorbed it from the Tungusic languages of eastern Siberia. *Parachute* and *commuter* were adopted earlier than we might expect (1785 and 1865), as was *electron* (1891), but of course, one can talk about something before it exists. *Communist* made its first appearance before Marx and Engels drew up their *Communist Manifesto.* It is perhaps also a surprise to find that *déjà vu* was until fifty years ago a specialized term of psychology, and that the Latin *Jesus,* ultimately from the Aramaic language spoken by Christ himself, established itself only in the sixteenth century, displacing the French *Iesu* and the common abbreviation *IHS.*

To paraphrase Wittgenstein, the limits of our language mark the limits of our world. At its most trivial there is the sensation that many readers will recognize: you come back from a foreign holiday with new terms of approval and terms of disgust, and at the same time you have certain new enthusiasms and an appreciation of new flavours – and possess new words with which to bring them to life. When King James VI of Scotland travelled to Oslo in the winter of 1589 to claim his bride, he returned with the toast *skol.* It's not hard to imagine what he must have got up to while he was there. Less than half a century later, Englishmen serving alongside Swedes during the Thirty Years War learnt the word *plunder,* which the Swedes had acquired from their German allies, and it was widely used during the Civil War, mainly in connection with the rapacious Royalist troops.[12]

More immediate examples are readily available. In the last few decades cheap air travel has made the world seem smaller, and few parts of the globe appear to be beyond our reach. Not many of the words we pick up on our travels survive the return journey: when you are in Bangkok it may be useful to know that a canal is a *klong*, and in Greece you may well discover that the word *malaka*, meaning 'wanker', is often used in all-male groups as a jocular term of endearment, but neither is likely to become a staple of your life at home. In general, loanwords cluster around a momentous event or a powerful phenomenon, not some brief encounter.

Essentially, there are two kinds of loan: words to denote phenomena that have never before been given expression, and words to denote phenomena for which there already exist quite adequate terms. In the second camp there are a number of striking subsets: words adopted because they seem especially colourful and felicitous, or for reasons of decorum, or in a spirit of technical exactitude, or for reasons of fashion. When a word is imported even though an equivalent term already exists, the result tends to be that the meaning of the older word changes.

There is, to use a well-worn phrase, a 'tipping point' where esoteric usage slips into the mainstream. Normally the transfer of a foreign word into English is effected by someone who has a good knowledge of both languages, but soon the word will be used by people who know little or nothing of the donor language and may even be unaware that the word is borrowed. As this happens, specialists worry about their language being cheapened by everyday use, and the layperson worries about being swamped by jargon. Here is the Roman poet Horace in the *Ars Poetica*:

> Why should I be grudged the right to add a few words to the stock if I can . . . ? It has always been accepted, and always will be, that words stamped with the mint-mark of the day should be brought into currency. As the woods change their foliage with the decline of each year . . . so words die out with old age; and the newly born ones arrive and prosper just like human beings in the vigour of youth . . . It is usage which regulates the laws and conventions of speech.[13]

More than this, usage is what makes words live. And usage will always prevail over theory.

At what point can a word truly be said to have been borrowed? One conventional view is that a 'foreign' word, even if in fairly common use, will be recognizable by its retaining a plainly un-English pronunciation and any accents or other diacritic signs such as, say, a circumflex; when it appears in print, it will be set in italics. But within the compass of such a rule there is, in practice, plenty of grey area. Most of us will accept that *elite* has been fully assimilated and that *égalité* hasn't, but what of *élan*, *esprit*, *entrepôt*, or for that matter *ensemble*? And, staying with French, what of *papier mâché*, which means something different to us from what it means in France, where it signifies little more than 'chewed paper'? (The French name for our papier mâché is *carton-pâte*.) We would tend to accept that *papier mâché* has been completely absorbed, but it does not fit the rule I cited a moment ago. Other examples are plentiful; the rule is flawed. *Vive la différence.*

The language scholar David Crystal provides the example of a purportedly English-language menu in a Nigerian restaurant including such items as *agidi*, *edikagong* and *foofoo*.[14] Someone whose first language is English and who is living in Nigeria or has Nigerian friends may be familiar with these dishes, but most English-speakers in Sunderland, Seattle or Singapore probably won't be. (*Restaurant*, we may note in passing, is pronounced in three distinct ways; none is quite the same as the French version, and each bears witness to a different degree of comfort with its Frenchness.) A list from 1969 of 'common Hawaiian loans in English' comprises 205 items, although on closer inspection the list consists of words with which few readers will be acquainted: representative examples are *malihini*, meaning 'a newcomer', and *humuhumunukunukuapuaa*, a type of fish with a snout like a pig's – the name maybe longer than the fish.[15] Many more readers, though, will accept that the Hawaiian *ukulele* is now an English word, and will be at ease with *aloha*, *hula*, *kahuna* as a word for an expert and the garland called a *lei*. We will tend to dispute the status of individual borrowings, as our experiences differ. An English-speaking native of East Harlem is more likely than I am to have picked up and accepted a Spanish word. On the other hand, having travelled quite widely in the British Isles, I am more likely to know a few words of Gaelic and Welsh.

Eventually a borrowed word may be 'conventionalized': its frequent use, together with changes in the way it is pronounced, means that it stops being considered foreign at all. Moreover, its meaning may rapidly alter after it has been assimilated. Even though a borrowing may begin with the need to remedy a particular deficiency in our language, the word acquired is highly susceptible to change, not only because it is novel, but also because it is isolated. Its links with the language from which it was borrowed are broken, and it has no semantic connections with other words in the language into which it has been absorbed.[16]

It is the borrowings from Latin, French and Scandinavian that have made the clearest impression on English, but many other languages have contributed: Greek, Italian, Spanish and Dutch have all been generous lenders, and among those that have provided at least a hundred borrowings we find, perhaps surprisingly, Russian, Urdu, Turkish and Malay. Some of the contacts have occurred within the British Isles: *penguin, corgi* and *flummery* are all borrowed from Welsh, while *puffin* and *bludgeon* appear to be Cornish, and *slogan* derives from a Gaelic battle cry. (Curiously, *penguin* derives from the Welsh words for 'white' and 'head', whereas of course penguins have black heads.) Others have been more remote: *elixir* is Arabic, *futon* Japanese, and *chimpanzee* comes from the West African language Tshiluba. *Sauna* is Finnish, *marmalade* is Portuguese (and originally referred to quince jelly), while *shibboleth*, which I used a few pages ago, is a Hebrew word for a stream, and enabled the people of Gilead to identify their Ephraimite enemies, who habitually mispronounced it. Some words' sources are unexpected. I can remember being surprised to find that *kiosk* is Turkish – as may be the card game *bridge* – and that *berserk*, like *geyser* and *narwhal*, is Icelandic: it seems to derive from the name of the bearskin coats worn by the fiercest Norse warriors. *Loan* itself is Norse. It has even been proposed – originally by Robert Ripley, in one of his widely syndicated *Believe It or Not* columns, and subsequently by people impressed by Ripley's suggestion – that *talk* is our one direct borrowing from Lithuanian. Sadly, the word does not come from this source, and there may in fact be no English word adopted directly from Lithuanian, though *eland*, the name of a type of antelope, may have come from the Lithuanian for a type of elk, via Dutch.

One of the effects of English's very diverse borrowings is that, while slivers of other languages look and sound familiar to us, there is no one language to which ours feels truly proximate. A German listening to a Dutchman will often be struck by the closeness of their vocabularies. Momentary illusions notwithstanding, speakers of English do not share this experience – except if they visit a few island communities off the coast of northern Germany.

While the adoption of foreign terms can facilitate traffic between the English-speaking world and other cultures, such language is sometimes used not in the interests of clarity, but for less democratic reasons. Loans tend to enjoy a certain mystical allure, and sometimes they are used to endow ordinary thoughts with extraordinary lustre. (*Allure*, by the way, is an example of a foreign word that has been adopted, has fallen into obsolescence, and has then been adopted afresh.) Elites, or those who consider themselves elite, reach for exotic vocabulary to impress those they consider their inferiors or to signal their distance from them. Perhaps a particular writer likes the German word *Weltanschauung*, believing that it projects her meaning more elegantly than the English 'world view': if she speaks it, though, she may be greeted with a few cheery *Gesundheit*s. Throughout the history of English, the decision of a speaker or writer to borrow a word – be it from Latin, Greek, Hindi or Japanese – has been divisive, possibly an act of snobbery or self-importance, and an at least covert statement about his or her education.

Naturally, words of this stripe are not used just in the interests of self-promotion. At their most valuable, they compress a great deal of information into a small amount of space. Looking at another German word that has been adopted into English, *Schadenfreude*, we can see that it expresses in very compact form an idea that would otherwise call for several words – along the lines of 'a nasty pleasure in other people's misfortunes'. According to the *OED*, it first crops up in an essay by the philologically minded cleric Richard Chenevix Trench in 1852, not long before he became dean of Westminster. A few years later Thomas Carlyle had a stab at a brief definition, suggesting it was joy not so much in making mischief as in seeing justice done. There is nothing intrinsically German about enjoying the misadventures of others, but this German word is more succinct than anything English can otherwise muster. The Germans also have a word that neatly conveys the idea of a song you are unable to get out of your head. This is *Ohrwurm* – literally, an 'ear worm', burrowing into the soft pulp of your brain. Of course the German language does not have a monopoly on this kind of concision. Terms from Latin can be every bit as spruce: at first blush, *procrastination* may seem a long word for an everyday phenomenon, but it would be hard to put the idea across any more briefly. By much the same token, the French have borrowed from English *le weekend* because it conveys the weekend's opportunities for relaxation and leisure more decisively than the native *la fin de semaine*.

Still, borrowed words are often redolent of the environment from which they were acquired. I may be able to refer to *moped* without thinking of Sweden – I mean the motorized scooter, not the past participle of *mope* – or to a *paper tiger* without any sense of its origins in the Chinese, but I am pretty much certain to be aware that in using *yin* and *yang* I am deploying Chinese terms, and to feel some intangible quality of Swedishness when referring to a *smorgasbord*. Such associations can give us great opportunities for nuance – for subtle gradations of register and meaning. As the horrible and bewilderingly well-informed narrator of John Lanchester's novel *The Debt to Pleasure* remarks, 'One should note that to be *bourgeois* is not at all the same thing as to be middle-class . . . Styles of self-satisfaction vary from country to country, just as to be bored is not the same thing as to suffer from *ennui*. The condition of feeling *einsam* is not identical with being lonely, and *Gemütlichkeit* is to be distinguished from comfiness.'[17]

Sometimes loanwords seem to manifest and affirm stereotypes: thus, regrettably, many British people are hostile to Germany and Germans, and their idea of Germany is immediately evoked by the words *Gestapo* and *Nazi*, by the dubious charms of *lederhosen* and *kitsch*, or maybe by the romantic pessimism of *Weltschmerz*. While this pattern of thought may seem odious and crude, the fact remains that what we take from a culture becomes what we know of it.

The ambiguity of those last few words is deliberate and fertile. For example, what we know of India is encapsulated in a vocabulary of Indianness which we sense we possess. And at the same time the aspects of Indianness that find their way into our language are 'becoming'; they are compatible with our needs and values, with what we want or feel able to believe.

This theme of appropriating what we find congenial is implicit in a further category: the loan translation or 'calque'. This comes from the French verb *calquer*, meaning 'to trace' (as in making a copy using tracing paper), and derives ultimately from the Latin verb *calcare*. Many English calques are sourced in French. When we speak of a *marriage of convenience*, the phrase is a version of the much older *mariage de convenance*. Other examples are *man of letters* (which renders *homme de lettres*), *to hold one's peace* (*tenir sa paix*), *bluestocking* (*bas-bleu*) and *the order of the day* (*l'ordre du jour*). So too we have *hit or miss*, *to learn by heart*, *a thousand thanks* and *to cut one's nose off to spite one's face*, all of which apparently 'trace' the form of French phrases. *Right here* may be another example, and *that goes without saying* is calqued on the French *cela va sans dire*, while *notwithstanding* is calqued on the Old French *non obstant*. As it happens, *loanword* is a calque of the German *Lehnwort*, and a couple of other instances of loan translations from German are *antibody* (which is based on *Antikörper*) and *wishful thinking* (from *Wunschdenken*), while, to give just one more example, *barefoot doctor* is a calque of a term in Chinese.

Uncovering the route by which a word has entered one's language offers several layers of reward. We may well enjoy knowing that *botulism* comes from a Latin word for a sausage, that *muscle* is related to *mouse* (a bunched muscle being a bit like a quivering mouse), or that *mortgage* literally means 'death grip': in each case the link is unexpected and droll. An *album* is, in the strictly etymological sense, something white, like a blank writing tablet, and *to prevaricate* means 'to plough crookedly'; *nickname* is a corruption of 'an ekename' (literally an added name); the noun *hyperbole*, which we take from Greek, conveys the sense of throwing something too far; and *cravat* comes from the French word for a Croatian, thanks to the French adopting this flimsy garment from Croatian mercenaries in the seventeenth century. The verb *to trounce* is related to *truncheon*.

Glamour is etymologically linked to *grammar* – an understanding of the workings of language was once seen as an occult accomplishment – and, similarly, there are forgotten links from *dainty* to *dignity* and from *cadence* to *chance. Cushy* comes from the Hindi *khush* meaning 'excellent', and has nothing to do with the word *cushion* (which for its part comes from Latin *culcita*, a mattress – also the source of *quilt). To doodle* originally meant playing the bagpipes, and can be traced to a Turkish word for a flute. Less startling is the information that *etymology* itself is a compound of the Greek for 'true' and 'word', but we may still be surprised that it was imported into English from French.

I could carry on in this vein for a long time. My point, however, is simple: words frequently come from unlikely places, and the unlikelihood is illuminating. Even when the sources are less surprising, the force of an etymology can be bold. The word *silk*, for instance, has made a long journey through Chinese via Greek and Latin to English. The word's journey evokes the romance of the Silk Road, and it is worth noticing too that the transition from the Latin *sericus* to the English *silk* – from an *r* sound to an *l* – may well have been produced by adoption into the Slavonic languages of silk's early traders in the Baltic. The word *empire*, which will come up frequently in the course of this book, derives from the Latin *imperium* and thus, inevitably, calls to mind the immense cosmopolitan might of the Roman people. The story of Rome – its imagery, its language – has been an inspiration for every imperial power since.

Sometimes the lexical archaeologists disagree: for instance, the end-of-year celebration known as *hogmanay* has been variously construed as a Celtic exclamation, a version of the Greek *hagia mene* ('holy month'), a rendering of the French druids' cry of 'Au gui l'an neuf' or a corruption of the Latin *hoc anno novo*. Deciding between competing explanations is usually a matter of identifying which account fits best with our understanding of history. But on the whole etymology is a more secure business, revealing the lustrous past concealed in every word. The poet Don Paterson suggests that 'Words are locked tombs in which the corpses still lie breathing.'[18] It is an image which nicely suggests the more macabre stories preserved in words.

Already I have referred several times to 'borrowing' and 'loan-words'. Both are misnomers: the language from which we acquire the word does not have to give it up. A word may be on proba-tion, and for a time it may have a disreputable or intimidating image, but we are not expected to return it. What, though, makes a loan-word stick? Most new words sparkle briefly, then fade. Those that endure are the ones that are useful, deal with matters of lasting significance, and achieve a high level of exposure. They tend as well to be easy to handle – or at least not furiously complicated. I may like *pinpilinpauxa*, which is the Basque for a butterfly, but I shall struggle to convince many other people of its usefulness.

To quote the French scholar Louis Deroy, 'L'emprunt est un intrus': 'The loanword is an intruder.'[19] Borrowed words do not slip into a language unnoticed; their arrival may be only gradual, but it is keenly felt. No loanword is ever universally welcomed, and each borrowed term is a tiny affront to the language that borrows it; yet a language totally hostile to change is a language in decline. As islanders, the people of Britain have long had a sense of their apart-ness, but this has fuelled rather than stymied an appetite for reaching across the seas to discover the many and alluring forms of 'other-ness'. For its part the United States, the world's most populous English-speaking nation, is also one of the most socially and ethnic-ally diverse, and its eclectic identity is grounded in the understanding that change will tend to bring about improvements.

There is another aspect to Deroy's observation: he implies that borrowing is not seamless, that its boundaries are ragged. When words are borrowed, they alter. This is true of their meanings as well as of their pronunciation. The degree to which this happens varies, but sometimes it is profound. Think back to *restaurant*, or compare, for instance, the pronunciations of these words, all of which are also derived from French: *marriage, garage, montage*. A loanword's level of acceptance is manifest in the way we articulate it. It is evident, too, in our willingness to use the word in ways other than that in which it was originally borrowed – as another part of speech, or in a derivative compound. Furthermore, we will happily use a word we recognize as borrowed to afford us what we think is insight into the culture where it originated. 'I know your words: I know your mind' goes the inevitable, dangerous, reasoning. Even if we feel confident that we understand, say, *jihad* or *lebensraum*, we should be wary of using *our* understanding of them as keys into languages and world views where their significance is far more complex.

Borrowing is not a one-way street. For instance, in Kashmiri you may hear a word like *bathroom* or *widow*, and in Serbo-Croat *shrapnel* or *scout*. In French, as I have noted, there is *le weekend*, along with *les bluejeans*, *le rip-off* and the calque *gratte-ciel* (skyscraper), which are seen by purists as grave embarrassments. The Swahili *madigadi* is a version of the English 'mudguards', and the same language takes the delightful word *kiplefti*, meaning 'traffic island', from the English 'keep left'. In Yoruba, a *square root* is *sikua ruutu*.[20] Russian borrowings from English include the slightly sinister *biznismen*, as well as *dzhemper* ('jumper') and *vokzal* ('station'). The last of these is a corruption of Vauxhall, the name of an area in south London once famous for its pleasure gardens; a Russian delegation of the 1840s stopped there and took this word, displayed on a sign, to be the generic name for a station. Borrowing is a subject that could fill volumes. But here we are concerned only with the traffic in one direction: into English.

Before we go any further, another word about terminology. Languages are not concrete, and it is not quite accurate to claim that a language 'alters' or 'spreads', or that it 'penetrates' a new area. When one says that a language changes, for instance, what one really means is that some parts of that language come to be used differently from the way they were previously used. Change results from human choice and from contact between individuals who speak differently. It begins with people, not with languages. Nevertheless, in the interests of concision, I shall throughout this book refer to the English language's 'changing', its 'conquest' of fresh territory, and its 'appetite', as well as to words 'entering' the language, and shall assume that readers recognize this as a kind of shorthand. I shall also try where I can to say something about the people whose actions and achievements are amalgamated – compacted, hidden – in the words concerned.

2. Invade

To enter in a hostile manner, or with armed force; to intrude upon, infringe, encroach on, usurp

From the Latin verb *invadere*, 'to go or walk in'

Sometimes it takes an outsider to recognize the heart of a country and its culture. Writing in the 1850s about his experiences of Britain, Ralph Waldo Emerson referred to the 'composite character' of its inhabitants. 'Every thing English is a fusion of distant and antagonistic elements. The language is mixed . . . [and] the currents of thought are counter.' The people combined 'contemplation and practical skill; active intellect and dead conservatism; . . . aggressive freedom and hospitable law'. 'Scattered by their wars and affairs over the face of the whole earth, and homesick to a man', they made up 'a country of extremes'. 'Who can discriminate them anatomically,' he wondered, 'or metaphysically?' 'Mixture', he concluded, 'is a secret of the English island.'[1]

This mixture is audible and legible in our daily use of English words. Often we have three terms for the same thing – one Anglo-Saxon, one French, and one clearly absorbed from Latin or Greek. The Anglo-Saxon word is typically a neutral one; the French word connotes sophistication; and the Latin or Greek word, learnt from a written text rather than from human contact, is comparatively abstract and conveys a more scientific notion. Consider, for example, the verbs *rise, mount* and *ascend*, or *go, depart* and *exit*. In each case, the first word has an Anglo-Saxon source and is informal, the second is French and comparatively formal, while the third is Latin and suggests something more specialized or technical. A more extreme example is *fire, flame* and *conflagration*; another, *holy, sacred, consecrated*. In this book you will frequently find the Anglo-Saxon *word* and the French *term*, but this is the last you will hear of the rather more intimidating Greek *lexeme*. One of the strengths of English is that it affords its speakers choices of this kind; the different levels of sophistication allow us great precision, and even if our exact wording is not consciously achieved, it reveals our attitudes, self-image and purpose.

Think about the distinction between *luck* and *fortune*, *fatherly* and *paternal*, *hearty* and *cordial*, or *almighty* and *omnipotent*. In each case the first, Anglo-Saxon, word is more direct, suggestive of something more primal, more resonant, more tangible. What about the difference between *altitude* and Anglo-Saxon *height*, or between *ordure* and *shit*? An *aroma* is quite clearly better than a *stench*. We may casually refer to these as synonyms, but we know they are not exactly interchangeable. Many Anglo-Saxon terms have deep emotional charge. Talk of one's *kin*, or of *home*, or of a person's *mother*, can, depending on context, be a sort of verbal handshake or wickedly inflammatory. Ideologues love to play on the associations of such words. Other especially emotive Anglo-Saxon words include *evil*, *freedom*, *weak*, *heart*, *lust*, *weep*, *strong* and *love*. The Anglo-Saxon part of the English vocabulary seems to earth us. Its matter-of-fact quality is at odds with the more academic colour of the French and Latin word-stock. There are plenty of French borrowings that are vivid rather than cerebral: for example, *glory*, *cruel*, *horror*, *guile* and *mean*. But the pattern is clear enough. Thus, typically, the Old English *dead* is balder than the French *deceased*, which is for its part softer and less technical than the Latin *defunct*.

The arrival in Britain of French and Latin words provided English with new semantic layers, and over the next few pages we shall see how this came about. The word *arrival* is itself an example – a Norman import, drawn from the Latin verb *adripare*, 'to come to shore'. Immediately we are reminded of the most famous example of words and conquerors appearing on British shores. 1066 is one of the few dates imprinted on the mind of anyone who has studied British history. Had Duke William of Normandy – or William the Conqueror, as we tend dramatically to call him – not invaded England, English would be a very different language.

Yet several of the key events in the history of English happened before the Norman Conquest. Two and a half millennia ago the

Celts were the dominant force in western Europe. Determinedly mobile people, they had provided the Romans with words for wheeled vehicles, and the relics of their culture unearthed by archaeologists include impressive wagons. They had begun to arrive in the British Isles by 2000 BC.[2] Broadly speaking, the languages of the Celts in Britain fell into two groups: the Brittonic, which consisted of Welsh, Cornish and Breton, and the Goidelic, comprising Irish, Manx and Scottish Gaelic. (We do not know about the languages that were spoken in Britain before the coming of the Celts, though the meagre evidence has not prevented speculation. Some have even postulated a link with Basque. Current fashion favours the nebulous name 'Early Indo-European'.) According to Graeco-Roman legend the Celts were 'people of alien behaviour, cruel, and prone to such savagery as human sacrifice'; 'fearless warriors', they were 'irrationally brave in the first onslaught but prone to wild despair when the battle turned against them.'[3] There was a good deal of truth in this, and, as Caesar and Tacitus would point out, their government was unstable, riven by disputes between competing factions. The rise of the Roman Empire curbed their influence, and between 55 BC and AD 410 England and Wales were occupied by the Romans.

Communication between Romans and the native Celts was sufficient to introduce some Latin into the vocabulary of their island colony.[4] Many of the people who ran Roman Britain were of British stock, but the language of government was Latin. Celtic languages registered this; for instance, the Welsh *ysgol*, 'school', derived directly from the Latin *schola*.[5] For readers familiar with Rosemary Sutcliff's classic *The Eagle of the Ninth*, memories may stir of leather-clad Roman frontiersmen conversing fluently with the native hunters, handing over their denarii for dogs and fighting-cocks. The reality was less charming: when not subduing recalcitrant tribes, the Romans busied themselves developing the road network, building sewage systems, and mining gold, lead, iron and tin. Then, after the legions were recalled to Rome in 410 to protect the city against marauding Visigoths, the administrative structures created by the Romans fell apart, and the result was a power vacuum.

According to a legend established by the sixth-century Celtic scholar Gildas, in his *De Excidio Britanniae* ('On the ruin of Britain'), the next wave of conquest was precipitated by military overlords who were desperate to repulse barbarian raiders in the north. Later accounts suggest that around 449 a warlord called Vortigern, harried by these Picts, called for assistance from abroad. The men who answered his call came to British shores in the guise of mercenaries, but soon revealed more rapacious motives: one pack of barbarians took the place of another. Excited by the prospect of fertile land and easy pickings, and under military pressure at home, a diverse group comprising mainly Saxons, Jutes, Frisians and Angles sailed from what we now know as northern Germany and Denmark.

Once ashore, these people's methods were savage. In his *Germania*, written around AD 100, Tacitus had noted their bellicose tendencies, and nothing had changed in the intervening years. Their ambitions were hawkish, and their influence spread fast. Modern accounts tend to present the migration as quick and coherent, whereas it is much more likely that the arrivals came in dribs and drabs. Nevertheless, the general pattern was that the Angles settled in what we now call East Anglia and fanned east and then north, while the Saxons focused on the south-east and the region that would come to be known as Wessex. The Jutes seem to have concentrated themselves in Kent and the Isle of Wight. The different tribes' patterns of settlement would be reflected in the development of different dialects. And today English-speaking visitors to the countries from which these people came occasionally hear snatches of speech that sound uncannily like English: for instance, the form of the Frisian language spoken on certain islands off the coast of Schleswig-Holstein contains some very familiar-looking words like *smoke, man* and *helpe*.[6]

Whereas the Romans had treated Britain as an imperial outpost, these newcomers settled permanently.[7] Estimates of their numbers vary: a figure of 10,000 has been put forward, but so has one of 200,000.[8] While there was probably a period of bilingualism, the Anglo-Saxons' forceful presence, together with the ravages of bubonic plague, ultimately ensured that little Celtic vocabulary was preserved in the language, although some of the mechanisms of Celtic rhetoric seem to have persisted, and in Cumbria, Wales, Cornwall and possibly also an enclave in the Fens the Brittonic languages held more firm.[9] Those elements of Celtic that do survive to the present day are mainly found in place names, such as Dover, Crewe and Penrith, or in the names of rivers, including the Wye and the Thames. A couple of widely acknowledged exceptions include *brock* (a badger) and *tor* (a high rock or a hill). Celtic words that were taken up by Old English – such as *deor*, 'brave', and *luh*, 'lake' – thereafter faded away.

The settlers did not all speak one tongue, but they all spoke Germanic languages. They had come into contact with Latin-speakers many times during the previous 500 years, and their languages had absorbed perhaps 300 Latin words. Whereas later borrowings from Latin tended to deal with sophisticated matters of scholarship or religion, these early ones – unusual in coming through personal contact, rather than through books – concerned everyday items. The Romans' aptitude for laying down paved roads is preserved in the word *street*, which derived from the Latin *via strata*, while their word for a rampart, *vallum*, is the source of *wall*. These words may have been reinforced in Briton by the presence of similar borrowed terms in Celtic.[10] This period of contact also introduced *mile*, from the Latin *mille passuum*, and hints of civilization in *trifot* (tribute), *belt*, *cup* and *portic* (porch). Although many early loans were connected with administration and the military, among the others were the words we know as *wine*, *butter*, *pepper* and *radish*. *Cheese* came from Latin *caseus*, and *kitchen* from *coquina*.

Settlers' different kinds of speech gave rise to the real diversity of Old English dialects. The word *English* comes from *Anglisc*, the name of the dialect used by the Angles, and both the country and its inhabitants came to be known as *Angelcynn*, 'the race of the Angles'. (*English* precedes *England*, which superseded *Angelcynn* in the eleventh century.) The form we now call Old English, which looks deeply alien to modern readers, was used for about 700 years after the coming of the Anglo-Saxons, and during this period changes happened only slowly.

The earliest speakers of English were illiterate pagans. There were traces of Christianity from the second century, and small Christian delegations travelled from Britain to continental religious councils early in the fourth century, but outside a few metropolitan centres Christian beliefs did not take a firm hold until much later. St Patrick began the work of Christianizing Ireland in around 430, and Irish missionaries travelled throughout Europe. Yet the defining moment was in 597, when St Augustine landed on the Kentish island of Thanet. He and his company of forty monks had been sent by Pope Gregory to convert the Anglo-Saxons. The inspiration for this, according to the Venerable Bede, writing more than a hundred years later, was an encounter at a Roman *market* (a word coming ultimately from the Latin *merx*, meaning 'merchandise') between Gregory and a gaggle of heathen English slaves. Struck by their fine appearance – '*Non Angli, sed angeli,*' he is supposed to have said – he decided to free their countrymen from the wrath of God. Augustine and his followers were generously received by Ethelbert, the king of Kent; a monastery was established at Canterbury, and soon, having apparently brought Kent under Christian authority, Augustine's monks were able to look further north. In 627 King Eadwine of Northumbria was converted, and within fifty years of Augustine's arrival Christianity had extended its reach through much of the island.

The monks brought with them the Roman alphabet, which displaced the Germanic alphabet of jagged characters (runes) as the chief medium for writing, and brought as well the custom of preserving learning in written form. Although most of their work was done in Latin, they introduced a few hundred words into the vernacular: new concepts required new terminology. *Deofol* (devil), *munuc* (monk) and *preost* (priest) seem to be pre-Christian borrowings, but among the fresh Christian additions were *Mass*, from the post-classical *missa* meaning 'dismissal' (the prayer at the conclusion of a liturgy), *halig gast* ('Holy Ghost', a calque of *spiritus sanctus*) and *cross* (from *crux*), which would slowly take the place of the older noun *rood* – a word preserved in the title of the *Dream of the Rood*, a visionary Old English narrative of the Crucifixion, and in the *rood screen*, the division in church between the nave and the choir. *Minster* was adapted from the Latin *monasterium*, while *martyr* came from Greek via post-classical Latin. A less morally resonant borrowing was an early form of *lentil*, the Latin root of which would later also provide us with *lens* – a device that gets its name through being the shape of a lentil seed. You might expect Latin to have coloured English more visibly at this time, given the deep impression made by Christian teaching, but English, ever adaptable, had its own ways of refashioning Latin concepts. For instance, the Latin *disciple* and the Romanized Greek word *apostle* begin to appear as Christianity is embraced, but their roles are often taken by the indigenous words *folgere, cniht, leornere, leorningcniht* and even the poetic-sounding *spel-boda*.

Bede refers in his *Ecclesiastical History of the English People* to the multilingualism of Britain in the eighth century: English, Welsh, Irish and Latin were in wide use, and the Pictish tongue was spoken in the northern part of Scotland. This seemed like something to celebrate. Bede wrote in Latin, which was the language of learning, of record, and of the Church.[11] The influence of Latin did not die out with the departure of the legions: Latin words were absorbed first as elements of the vocabulary of the Anglo-Saxon invaders; then through the work of Christian missionaries during the period of Anglo-Saxon rule; then after the Norman Conquest, often via French, in connection with matters of medicine, law and religion; during the Renaissance, with the reawakening of classical learning; and as specialist terms obtaining only in certain domains, such as botany or jurisprudence. A glossary surviving from around 680 provides English explanations of Latin words, and shows among other things an attempt to copy Latin categories of occupation and profession. One example is the use of *egderi* for a man who operates a harrow, apparently on the model of the Latin *herpicarius*.[12]

The next period of foreign influence began in a blaze of violence. The first Viking attack on England was recorded in 789. Three ships arrived at Portland in Dorset; the local reeve, Beaduheard, mistook them for traders, rushed to meet them, and was slaughtered. More significant incursions began with a raid on Lindisfarne, which is mentioned in the *Anglo-Saxon Chronicle*'s entry for 793. That year 'terrible portents came about over the land of Northumbria, and miserably frightened the people.' 'Dragons were seen flying in the air,' and there soon followed 'a great famine'. Then 'a little after that . . . the raiding of heathen men miserably devastated God's church in Lindisfarne.'[13] The following year Vikings plundered the monastery at Jarrow, where Bede had written his *Ecclesiastical History*. Later raids were more intense, and the invaders stayed for longer; in 851 a group wintered on the island of Thanet, and between 865 and 869 significant inroads were made in East Anglia, Mercia and Northumbria. Plunder and the desecration of religious sites were rife; whole communities were wiped out.

Why did the raiders come? One standard account suggests the multiplicity of possible explanations: 'Famine, pestilence, cataclysmic natural disasters in their native land, over-population as a result of the widespread practice of polygamy, the custom of driving out younger sons to fend for themselves, the cutting off by the Arabs of the old trade connections with Byzantium, an obsessive mania to destroy other people's property, a fanatical loathing of Christianity, and an insatiable appetite for high adventure.'[14] This was a period of tribal movement – of restlessness and displacements. Britain was not the only territory to face the Viking menace: Charlemagne had to upgrade the Frankish coastal defences to secure them against Scandinavian pirates, monasteries in Ireland and on the Loire were attacked, and Vikings settled on the southern coast of the Baltic and in eastern Europe. Later Paris was looted, and Charles the Bald had to pay the plunderers 7,000 lb of silver to withdraw.[15]

During the ninth century these mainly Danish invaders settled in Britain, concentrating at first on the accessible northern and eastern reaches, and making the greatest impression in what are now Yorkshire and Lincolnshire. In time they took London and Canterbury, and their ambitious gaze turned west towards the kingdom of Wessex. Yet, though they came as pirates, their contributions in time became more positive. They did not eject the English from their homes, but created new urban centres and strengthened the market for property, as well as providing richer opportunities for traders and craftsmen. Collaboration thrived. For instance, Northumbrians welcomed Viking support in their quarrels with the West Saxons, and more than one archbishop of York actively co-operated with the city's Scandinavian conquerors.[16] Many Vikings converted to Christianity and assumed 'local' identities – an indication that status mattered more to them than their innate ethnicity.[17]

The vocabulary of farming suggests another area of collaboration: surviving dialect words such as *lathe*, a barn, and *lea*, a scythe, came straight from Norse. Although there were abundant differences between Norse and English, the two groups could understand each other. The language scholar Roger Lass suggests that we can imagine their levels of mutual comprehension by reaching for a modern example from South African English, where borrowings from Afrikaans colour a simple question about why someone has failed to put sausage on the grill: '*Ag*, man, why didn't you put the *boerewors* on the *braai*?'[18]

Words of Scandinavian origin rarely look or feel foreign to modern English-speakers. They have been completely assimilated, and most denote everyday objects. Yet different habits of pronunciation meant that a borrowed word, though shared between communities, could evolve in different directions. Thus *shirt* and *skirt* are different flowers of the same root, and so are *scrub* and *shrub*. Here we have a clue to the abrasive nature of the two groups' interactions. As Bruce Smith writes, 'each culture has its own distinctive way of understanding the world through sound,' and accordingly 'the borders between cultures become, potentially at least, sites of noise, confusion, pandemonium.' Settlers and colonists will always try to impose on their conquered lands a particular 'acoustemology' – a recognition that people establish their culture through sound.[19] The Greek historian Herodotus made the startling claim that the desert people known as the Garamantes squeaked like bats; the noises they made were an integral part of their aura of belligerence. Things said and things heard are challenges: sounds are evidently outside us, yet we experience them as though they are *inside* us. The Norse settlers' acoustic onslaught was the most intimate kind of affront. Just sample the guttural force of *konungr*, the Norse for 'king', and *hrafn*, meaning 'raven', or the abrupt stab of the adverbs *ok* and *mjök*, meaning 'also' and 'greatly'.

Emerson could write lyrically that 'The Scandinavians . . . still hear in every age the murmurs of their mother, the ocean; the Briton in the blood hugs the homestead still.' Less appealing, yet no less salty, was his reference to the Norse legacy he could read in the features of a 'misshapen hairy Scandinavian troll . . . whose speech is a brash of bitter waters'.[20] Emerson's words evoke the nature of the two cultures' confrontation. The verb *to amaze*, a perpetual feature of our daily conversation ('I'm amazed you can speak six languages'), dates back to these bristling encounters, and modern etymologists point out its links with two Norwegian verbs that denote bustling and dreaming, a Danish term for bother, and a Swedish word for sunning oneself. Imagine being in the middle of this triangle of languages: as you juggle the different senses, you act out the adjudicative experience of encountering new words. When words are learnt through conversation, as they were from the Norse invaders, the urgency of that confusion and the quick dialogue of intuition and judgement are all the more extreme.

Resistance to the Vikings was mobilized by King Alfred. He forti-fied the English law, encouraged shipbuilding, and revived learning. He acclaimed wisdom as 'the loftiest of virtues', and his reputation for prudent intellectualism spread far beyond his kingdom. Above all, he fostered a sense of national identity. Alfred felt able to refer to his language as English, and his thriving West Saxon kingdom, based in Winchester, enhanced the status of the vernacular. He promoted education and the translation of Latin texts, sometimes enlisting the help of foreign scholars, and, noting a decline in the knowledge of Latin, he established the idea that English could take its place as a suitable medium for intellectual argument as well as for the business of the court. This revival of learning ushered in Latin loans, and sometimes English words, especially abstract ones, were formed on Latin models. Thus a verb like the Old English *utdraefan* was based on the same Latin concept that gives us the modern English *expel*; the word's constituent parts are native, but the compounding of *ut* and *draefan* is inspired by the Latin. The 'learned' aspect of English was steadily augmented in this way, and under Alfred's aegis the burgeoning West Saxon dialect promised to become the language's standard form – a process which became conspicuous from about 975, but was abruptly checked by the Norman Conquest.

Alfred's drive for English unity was pragmatic. In 878 he and Guthrum, king of the East Angles, entered into an agreement, commonly dubbed the Treaty of Wedmore, which ended a quarter of a century of especially vicious plunder. Alfred formally conceded to the Vikings a large part of the Midlands and northern England, which was to be known as the Danelaw. Its most important communities lay in Leicester, Nottingham, Derby, Stamford and Lincoln. Derby's name is telltale; that terminal -*by* is a clear sign of Viking influence, and can be seen in the names of other communities in the north of England and the Midlands, such as Corby and Rugby. One of the consequences of the agreement was that in the northern part of the country the Norse language became dominant, and, while Alfred's resistance ensured that English kept its core of Anglo-Saxon, across the whole country many Anglo-Saxon words gave way to Norse. The verb *to call*, which first appears in a poem written after the Battle of Maldon in 991, is a striking example, and the poem highlights the loquacious contact between Anglo-Saxons and Vikings. As violent clashes with the Norse settlers became rare, however, trade flourished, and the linguistic infusions came in a wider range of flavours. Among the borrowings from this period are *gasp*, *rake* and *scare*, along with such commonplace nouns as *root* and *sky*, the adjectives *loose*, *tight* and *weak*, and the pronoun *both*. The Norse *vind-auga* ('eye of the wind') became *window*. Phrasal verbs (*put up*, *put away* and so on) may also have come from this source. Most strikingly, Norse pronouns such as *they* and *their* displaced Anglo-Saxon ones.

Another of the Viking contributions to English was a move away from inflexional endings, which were an obstacle to communication between speakers of Norse and speakers of English. As Matthew Townend explains, Norse and English words were often similar, but their endings were different. Accordingly, 'In a situation in which speakers of the two languages were repeatedly in contact with one another, on a daily or even a domestic basis, it is quite possible that these inflexional differences became eroded or ignored, as they played no role . . . in effective communication.' Instead, other means of 'expressing grammatical relationships came to be more prominent – above all, the method of a relatively fixed word-order'.[21]

There are two main periods of borrowing from the Scandinavian languages. The first introduction of Scandinavian words followed the northern raids at the end of the eighth century and lasted for a little over 300 years. Some of the new terms had to do with the invaders' unique equipment – the names of the vessels they came in – or with their systems of government. It is to this early Scandinavian presence that we owe the words *hustings*, *law* (from the Norse *lagu*) and *wrong*, as well as *husband* and *outlaw*. The establishment of *law* owes much to the powerful homilist and legislator Archbishop Wulfstan of York, whose insistence on *lagu* pushed aside the Anglo-Saxon word *æ*; he also seems to have created the specialized legal sense of *cost* – 'a condition'.[22] Meanwhile, words such as *dreng* (warrior) and *cnearr* (a kind of small ship) were absorbed in times aquake with fear of Nordic military might.

The second period of borrowing, between the accession to the English throne of the Danish king Cnut in 1016 and around 1150, delivered words of a more domestic stripe: *knife*, *skin*, *score*. Other words acquired in this period are *leg* and *same*.[23] *Akimbo*, which might be imagined to be Hindi or Japanese, appears also to derive from a Norse or Icelandic term heard at this time, although it did not achieve its present spelling until the eighteenth century. Whereas in the previous phase English-speakers had adopted Norse words out of deference to their new masters, now Norse-speakers were switching to English and interfering with its vocabulary. What did they feel the need to bring in? As Simon Winchester nicely remarks, 'we can somehow understand that the gloomy antecedents of Ibsen would have given to English the likes of *awkward*, *birth*, *dirt*, *fog* (perhaps), *gap*, *ill*, *mire*, *muggy*, *ransack*, *reindeer*, *root*, *rotten*, *rugged*, *scant*, *scowl*, and *wrong*.'[24] Even grimmer loans from this source include *muck*, *scab* and possibly *scum*.

A different perspective is offered by Helena Drysdale, who alludes to the lasting 'northern connection' between Britain and Scandinavia, and remarks of Sweden, 'Muesli, yoghurt, fresh milk, brown bread, comfortable clothes: I felt more at home here than in France.'[25] The sentiment rings true; the temperamental kinship between Britons and Scandinavians is a kind of open secret.

Although substantial during this second period up to 1150, the Scandinavian contribution to English then faded; Norse continued to be spoken in some northern areas well into the twelfth century, but fell away as the settlers gave up their language in favour of

English – and then as French asserted itself.[26] The total legacy amounts to about 2,000 words in use in Standard English today, with as many more hanging on in the regional dialects of Cumbria and the north-east, such as *beck*, a stream, and *keld*, a fountain or spring.

We get a sense of what was important in Anglo-Saxon life from some of the areas where its vocabulary was most concentrated. It is often claimed that the Inuits (or Eskimos, as they are wrongly called) have a vast array of words for snow, and the claim seems plausible, for they are likely to label different types of snow the way a geologist discriminates between types of stone. Yet whereas the image of the Inuits as connoisseurs of snow is actually quite doubtful, Anglo-Saxon provides a pleasingly authentic example of this sort of lexical clustering: its more than thirty words for 'warrior' reflect its pugnacious culture, and the profusion of seafaring terms is a reminder of Viking wanderlust, an addiction to seaborne adventures that has infiltrated the very heart of the British consciousness.

Pick up certain words, study them, and you can almost hear the rush of the sea inside. *Storm*, *sail*, *oar* and *mast* are stately and spacious. So is *sea* itself. The names for the four points of the compass are much older than the compass itself. Given their skill as sailors, we should not be surprised that the marauding Scandinavians intro-duced to the Anglo-Saxon stock of sea terms a fleet of new ones, such as *billow* and *raft*. In passing, it is worth noting how many everyday idioms derive from the language of the sea. Some of them retain an unambiguously nautical air, as when we talk of *plain sailing*, *stemming the tide* or *clearing the decks*. Others show their colours a little less clearly – *to show one's colours* is indeed one such example, and so are *to touch bottom*, *in the offing* and *distress signals*. Then there are those phrases somewhat less plainly nautical in origin, which are nevertheless exactly that: *under way*, *to break the ice*, *to keep abreast of something*, *to find one's bearings*, *second-rate*. This imagery is a relic of a now-desiccated maritime Britain. We may no longer agree with Ernest Barker's claim that 'the Englishman . . . hears the surge and thunder of the sea, and tastes its savour, however far inland he may be,' but nowhere in Britain is more than 70 miles from the sea.[27] For a modern Anglo-Saxon, the coast remains close, and the prospect of riding the waves seems alien only to a few.

The most commonly used words in English today are relics of Old English: they include *the* and *that*, *of* and *from*, *in* and *by*, *to* and *with*, and of course *and*. The most commonly used noun is *word* – a telling indication of the amount of energy we expend discussing language. The dozen most common verbs are *say, get, go, know, think, see, make, come, take, want, give* and *mean*. Ten of these were part of the native stock of Old English – the exceptions are the Norse loanwords *want* and *take*.[28] Other words of great age include *town, earl, thief* and *theft, yoke, wood, throat* and *church*. The names of many animals – for instance, *mouse, wolf, hare* and *cow* – are similarly venerable. The terms we use for natural features, such as *hill* and *stream*, are mostly Anglo-Saxon too.

The literature of the period is reticent, laconic and metaphorical. Sentiment is often kept at bay, while candour is paramount. Puns exploit words' several layers of meaning, and heavily alliterative structures are favoured. Our impressions are incomplete, however, as only 30,000 lines of Anglo-Saxon poetry have survived; the 3,182 lines of *Beowulf*, preserved in a single fire-damaged manuscript, represent by far the most substantial example and have a distinctly Scandinavian aroma. Clearly, a poem will make use of a rich selection of vocabulary, so this most accessible of Anglo-Saxon texts is not necessarily a reliable guide to the modes of everyday speech. All the same, the poetry sings to us of an age preoccupied with courage and honour, as well as with the alien presences lurking at the margin of society; Beowulf makes a point of talking up his physical strength and his skills in fighting giants and water-monsters, yet he would sooner be peaceable than violent. There is plenty in *Beowulf* that we can recognize – the monster Grendel inhabits the 'moras' and the 'fen', for instance – but besides numerous strange-looking words there are bewildering features such as a minute distinction between different types of man: *ceorl* and *wer*, *beorn* and *rinc*, *gome* and, not entirely reassuringly, *man*.

Alongside this creative writing about heroic champions and journeys grew a new culture of scholarship. In the later part of the tenth century the monasteries underwent dramatic reform, becoming major centres of literary endeavour. At Ramsey in the Fens, for instance, the direction of Oswald, archbishop of York, ensured close contact with France; Oswald had imbibed the spirit of reform while a monk at Fleury-sur-Loire, the capital of Benedictine scholarship. At the heart of the reform movement was a focus on assembling and reproducing seminal texts: the teaching of mathematics, history, ancient literature and Bible study was much improved. The revival of monastic learning – encapsulated in the new prominence of the word *school* – helped boost both the preservation of Latin texts and the status of Old English as a language in which to craft works of literature. Its fruits were delicious. In all, it resulted in about 450 Latin words finding their way into English texts before the end of the Old English period, and three-quarters of these were taken into general use.[29]

Meanwhile, shifts in political power were gestating. At the beginning of the eleventh century Ethelred, known to posterity as 'the Unready', was on the throne. It was claimed that he soiled the font during his baptism, and that this was a portent of the English monarchy's demise. The story is almost certainly apocryphal, but, despite the efforts of his more inspiring son Edmund Ironside, the fortunes of his house collapsed: in 1016 the throne passed to Cnut, who married Ethelred's Norman widow, Emma, the following year. Cnut jointly ruled in England and Denmark, and was King of Norway for the final seven years of his life. England was his main focus; his nineteen-year rule was skilfully oppressive, notable for heavy taxes and the artful piety he exhibited in order to placate influential churchmen. However, all his children died without issue, and in 1042 the Danish line fizzled out, allowing Emma's son by Ethelred, Edward, to become king.

The more genuinely pious Edward the Confessor, having grown up in Normandy, insinuated new influences. His court attracted Norman visitors, and he appointed a Frenchman to the bishopric of London and then to Canterbury. Since his Norman confidants spoke French, ambitious English noblemen made stuttering efforts to ingratiate themselves by doing so too. This Norman presence is evident in the splashes of French found in Old English. *Prut*, meaning 'proud', came from the French word *prud* and spawned *prutness* and *prutlic* and the damning *oferprut*. The first recorded use of the French word *cancheler* (which would morph into *chancellor*) is in a pre-Conquest charter, and documents of this kind increasingly showed the influence of French handwriting.

The royal succession was to be tangled, for half-Norman Edward lacked a true heir. Of his relatives, the most immediate candidate was Edmund Ironside's son Edward, but he was exiled in Hungary, which hardly made him a credible successor, and after this Edward's death the role devolved on his young son, Edgar the Atheling. Edgar's claims were ignored, and it was Harold, son of the powerful Earl Godwine of Wessex, who was crowned at Westminster when the Confessor died in the first week of 1066. William of Normandy, who believed he had been promised the throne, challenged Harold's election by the English magnates, and began a determined campaign of diplomacy and propaganda.

The *Anglo-Saxon Chronicle* for that year records that William sailed to Pevensey, and that 'this became known to King Harold and he gathered a great raiding-army, and came against him at the grey apple tree.' There was 'great slaughter' on both sides, but eventually 'the French had possession of the place of slaughter, just as God granted them because of the people's sins.'[30] The remark about English sins can be interpreted as a criticism of the supposedly decadent English Church or as a reference to the story that before Hastings the English feasted drunkenly while the Normans prayed. What is certain, though, is that the Normans believed that God awarded victory to those of whom he approved. Their success in battle licensed a self-righteous confidence, and began a period of French political and cultural dominance that lasted for 300 years.

The Normans, it should be emphasized, were not exactly French. They were, in fact, of largely Scandinavian origin, and their name points to their Norse antecedents. They had migrated to France only in the ninth century, and had been granted a pocket of land around Rouen by King Charles the Simple. This concession in time expanded to include Evreux, Bessin and the Cotentin peninsula. The Norsemen embraced Christianity and the French language, as well as French habits and manners. Flexible and enterprising, they looked abroad for further gains.

William turned their aspirations into reality. He obtained a papal blessing and drummed up an army of invaders. Some of them were recruited beyond Normandy – many were short of useful employment and therefore on the lookout for any opportunity that smelt of money. Yet they were men of war, even if not necessarily men of standing. They brought their horses with them, and their expertise on horseback and superior ballistics proved decisive at Hastings: mounted troops shocked the Saxon infantry. They also, inevitably, brought their language, a dialect of what was later recognized as the *langue d'oïl*. It did not flood across Britain, but its effects were soon obvious.

Rather than overwhelming the entire Saxon nation, the invaders simply pushed aside its aristocracy. Forest and fields were carved up. The Domesday Book would show, twenty years after the Conquest, that less than a tenth of the land remained in the hands of the Anglo-Saxon noblemen. The very fact of this document's creation signalled the humiliation of the native people; 'Domesday' meant 'day of judgement', and a record of this kind was, in the words of the historian Michael Clanchy, 'a product of distrust rather than social progress'.[31] The Domesday Book, though written in Latin, was symbolic of the new regime's particular brand of thoroughness. Its name, which was rooted in Old English, represented the attitude not of those who created it, but of those whose holdings it so decisively adjudged. In the years following its compilation, it was not often used, but the process of making it intimidated the people. Furthermore, it linked written records with the exercise of royal power. After Domesday, documents came to be seen as vital administrative tools: records were kept of court sessions, land transfers and enclosures, apprenticeships, conscription and taxes.[32] Most of them were written in the French dialect that has come to be known as Anglo-Norman.

Seen from the vantage point of the present, the Domesday Book highlights the way land was reapportioned after the Conquest. It even introduces a new term of land measurement, the *carucate*, an area of 120 acres (as much land as could be ploughed in one year with a team of eight oxen), and we can trace the phrase *no man's land* to the same massive text.

The glut of administrative writing that followed shows that

political changes were rapidly effected, but it took time for the change of regime to stamp its presence on the language. It is likely that in William's England there were fewer native French-speakers than there had been Norse-speakers during the reign of Cnut: French could not supplant English as the language of those beyond William's court. Moreover, fundamental differences between English and French meant that it was not easy to become bilingual. The individuals who did so tended to be at the higher end of the social scale. Yet within three generations of the Conquest most noblemen were comfortable in either language. One recent account states that after the Conquest 'those who normally fought used French, those who worked, English, and those who prayed, Latin.'[33] Another, older, account suggestively posits that 'The overlords spoke Norman French, as the white settlers of Kenya speak modern English.'[34] The three languages mingled and interpenetrated in complex ways. By the end of the twelfth century the status of French was close to that of Latin − a language of administration, culture and learning, but not of common daily speech. In the wake of conquest, even as French becomes the language of power, 'Old English phrases, syntax, and idioms remain the expressive baseline of the land.'[35]

As Richard Bailey has pointed out, in the period following the Conquest new words sprang up for 'those who mediated across the boundaries which language could create'. One example was *latimer*, a corruption of *latiner*, and another was *translator*, a term imported from French. A further word of this type was *drugeman* − plainly the same as *dragoman*, a word we shall meet in due course, but modelled in this early form on the Old French *drugemen*. Later, 'the bilingual facilitator' came to be called a *truchman* or *linguister*.[36] Especially important were clerks and scribes, capable polyglots who wrote up documents − prototypes of the modern bureaucrat. But they were not the only ones who had to reach across the boundary for professional reasons. A merchant or a household servant would have needed a working knowledge of both languages, and so would a wet nurse. As they switched between the two, French words slipped into English usage, and, undoubtedly, words from English and other British languages were absorbed, in Gallicized forms, by Anglo-Norman. Individuals would not have used words in this way self-consciously, and their sense of the boundaries of 'their' language would have been quite fluid. In time, the languages merged.

When you achieve power, in any situation, you create not only new laws, but also a new language of rule and new words for those you rule. It is something of a cliché that 'language is power'; it is more useful to see that power is in part a feat of language. Forms of language are used to protect a society's dominant group. The Normans introduced new job titles, such as *assizer* and *alnager* (a quality controller in the wool trade), and the king's *exchequer* took its name from the counting table, draped with a squared cloth that resembled a chessboard, where revenues were piled and totted up. They introduced the concept of *tenserie*, which was protection money. They used local labour to build castles, which they then staffed with their own men. The word *castle* can be found in Anglo-Saxon translations of the Gospels before the Conquest, but there it signifies a village; only after the Conquest does the word take on a more forbidding aspect.

The whole character of the invaders' military efforts was impressive. Their expertise is implicit in the copious new language of warfare that they introduced. This comprised such words as *fortress, conflict, siege, assault* and *armour*, along with the punitive *prison* and *tax. War* itself is a Norman word – the Germanic tribes had had no single word that conveniently conveyed its meaning, while the Latin *bellum* had always been awkward, given its proximity to several words meaning 'beautiful'. Unsurprisingly, the entire vocabulary of castle-building was Norman, and, although the basic parts of a man's armour kept their Anglo-Saxon names (*shield*, for instance), the Normans' more sophisticated equipment enriched the lexis of combat with a host of fantastic items like the *ventail*, a piece of armour for protecting the neck, and the *rere-brace*, which protected the triceps.

Few manuscripts survive as testimony to the cultural and linguistic traumas of the period. This shortage of documentation means that the earliest citations we can find for some French loanwords are not until several hundred years after the Conquest, although we can infer that many were adopted much earlier. Of course, few borrowings were immediate: it needed at least two generations of bilingualism to break down the essential English mistrust of French words. As one historian argues, 'The true fusion of French and native elements seemingly took place only after English had risen again from the thraldom to which William's Conquest had consigned it.' As a 'slave tongue' it 'sullenly kept to itself', but as 'the free tongue of independent men' it was both resurgent and absorbent.[37] By 1150 Old English was in effect obsolete, although Old English texts continued to be copied in the thirteenth century. It was superseded by what we call Middle English, into which a wealth of Anglo-Norman was absorbed – not as ornament, but organically. Middle English is, as its name suggests, the transitional phase between the strongly inflected Old English and its very modestly inflected Modern successor. Grammar was changing, and so was pronunciation. Word order now clearly governed the meaning of sentences, and the role of prepositions became greater. Vowel sounds lengthened. These were not direct consequences of the Norman Conquest, but the French administration recorded the changes.

The augmentation of English vocabulary was an integral part of this change. Many of the French words that entered English were imposed rather than assimilated. Respect was institutionalized, and there developed a whole new language of master-servant relations, manifest in the advent of French words like *allegiance*, *fealty* and *homage*. Indeed, *master* itself, though assimilated from Latin before the Conquest, was reinforced by the Norman term *maistre*, and *servant* is Norman too. The Old English *cniht* (knight) held out against the comparatively awkward word *chevalier*, but there were plenty of new titles, ranging right across the social spectrum from *marquess* and *viscount* to *page* and *serf*.

The opulence and hierarchical nature of the Anglo-Norman household are suggested in the newly imported words *banquet*, *butler* and *page*, and other novelties in this field included *cellar*, *dinner*, *goblet* and *chimney*. Do these words *feel* French? Not at this remove. But then neither does the French of French-mediated names that came in at the same time, like William, Robert, Alice, Richard, Henry, Hugh and Matilda.[38] The practice of using surnames was also a Norman phenomenon, and increased significantly in the twelfth century; by 1300, only 1 per cent of the population lacked a surname.[39] Meanwhile, the names the Normans gave places, such as Beaulieu and Richmond, contained unmistakable judgements about the allure of their new estates. The words fell like snow, covering what was there before. (The image is George Orwell's, not my own.) For instance, the French loan *riche* overlaid Old English *rice*, which had the meaning 'powerful' and conveyed a sense of nobility; initially the French loan reinforced the existing term, but then the older connotations melted away, and *rich* increasingly had to do with material possessions, not personal qualities.

The word-stock registered as well the gamut of Norman leisure activities and accoutrements. In the Middle English period, when acquisitions from French were abundant, new terms sprang up in literature and music, in fashion and architecture – and these channels have stayed open ever since. *Gown* was one such import; others were *cloak, garter, satin* and *ermine. Fashion* itself was French, as was *style.* This channel of influence has never closed, and it is to French that we owe altogether more recent loans like *blouse, gauze* and *moustache.* The sixteenth-century traveller Fynes Moryson touched as neatly as anyone has done on the advent of French style:

> The wise Romans as they inlarged theire Conquests, so they did spreade theire language, with their lawes, and the divine service all in the lattene tongue, and by rewardes and preferments invited men to speake it, as also the Normans in England brought in the use of the French tounge, in our Common lawe, and all wordes of art in hawking, hunting, and like pastymes.[40]

Hawking and hunting had been popular before the Conquest, but their vocabulary was now overhauled. The falconer's vocabulary for different types of bird is thus heavily French – *peregrine, gyrfalcon, saker, lanner, merlin, hobby* – although *goshawk* is Old English and is found in an early eleventh-century glossary of Latin. The expressions *to turn tail* and *pride of place* also derive from the Norman practices and doctrines of hawking. The adjective *haggard* is related to the French name for a wild bird captured as an adult, while also influenced by the Teutonic *hag*, a wild-looking woman. Heraldic devices, which proved helpful in identifying men who were clad in otherwise anonymous armour, took their names from French, as we can see from the names of their 'tinctures' (*vert*, *azure*, *argent*) and partitions (the *chevron*, for example, and the *bordure*).

At the same time, French terms suggested the changing contours of day-to-day morality. There were new ideals of behaviour. The language of status became the language of moral excellence, while low status was equated with low moral standards. The etymologies of *chivalry* and *courtesy* show up their aristocratic temper, embedding the values of horsemanship and the royal court. By contrast, the Anglo-Saxon *churl* and *knave*, formerly markers only of inferior status, became terms of condemnation.[41] Other new words included *courage* and *virtue*. I shall say more about the former in a later chapter; as far as *virtue* is concerned, the key thing to spot is that it is ultimately connected to the Latin *vir*, 'man', and to be virtuous was originally to be strong, to show a capacity for action. Later, the same type of distinction was made between urban polish and rude rusticity. We see something of the new moral colour in the *Ancren Riwle*, a manual for aspiring female hermits dating from around 1230, which introduces a host of new words: *apocalypse*, *comfort*, *discipline*, *guile*, *purgatory*, *virtue* and *hypocrite*, plus an early, isolated, sighting of *scandal*. It also features some novel calques of French expressions: *to make moan*, *to make profession*, *to cry mercy* and *beforehand*. (Other such calques tended to be modelled on expressions that used the verbs *avoir* and *faire*. For example, *to have mercy* and *to make peace*.) At the other end of the spectrum there were new and distinctive Anglo-Norman terms of abuse, notably *bugger* and *bastard*.[42] *Bugger*, it should be pointed out, was a word for a heretic – literally, a Bulgarian.

While many of the new words related to the lives and concerns of the aristocracy, others had to do with the most ordinary matters. A comprehensive list would be overwhelming, but examples include *fruit* and *vegetable*, *place* and *number*, *pleasure* and *pain*. Although the Normans introduced new concepts, to a greater degree, as these novelties suggest, they brought fresh ways of expressing existing ones. Some were freighted with moral significance; for instance, *kynde* frequently gave way to *nature*, a word with more obviously religious overtones, which suggested a link between a thing's attributes or character and certain deeper, God-given, principles. *Cattle* became the standard word for personal property, and, because livestock tended to make up the chief part of a person's movable goods, it came to be used almost exclusively of domesticated animals – not just cows, but also pigs, goats, sheep and even bees. Parts of the body generally kept their Anglo-Saxon names, but the French *face* managed to displace *onsene* in casual speech.

The Norman influence pierced even the heart of family life: *nephew, niece, cousin, aunt* and *uncle* displaced existing terms, although the Saxon words for the most intimate relationships – *mother, father, sister, brother* – remained. *Nephew* superseded the compound mouthfuls *brothorsunu* and *sweostorsunu*, and, downplaying the ties of kinship so obvious in the Old English, perhaps implied among other things a recalibration of the nurturing uncle-nephew relationship – one to which the Anglo-Saxons had attached special significance. Moreover, while *mother-in-law*, *sister-in-law* and their like were made up of English words, they were actually calques, recreating the shape of terms used in French.

Norman settlers soon began to intermarry with the natives. The chronicler Orderic Vitalis, born in 1075, was the child of such a marriage, though he habitually referred to himself as 'Vitalis the Englishman'. Nothing more urgently accelerates the need for successful communication than the heat of sexual desire. For many Normans, the Englishwomen were sleeping dictionaries. The children that resulted from these unions picked up elements of both languages, and switched, like latimers and linguisters, between the two. As they did so, some of the French words they used ceased to be thought of as French, while others acquired subtly new senses.

For a picture of the influence of French, we may usefully look at two different versions of *Brut*, a poem which offers an account of British history and was the work of a Worcestershire cleric known to posterity as Layamon. Whereas in a version dating from around 1200 we find the words *marmon-stane, munuccliff, milce* and *boc-runen*, an updated text produced half a century later replaces them with terms we will recognize much more readily: *marbre* (marble), *abbey, grace* and *letter*.

Of the approximately 27,000 words identified in the *OED* as having first been used between 1250 and 1450, more than a fifth have French origins, and more than three-quarters of these are nouns.[43] About half of all words in common use are nouns, and the introduction of new nouns – so many of them material – marks the discovery of new things, new experiences, new attitudes.

Nouns have always been the part of speech absorbed in greatest number; verbs and adjectives are the only other groups where loans are at all common. The adoption from other languages of parts of speech other than nouns is evidence of a deep connection – an engagement with concepts, rather than just with 'stuff' – but nouns, though they may give less pleasure than adjectives and adverbs, mark the space we inhabit and the objects that earth our perceptions. Here they reinforce our understanding of what the Normans introduced to Britain: castles and cavalry, feudalism, new systems of land tenure and government, new styles of church and name, writs, courts and prisons, as well as rabbits and cider-making. These last two novelties merit a brief digression. Today, after all, the French name for a rabbit is *lapin*. But a connection with our word *rabbit* is suggested in *rabouillère*, the burrow where the female rabbit brings forth her young. As for the cider-making, the Norman terms could not displace the old words *apple* and *orchard*, but *cider* itself was Norman, and so was its pear-based cousin, *perry*.

The public profile of English had diminished. It was still used in private, but its character was changing; noticeably, for instance, the old clusters of consonants were being broken down. Of the areas to escape French influence, two of the most important were seafaring and farming, both of which were long-established components of English identity into which the Normans could introduce no significant innovations.

The French language that came to Britain with the Conquest comprised the forms spoken in Normandy, Brittany and Picardy. The Normans made up the largest contingent of the invading army, and for a couple of generations, it seems, the French spoken in England was not very different from that spoken in Normandy. (Histories of English have tended to be dogmatic on the point, which seems dangerous, since there are, perhaps needless to say, no audio recordings of the Norman knights travelling through the south of England, and the evidence we do possess is the work of scribes, an anonymous and mobile class.)[44] In 1154 the accession of Henry II relocated the Crown's political base to Anjou, and this conferred new prestige on the dialect of central France, which was also spoken in Paris. Henry could speak little or no English, though he could understand it; his wife, Eleanor of Aquitaine, had no grasp whatsoever of the language. Many found themselves inconvenienced by this shift. One of its likely effects was a decrease in the status of Norman French, which came to be regarded as rather rustic and uncouth by those who spoke the Parisian form – a group that included an increasingly large number of England's courtiers. A well-known French poem of the period denigrated the '*faus franceis . . . d'Angleterre*' – proof of the divergence.[45] Increasingly, Norman French was marginalized: people bilingual in English and Norman French found the latter less useful, while Parisian French, though exalted, seemed alien.

Yet, as Norman French was losing its vernacular currency under Henry, it was becoming the language of the law, displacing Latin. While some of the law's old mechanisms remained, the terminology was refined, largely so as to disempower English-speakers. The Norse word *law* survived, but a new jargon engulfed every dimension of its practice and enforcement. Much of this endures: *jury, justice, plea, plaintiff, lease, larceny* and *crime* are all from French. So are *real estate* and the curious word order of *court martial*. Furthermore, specialist terms such as *suit, impeachment, assault and battery* and *rape* were specifically Anglo-Norman, their forms different from those found in the French used on the Continent.[46] As English law became more sophisticated, so the gulf between the artificial Law French and the spoken language widened, and the legal uses of French grew increasingly specialized. Geoffrey Hughes observes that 'the old direct and familiar native terms were replaced by new opaque equivalents.' This cultivation of a less than transparent language of administration would over time establish itself as 'a general model in the development of professional language in English'.[47]

Behind the everyday appearance of *council, county* and *custom* lies a recognizable substrate of otiose bureaucracy. All are French imports, along with such financial terms as *price, receipt, revenue* and *budget*. The last of these derives from the French diminutive *bougette*, which can be traced back to the Latin *bulga*, 'a leather bag'. The word *tort*, still used to signify any breach of a legally imposed responsibility, was current in French in the eleventh century and retained its Latin connotations of twisting (not just of wronging, but also of wringing), while the first uses of the French-derived *heir* and *appeal* were in legal contexts. Surprisingly, *hotchpotch* derives from *hochepot*, a French legal term for the gathering of properties to make it possible to divide them equally; out of this came its use for a dish comprising a jumble of ingredients, and by the sixteenth century it could signify a medley or farrago of any kind.

The *Dialogus de Scaccario*, produced by Henry II's treasurer Richard FitzNigel around 1177, is a fascinatingly lucid account of the operations of the exchequer. It also sheds light on the merging of English and Norman identities. In the guise of the 'Master', FitzNigel explains that in the aftermath of the Conquest 'what were left of the conquered English lay in ambush for the suspected and hated Normans and murdered them secretly in woods and unfrequented places as opportunity offered.' When a Norman was found killed 'without his slayer being known or revealing his identity by flight', the hundred (i.e. local subdivision of the county) where the crime was discovered had to pay 'a large sum of assayed silver, £36 or £44 according to the locality of the murder and the commonness of the crime'. But at the time of his writing, the fine is exacted 'whoever is found slain': after more than a hundred years of social contact and intermarriage, the 'nations are so mixed' that among all but the lowest orders of society 'it can scarcely be decided . . . who is of English birth and who of Norman.'[48]

Henry II's youngest son, John, would see this at first hand. He inherited the kingdom from his brother Richard, who had spent no more than 5 per cent of his ten-year reign in England. John, by contrast, explored his mixed kingdom. But then he had to: having lost ground in France to his rival Arthur of Brittany, he lost more as a result of poor strategy. In 1200 John took as his second wife the 13-year-old Isabella of Angoulême. His choice was fuelled by lust, and it was rash, for Isabella had been betrothed to another man, Hugh de Lusignan. Hugh appealed to the judgement of King Philip Augustus of France, and Philip, riding roughshod over the law, pronounced John a rebellious vassal and confiscated his French lord-ships. Despite John's attempts to cling on to Normandy, Philip seized it, marching triumphantly into Rouen in June 1204. Thereafter, only the Channel Islands stayed loyal to John, and although he twice tried to make inroads in Poitou he failed to gain a new foothold in France.

The English Channel now seemed a wider gap than at any point in the previous 150 years, and the gulf increased under John's son, Henry III. Although the Francophile Henry's marriage to Eleanor of Provence introduced a fresh wave of French courtiers, resistance to their influence brought about a surge of nationalist feeling. Moreover, Henry's awareness of his country's Anglo-Saxon past is evident in his politic decision to name his first son Edward, after the Confessor. And whereas John's Magna Carta was written in Latin, the draft constitution to which Henry subscribed in 1258 under the Provisions of Oxford was pointedly drawn up in Latin, French and English. This was a feat of propaganda, determinedly inclusive. Copies of the English version were sent out into every county, to be promulgated by the local sheriffs.

Henry's son Edward was to be a passionate defender of English, and later, during the Hundred Years' War (1337–1453), burgeoning English nationalism fostered an increased respect for the vernacular. Writing home during his French campaigns, Henry V chose English, and his travelling secretariat played a crucial role in the develop-ment of its standard form. In 1362 the Statute of Pleading was enacted, and, at least in principle, English became the language of Parliament and of the law. Yet ironically, even though it declared that all pleas should be couched in English and promoted the idea that using English in courts would dispel confusion, the Statute was written in French and stipulated that court records be kept in Latin. Its rhetoric was firm, but the closed ranks of the legal profession shunned much of its logic. For another 300 years lawyers would continue to do a great deal of their writing and thinking in French, and they would supplement it with generous helpings of Latin – words like *affidavit* and *subpoena* – which conveyed an air of precision and authority unavailable to English. To this day the language of the law proves prolix, repetitious, archaic and theatrical, as indeed do many of its quite mystifying processes and practitioners. Legal terminology retains quite a number of bilingual doublets, such as 'keep and maintain', 'goods and chattels' and 'will and testament'. Lightly disguised French terms such as *larceny* and *devise* have proved remarkably durable alternatives to *theft* and *bequeath*.[49] Nevertheless, by the second half of the fourteenth century the legal position of English was greatly strengthened, and by the early part of the fifteenth legal documents were more likely to be in English than in French. At this time we also see a dramatic rise in the volume of wills and letters composed in English.

The Normans' legal apparatus engendered political unity. The disparate parts of England had been drawn together in the century before the Conquest, and now under Norman rule this togetherness tightened, bringing the antipathies between the English and their Welsh and Scottish neighbours into sharper relief. But the Conquest was only slowly completed: rebellious elements in the north-west and in Wales resisted Norman rule, and it was not until 1284 that Wales was incorporated into England under the Statute of Rhuddlan, which introduced the mechanisms of English law and smoothed the way for English settlers. In Scotland, pressures exerted by the Norman administration gradually pushed Gaelic-speakers north into the Highlands. The reign of Malcolm Canmore, who had an English wife, saw an increase in 'anglicization', and familiar patterns of land tenure were superseded by Anglo-Norman feudalism. In the *burghs* – urban communities established by royal charter – English and French were in frequent use, and the Scottish Church assimilated English practices and the English calendar during the twelfth century. Later, the English-language Bible would enhance the status of English north of the border: a law passed in 1579 obliged every householder worth 300 marks to possess a Bible, and in practice this meant an *English* one.[50]

Another significant development, in 1169, saw adventurers from Pembrokeshire – some of whom spoke English – land at the south-eastern tip of Ireland near Wexford. Although the language did not establish itself decisively in Ireland until the seventeenth century, following James I's encouragement of Scottish settlement in Ulster and Oliver Cromwell's military victories, English was seeded there by this twelfth-century invasion. Nearly 200 years later, in 1366, its position was enlarged by the Statute of Kilkenny, which marked a cogent attempt to quench Gaelic, insisting that the Irish people accept English names, English speech and the English way of riding horses. Thus English first jutted into the Irish consciousness during the reign of Henry II – another Norman success.

While Latin remained the language of the Church, and held sway for a large part of the millennium as the language not just of the clergy and lawyers, but also of physicians, a good deal of ecclesiastical language was imported. Although the simple, vital concepts – *God*, for instance, and *sin* – retained their old names, the mechanics of faith and observance were explained afresh. The Normans had brought their own clergy, and their clerical vocabulary was abstract: *sacrament, saint, nativity, grace, miracle, sermon, mercy. Charity* displaced the appealing *mild-heortnes.* Later additions included *salvation, purity* and *devotion.* The Norman construction of cathedrals, as at Durham, Ely and Winchester, echoed this new language of piety.

Although out of doors the French influence was imposing, it was felt with more relish in the kitchen. The Normans liked their food well seasoned. According to romantic tradition, the Saxons caught the animals (*sheep, cow, pig, deer*) and prepared them – by boiling, roasting or frying (all Norman terms) – for the Normans' table, where they reappeared as *mutton, beef, pork* and *venison.* In *Ivanhoe,* Sir Walter Scott shows grunting Saxon *swine* being briskly transformed into *pork* for the Norman repast. Yet by the time the word *pork* came into common use, in the thirteenth century, the social model suggested by Scott was a thing of the past. Furthermore, words such as *mutton* and *beef* were used of the animals as well as of their meat hundreds of years after the Conquest, and their restriction to meat was not finally achieved until the eighteenth century.[51] We can see this persistence very clearly in the case of *venison*, which we encountered earlier, on Samuel Sewall's plate at breakfast. In the Douai Bible of 1609 there is a reference in the first Book of Kings to 'venison of hartes, roes and buffles', and in his classic of social criticism, *Walden* (1854), Henry David Thoreau refers to a 'poor wee' hare as 'wild free venison'. The meaning of *deer* has altered, too, which explains the reference in *King Lear* to 'mice and rats and such small deer' – and the homilist Aelfric of Eynsham's using this word of an *ylp* (short for *ylpend*, 'elephant'). But even if the distinction in language between the living creature and the meat for which it was killed is not so nicely a Norman achievement as is often argued, it is clear that the vocabulary of the kitchen was massively augmented by luxurious Norman appetites. In the period following the Conquest, novelties included *liquorice*, *claret*, *gravy* and *mustard*. As one commentator says poetically, 'The English laboured, the French feasted.'[52] Moreover, the Normans retained troupes of professional entertainers to enliven their feasts. Their various designations – *goliard*, for instance, and *troubadour* and *jongleur* – are now imperfectly understood, but the names recall an age when French was becoming the European language of art, music and entertainment.

It is within this field that borrowings from French have continued most steadily. France is of course Britain's nearest neighbour, and French has long been the living foreign language most widely taught in British schools. It has maintained its prestige by playing a leading role in the lexis of fashion and high art. Think, for example, of these more recent French borrowings, all of which have kept their French pronunciation: *ballet*, *promenade*, *croquet*. Then there are those which are pronounced the French way by some speakers and in a more English manner by others: *envelope*, *trait*, *valet*. In many cases the French stress has been kept, though the pronunciation has been anglicized: examples are *gazette* and *grimace*. (The former has its real roots in Italian, possibly in *gazzetta*, 'little magpie': the sixteenth-century Venetian news-sheets were eclectic collections of information for an audience of chatterers.) And then there are other words, less likely to be recognized as borrowings, where the stress has sharply altered from the original: *palace*, *beauty*, *service*.

Complaints about borrowing from French have been clamorous for much of the last millennium. We shall see a particular anxiety about them later when we look at the nineteenth century. To this day many people consider them pretentious. The standard argument has always been that Anglo-Saxon words are pure and French ones artificial, barbarous and infused with the dark scent of depravity. But purism itself carries a whiff of the absurd. Much of what is condemned as wrong was standard in the past, and the very language that is now held up as 'pure' is itself likely to have been imported in its time. What passes for vigilance is often just intolerance in disguise.

At any time there will be a number of new words or new usages that attract particularly violent condemnation. Yet often they only appear to be new. I'll admit that the first time I saw the word *architect* used as a verb – in an advertisement by a management consultancy, and of a business strategy, not a building – my brow furrowed. Yet later I found it used as a verb by Keats, who also used *architecture* in this way. Had I been too quick to bridle at a perceived solecism? I now think I had, notwithstanding the fact that Keats was pilloried by contemporary reviewers for his profligate way with verbs. We frequently hear pronouncements about what words 'ought' to mean, and these often make studious reference to etymology, as if words must cleave to their etymological roots. But could we find anyone who would insist, in a spirit of etymological nicety, that a *candidate* must be dressed in white, or that a *school* should be, as it was for the ancient Greeks, a place of leisure? As C. S. Lewis pointed out, 'Statements that honour, or freedom, or humour, or wealth, "does not mean" this or that are proof that it was beginning to mean, or even had long meant, precisely this or that . . . We are in fact resisting the growth of a new sense.'[53] Our communicative procedures evolve, as we have done and (slowly) continue to do.

None of this is to say that we need no guidance on matters of usage. There are compelling reasons for punctuating and spelling according to particular conventions, as there are for wanting a large degree of stability in our language. But fighting battles about individual words and tiny increments of semantic change is bootless. There has long been – and in some quarters there remains – an appetite for employing Anglo-Saxon words where more recent imports are the norm. The nineteenth-century clergyman William Barnes preferred *wheelsaddle* to *bicycle* and *folkwain* to *omnibus*. By the same token *forceps* would be *nipperlings*, and *pathology* would be *painlore*. Some of his new words recalled the language of Old English poetry: he proposed *glee-mote* in place of *concert*, and the wonderful *cellar-thane* instead of *butler*. In the sixteenth century John Cheke had tried something similar in translating passages from the Bible:

for example, he coined *gainrising* in place of *resurrection*. More recently the historian and broadcaster David Starkey has declared that 'the word *liberation* is a foreign word, and . . . it's very inappropriate to our own context . . . I actually believe in a good English word, and it's called *freedom*.'[54] Here we have, once again, the familiar notion that the older word is more authentic, more true to something intrinsically English, less smudged by its foreign associations – which in this case are to do with the French Revolution.

But how pure are the purists? Daniel Defoe could refer in his poem 'The True-Born Englishman' (1700) to the 'heterogeneous' island people: given their origins 'in eager rapes' or 'furious lust' and the repeated infusions of foreign blood, it was all too easy to see that 'A true-born Englishman's a Contradiction, / In speech an irony, in fact a fiction.' As for the language this Englishman spoke, it was best described as 'your Roman-Saxon-Danish-Norman-English'. Defoe had pertinent and immediate reasons for writing this – after all, at that time the English throne had recently passed to a Dutchman, William of Orange – but his words stand as a deft summary of the miscellaneous nature of English and its speakers. He identifies some of the traits the English have been bequeathed by their ancestors: there is Roman valour, Nordic glumness, the sour manner of the Picts, Saxon honesty, and Norman falsehood. The different 'customs, surnames, languages, and manners' of these groups contribute to an 'amphibious' national character. Defoe's lines manage both to satirize conceited English self-regard and to demonstrate his confidence in the expressive potential of English.

The debt to French, and the resistance to it, is a subject to be revisited later on. Yet while French percolated through English, there was at the same time another, much more remote, source of new words that was beginning to involve itself in the language.

3. Saffron

A product consisting of the dried stigmas of a kind of crocus. It is used as a flavouring and dye, and was formerly used as a medicine.

The noun ultimately derives from the Arabic *zafaran*, the origin of which is unknown. Etymologists sometimes make an erroneous connection between *zafaran* and the word *asfar*, 'yellow'.

In San Francisco Bay there is a small island which from 1850 to 1963 served as a prison. Its name is Alcatraz. It was christened by the Spanish seaman Juan de Ayala, who landed on its rocky shore in 1775; struck by its sizeable pelican colony, he dubbed it La Isla de Alcatraces – in Spanish, *alcatraz* is the name of that gregarious bird with its bucket-shaped bill. If we trace this word back further, we find its source is *al-qadus*, the Arabic term for a bucket attached to the sort of waterwheel used for irrigation.

This may seem little more than a curious nugget of trivia, but it opens up a significant lexical field, as we can see when we consider some of the other English words that begin *al-*. In an age when *al-Jazeera* – literally 'The Peninsula', after Qatar, the peninsula where it is based – is a hugely popular Arabic television channel and *al-Qaeda*, 'The Base', a globally infamous Islamist group, we may be more alert to the possibility that words of this type have Arabic roots. It is from Arabic that we have derived *alkali*, *alchemy* and *almanac*. *Alcohol* is related to *kohl*, the sooty powder used as a cosmetic in the Middle East.[1] And *ealfara*, an obsolete Old English word for a packhorse, which seems to have been the first borrowing from Arabic, derived from *al-faras*, 'the horse'.[2]

The noun *algorithm* has become quite common in an age of computerized calculations, although it did not make its first appearance until 1957. Previously the word had been *algorism*, which was a corruption of the final part of the name of a ninth-century mathematician, Muhammad ibn Musa al-Khwarizmi: the Latin *algoritmi* was an approximation of al-Khwarizmi, which meant 'the man from Chorasmia' (today the Khorezm province of Uzbekistan). Another English word imbued with a legacy of misunderstanding is *admiral*. This is an anglicized version of *amiir al-bahr*, which literally means 'commander of the sea'. It is the word *bahr* that means 'sea', but this is the part that English has relinquished. Thinking of words of this stripe, we should note that the first appearance in English of *algebra* (Arabic *al-jabr*) was in 1541, when it was used to mean 'bone-setting'. The refined organizational work of a mathematician working with complex formulae is not unlike the fastidious prestidigitation of a bone-setter. And if we look to other European languages, in particular Spanish, we can see this link preserved.

All these words retain the Arabic definite article and are thus quite easily spotted. Yet many of English's borrowings from Arabic are not of this pattern and would not commonly be recognized as having such a source. While words connected with the Muslim faith – *Allah*, *Qur'an*, *Ramadan* – are all plainly Arabic in origin, as is the word *Arab* itself, what of *carcass*, *syrup* or *mattress*? Each of these can be traced to an Arabic root. *Mattress* derives from an Arabic phrase meaning 'the place where something is thrown': it seems that medieval travellers to the Middle East noticed the Arab habit of sleeping on scattered cushions. Here, then, is a classic example of something we take for granted having a source – now forgotten – in European encounters with that amorphous construct 'the East'. (And, while we are about it, there is a certain irony in the name of Marco Materazzi, the Italian footballer most famous for falling theatrically to the turf after being butted by Zinedine Zidane in the 2006 World Cup Final, deriving from a word for something thrown to the ground.)

When we think about European encounters with the East, we would do well to picture the relationship from the other side. Europe, so easily thought of as a big place, especially when we are talking up its diversity, can also be seen as a small one. In Fernand Braudel's chastening phrase, 'Europe is an Asian peninsula.'[3] It is a given that Europeans underestimate the scale and resources and history of Asia – and do so recklessly. By looking at English's Arabic connection, we can begin to correct this.

Sugar, for instance, is one of those articles we think is ours by right and can barely imagine being without. But it was introduced to western Europe by Berbers only at around the time the first Viking ships were harrying England. Its name derives from the Arabic *sukkar*.[4] *Apricot* comes from Spanish, yet can be traced back further to *al-burquq*; the fruit was known to the Greeks, but was popularized by Arabs who introduced it into Andalucia and Sicily. The *lute* took its name from the Arabic *al-ud* (or from an older Persian term); today visitors to the Middle East can hear music played on a modern fretless version of this called the *oud*.

Examining the Arabic element in English, we sense how important the Arab peoples were in bringing ideas and goods to the West. They were also the essential intermediaries in the flow of commodities between the Mediterranean and the Far East. Wood, iron, linen and money were ferried in one direction, and silks, spices, sugar, glass, gems and finely worked metal came back in the other.[5] Etymologies hint at the channelling of disparate cultures that the traders achieved. Among the spices were *cinnamon*, which gets its name via Greek from Hebrew, and *ginger*, which can ultimately be traced to Sanskrit, while *marzipan*, which came later, may have taken its name from a Burmese city known for its handsome storage jars. Meanwhile, Arabic passed on the intellectual legacy of antiquity, and especially the rewards of Persian culture. The civilization of the Mediterranean was competitive, hybrid and prosperous; the Renaissance had its roots in this fertile exchange.

The language of the Arabs – part of the Semitic division of the Afro-Asiatic family, named after Noah's second son, Shem – is recorded roughly a millennium before anyone spoke English. It has imprinted itself significantly on the vocabulary of more than a dozen languages, among them Spanish, Turkish, Urdu, French and Swahili. Although English lags behind these, it is striking that so many of the words we have taken from Arabic denote everyday phenomena. Most are nouns. *Crimson*, which comes from the Arabic *qirmizi*, is unusual in this group in being in English both noun and adjective. *Qirmiz* was the name of a louse which was ground up to produce dye of this hue. A Spanish ship set upon by pirates off Sandwich in 1228 reportedly contained 100 lb of *qirmiz*.[6] And *crimson* is not alone: the language of colour brims with Arabic. Before 1200, Egypt and Syria were regarded as important sources of the best kinds of cloth; by 1300, English merchants (and artists) were more interested in Egyptian and Syrian dyes, and they sold to the Levant cloth that they had immersed in these dyes and had indeed sometimes produced using raw fibres sourced in the Near and Middle East. Thus around 1200 we find the first reference to the coarse cloth called *fustian*, which took its name from *fustat*, a word for a large tent or canopy made of haircloth. *Fustat* was so called after a suburb of the 'virtual capital' of the Islamic world, Cairo.[7] Not long after this we borrowed *cotton*, which derives via French and Spanish from the Arabic *qutn* or *qutun*; it had been introduced to Iraq, from India, around AD 600, and had spread to Europe by the tenth century. With cotton came colours and dyes: first *saffron* and *scarlet*, then *azure* and *henna*.

Arabic was spread by religion, though we should be clear that the rise of Islam breathed life into civilizations that already existed. The religion's rapid ascendancy after the death of Muhammad in 632, at a time when Christianity was fanning through England, took Arabic to the fringes of the Black Sea, west as far as Tangier, south beyond Egypt, into Sind and the Punjab, and beyond Persia as far as the (now desperately shrunken) Aral Sea in the north of modern Uzbekistan. There are records of Arabic as early as the fourth century BC, but it was this seventh-century spiritual advance that spread it far beyond its heartland in Mecca and Medina. To those who heard the finely wrought language of Islam, there seemed no credible explanation save divine inspiration. Moreover, the religion's teachings were concentrated in the immutable text of the Qur'an, a work whose name, meaning 'Recitation', announced the importance that it would place on words, reading and public performance. Wherever Islam went, Arabic established itself – at astonishing speed.[8] Yet only slowly did Islam penetrate Western minds as 'an intellectually identifiable fact'.[9]

One obvious area of contact between English-speakers and these Arabic-speaking Muslims was the Crusades. This succession of penitential wars occupied the thoughts of western Europe for a period of around 400 years – and even as late as the final years of the seventeenth century the Ottomans were being attacked by crusaders. The Crusades have traditionally been viewed as campaigns conducted by Christians motivated by the need to recover the holy sites in Jerusalem. But holy war penetrated a range of other regions, including North Africa, the Balkans and Poland, and the real definition of crusading is fluid. In its original conception the First Crusade, summoned by Pope Urban II to demonstrate his own political and moral authority as well as the authority of Christendom at large, was to comprise a body of disciplined, well-armed warriors. In reality it proved to be 'an enormous rabble of zealous but for the most part uninstructed fighting men, unamenable to imperial control, who . . . blundered on down into Syria and Palestine where they captured Jerusalem'.[10] This was achieved in July 1099: the celestial city was ransacked, and its Jewish and Muslim inhabitants were massacred.

Before the Crusades, British knowledge of the territory east of the Bosporus was fragmentary at best. In Shakespeare's *Macbeth*, set in the eleventh century although written in 1606, one of the witches boasts of sexually tormenting a sailor who has travelled to Aleppo, and in the play's closing stages Lady Macbeth, reflecting on her guilt, says that 'all the perfumes of Arabia will not sweeten this little hand.' While Shakespeare knew something of Aleppo and Arabia, his characters would have been ignorant of them. In the eleventh century there was no accurate recent information about either Africa or Asia, and those who wished to learn about those two vast continents had to consult old accounts such as those of Pliny the Elder and St Isidore of Seville. The power of the Muslim world and the Byzantine Empire was immense and inscrutable. The Western impression of Africa and Asia was that they were hazardous and uncivilized, full of gargantuan lizards, men with the heads of dogs, eels many hundreds of feet long, and creatures like the Monoceros, which was alleged to have a stag's head, the body of a horse, and feet like an elephant's.

The Crusades shifted the balance of power in the Mediterranean, and helped remedy some of these skewed notions. Even if many of the old ideas hung on tenaciously, the crusaders were at least aware of Islam and Muhammad. The First Crusade brought a large amount of land under Western control, and, while these gains were vulnerable, the new waves of pilgrims who flooded to the Holy Land were able to pen accounts that afforded a much more accurate picture of the region. Tales of wonder remained popular, and garbled polemics frothed with racist drivel, but the increased presence of Christians beyond the eastern Mediterranean 'stimulated a small industry of written information', which from the thirteenth century paid keen attention to the geography, politics, economy and social lives of Muslims, Mongols and the Asiatic peoples.[11] The twelfth-century historian William of Tyre in his *Chronicon* (now lost) offered a detailed portrait of Lower Egypt, Edessa and Damascus. In the thirteenth century William of Rubruck travelled as far as the Mongol capital, Karakorum; he expected to see freaks and monsters, but encountered nothing of the sort, and his writings were distilled by Roger Bacon in his encyclopedic *Opus Maius*.

Yet even fresh productions could prolong outmoded images. The Hereford *Mappa Mundi*, produced in the 1280s, affords a wealth of information about the routes of trade and pilgrimage, but it incorporates very few of the recent findings and depicts Africa and Asia as the home of exotic and monstrous beings and of sites mentioned in the Bible, such as the Tower of Babel.[12] (*Mappa*, incidentally, was post-classical Latin: the word had once signified 'cloth', and the vellum on which the Hereford map was drawn was close in dimensions to the sheet you might fit on a modern double bed.) One picture shows a venomous dragon; another a one-legged monster with eight toes on its single foot. Here is Calvary; there the Garden of Eden.

The presentation of the peoples of the East as monstrous and malformed was politically convenient. Comfortingly, too, it reinforced Europeans' sense of their own excellence and privilege. According to Bartholomaeus Anglicus, in his *De Proprietatibus Rerum* (dating from around 1250), the people of Albania were huge and fair-skinned, and were accompanied by giant hounds. In India there were white lions, together with gigantic worms and snails; the people were pale-skinned, with long, thin beards. Libya and Ethiopia for their part were home to small dark-skinned people, many of them misshapen.[13] A person who might now be categorized as a Muslim was known as a *Saracen*, a name which seems to have derived from a Greek term for 'easterner' and may ultimately have originated either in the Arabic for this, *sharqiyyin*, or in another Arabic word for a 'marauder'. It served, from the tenth century at least, as a derogatory catch-all for Muslims, nomads, pagans and aliens. It was a limiting word, insensitive to the diversity of these peoples; initially picked up from conservative Latin writings, and used to play up the differences between Christians and Muslims, it was believed, quite wrongly, to have been a name these peoples had given themselves, in reference to their alleged descent from Sarah, the wife of Abraham in the Old Testament. For most Europeans before the seventeenth century, there were scant opportunities to challenge such images, and few reasons to think it necessary to do so.[14]

Perceptions of the East were always channelled through particular forms: travelogues, fables, polemics. In 1298 the Venetian Marco Polo, languishing in a Genoese jail, dictated to one of his fellow prisoners an account of his lengthy travels in the East, jewelled with the marvels and mysteries of India, China, Persia and Tibet. His extravagant tales, though damned by many as a tapestry of lies, inspired countless travellers to head east. The volume known as *The Travels of Sir John Mandeville*, which began to circulate around 1356, was a standard account of the East for several generations. It is the work (in French) of a man claiming to be an English knight; little is known of the author, but in eighteenth-century illustrations he is presented as a swaggering buccaneer with a parrot and a blunderbuss. He claimed to have travelled for thirty-four years, having originally set out simply to explore the Holy Land, although it is doubtful that he did anything of the sort. His book offered descriptions of India, China and Tibet, and contained appetizingly extravagant visions of the East, complete with cannibals, 'very handsome' pygmies, and men whose testicles dangled near their feet. The English version of his text contains the first references to Nubians and Numidians, as well as the first to a mosque (spelt *Moseak*) and to lemons. Rather appropriately, we can also find there the first use of the adjective *aromatic*. The veracity of Mandeville was often questioned – and was finally trashed by Victorian critics – but his claim that it was possible to circumnavigate the globe proved hugely seductive for readers of his work. The book enjoyed great popularity long after its publication: Christopher Columbus had a copy with him when he crossed the Atlantic in 1492, and Martin Frobisher read Mandeville while seeking the North-West Passage in the 1570s.

Mandeville's vision was at once sinister and alluring. It promoted the idea of a dangerous yet ambrosial Elsewhere. Those who lived at the world's margins were dark and deformed, apparently descended from Noah's son Ham, whose progeny had been cursed after he saw Noah naked. But at those very margins there were plants of mind-boggling deliciousness. In the Far East fish sacrificed themselves upon the shore, and the eager traveller would come upon snails so large that three or four men could huddle inside their shells. Little evidence was adduced in support of these claims. But little was needed to make the stories stick. In the first century AD the Greek Strabo had written in his *Geographica* that the natives of Ireland were cannibals, many of whom had a taste for incest and devouring their dead fathers, and despite admitting that he had not a single witness he succeeded in popularizing this unpalatable image. Gerald of Wales and the Benedictine monk Ranulph Higden, more than a millennium later, perpetuated the idea. Inevitably, there were even greater wonders further afield: harpies and serpents, and creatures capable of speaking all the world's languages.[15]

Where medieval authors of travel books and bestiaries offered extravagant images, those who had participated in the Crusades were well placed to point up their inaccuracies. But, while they could report what they had seen, their experiences were limited by language. The knights in *Ivanhoe* who speak Arabic are Sir Walter Scott's fantasy. In reality, crusaders did not go native and learn the intricacies of Arabic – though there were a few exceptions, like Reynald of Sidon and Humphrey of Toron, who were able to converse with the Muslim resistance leader Saladin in his own tongue. For the most part the newcomers employed interpreters and go-betweens – a distinctive feature of the Near East, as so many different languages were spoken there. Turks, Armenians and Greeks could have as much difficulty with Arabic as did those from further west: the crusaders were not alone in needing help.

By the fourteenth century we find the word *dragoman*, from the Arabic *tarjuman*, established as the preferred term for an interpreter or go-between employed in countries where Arabic, Persian or Turkish was spoken.[16] Dragomen were often refugees who had fled Christian Europe and settled in Muslim countries; among them were Jews from Spain and Italy. The reliance on these interpreters meant that crusaders' understanding of the East was perpetually mediated. Eventually, European countries doing business in the Near and Middle East became nervous of this heavy reliance on dragomen, and efforts were made to train what the French liked to call *les jeunes de langue*. Yet for many generations before these 'language cadets' became a useful fillip to diplomacy, the go-betweens served not just as translators, but also, unofficially, as ministers of foreign affairs.[17]

The linguistic legacy of the Crusades is sometimes unexpected. For instance, the mechanism known as a *capstan* seems to have got its name as a result of crusaders' contact with shipmen in Barcelona or Marseilles in the early fourteenth century, while *house*, the name of a covering used to protect the flanks of a horse, looks to have been a crusader corruption of the Arabic word for this, *yushiah*. *Popinjay* was modelled on an Arabic term crusaders heard: the Arabic name for a parrot, *babbaga*, was meant to imitate its jarring chatter. The noun *hazard* may derive from *al-zahr*, meaning 'die' (as in dice), but a more seductive story is that it comes from the name of a Palestinian castle, Hasart. The second of these explanations was furnished by William of Tyre, who claimed that it was during the siege of this castle that a game known as *hazard* was devised in order to while away the empty hours. The game is mentioned by Chaucer in *The Canterbury Tales*; one of those to refer to it is the sleazy Pardoner, who brackets it with brothels as a corrupting influence on the young. We should hardly be surprised: many of the crusaders were more interested in corruption than in religion, and they were apt to talk about the spices and other otherworldly luxuries they had encountered on their travels. In doing so, they inspired fantasies of the opulent East.

A few Arabic words entered French at that time, and from there spilt into English: *bédouin* is perhaps the most enduring example.

Meanwhile, the large number of French crusaders established in Arab minds a special sense that Europeans were Franks – hence the Arabic term *feringi*, used of Europeans in general, and hence too the term *lingua franca*, to denote 'an unofficial language of wider communication, which was first used in the Levant'.[18] During this period *miscreant* (from the French *mécréant* and literally meaning a misbeliever) also comes into use, and we acquire via French the sibilant Arabic *assassin*.

It is usually claimed, rather enticingly, that this word meant 'a hashish-eater', and the element of crazed dedication is present in the *OED*'s explanation that the word was used to refer to 'certain Muslim fanatics in the time of the Crusades, who were sent forth by their sheikh . . . to murder the Christian leaders'. Other evidence suggests that the Hashshashin were a group of militant Nizari Muslims, active in the twelfth and thirteenth centuries, who preyed mainly on the Abbasid caliphs; their most celebrated leader was the Iranian holy man Hassan i Sabbah. There is little proof that the Hashshashin habitually used stimulants to inspire their attacks: the myth stems mainly from the account of their activities by Marco Polo. Still, the Hashshashin were undeniably ruthless and murderous, and their exploits live on in the imagination. The word derived from their fearsome name took some time to be wholeheartedly adopted into English. It is found in Latin texts by English authors in the thirteenth century, but the *OED*'s earliest citation for its use in English dates from 1531. *Assassination*, for its part, seems to be Shakespeare's coinage: it appears in one of Macbeth's soliloquies, a five-syllabled novelty that signifies the overreacher's fervid probing of his own conscience.

Words such as *hazard* and *assassin* testify to the crusaders' experience, yet, as I hinted a moment ago in noting the roots of *crimson* and *cotton*, the chief conduit of Arabic into English was peaceful, not blood-stained. For the crusaders were not the only travellers to encounter Muslims: there were also pilgrims and peripatetic clerics, diplomats and sociable nobles – cushioned by as many servants as they could afford, their purses as fat and their credentials as impressive as possible. Above all, there were traders, for whom risk was justified by financial opportunity.[19] While short-haul trade could be carried out by the people who produced the goods that were for sale, long-haul trade called for entrepreneurial specialists. It involved migration, which was often though not always permanent. When the Greeks were restored to Constantinople in 1261, the Black Sea opened to Europeans, who established trading bases on the Crimean coast and at Trebizond. Other routes developed: to Cyprus, Beirut and Alexandria.

Right across the Mediterranean, English traders were viewed with suspicion. Giovanni Frescobaldi, a Florentine writing in the early fourteenth century, offered representative advice to anyone who dared make the crossing to England: 'Wear modest colours, be humble, be dull in appearance but in fact be subtle: if the Englishman [tries to] floor you, woe to him!'[20] Trade tested the myth of English aggression. Business with the Levant created many more points of contact between English-speakers and the Arabic-speaking peoples of North Africa. By the middle of the twelfth century the traffic in Eastern luxuries was well developed; to the familiar appetite for pepper were added tastes for Tibetan rhubarb and Nepalese spikenard.[21] Henry III enjoyed the spicy taste of the dried berries of *cubeb*, which was probably imported from Java via Aden and gets its name from the Arabic *kababah*. By the early fourteenth century another Florentine, Balduccio Pegolotti, could compile a list of Oriental, Arab and African spices traded, comprising 288 different items.

In this dynamic market, payments and bribes were often made by *sakk*, a form of money order which gives us the word *cheque*.[22] Textiles and victuals and luxury goods were paid for in this way. Similarly, *tariff* comes from the Arabic for a definition or notification, and *carat* from a word for the weight of four grains (roughly a quarter of a gram, although now a carat is exactly a fifth of a gram). A later acquisition was *average*, which used to have a more specialized meaning than it does today. An average in the sixteenth century was a financial loss evenly shared by buyers and sellers when a cargo was mislaid. It can be traced back to the Arabic *awariyah*, 'damaged goods'. Among the testaments to the complex cross-currents of trade are dictionaries such as the *Rasulid Hexaglot* – a fourteenth-century vocabulary of Arabic, Persian, Mongol,

Turkic, Armenian and Greek – and, from the same period, the seven-language dictionary of Badr al-Din Ibrahim, which included Aramaic and Latin.

The ethnographer Shelomo Goitein, who translated several dozen letters written by traders of the eleventh, twelfth and thirteenth centuries, explains, 'In the Middle Ages, textiles were the number one item of commerce in both general and luxury goods. According to a Muslim legend, Abraham was a clothier . . . The pious and learned Muslims who mostly found their livelihood in the bazaars of the clothiers, simply could not imagine that Abraham, the father of faith, could have done anything other than trade in textiles.'[23] The letters themselves speak of a kind of Iraqi taffeta called *attabi* (in English *tabby*), and refer to a stone frying pan as a *tagine*.[24] They are full of talk about silks – the heavy material known as *ibrisim*, the light one called *khazz* – and other commonly traded goods: types of fragrant wood, pearls from the Arabian seas, rose marmalade from Syria, and Egyptian dyed purple wool. Here too are knuckles of Tunisian honey, flax and camphor, and chests crammed with corals, saffron, shelled almonds, and olive-oil soaps. Words learnt from Arabic by traders included *amber*, *syrup*, *mohair* and *damask*. *Caraway* comes from medieval Latin *carui*, but ultimately from *al-karawiya*; dirtily musky *civet* can be traced to the Arabic *zabad*, itself possibly connected to the savoury *zubd*, meaning 'froth', or *zubda*, meaning 'extract' or 'quintessence'; and fragrant *jasmine*, which comes to us through French, has its roots in the Arabic *yasamin*.

The Arabic-speaking world was a trader's delight. Its hub was the *suq* – in English commonly spelt *souk* – where transactions were carried out. Within its compass merchants from outside the Arab world learnt words to do with animals (*giraffe*, *gazelle*, the stork known as a *marabou*), plants, chemistry (*borax*) and clothing (*sash*). Arabic words for foodstuffs, alluringly simple, also gained currency. *Naranj* was the Sanskrit word for the citrus tree and its glowing fruit: in Arabic it kept this form, but in English 'a naranj' soon mutated into 'an orange'. Other names of fruits and vegetables include lime (*limah*), endive (*hindab*), artichoke (*al-kharshuf*), which was introduced to England in the reign of Henry VIII, and possibly spinach (which may ultimately have been derived from the Arabic *isfanaj*). English *cork* comes from the Spanish *corcha*, but can be traced to the Arabic *qurq*. The name of aromatic *galingale*, used by Chaucer's ulcerous Cook and sprinkled in the land of Tennyson's lotus-eaters, is believed to have travelled by way of Arabic from the Chinese. Arabic–Chinese contact is exemplified by the experience of Ibn Wahab, who visited China in 872 and was impressed to find that the emperor Yi Zong had a good knowledge of the basic tenets of Islam. Even at its most introverted, China would send out emissaries to gather intelligence about other societies and their learning, and the Arabic world was one obvious destination.

While the eastern Mediterranean attracted commercial and religious adventurers, the main source of Arabic words was contact with bilingual Spain following the so-called Moorish conquest – and also, to a lesser degree, contact with Sicily (formerly under Muslim rule) and with polyglot traders from Venice and Genoa. Merchants picked up Arabic words or Spanish words tinged with Arabic, and spread them among their associates and customers. Muslim Spain was a vital connection between East and West: a stop-off for goods on their way to North Africa and Egypt, and the hub from which Eastern goods were redistributed to England, France and Italy. Iberian goods were also prized. Trade in Spanish textiles was fruitful under Muslim rule. Figs came from Granada, wool and soap from Castile, olive oil from Seville.

There were intellectual and cultural contacts, too. For half a millennium Spain was a hive of Islamic culture. The Muslims arrived on the Iberian peninsula in 711, when an army of Arabs and Berbers under Tariq Ibn Ziyad invaded, crossing the Strait of Gibraltar and brushing aside the corrupt Visigoths. A second wave followed, commanded by Musa Ibn Nusair; they quickly took control of Toledo and Zaragoza. In the years that followed they attempted to extend their authority into France, but after defeat by the Franks at Tours in 732 – a moment often characterized as 'saving' northern Europe from Islam – they concentrated on their Spanish gains. At first Spain was merely an obscure outpost of the Umayyad caliphs, who were based in Damascus. But when the Abbasids supplanted the Umayyads, in 750, they began a campaign of persecution, and the teenage Umayyad prince 'Abd al-Rahman fled to Andalucia.

There he was able to establish what was in effect a new western caliphate, an Umayyad emirate politically independent of the new power base in Baghdad.

The Arabic influence was profound. The conquerors married the conquered, disseminating their ideas and the vocabulary they used to express them. Bilingualism was widespread, falling off only in the twelfth century. The golden age of Moorish culture in Spain lasted a little over a hundred years, from 929, when 'Abd al-Rahman III pacified and united the conflicting factions of Andalucia, to 1031, when the Umayyad caliphate collapsed. This period was characterized by the growth of the region's towns: as Spain was 'Arabized', there were significant advances in legal practice, the writing of history and poetry, decorative art, astronomy, mathematics and medicine, and these were concentrated in urban communities. One historian of Islamic Spain notes that, of the large number of Arabic words in modern Spanish, 'Very many are connected with commerce, and with . . . travelling, weighing and measuring, and keeping order in the markets and in the town generally.' A well-known example is *aduana*, meaning a customs house, which stems from the Arabic *diwan*. 'Another sphere with many words is house-building; the words are mostly for parts of the house or its furnishings which indicate a degree of comfort beyond the bare necessities.'[25] One example that springs to mind is *alcoba*, which can be traced back to the Arabic *al-qubba*, meaning 'the vaulted room', and is the source of the English *alcove*. Place names also testify to the Arab influence. Besides Gibraltar – from *Jabal Tariq*, 'the mountain of Tariq' – examples include Trafalgar, from *al-taraf al-agharr* ('the handsome cape'), and Guadalquivir, from the Arabic for 'the great river'.

In all, modern Spanish contains about 4,000 Arabic loanwords, such as *gandul* meaning 'lazy' and *baladi* meaning 'insignificant'.[26] One of the more conspicuous examples is the formal second-person pronoun, *usted*, which derives from *ustadh*, a courteous term of address in Arabic. In *The Wealth of Nations* (1776) Adam Smith mentions the *alcavala*, a Spanish property tax which takes its name from the Arabic *al-qabalah*, meaning a duty, levy or liability. Those words learnt by English-speakers were often associated with Spain, but the culture in which they originated was an Arab one. *Arsenal* entered English from Italian, but stems from an Arabic word for a workshop; the paths taken by *sirocco* and *talisman* are similar, while *calibre*, acquired from French, can be traced to the Arabic *qalib*, a mould used for casting metal.

Later, decadence and a long programme of Catholic reconquest eroded Arabic influence. Yet its legacy continued to be felt until the late fifteenth century, when the Inquisition was set up. The year 1492 proved momentous in Spanish history: Granada was captured by Ferdinand, king of Castile; the Christians expelled the Jews from Spain (or forcibly converted them); and Christopher Columbus discovered America. The importance of the first of these events is obvious, but the other two were also critical: the religious pluralism of Spain was abruptly brought to an end, with Christianity established as the only acceptable faith; and the discovery of the New World was symptomatic of the increasing strength of Christian Spain, which made Muslim retaliation pointless, as no Islamic state could muster a response to the Spanish Christians' might.[27] Spanish national identity was given focus: now it really meant something to be 'Spanish'. The Muslims in Spain were compelled to renounce their Arabic culture in the sixteenth century, and were finally expelled in 1609, although by then there were graver threats to the country's majesty.

Under Arab rule, Muslim, Christian and Jewish communities had lived side by side. Their coexistence was not quite harmonious, but it worked. Languages commingled: Andalucian Arabic, classical Arabic, Latin, Hebrew and a primitive form of Castilian. As a result, those who were not Muslims offered little resistance to Arabic words and thought. The Islamic legacy can be seen today in the Great Mosque at Cordoba, in Seville, Toledo and Valencia, and in Granada's Alhambra (literally, 'The Red').

Arabic learning was formidable. Alchemy was popular in the ancient world, and the language of alchemy can be seen in written works of the fourteenth century, reflecting the achievements in the field of figures like Roger Bacon and Nicolas Flamel. The word itself first appears in a literary context in *Piers Plowman* (*c.*1360). Chaucer refers to an *alembic* (which comes from *al-anbiq*, a 'still') in *Troilus and Criseyde*, which was written in the 1380s. He mentions *arsenic* in *The Canterbury Tales*, and is the first English author to refer to an *almanac*. The distinction between science and magic was not always made sharply. Words that now belong to science once belonged to alchemy. One example is *test*, as in 'test tube' and 'test specimen', which originates in *testa*, the Latin name of the pot in which alchemists cooked up their potent mixtures. Other words of Arabic origin that come out of alchemy, though they now relate mainly to mathematics, are *zero*, *cipher*, *zenith* and *nadir*, all of which blazon the Arabs' powers of abstract thought.

English visitors to Spain were impressed by the Muslims' arithmetical skills and their practical application of these skills in land surveying, crop rotation, and the planting of orchards. Chronic water shortages necessitate technological ingenuity: the Muslims in Spain were masterly constructors of canals, irrigation works and even aqueducts, while a mixture of practical and aesthetic concerns informed their passionate interest in the design of gardens. Logic, geometry, anatomy and music were other areas of close study, while their expertise in chemistry, shaped by Greek and Persian traditions, informed a sophisticated understanding of medicine. They may even have developed a prototype of the modern fountain pen, almost a thousand years before such a device was patented in Britain.

A key figure in transmitting the more arresting details of their expertise back to England was Adelard of Bath, a twelfth-century scholar who studied mathematics and physics, under the influence of Arabic doctrine, at Laon in France and in Syria, as well as probably in Spain. He translated important Arabic works of mathematics and philosophy, and produced a textbook about the abacus (the name of which comes from the Hebrew *abaq*, meaning 'dust', and originally signified a board covered with sand in which one could draw figures with one's finger). He also wrote a treatise on the astrolabe, a kind of primitive computer that made it possible to work out the altitude of the celestial bodies and was a valuable aid to navigation. Adelard tapped into the Arabic interest in astronomy and astrology; in the deserts Arab travellers had needed a good knowledge of the stars, and clear desert skies had helped astronomers draw up the rudiments of the impressive celestial maps that later earned them tributes from Copernicus and Kepler. (Lest we forget the cultural importance once attached to astrology, pause for a moment to reflect on the roots of such familiar words as *martial, saturnine, mercurial* and *jovial*.) Arabic proficiency in this area led to the building of the first European observatory, in Seville, around 1190; when it was completed, this 320-foot minaret, the Giralda, was the tallest structure in the world, and it still dominates Seville's skyline.

The difficult journey to the shrine of St James at Santiago de Compostela was an alternative route into Spanish culture for adventurous Englishmen at this time. Ansgot of Burwell is the first Englishman known to have visited the shrine, some time around 1095, and many more pilgrims followed. The first translation of the Qur'an – into Latin, with pedantic notes in the margin – was made by an English archdeacon at Pamplona, Robert of Ketton, in 1143.[28] Moreover, Robert was one of a network of translators whose work helped spread the rewards of both ancient and contemporary learning right through the rest of Europe. The process was by no means rapid, but it was indicative of the feeling that Arabic learning needed to be understood – even if only to be rebutted, as by Peter of Cluny in his polemical and somewhat briskly titled *The Abominable Heresy or Sect of the Saracens*, written around 1150.[29]

Subsequently, regard for Arabic scholarship has fluctuated. One notable flowering occurred during the middle years of the seventeenth century, when the academic study of Arabic flourished. William Laud, while chancellor of Oxford University, advanced the language's standing there, collecting important manuscripts. Meanwhile at Cambridge a keen understanding of Arabic was initially seen as helping to defend the position of Christianity. For scholars intent on scientific progress, Arabic was crucial to unlocking the secrets of Islamic scholarship in this field. The publication of Edward Pococke's *Specimen Historiae Arabum* in 1650 stands as a moment of particular note: Pococke's book was a brilliant celebration of Islamic culture's previously neglected achievements in fields such as zoology, philosophy and geography.[30]

Yet, while many of the elements of Arabic that have found their way into English have been technical in character, many more have been bound up with the romance of the East, that highly selective delight in its otherness. In the sixteenth and seventeenth centuries, when it was still immensely useful for a trader to know Arabic, the study of the language was also promoted by enthusiasts who admired the copiousness of its vocabulary. There has been a popular myth that every Arabic word can denote itself, its opposite and a kind of camel. Among the peoples of the Arabian Peninsula, *zabab* can mean 'messenger' or 'huge deaf rat'; another example, quite well known, is a word I cannot transliterate (roughly, it is *rass*) which can signify eating a lot, eating a little, or a camel with a good deal of hair behind its ears. The sense that the expressive possibilities of Arabic are infinite has perennially inspired those who have experienced the Arabic-speaking world.

The travel writings compiled by Samuel Purchas, which appeared between 1613 and 1626, contain a notably large number of Arabic and Persian words, ranging from the familiar *sherbet* to the more exotic *bezesteen*, a Turkish marketplace. Purchas also introduces *oasis*, which, though borrowed by English from the Greek of Herodotus, stems from a long-lost Egyptian word. *Yoghurt* is first used by Purchas, and so is *sofa*. The latter's meaning looks close to the one we now enjoy, but when we find Lady Mary Wortley Montagu writing in 1717 about 'sofas of marble' we gather that the word did not at the time mean what it does today. In fact it was initially used of an area of floor that had been equipped with carpets and cushions to make it comfortable. As it happens, the *OED*'s first citation for the word in its usual modern sense dates from the same year as Lady Mary's 'sofas of marble', and this meaning soon became the norm. When a character in a novel by Samuel Richardson – or indeed Casanova in his diary – collapses on a sofa, we can be pretty sure it is a soft couch rather than the partly cushioned ground. Lady Mary writes also of going into a spectacularly decorated *harem*; in this case the word is not so new. First cited in Sir Thomas Herbert's *Travels* (1634), it denoted initially a section of a dwelling reserved as a sanctuary for women. Later it acquired the sense that English-speakers now tend to use. This sense is present in Arabic, but there the enclosure and the women it contains are distinguished only very subtly, if at all.

Creative writers have revelled in using Arabic words to light up their prose. James Morier's *The Adventures of Hajji Baba* (1824) is dotted with words from the Middle East, such as *kismet, muezzin, shalwar* and the Turkish *baklava*. So, a little more surprisingly, are the novels of Thackeray, where a character may imagine himself puffing on the water pipe known as a *narghile*, and where we find references to a *harem* of friendships and an *otto* of whisky (a play on the better-known *attar*). More recent examples are Frank Herbert's six *Dune* novels, published between 1965 and 1985, which redeploy a number of Arabic words and suggest a solid knowledge of the Qur'an as well as a particular interest in Iraq.

A keener, less reverent, knowledge of the word of Allah resulted in the noun *fatwa* dramatically entering public consciousness in 1989 when Ayatollah Khomeini of Iran ruled that Salman Rushdie's novel *The Satanic Verses* was blasphemous. The word was commonly assumed to mean 'death sentence'; in reality, a fatwa is simply a judgement passed – typically by a jurisprudential scholar called a *mufti* – under sharia law. Current world events are familiarizing people who speak not a word of Arabic with concepts such as this body of Muslim law, the school called a *madrasa* where it may be taught, the oral traditions of Islam known as *hadith*, the *hajj* that Muslims are expected to make at least once in a lifetime to Mecca, the *imam* or prayer-leader, and various types of veil and overgarment such as the *niqab*, the *jilbab* and the *burqa*.[31] How long before we are equally conversant with *shahada*, the act of testimony by which a person becomes a Muslim, or *hujja*, the Prophet's proof of his existence, articulated by the imams in their teaching?

Arabic was always, before all else, a sacred language, and Europeans who visited the Near and Middle East came across more common vernacular tongues, notably Turkic and Persian. The latter, an Indo-European language today spoken chiefly in Iran, was first directly encountered during the Crusades, when Europeans met the Seljuks of Anatolia, and it was in the urban centres of this same region, as Turkic increasingly displaced Persian in the thirteen and fourteenth centuries, that the language we would now identify as Turkish was heard. While superficially its legacy is modest, Persian made its presence felt subtly – as a language of scholarship and sophistication, and through its kindred tongues, such as Sogdian, 'the lingua franca of the Silk Road . . . in the eighth to tenth centuries'.[32] After Baghdad became the capital of the Abbasid caliphate in 762, the Muslim Empire was increasingly open to Persian cultural influences, and looked to the east rather towards the Mediterranean. The Persian legacy would include, among many other things, the *shiraz* grape, the paisley design (though its name is Scottish) and the *parting shot*, originally a 'Parthian shot'.

Later, Persian filtered into India. The Mughals, whose empire was founded by Babur in 1526, pressed Persian and Arabic words into use in the native languages, and the status of many Persian loan-words in English was reinforced when they were re-encountered in India. *Tandoor* today denotes a clay oven, and has been borrowed into English from Urdu or Punjabi, but in the seventeenth century it was a table with a brazier under it, where people sat to keep warm on cold nights, and this word was learnt from the Persians, to whom the practice and the word had passed from ancient Assyria. Words like *kiosk*, *hookah* and *divan* were learnt in Turkey, and *caravan* was picked up in North Africa; but English-speakers met with Persian items such as *bazaar*, *jackal*, *seersucker* and *shawl* further east. *Khaki* was another; it had its origin in a Persian word for dust, but became well known only after the British commander Harry Lumsden garbed his Indian recruits in loose drab uniforms in the 1840s. Discoloured by imperial use, many such words eventually came to be used in thoroughly un-Eastern contexts: Thomas Hardy could write of the *attar* not of roses, but of applause; Macaulay of a *bazaar* at Tunbridge Wells; Thomas Jefferson of the *janizaries* of the British navy.

Viewed from above, the Persian contribution to English is close in character to that of Arabic. Colours, scents, materials and luxuries figure prominently. Thus *candy* comes from the Persian *qand*, meaning the juice of sugar cane, and *taffeta* can be traced to *taftah*, the Persian word for shining spun cloth of either silk or linen. *Musk* leaks from Persian through Greek and Latin; in the background seems to be the Sanskrit *muska*, meaning 'scrotum'. *Tulip* is a Turkish corruption of the Persian *dulband*, meaning 'turban'. *Lilac* comes from the Persian *nilak*, meaning 'of a blue shade'; as one study of etymologies explains, 'Before it started its wandering en route to English, the Persian form of the word underwent an assimilatory sound change by which the *n* shifted to *l* by way of anticipating the following consonant.'[33] A later tribute is *margarine*, invented by Hippolyte Mège-Mouriès in 1869. Its name is far lovelier than its taste – if only we could dissociate the two – for the source of *margarine* is the Persian *murwarid*, meaning pearl. The name occurred to Mège-Mouriès as he saw myriad pearly droplets gleaming in the fatty acid which was used to make it.

Finally there is *chess*, a game which originated in either India or Iran and takes its name from French. *Chess* is far removed from the Persian word for the game, *shatranj* (the sound of which does seem to be preserved, however, in the Portuguese *xadrez*), but that is because in most European languages chess has been known by the name of one of its pieces, the king (*shah*). It is quite widely known that the chess terms *check* and *checkmate* derive ultimately from Persian: you call 'Check' to alert your opponent to the danger you are posing to his or her king (*shah*), and when you make your winning move the cry 'Checkmate' (*shah mat*) signals that 'the king is dead.' An explanation for the game being known to Europeans by the name of just one of its six types of piece is that early travellers to the Middle East brought back the most handsome figurines – finely carved kings – as mementos of their time there. Before the game was well known, its most potent piece was a totem of its appeal.

Chess is of course a game of war: pieces are seized, and a few are promoted; positions are fortified or surrendered; kings – much less mobile than their minions – need careful screening from attack; and victory begins with an opponent's blunder. As a metaphor for empire-building and the intricacies of Middle Eastern culture, it is exquisite.

4. Volume

A collection of written or printed sheets bound together so as to form a book

From the Old French, and ultimately from the Latin *volvere*, 'to roll'. The image of a roll of parchment lies behind the word's use to denote a book. It is only since the nineteenth century that *volume* has conveyed the sense 'strength of sound'.

We have moved a long way from the language of the Norman kitchen, but chess does link us back to the Norman exchequer, as well as to Middle English and two significant figures in its development. One of these is Geoffrey Chaucer, whose ailing Cook and moralizing Pardoner we have already met. In Chaucer's *Troilus and Criseyde*, a defiant Criseyde declares, 'Shal noon housbonde seyn to me "Chek mat!"' Chaucer clearly expects his audience to understand this reference. In the earlier and less well-known *Book of the Duchess*, completed around 1369, the game provides him with an extended metaphor for the precarious give and take of courtly love. The metaphor, adapted from the popular thirteenth-century *Roman de la Rose*, has since been frequently reworked: characteristically, Chaucer both registers fashion and popularizes it.

The other notable figure is the printer William Caxton, whose achievements will be examined towards the end of this chapter. For now, it will suffice to say that Caxton initially targeted an elite, courtly market; it was with this market in mind that he printed his second English book, a translation of the earliest important European work about chess, which had been written by the Dominican monk Jacobus de Cessolis. It took Caxton some time to recognize that he could successfully sell books to other types of reader. His evolving sensitivity to the market for his products was part of a larger, subtle cultural shift in which new concepts of reading, writing and publishing developed. Furthermore, both he and Chaucer played vital roles in consolidating national identity and in nurturing a more cosmopolitan notion of English and its uses.

New words of the period reveal the growth of a noble, refined register – and of an English thus richer in nuance and scope. The language was being turned to an increasing range of uses – sermons and works of history, treatises and legal documents, drama, fiction and philosophical papers – and these disclose changing patterns of thought and behaviour, a greater cosmopolitanism, and a more literate, rational world view. Among other things, there was a more confident awareness of people as individuals. One aspect of this was a keener perception of authorship, of the creative role of figures such as Chaucer. Another was a higher valuation of youth, of its romantic potential and the rewards of youthful good health. This was bound up with a keener sense of the passage of time and a more accurate regulation of it. By the end of the fourteenth century the sound of a bell tolling the hours was a common one in English towns, and mechanical clocks were becoming objects of civic pride. The practices of time-keeping and time-saving made the airy promises of eternity seem less important than the regular, rational affairs of industry and trade.[1]

The period's spirit of inventiveness was evident in feats of architecture and engineering, such as those learnt from Islamic Spain: the harnessing of water power, improved techniques of mining and quarrying, the building of bridges. Innovations in medicine were frequent, too. In the early medieval period they went hand in hand with improvements in the practice of surgery, and they started to take place on a new stage: the *hospital*. The word originally denoted a lodging for a pilgrim en route to Rome, Jerusalem or the shrine at Santiago de Compostela, or a place of entertainment for other travellers such as crusaders. It derived, via French, from the Latin *hospes*, which could denote either a host or a guest. Bound up with this, of course, are the words *hotel*, *hostel* and *hospitality*. Early in the fifteenth century a *hospital* became an asylum for needy individuals – the old, the sick, the poverty-stricken – and also, around the same time, the name of an institution where medical treatment was available. This last concept was learnt during the Crusades from the example of Persian and possibly also Iraqi treatment centres, but we can trace the phenomenon further back, to Rome and the *valetudinarium*, where injured legionaries were nursed. Evidently, between the eleventh and the fourteenth centuries there was a fundamental change in the nature of hospitals and the services they offered: 'the emphasis shifted away from merely preparing the soul of the patient for death.'[2] This culture of caring for the sick was increasingly material: medicine involved a more sophisticated range of tools and closer documentation.

In step with this greater emphasis on physical intervention, there was a sharper sense of the complexities of the mind. One of the most popular works in Middle English was *The Pricke of Conscience* (*c.*1350), a long poem widely and wrongly attributed to the prolific Yorkshire hermit Richard Rolle. Its author was not the first to speak of *conscience*, our internal witness – the word was introduced from Latin, via French, in the thirteenth century. But this didactic text, which exists in well over 100 manuscripts, boosted the profile of *conscience*, which displaced the lovely early Middle English term *inwit*. And whereas in Latin *conscientia* had conveyed something abstract, not far removed from *knowledge*, in English it signified an attribute of the mind, the moral faculty. The first place it appears in this sense is the *Ancren Riwle*. By the time of *The Pricke of Conscience*, a century later, its new meaning was entrenched. It was symptomatic of a whole new dimension of English, articulate about the inner world of thoughts and feelings.

The author of *The Pricke of Conscience* is alive to the limits of his audience's understanding, stating that he wrote for 'lewed men'. A note of explanation: to call a man 'lewed' or 'lewid' had long been the equivalent of saying he was, in today's English, a *layman*. The word was also used to pinpoint a person's origins: the *lewed* were the English, not their Norman overlords. But the word was just starting to be a pejorative term – as it would increasingly become after the Reformation. (We can be sure, incidentally, that the author was sensitive to *his* audience, for writing remained a skill monopolized by men.) So, *The Pricke of Conscience*, which was read more widely in the fourteenth century than any other spiritual treatise, displayed a self-consciousness about its readers and – a bigger group – those who were to listen to it being read. To many people the vocabulary it used would have seemed quirky, possessing as it did traits unique to Northumbria, even when copied and modified by scribes as far away as Suffolk and Devon.

Throughout the Middle English period the differences between English's dialects are dramatically visible in written texts. For instance, the famous poem *Sir Gawain and the Green Knight* displays the dialect characteristic of the north-west Midlands (in fact Cheshire or southern Lancashire), and thus shows clearly the influence of Norse, notably in its grammar, which preserves few Old English inflexions. A seminal work of a slightly earlier date, known as *The Ormulum*, is a series of verse homilies composed by a Lincolnshire monk. It parades the palpably different dialect of the east Midlands, which nonetheless has its own special tincture of Norse words like *scone* (meaning 'beautiful') and *flit*. In the *Cursor Mundi*, a religious epic produced in Durham around 1300, we can discern the north-east dialect – and we find the first surviving reference to *ivory*, which was then sourced from walruses. A copy produced in the south of England in the fourteenth century differs from it noticeably, containing fewer Norse words and more Anglo-Norman ones. John Barbour's patriotic poem *The Bruce* (1376) is in the Norse-flecked dialect of south-western Scotland; its language contrasts with that of the scholarly writings of John Trevisa, which were written in Cornwall and manifest the dialect of England's south-west, which even in the 1380s had yet to embrace the Norse pronouns *they* and *their*. Trevisa makes reference to the 'scharp, slyttyng and frotyng' speech of northerners, which he attributes to their proximity to 'strange men and aliens' and distance from the centres of royal power.[3] We certainly don't need to know the exact meaning of his words to capture their biting gist. 'Frotyng' is especially alarming.

Culture at this time remained chiefly oral. However, we rely on written texts for a sense of what this oral culture was like. One thing that is abundantly clear is that, although it was rare for writing in dialect to be stigmatized, contemporary commentators fretted about the seeming disunity of England and about the state of its language. Those using English often found it necessary to explain why they were doing so.

Nonetheless, English was in the ascendant. There was an increasing confidence about what sort of ideas could be successfully conveyed in it. The language was gaining ecclesiastical support: it was the ideal vehicle for giving basic religious instruction. In 1385 Trevisa could comment that the pupils at grammar schools were ceasing to learn French, and could trumpet the quality of his own English by emphasizing its difference from 'old and ancient' versions. English was the 'cradle tongue': to know the French of Paris was an accomplishment, and by the end of the fourteenth century even 'gentlemen' were ceasing actively to encourage their children to learn it. Significantly, Trevisa's finest work was his translation into English of the *Polychronicon*, a 'universal history' by Ranulph Higden, and he planned as well an English version of the Bible. Trevisa had travelled far beyond the confined world of his Cornish youth – as a student to Oxford, and later much further (he is able, for instance, to speak from experience about the quality of the hot baths at Aachen in Germany and at Aix-en-Savoie). Yet English was by no means universally spoken in Cornwall at the time, and it was important to him that the people of his native region should participate in the new world of opportunities whose rise was explicit in the rise of vernacular English.[4] Moreover, while the victories against France at Crécy in 1346 and at Poitiers in 1356 amplified nationalist feeling, and a new merchant class was getting rich from servicing the needs of England's armies, famine and pestilence – notably the Black Death – were eating away the fabric of the feudal system. The masses were increasingly vocal, and they spoke English.

It was thus a polemical statement, rather than merely a statement of fact, for the author of the *Northern Homilies* to state that he writes 'On Ingelis tong that alle may / Understand quat I wil say'.[5] When Richard II met with Wat Tyler and his followers at Smithfield during the Peasants' Revolt of 1381, he showed his political nous and instinctive pacifism by addressing the crowd in plain English. The crowd, after all, were as resentful of the prissy language of officialdom as we are of its twenty-first-century counterpart. Just as striking was the decision of his successor, Henry IV, to use English for his coronation speech – and for his will. The language makes its first appearance in parliamentary records in 1388.

Parliament is by this time an established word. It comes from the eleventh-century French word *parlement*, and appears in Anglo-Latin jargon as early as 1216. From the late thirteenth century its meanings in English and French diverge: in the former it is a legislature, whereas in the latter it signifies a judicial body. Its development is a symptom of the period's changes, for while the chief source of new words in Middle English was borrowing, the borrowed words took on new characters and new dimensions. About a quarter of the total vocabulary of Middle English was imported, and of the 10,000 or so words adopted from French during this period around three-quarters have survived to the present day. The meanings of some have shifted a great deal, and others have fallen out of use, but French, as we have already seen, provided a vocabulary of refinement and regulation. Modelled on French, diminutive words ending in *-let*, such as *gauntlet* and *hamlet*, gained currency at this time, and paved the way for others, much later, quaintly based on their model – *ringlet, leaflet, booklet, starlet*.

The copious borrowings from French meant that words from other languages, notably Latin, could be quite readily accepted: borrowing was rarely felt to give cause for concern. Words adopted straight from Latin include *et cetera* and *index, limbo* and *incubus, malefactor* and *inferior*. Writers of the period were keen on Latin prefixes – *ob-, contra-, super-*, and so on – which they grafted on to the front of favourite verbs. John Trevisa took over many Latin words, as did other educated English-speakers of this time, to fill gaps in the technical, philosophical and theological vocabulary of the vernacular: a brief selection of examples found in Trevisa's writings could include *complement, denomination, expedient, occasional* and *plural*.

Commercial activity was on the increase. English merchants found new opportunities to sell their wares into Prussia, Poland and western Russia, into Norway, and, later, into Iceland. Their activity was increasingly systematic, and they developed mechanisms for preventing fraud. Thus in 1312 a convention of pepperers, ironmongers and apothecaries established the *avoirdupois* system of weight measurements, which would be used for dyes, metals, drugs and spices.[6] As merchants became increasingly specialized in their crafts, they organized themselves into guilds and alliances. The specialists acquired Anglo-Norman names: the *mercer* dealt in fabrics, the *haberdasher* in small articles of dress, the *chandler* in candles, the *currier* in dressing the hides prepared by a *tanner*. (We may note in passing the large number of 'occupational' surnames in English: not just Mercer and Chandler, but also, for instance, Smith, Turner, Taylor, Beadle, Ostler, Butcher, Mason and Weaver. Another is Chaucer, derived from the French *chaussier*, a shoemaker.) Their professional alliances were continually being rearranged, and the different groups frequently collaborated; a fishmonger and a salter might work together in trading fruit, while a mercer might import hats, mirrors and wax.[7] One of the effects of this was that, at the same time as the different groups of merchants were developing increasingly specialized vocabularies, these vocabularies were intermingling. Urban communities outside London were growing, mainly around natural harbours – as in Bristol and Southampton – and were frequently visited by foreign merchants. From Castile came fruit and salt, saffron, iron and leatherwork; from Portugal, cork, wax and sugar grown in Madeira. After the Black Death caused a shortage of retail goods, Edward III liberalized trade, and the right of foreign merchants to traffic in goods such as fruit and furs (the latter's name related to a French word for a sheath) was reinforced by royal proclamation under Richard II in 1378.

Wine was one of the most enthusiastically consumed imports – next to no wine was produced in Britain – and it is fitting that the central literary figure of the period, Chaucer, was the son of a London vintner. Chaucer's father would have associated with men from Gascony, Italy and perhaps also Germany, and from an early age his son was exposed to foreign languages. Indeed, his first courtly poems may have been composed in French. Chaucer used the east-Midland dialect common among the merchant class of London, a city that was even then a linguistic hotbed, resounding with street talk, the cries of merchants and dissidents, slogans, modish put-downs, and the chatter of short-term visitors and immigrants. It was to Chaucer's London that Dick Whittington travelled to sell his precious silks and velvets.

Instead of following his father into the wine trade, Chaucer chose a political and administrative career, and he is the first author to refer to an *ambassador*, *exchange*, *attention* and *government*. He may well have served under the Black Prince in France, and we know that he travelled in Flanders and Spain, as well as making several trips to Italy, notably to Genoa to negotiate with the doge over English rights of access to the port there. In 1378 he became 'comptroller' of the port of London, and that same year he was sent by Richard II to Lombardy on state business. He was thus well placed to augment his personal vocabulary, and this enabled him to be unusually inventive with language.

For as long as language has existed, particular individuals or social groups have been in the vanguard of linguistic innovation: today's specialist term or snippet of arcana is tomorrow's buzzword or common parlance, and we, as speakers and writers, are the conduit between the language of today and that of tomorrow. Chaucer is one of those individuals whose use of language looks, from the vantage point of the twenty-first century, radical.

Lexically rich, Chaucer's mature writing is couched in a natural, fluent style that can mask the real extent of his technical virtuosity. His fellow poet Thomas Hoccleve characterized him as the 'first fyndere of our faire langage' – the first, that is, to understand and reveal its power. Whether or not Chaucer performed such a role, his veneration as a kind of founding father was vital to those who argued for English's value. His work levying customs on exports passing out of London allowed him to observe at first hand the growing role of English in business and politics: he chose to use it as the medium in which to parade his imagination. He was keenly aware of classical literature, and his often sceptical responses to his literary precursors informed his attempt to create a literature in English that could rival the works of Ovid or Virgil. There are Latin words and phrases in his writings, along with borrowed rhetorical figures and formulae – *mea culpa, amor vincit omnia, in principio*. He gorged on Dante, Petrarch and Boccaccio, and turned to them for flashes of Continental erudition – lifting the word *permutacioun* from the *Inferno*, for instance, and taking his concern with *gentilesse* from Dante's *gentilezza* in the *Convivio*. Yet above all he was eager, like his peers John Gower and William Langland, to promote the vernacular.[8] In so doing, he hoped to secure a place for English literature on the international stage.

Bringing in new words was a way of empowering English. Although Gower chose to write his first substantial poem in French, he was the last major English author to write in the language, and his masterpiece *Confessio Amantis* was composed in English and dedicated, pointedly, first to Richard II and later to Henry of Lancaster, who was soon to become Henry IV. In championing the vernacular, as Dante had done in Florence, these authors and their writings posed a threat to the existing cultural elite – the cadre of privileged churchmen who relied for their status on being able to reveal to the masses the contents of that numinously non-vernacular work, the Bible. By contrast, the nation's political elite began in the early part of the fifteenth century to promote vernacular writing – a vital endorsement of the national language.

Chaucer's poetry was intended for oral performance – he was writing not for posterity, but for a known coterie of courtly acquaintances – yet after his death in 1400 his oral works were disseminated in manuscript. Fifty-five copies of his most enduring work, *The Canterbury Tales*, survive from the fifteenth century. Ostensibly a record of speeches made by a large group of pilgrims on their way to Canterbury to visit the shrine of Thomas à Becket, *The Canterbury Tales* is an opulent and frequently hilarious vision of fourteenth-century England, which ranges across the social spectrum – and across the whole spectrum of fourteenth-century language. While often manifestly traditional, Chaucer's English also displays the language's evolving vocabulary, and indeed, with shrewd delicacy, he presents himself as a refiner of English's rudeness.[9] In his eyes, new words of foreign origin enhanced the dignity of written English. His writing is full of 'local' novelties – words he uses only once – yet there are numerous occasions when his exuberance throws up a word that has since caught on. Among the huge number of words that first crop up in Chaucer we might pick out *accident*, *intellect*, *galaxy* and *famous* – or *bribe*, *moral*, *magic* and the verbs *resolve* and *refresh*. The famous opening of the general prologue to the *Tales* is littered with terms drawn from French, italicized in the extract below.

Whan that *Aprill* with his shoures soote
The droghte of *March* hath *perced* to the roote
And bathed every *veyne* in swich *licour*
Of which *vertu engendred* is the *flour*;
Whan *Zephirus* eek with his sweete breeth
Inspired hath in evry holt and heath
The *tendre* croppes, and the yonge sonne
Hath in the Ram his halfe *cours* yronne,
And smale foweles maken *melodye*,
That slepen al the nyght with open eye –
So priketh hem *nature* in hir *corages* –
Thanne longen folk to goon on *pilgrimages*.
And *palmeres* for to seke *straunge* strondes.[10]

Of these words, the noun *corage* especially merits a closer look. We may assume that it has a sense much the same as the modern 'courage', but the word has three layers of meaning, suggesting the human 'heart' (iconic seat of our emotions), the military resilience of 'valour' and the sharp pangs of 'lust'. In the Middle Ages it suggested 'interior intellectual and emotional states', but in post-medieval contexts the focus shifted to 'outward conduct, especially in combat'.[11] For Chaucer, then, its meanings were thickly tangled. In later usage it was more clearly associated with physical and mental fortitude, but its medieval connotations were resuscitated in the Renaissance. When Bottom in *A Midsummer Night's Dream* agrees that he and his fellow actors should decamp to the forest in order to 'rehearse most obscenely and courageously', the earlier complexity of *corage* is audible. Perhaps this can help us understand why the word *courage* is almost invariably used about men.

Chaucer's writing reveals a language in flux. A literary magpie, he borrows from Latin, French and Italian to enhance his poetic diction and his audience's awareness of his erudition. From Latin he takes technical terms or sophisticated ones: *magnificence*. His French borrowings hint at the contemporary concern with *curteisie* – and his own concern with making his verse congenial to the educated figures who, like him, were to be found at the periphery of court life. He took from French a vocabulary of the abstract, comprising nouns like *argument, disposition, impression, liberty, resemblance* and *solitude*, along with adjectives such as *outrageous*. Though not always the first to use such words, he encountered them in French texts rather than English ones. He can gloss the puzzling new French-derived *mansuetude* with the more familiar French word *debonairetee* – and can pun on *debonair*'s etymology in writing of a 'deboneire wynde' (that is, one containing 'good air').[12] He is the first to write of either *tragedie* or *comedie*, to refer to *poetrie* by that name, and to use, in a rather more technical sense than we are used to, the noun *consequence*.[13] His works also contain our first sightings of calques from French such as *on pain of*, *to do one's business* and *to have recourse*, which together hint at a legalistic world of constraint, commerce and complaint. In *Troilus and Criseyde* he renders the French words *jeu parti*, 'a divided game', as 'Iupartye', and this becomes the familiar *jeopardy*.

It was not just writers with court connections who deployed sophisticated French vocabulary. William Langland was an obscure figure, a minor cleric from the west Midlands, possibly a hermit or dissident, and certainly unbeneficed – a slipshod outsider. Yet *Piers Plowman*, the long allegorical poem of which he is generally reckoned the author, is difficult and energetic. Its language reflects the poet's desire to develop an English vocabulary suitable for dealing with thorny theological issues, and is densely populated with French and Latin verbiage as well as with literary and scriptural allusions.

Back to Chaucer, though. At the end of his romance *Troilus and Criseyde*, which he modelled on a work by Boccaccio, he makes reference to the 'gret diversite / In Englissch and in writyng of oure tonge'. He offers his book to the entire nation, conceiving of himself as a national poet rather than a regional one or a specialist, and he exploits this 'gret diversite' to achieve literary effects. The Host in *The Canterbury Tales* intervenes in one tale to upbraid its narrator for using 'drasty speche' – perhaps this is coarse-sounding English, where some sort of alliterative finery would have been expected and preferred, or perhaps it is an excess of flatulent Frenchness. Either way, the Host's judgement is stinging: 'Thy drasty rymyng is nat worth a toord.' *Drasty* means 'trashy' or 'dreggy', and seems to have been used mainly in the context of brewing, so it is an appropriate word to come twice out of the mouth of the Host, who is after all an innkeeper. For its part *toord* is pungently self-explanatory. Chaucer makes a point of setting trash alongside jewels.

Right through the poet's *oeuvre* there is this mix of registers. There are technical words aplenty, as in his translation of Boethius's high-minded *The Consolation of Philosophy*, or in a reference in *Troilus and Criseyde* to *ambages* (a Latin word for circumlocutions), yet in his earthier works readers do not have to look far to come across the words *pisse* and *ferte*, and Alison in *The Miller's Tale* giggles 'teehee' after contriving to have dainty Absolon kiss her *erse*. The Parson refers eleven times to *misericorde*, a weightily religious alternative to the everyday *pitee*. The Knight, who has visited Egypt, Prussia, Lithuania and Moorish Spain, seems to be a relic of a bygone age, and his language is archaic. The Pardoner, who passes off pig's bones as holy relics, drops in Latin words to 'saffron' his sermons.

The diversity of Chaucer's language reflects the breadth of the society he depicts. Characters speak in clearly identifiable voices, indicative of their varied origins and enthusiasms. His close experience of London life and the city's many forms of English fed into this diversity of colours and flavours. In 'The Reeve's Tale' he pokes fun at the northern speech of two Cambridge students, John and Aleyn; the humour comes at the expense of their regional pronunciations, rather than their social class. What is more, the language used to describe characters says something of their values and aspirations. We are told that Madame Eglentine the Prioress speaks French fastidiously yet with an unmistakable east-London accent; appropriately, the language used of her is clotted with pretentious French diction. By contrast, Robyn the ribald, thieving Miller, who breaks down doors with his head, is sketched with a series of blunt, mainly Saxon, monosyllables – 'ful byg he was of brawn, and eek of bones'. Chaucer's pilgrims are characterized by what they do, and the same is frequently true of the figures who appear in the pilgrims' tales. Professional jargon, often thick with terms drawn from French, helps define them. (It is no coincidence that *jargon* was adopted from French in the age of Chaucer, to denote the twittering of birds and other forms of unintelligible chatter.) Where once the sophisticates simply spoke the French language, now they needed to steep their

English in fancy Gallicisms. *Chevysaunce* is a good example – a specialist legal term used by the Shipman to suggest the opaque dealings of the merchant class.

Chaucer demonstrated the vitality of English, then, and its range. This was not universally popular. To many of his peers, English could never have the refinement of Latin and was no more than an 'upstart language', with neither the elegance nor the resources of other tongues.[14] Later commentators were scathing about his innovations. Stephen Skinner, a noted linguist of the seventeenth century, voiced the not unusual view that, by bringing 'whole cart-loads' of foreign words over from the Continent, Chaucer had damaged English, 'smearing rouge over its natural colours and putting a mask over its true face'.[15]

Where Chaucer revelled in the variety of Middle English, religious writers worried that it compromised the integrity of their work. John Wyclif pressed for the scriptures to be available to people who knew no Latin, and the manuscript translations of the Bible that he instigated are characterized by a conflict between slavish adherence to the strictures of the Vulgate's Latin word order and an earnest striving after appropriate idioms. The language of the period seemed at times too volatile to convey the necessary authority, but Wyclif's translations reached a larger audience than any previous work in English. They contain some delightfully graphic terms, such as *arse-ropes* (intestines), and Wyclif is the earliest recorded user of many alien items, among them *behemoth*, *chimera*, *puberty*, *civility*, *zeal* and *alleluia*. He also brings in *character* – minus the *h* – on the model of Latin, although it derived ultimately from the Greek term for a branding iron. Initially it meant simply a 'brand' or 'distinguishing mark', and it came to signify the sum of an individual's qualities only in the seventeenth century.

Latin was vital to the endeavours of one of Chaucer's keenest contemporary admirers, John Lydgate, who devoted much of his energy to turning classical prose into English verse. He developed for the purpose an aureate, sugary style which made generous use of terms borrowed from Latin, characterized by the critic Seth Lerer as 'shimmering high-concept words'.[16] Condemned by the nineteenth-century critic Joseph Ritson as 'a voluminous, prosaick, and drivelling monk', Lydgate was undeniably overproductive, but his writing was at its best grandly dramatic, and his style, rather than being tediously habitual, was pointed or moderated according to the nature of his material. Some of his coinages – *momentaneous*, *palaestral* – stray too far in the direction of obscurity, but there are others – *opportune, melodious, mutability* – that prove eminently useful today.

Lydgate's euphonious elaborateness influenced a group active in the late fifteenth century known as the Scottish Makars, chief among them William Dunbar and Robert Henryson. Dunbar is a virile poet, but among the many voices of which he is capable the most striking is an enamelled, ceremonial one, audible in 'The Golden Targe', where dawn's 'perly droppis schake in silvir schouris' and the sky is 'The cristall air, the sapher firmament . . . redolent, / With purpur, azure, gold', bright with the 'armony' of birdsong and sunbeams 'birnyng as ruby sperkis'. Latin flourishes of the kind favoured by Lydgate and his inheritors were calculated to appeal to a public well versed in the language. The emergence of grammar schools and the strengthening of the universities in the fifteenth century ensured there was a sizeable audience attuned to this kind of rhetoric.

Ceremonial Latin touches were evident, too, in official letters. The English used by Henry V in his correspondence contains studied repetitions and is busy with Latin borrowings.[17] Still, Henry's decision to use English is symbolic: this was the language of a nation quite independent from France. English was a means of binding together the country's disparate social groups when they were faced by a foreign enemy. In Shakespeare's play about Henry, this spirit of nationalism is both highly visible and repeatedly undercut, and the drama highlights the sheer range of people Henry rules. Yet Henry draws them together, forging a community spirit in his celebrated St Crispin's Day speech with its rallying talk of a 'band of brothers'. It is to Henry's reign that we can trace the notion of the 'King's English' – a telling realization of state patronage, albeit not expressed in these exact words until, ironically, the reign of Queen Elizabeth.

While figures such as the Scottish Makars experimented with the language's resources, technology accelerated the spread of English. It quickened national consciousness of the language, disseminated texts more widely while also creating new kinds of text, and played a crucial role in standardization and in preventing the inevitable distortions of oral and manuscript transmission. It also led to richer cultural cross-pollination, greater opportunities for comparing texts, better organization and cataloguing of scholarship, and a keener awareness (and criticism) of literary style. Of course I am thinking here about the impact of print. For right across Europe an epochal development in the moulding of languages was the development of printing using movable type. This began – some 400 years after it was first developed in China – with Johannes Gutenberg in 1447.

In truth, the print revolution could not have happened without the growth of papermaking. In the twelfth century, merchants who traded with Arabs introduced paper to Italy. It was cheaper than vellum or parchment, and, because it could not be reused, whatever was written on it was destined to last as long as the paper itself, rather than just until a scribe needed to scrape it clean to make way for something new. Soon its manufacture flourished in Ancona, Genoa and the area around Lake Garda, and Italian paper-makers spread the skills of their trade into France, where the main centres were Paris and Troyes. The first German paper mill began production in 1391; the first in England apparently in 1495. At the same time, the copying of texts was more and more being done not by monks, but by secular scribes who were working for commercial gain.

Before the invention of printing, new words were trafficked by people, in person or by means of treasured manuscripts: after it, they were conveyed by books. Printing opened up the English lexicon, by allowing readers access to a wealth of new works that were studded with appealing, useful, novel words. As the historian Lisa Jardine has observed, 'Printed books permanently altered the way information was distributed around Europe.' After all, while 'men of dangerous or dissident ideas could be kept out of areas whose authorities did not approve of them . . . their books, it quickly became clear, could not'.[18] Furthermore, printed books possessed 'cachet and desirability', and their 'distinct existence' had the effect of making a written work a 'defined entity, with a clear beginning and end'.[19] Although at first most printed works dealt with religious subjects, the range of printed material soon increased, and the new technology made writers feel powerful. Printing diffused knowledge and stimulated the development of national literatures. It also enabled individuals to build private libraries – their contents determined by personal taste rather than by the dogma of institutions.

In England the first press was set up in 1476, by Caxton. While this is widely known, it is worth pointing out that by 1480 there were more than a hundred printing presses across Europe. Almost half of these were in Italy, and about a third were in Germany, but printing had also reached Poland, Bohemia, France and Spain, among others, and there were presses at Krakow and Lyons before there was one in London.

Caxton was not one of history's trailblazing geniuses; rather, he was an ambitious and astute opportunist cashing in on a gap in the domestic market. Having made money as a mercer, he decided to invest in a press. He learnt the techniques of the craft at Cologne, at a time when in England printing was still thought of as a noble mystery. Having witnessed at first hand the lucrative trade in fine manuscripts, he saw ample opportunity for profit. His own reading, which was conservative, influenced what he printed; he enjoyed French works of chivalry, but knew little of Italian literature. Yet he also played on the snob appeal of Continental works: whatever was fashionable in Flanders and Burgundy was likely to go down well with English readers who aspired to sophistication. In 1474 he set up a press at Bruges and printed *The Recuyell of the Historyes of Troye*, a long and popular courtly romance which he had translated from the French while living in Cologne. Two years later he returned to London with his press and set up shop at the sign of the Red Pale near Westminster Abbey, close to the offices of government. Over the remaining years of his life he produced a total of 103 printed works, including two editions of *The Canterbury Tales* and one of Sir Thomas Malory's *Le Morte D'Arthur* – the latter a work heavily indebted to French sources, which happens to contain our first sightings of the French loanwords *summit* and *infidel*.

Caxton's writing consisted mainly of translation. Besides rendering into English two French versions of Jacobus de Cessolis's book about chess, he transported from Dutch the story of Reynard the Fox, notable for establishing the English spelling of *ghost*. He seems to have had no experience of translation before setting up his press, and he was not particularly good at it. In common with many other translators of the period, he transplanted words directly from the French or the Latin. Translations flooded the language with new terms; Caxton's contributions were not especially numerous, but included words lightly altered from French (*brutish*, *ample*, *viceroy*) and a few just crudely transposed.

No great stylist, Caxton had little real learning and his cast of mind was plainly medieval. Yet, without explicitly making a case for it, he was an innovator in suggesting some of the fresh directions in which the language could evolve. He showed the different functions it could perform. In personal vocabulary we see the evidence of his time in Belgium. He likes the word *spincop* – from the Flemish *spinnekop* – as an alternative to *spider*, and uses a few other unusual words of Flemish origin, including *okselle* meaning 'armpit', *mecop* instead of *poppy*, *unberisped* to mean 'unreproved', *visevase* ('a vain or empty matter' – compare the modern Dutch *viezevaas*, 'a prank') and *butter* as a word for a cheat. One word he alone seems to have picked up from Flemish is the verb *bedwynge*, which he uses to mean 'restrain'. None of these adoptions really caught on; rather, they are indicative of Caxton's clumsy way with language.

Yet crucially, even though Caxton had doubts about English – which he considered 'imperfect', 'rude' and 'simple' – he chose to print books in the vernacular. He was interested in enshrining a standard form of the language. This was not out of any very noble philosophical calling, but simply because he was a businessman and wanted his products to last well and reach a large audience. He wrote promotional epilogues and prefaces for the books he published, and sought out influential patrons: he was a marketing man, intent on making money, and the forces of the market determined what got published and how it was presented. I should add that Caxton did not refer to his business as *printing*; rather, he called it *imprinting*, and the shorter word that we now use began to catch on only in the following century. Nor did he employ the verb *to publish*. This word, acquired from French but rooted in the Latin, was not used of the issuing of books for sale until about half a century later.

The distribution of printed books written in English focused attention on spelling reform and grammar. It also fostered a belief in English as a legitimate medium for literature and works of reference or philosophy. This, in turn, led to what academics call 'elaboration': English came to be used for a greater number of different purposes, and especially for refined, prestigious ones. When Henry VII called for the Statutes of the Realm to be printed by Caxton in English, he was increasing the law's audience and severing its old ties with French. He was also enlisting the power of print. As the uses of the vernacular grew more numerous and diverse, its vocabulary burgeoned. Moreover, the rise of printing meant that gradually, right across Europe, the literary world fragmented; rather than being unified by the intellectual culture of Latin, Europe now became a patchwork of increasingly robust vernacular languages. As Elizabeth Eisenstein reports, 'Typography arrested linguistic drift . . . and paved the way for the more deliberated purification and codification of all major European languages.'[20] Printed books were essential to nations' different myths of identity. They realized among their readers a sense of national community; readers were rarely able to see the cohesion of such communities, but the written word made it possible to *imagine* them.

After Caxton's death in 1492, his business passed into the hands of his foreman Wynkyn de Worde, who published more than 700 titles in a period of about forty years. He came from Alsace – in common with most printers in England, he was a foreigner using foreign equipment – and had served as an apprentice to the type-founder Johannes Veldener. Whereas Caxton had concentrated on courtly writings, Wynkyn offered printed editions of religious and devotional works, and later began to publish poetry and educational primers. He also introduced italic type to English printing. Other new typefaces made it possible to print an increasing variety of texts. In 1519 the first Greek typeface was introduced. A Hebrew face followed in 1592, and an Arabic one in 1617. Anglo-Saxon type was commissioned in 1567, and an Irish face was introduced in 1571 so that a Gaelic version of the catechism could be printed.[21]

Between 1500 and 1600 as many as 200 million printed volumes were produced in Europe. It was around 1530 that printing and typefounding became distinct businesses, and from this point on the names of the most successful typefounders would live on as the titles of the faces they created: among them Claude *Garamond*, Francesco *Colonna*, Giambattista *Bodoni*, and several generations of the *Caslon* family.

In 1516 Erasmus of Rotterdam, who had made several visits to England in the previous two decades, called for new versions of the scriptures that would make them as accessible to a ploughboy as to a bishop. William Tyndale's New Testament (1525) answered this call. Tyndale failed to find support at home for this project of empowering ordinary people, and his lucid version of the Gospels had to be published in Germany. His vigorous insistence on Church reform led eventually to his being thrown in jail; in October 1536 he was strangled and then burnt at the stake. Nevertheless, Tyndale's legacy is clear. His style was beautifully simple, direct yet deep, its cadences a lasting influence on English religious diction. He coined the words *atonement* and *scapegoat*, among others, and came up with many enduring phrases – 'my brother's keeper', 'a law unto themselves', 'the salt of the earth'. Tyndale found fresh uses for many words that already existed; one example is *beautiful*, which had previously been used only of the human face or form, but which he applied to painted tombs (the white sepulchres attractive only on the outside). His was the Bible that opened the floodgates for a whole generation of Bibles that made English the language of English religion. His work was supplemented by Miles Coverdale, who added some more ceremonial touches and dropped some of Tyndale's more radical interpretation.

The increasingly sturdy image of English that we see in Tyndale's prose went hand in hand with an increasingly confident sense of what it meant to be English. Sir John Fortescue's treatise *De Laudibus Legum Angliae* (completed in 1471) exemplifies this: its title boasts – in Latin, admittedly – of the excellence of English law. One of the principles Fortescue admires is trial by jury. This was a cornerstone of national identity. In due course Fortescue managed to analyse the problems of his country's government in

English, providing early sightings of *larceny, feasible, endowment* and *advertisement.*

At this time a standard version of English was crystallizing, which privileged eastern and central spellings. London's political and judicial administration and the vernacular Bible were its pillars. A form of English suited to 'official writing' was developed early in the fifteenth century by the scribes who worked in the offices of the Court of Chancery, Parliament, the Signet and the Privy Seal. They laboured to avoid the obscurity that had smutted the prose of their predecessors. Yet we should be wary of overvaluing the influence of the Chancery style. Most likely the Chancery scriveners were approving a form in wider use: they endorsed an English already prevalent among teachers, churchmen, lawyers and merchants.

The emergence of what we call Modern English (or sometimes Early Modern English) is conventionally dated to somewhere between 1450 and 1500, with Caxton's introduction of print technology serving as a convenient cut-off halfway between the two. Straddling the border between the old and the new is the poet John Skelton, who was born around 1460 and died in 1529. This ambitious Yorkshire maverick is the first notable English author to have been active wholly in the age of print, and, while his works have more than a touch of medievalism, his vocabulary is modern in its range. When he describes someone clumsy as a *knuckylbonyard* or calls a fool a *hoddypoll* he sounds simple and rustic, yet he is the first author to write of *contraband, idiocy* and *declamation* – and to mention a *shuttlecock* or have a character cry *boohoo.* Much of Skelton's work consisted of Englishing important Latin texts, and he continually found himself negotiating between the elegance of novel ornament and the simple force of older language. As a poet, he was also, he believed, a kind of historian; the words he chose would have mnemonic intensity – and needed to if they were to be heard above the din of other men's lies and mistakes. He was forever reworking his writings, and his determination to show his control over his output is evidence of a sneaking sense of his audience's greater role in constructing its meanings. Skelton wanted his language to display the rhetorical balance of classical literature. To this end, in a single translation published in 1485 he could deploy more than 800 original borrowings from Latin.[22]

Such a glut of Latinism draws attention to another area of increasing anxiety. The durability of Latin literature seemed to say something about the force of Latin itself, but appropriating Latin terms was a dangerously recondite way of bolstering one's own authority. What was Skelton thinking? Concerns on this front were set to increase. The language of the sixteenth century's intellectual renewal would be passionately contested, and in the century that followed English would engage with many other tongues. It is into that period that we now venture, by three routes: exploring the broadening geographical horizons of English, its domestic flux, and then, more closely, its passage into America.

5. Bravado

An ostentatious display of courage or boldness; boastful or threatening behaviour

From the Spanish noun *bravada*, meaning 'swagger', 'boasting' or 'bravery'

First, then, the broadening geographical horizons. In 1603 the poet Samuel Daniel, a minor courtier who had travelled to France and Italy on state business in the 1580s, produced an essay entitled *A Defence of Ryme*. There he argued that the English were too smitten with Greek and Latin learning and should trust their own artistic discretion. He characterized the desire to emulate the Ancients as 'a winde, but of the worst effect': much of what passed for eloquence was really just flatulence. Daniel had long sensed that the uses of English were restricted, yet he had also been coolly aware of new opportunities for his language. In the dedication of his play *Cleopatra* (1594) he had written, 'O that the Ocean did not bound our style / Within these strict and narrow limites so', and had expressed the hope that in the future someone would 'Unlocke these limites, open our confines' to 'inlarge our spirits, and publish our designes'. More arrestingly, in his poem *Musophilus*, published in 1599, he returned to this theme, wondering prophetically,

> And who in time knows whither we may vent
> The treasure of our tongue, to what strange shores
> This gaine of our best glorie shal be sent
> T'enrich unknowing Nations with our stores?

When Daniel penned these lines, English had already been imposed on migrant families in Ireland, on Welshmen seeking office, and on Cornish-speakers. But soon it would be thrust much further afield, and in the process it would absorb a host of unfamiliar new words. The bold creativity of poets like Daniel, who revelled in dreaming up fictional landscapes, can be understood as a rehearsal for the real business of claiming and peopling new worlds.

In Shakespeare's *Richard II* the Duke of Norfolk, faced with the prospect of exile, reflects sadly that 'My native English, now I must forego,' and follows this with thirteen lines expanding on the theme. 'My tongue's use is to me no more,' he despairs; the worst of his fate is that it 'robs my tongue from breathing native breath'. At the time Shakespeare wrote this – some 200 years after the real-life Norfolk's expulsion – there were still no English-speaking communities abroad.[1] But within 100 years such communities had developed in the Caribbean, Ulster, India, on the Gold Coast of West Africa, and in America; within 200 years in Canada, Australia and Malta; and within 300 years in South Africa, Singapore, New Zealand and Uganda, to name a few. Those communities were seedbeds for new vocabulary.

In the sixteenth century, the size of Europe's known world doubled. The large-scale exploring carried out in the Renaissance was a form of experiment, and those who played a part in it were acutely conscious of being involved in a grand new enterprise and a rich historical moment. The chief reward of discovering new territory was financial. Fantasies of lost worlds and unknown pleasures (El Dorado, the Seven Cities, Atlantis, Avalon, the milk and honey of Cockaigne) were – and are – grounded in the lust for power and riches. The example of Italy was captivating: the blossoming of Italian art in the fourteenth century had coincided with the growth of trade and travel, and Italian manufacturers, having learnt to imitate the designs of imported oriental luxuries, had become first competitors and then leaders in the international market for expensive goods.[2] They are up there still, as a walk down Bond Street, Rodeo Drive or Shanghai's Nanjing Road will confirm.

In the early part of the sixteenth century, English trade grew, with the Levant a significant new focus. Cyprus, Crete and Beirut were all popular destinations for traders who sailed out of London, Bristol and Southampton, looking to source timber, copper and luxuries. Turpentine from the Aegean island of Chios was sought after; the island's wine was also prized, and so, later, was its *mastika*, a spirit or liqueur flavoured with the resin of the mastic tree. Yet by the middle of the century English ships were a rare sight in the Mediterranean, forced out by Portuguese, Turkish and Armenian rivals. While the lack of political cohesion in Germany presented one alternative opportunity, others were urgently needed. England felt isolated, especially after Pope Pius V excommunicated Queen Elizabeth in early 1570; English merchants were debarred by papal bull from trading in Catholic Europe, and were thus obliged to seek out markets further east.

Between 1556 and 1581 audacious efforts were made to galvanize eastward trade by establishing a trading connection across the Caspian Sea. The Muscovy Company was granted a charter in 1555; eleven years later it changed its name to the Russia Company, reflecting the increasingly broad compass of its interests. Words borrowed as a result of this connection included *rouble, czar, kvass, beluga, horde* (really a Turkish word), *knez* (a 'duke' or 'prince') and *verst* – the last of these a Russian measure of distance, equal to two-thirds of a mile, and, like the other borrowings from Russian at this time, indicative of exclusively Russian concerns. Meanwhile, for those prepared to navigate the Baltic, in spite of this route's daunting reputation, there was the guarantee of lucrative markets for cloth, lead, coal, tin and rabbit skins.[3] In 1577 John Hawkins, having already shipped currants from Cephalonia, proposed a potentially rewarding entry into the Ottoman market for such commodities. Others exported munitions. The trouble was that in doing so they were muscling in on opportunities that had traditionally been exploited by the Venetians and the Genoese. Throughout the 1570s, when surging demand for lead and tin promised to revitalize English shipping in the Mediterranean, the efforts of English merchants were endlessly hampered and undermined by aggressive, established competitors.

Nevertheless, there were successes. The Levant Company was granted a royal charter in the early autumn of 1581, and its profits bloomed. As Fernand Braudel explains, this was due to 'the excellence of the ships, the low price of their cloth, and the quality of their organization'. In addition, its sailors made use of an 'ingenious' convoy system (from 1591) and enjoyed a greater reputation for honesty than French or Venetian merchants.[4] At the same time, English privateers made a point of savaging Venetian and Genoese merchantmen. They set upon exhausted Portuguese returning from the East Indies. They tangled with Barbary corsairs off the coast of North Africa: while captured Englishmen were shut up in jails or sold at slave markets, defeated 'Turks' and 'Moors' (words that were used with casual abandon) found themselves hauled to English jails.[5] The noun *pirate*, derived from French, achieved real currency at this time, and expanded to include pirate ships as well as those who manned them; the word was first used as a verb late in the sixteenth century.

All the while, grander designs were afoot. By the 1570s the English were beginning to imagine for themselves an overseas presence to compete with Spain's – a Protestant empire. Queen Elizabeth's excommunication had led to an upsurge in patriotism. In the years that followed she became an almost mythical figure – her mystique and power captured in a succession of portraits which show her fabulously attired and decked with jewels. The astrologer and royal adviser John Dee, who was the first person to refer explicitly to an English 'empire', took a leading role in defining the imagery of these portraits. From 1579 onward they contain what Roy Strong has justly called 'a heavy symbolic overlay in terms of imperial pretensions stemming from maritime power and from a reassertion of dominion based both on the imperial descent of the Tudors from Brutus and on the conquests of Arthur'.[6] It seems material that it was during Elizabeth's reign that Shakespeare wrote his history plays, which construct an unambiguously regal image of England. The word *patriot* was imported from French; one of its earliest recorded appearances is in Ben Jonson's *Volpone* (1605), where talk of patriots is deemed sufficiently strange that the word requires a gloss – 'sound lovers of their country'. It was soon common, yet in French its use fell away, and in the middle of the eighteenth century, when French authors readopted the term, it was considered a nasty Anglicism.[7]

The belief that there was a connection between the Atlantic and Pacific oceans, affording an alternative sea route to the Orient, had inspired previous generations and now impelled a succession of journeys westward. While the magical prize that was America would become the focus of English ambitions, initially the intended goals were India and Cathay (as China then was known). John Cabot left Bristol with eighteen men in 1497 and, having discovered Newfoundland, returned with claims of having located the kingdom of the Great Khan and reports of excellent cod, timber and silks. His son Sebastian was commissioned by Henry VIII to visit the Malay Archipelago, but irked his sponsors by instead channelling his energies into searching the River Plate for silver. (Neither Henry nor Sebastian Cabot would have spoken of an *archipelago*. The noun derives from Italian, though clearly modelled on Greek. It can be found in a Venetian legal document dating from 1268, but was adopted into English only in 1600, by Richard Hakluyt.) More famously, between 1577 and 1580 Francis Drake circumnavigated the globe, impudently snatching Spanish treasure whenever he could. (Again, the key word is an anachronism; the verb *to circumnavigate* was not adopted until fifty years later.) Drake made several import-ant discoveries along the way: it became apparent that Tierra del Fuego, which had previously been thought to be the tip of a remote continent, was an archipelago, and Java turned out not to mark the edge of a southern continent, but to be a large island.

For sixteenth-century adventurers, the best chance of getting rich lay in satisfying the contemporary mania for spices. Sebastian Cabot's proposed journey to the five angrily volcanic islands known as the Moluccas was sponsored by the Crown because cloves were known to grow there. These aromatic red-brown buds were highly valued – as a flavouring in the kitchen, and also as a perfume and a medi-cine. The European appetite for such delicacies initiated a spice race, in which English merchants vied with the Dutch and the Portuguese for a share of the huge profits available.

As we have seen, the English appetite for spice can be traced back to the Crusades. But the English were not alone in craving it, and this raging desire – not just for cloves, but for a host of other spices – animated the whole business of empire-building. Some cravings seemed positively perverse. *Coriander* takes its name from the Greek *koris*, a bedbug: the unripe leaves and seeds of the plant were long claimed to smell just like a crushed bug. Still, it was an object of desire, along with chilli, cinnamon, ginger, nutmeg and mustard. As Jack Turner, a fine historian of the phenomenon, observes, 'Columbus, da Gama and Magellan, the three standard-bearers of the age of discovery, were spice-seekers before they became discoverers.'[8] For instance, when Vasco da Gama eased into Calicut in May 1498, four months after dramatically rounding the Cape of Good Hope, it was with the intention of acquiring not only precious stones, but also Moluccan cloves and pepper from Kerala. And that was not all: to the west, there was the promise of furs – mink, otter, bear, black fox and beaver. There was also, as John Cabot had suggested, Atlantic cod, a meaty fish that swam with its mouth open and was easy to catch. The fish appealed especially to Catholics, who were forbidden from eating meat on as many as 165 days a year.

In the fifteenth century, competition between the Spanish and the Portuguese for control of the Atlantic had opened up the fertile Americas. From the moment in 1434 when Gil Eannes, a sailor in the employ of Portugal's Prince Henry the Navigator, succeeded in passing south of Cape Bojador – for years known as the Cape of Fear, 'a psychological as well as a physical barrier to sailors' on the Atlantic[9] – a whole new arena of possibilities was open. The courtly Pedro Alvares Cabral began the settlement of Brazil, having arrived there by accident; Brazilian gold would ultimately pay for a range of English exports to Portugal, and would help cement the position of the English merchants at Lisbon. For the Spanish, the cautious yet restless Hernan Cortés subdued the Aztecs in the space of two years, and Francisco Pizarro, his imitator, conducted a steely campaign of terrorism to conquer the even richer empire of the Incas, while Venezuela – dubbed the Tierra de Gracia by Columbus – was colonized in 1522.

The resources of Central and South America were mercilessly exploited. Assisted by local allies, West African auxiliaries, and the ravages of smallpox and typhus, the conquistadors carved a passage through the continent, their steel swords literally shattering the copper-tipped axes and obsidian weapons of the native inhabitants.[10] They benefited, as others had before, from bilingual facilitators. One such go-between was Jerónimo de Aguilar, a Spaniard who had been shipwrecked on the Mexican coast and had spent most of a decade living in a Mayan village. Men like Aguilar could drill and regiment the natives: the rewards soon followed. The Spanish sent silver from Peru to be minted in Antwerp. Fine gold ornaments were melted down and sent home to glut the royal coffers. Bullion was humped across the Panama isthmus, and in Cartagena, Veracruz and Havana the spoils of conquest – not just gold and silver, but also skins and foodstuffs and dyes such as *cochineal* (first attested in 1586) – were collected in preparation for the long sea journey to Seville. Later there was *vanilla*, named by Willem Piso, a doctor in the service of the governor of Brazil; the Spanish made it popular in Europe, and 'jealously guarded' its source.[11] Its name in Nahuatl, the tongue the Spanish dubbed *lengua mexicana*, was *tlilxochitl*, meaning 'black flower'. This was difficult to say; the less beguiling Spanish alternative means 'little sheath'.

Colonialism was claimed to be a civilizing process. In his 'apologetic' history of the conquistadors' achievements, Bartolomé de las Casas cited Gregory the Great's decision to send St Augustine to England as a precedent for this. He had clearly read his Bede, and insisted that just because the sixth-century English had practised bestial customs it had not meant they were contemptible: Augustine had been sent to free them from the stigma of barbarianism. So too the peoples of the Americas were to be liberated from vicious primitivism by European morals, manners and learning. The conquistadors had received a papal blessing to legitimize their campaign. They carried copies of the *requerimiento* drawn up by the eminent jurist Juan López de Palacios Rubios, which reassured them that their acts had divine authority. Native inhabitants were expected meekly to submit to it. Of course, what really unfolded was a succession of atrocities: financial and sexual urges supervened on spiritual ones.

Its methods were questionable, but imperial Spain was the chief European power. For the English, trade, diplomacy and conflict were the main routes of contact with this prosperous empire, and Spanish words began in the sixteenth century to percolate through English. Hence, for example, *armada*, *galleon* and *contraband*. So too *hammock*, from the Spanish *hamaca* – a necessity for sleeping in hot climates, which struck Columbus as impressively hygienic. For English traders, Spain's ports were a vital source of goods from the East and the Americas, while Spanish merchants dealt in English textiles.

Given Spain's might, alliances were crucial, and successive English monarchs grappled with the issue. Henry VIII's first queen was Catherine of Aragon, and in the early part of their marriage Anglo-Spanish relations prospered. When Catherine experienced difficult pregnancies – of which there were several – Spanish doctors were brought over to examine her. A new bond between the two countries was concluded in 1515, and, although this was unstable, Catherine was able to extend patronage to the Valencian philosopher Juan Luis Vives and to other Spanish humanists. Spanish mystics such as San Juan de la Cruz influenced English poetic taste. More parochially, there was a persistent craving for Spanish fashions – supple gloves and perfume from Cordoba, stiffened bodices, and the hooped dresses known as *farthingales* (their name a corruption of the Spanish *verdugado*). But when Henry broke with the Catholic Church in order to annul his marriage, the relationship soured. His only legitimate son, the Protestant Edward VI, was highly educated yet unable to assert himself, and died of tuberculosis aged just fifteen. Edward's Catholic successor, Mary, who was Henry's daughter by Catherine, promised to lubricate the relationship through her marriage to Philip II of Spain. English traders felt they had reason to be optimistic, but the wider reaction was xenophobic. The commercial concessions the merchants had hoped to receive from Philip were never granted, and Philip's resistance stimulated the independent spirit that would animate English ventures in the Americas.

With the accession of Mary's Protestant half-sister Elizabeth in 1558, and as England's political alliances looked increasingly fragile, hostilities became inevitable. Elizabeth's truculent policy in the Spanish-controlled Netherlands and her indulgent attitude towards English pirates provoked wrath abroad. She was rarely quick to make decisions, and may best be characterized as a political survivor rather than as a pioneer. But the complex iconography that grew up around her made her appear at once threatening and vulnerable, and it signalled a change in the temper of the nation. Something that approached a cult of the Queen developed, and the almost religious ceremony that revolved around her seemed an affront to the Roman Catholic celebration of the Virgin Mary.

The ritual veneration of Elizabeth – as the bride of Christ or of the English nation, as God's own daughter and agent, and as a warrior, phoenix and living saint – was a statement of Protestant allegiance and of patriotism.[12] The execution of her cousin Mary, Queen of Scots, in February 1587 was seen throughout Europe as a religious gesture, not a punishment for treason: Mary was represented as a martyr, while Elizabeth became the target of violent Catholic invective, which characterized her as a monster, an adulterer and the product of incest. One account of the history of English suggests the temper of the times in a single, made-up sentence that buzzes with Spanish loanwords: 'The war was fought by trade *embargos*, as well as by *desperados* who stormed the *barricades* with *bravado*.'[13]

Linguistically, the Americas were to be the grand stage for confrontations between English and Spanish, and the English adventurers who trampled this stage came from a country that was in the process of discovering its own identity – somewhere in the middle of a triangle bounded by the Church, the monarchy and the political class. Language was instrumental in realizing this national identity, yet was also, as we shall see, an ideological battleground. Those who ventured far abroad were involved in promoting the national consciousness, but also in adding to it. Unlike the Spanish, the English were not conquerors seeking vassals. Rather, they were planters looking for land, supposedly green-fingered and eager to nurture growth. New experiences were cultivated or soaked up, not scythed down. English seafarers adopted many of the Spanish terms for articles found in the New World. After all, the Spanish had got there first. Many of the new words were first recorded by Richard Hakluyt, whose *Voyages* collected these pioneers' first-hand accounts. Hakluyt's writings include what are almost certainly the first mentions in English of the *sombrero* and the *llama* – from Spanish and from Peruvian Quechua (via Spanish), respectively – and of *Eskimo*, which comes from the Abenaki language of the American north-east and means 'eaters of raw flesh'.

Many sixteenth-century imports from Spanish related to animals (*armadillo*, *mosquito*); plants, food and drink (*guava*, for instance); and places (*Carib*, *El Dorado*). Others denoted ranks, types or traits either common in Spain (not just *bravado*, but also *cavalier*, *grandee*, *major-domo, miser, padre*) or discovered by the Spanish abroad. Spanish clothes made a strong impression (hence not just *sombrero*, but also *cape*), and so did their forms of entertainment, such as the *guitar* and *castanets* – the latter from a diminutive form of the word for chestnuts, presumably because the instrument made a sound like hard nuts rattling. It is not difficult to imagine the experiences which gave English adventurers the opportunity to absorb words such as *peccadillo* or *hurricane* (which was at first, thanks partly to Portuguese influence, spelt *furicano*). Then there is *bizarre*, adopted from French but made more popular by its associations with the Spanish *bizarro* meaning 'brave' – a term for its part rooted in the Basque word for a beard, presumably because bearded men were thought to be spirited, all bristle and gristle.

Besides the Spanish, there were contacts with French and Portuguese settlers. These threw up puzzling new words, and many of the terms acquired from Spanish, French and Portuguese had their roots in Native American tongues. Speakers of Arawakan languages were the first indigenous Americans encountered by Columbus, and from these languages the Europeans took words such as *iguana, mangrove, mahogany* and the already mentioned *guava*. From Carib came *cayman, manatee* and *peccary*, along with *yucca* and *savannah*, and from the now-extinct Taino language of Haiti *canoe, cassava, maize* and *papaya*. The Spanish also adopted from Taino the word *guayaco*, the name of a tree which oozed a resin that was believed to have medicinal value. Its first appearance in English, as *guaiacum*, was in 1533 in a translation by Thomas Paynell of a Latin treatise about the plague; the possibility of finding in the Caribbean and America remedies for common or fatal ailments was to be mentioned time and time again in promotional pamphlets.

Nahuatl was an especially rich source, providing *chilli, cocoa* (which was believed to cure tuberculosis), *coyote, guacamole* and *peyote*. It was also the source of *tomato*, though initially tomatoes were often called 'love apples' on account of their alleged aphrodisiac properties. This may go part of the way to explaining why in Italian the seemingly mundane tomato is called *pomodoro*, 'apple of gold'. In Britain and America the fruit's popularity was slow to rise, because of its less than inviting kinship with deadly nightshade. Another word acquired via Spanish is *avocado*, which, thanks to its shape, takes its name from the Nahuatl for a testicle. (The more lovely *orchid* also draws its name from a word for this part of the body. Here the source is Greek, and again shape is the key: orchid bulbs look alarmingly anatomical.) *Buccaneer* derives from a French corruption of the Tupí Indians' name for a method of curing their meat, and Portuguese contact with the Tupí in Brazil yielded *cashew, jacaranda, macaw, maraca, piranha, tapioca* and *toucan*. Pizarro's inroads in Peru explained the Spanish adoption of the Quechua words *condor, guano, puma* and *quinoa*, and of the words *alpaca* and *pacay* (a pulpy fruit) from the Aymara language spoken by the people living on the plateaux around Lake Titicaca. *Jaguar* was adopted from one of the several dozen Tupí–Guaraní lowland languages, where it signified nothing more precise than a carnivorous creature. Another discovery was the raintight blanket the Spanish called a *poncho*, which they appear first to have seen in Peru; British observers, less impressed, were still examining it with somewhat sceptical curiosity in the middle of the eighteenth century.

Encounters with the Portuguese were scattered and less frequent, but led to the adoption of such words as *auto-da-fé, assegai* (a hardwood spear), *marabout* (a Muslim African mystic), *madeira, albino* and *yam*. As their nature implies, one area of contact was West Africa. The Portuguese had been 'the first European power to project themselves, and their language, . . . into the world at large'.[14] They had established coastal positions between Cape Verde and Benin, and pepper, ivory, gold and slaves were their chief commodities. In the minds of their European rivals, these strategic footholds were impressive; the fort at São Jorge da Mina, for instance, was 'a fantasy city of turrets and spires, painted by mapmakers to resemble a sort of Camelot with blacks'.[15]

English adventurers were not quick to follow the Portuguese example. An early proposal to tap the African market was vetoed by Edward IV in 1482, and it was only in the 1530s that William Hawkins made the first documented English visit to West Africa, on his way to Brazil. Later, Hawkins engineered trade, sending a strange cargo that included nineteen dozen nightcaps in return for a number of elephant tusks. This bounty was sufficiently impressive to inspire at least a dozen English vessels to sail for Guinea between 1553 and 1565. The climate and tropical diseases took their toll on their crews, and those who returned expressed astonishment at the sight of the nearly naked tribesmen. They also noted details of the language these men spoke – a pidgin dotted with Portuguese words.[16] But Portuguese was mainly met with later, on the spice-laden fringes of the Indian Ocean, and we must wait to deal with that.

In the Americas, the most inspiring achievement of the Portuguese was the intensive cultivation of sugar, which they had pioneered in Brazil. The English learnt from their example. In the Caribbean, piracy was lucrative; buccaneers moved in swarms, launching audacious raids. The English busied themselves with 'the collective larceny of Spanish assets'.[17] But on land, sugar was the key to English prosperity. It was first planted on Barbados in 1643, and within half a century it covered 80 per cent of the island; refined sugar, *molasses* (from the Portuguese *melaços*) and *rum* (perhaps a West Country word) accounted for almost all Barbados's exports. As other Caribbean islands were permanently occupied – Antigua, Nevis, Montserrat – the highly profitable sugar cane was planted there too. St Kitts, initially a tobacco island, became an intensive sugar plantation. Jamaica was seized from the Spanish in 1655, and formally ceded in 1671, by which time it was home to fifty-seven sugar refineries as well as new and fruitful cocoa plantations.[18] Much of the cheaply produced rum was ferried to the Gold Coast to be bartered for slaves or even gold. Slaves were vital for the plantations' development, as the harsh conditions discouraged free men from working there. A plantation of 100 acres needed 150 strong labourers.[19] From the Spanish the English took the words *negro* and *mulatto*, the latter used of any child fathered by a Spaniard on an African woman, and they borrowed too the Spanish habits of discrimination and subjugation.

When the first English settlers landed on Barbados, in 1627, the party included ten Africans seized from a Portuguese vessel in the Atlantic. Over the next few decades, the numbers swelled. At first the Dutch West India Company dominated the slave trade; then, from 1663, the Company of Royal Adventurers Trading into Africa muscled in. In 1670 the white population of the West Indies was

41,400, as against a black population of 51,900; fifty years later, the white population had shrunk to 34,200, but the black population stood at 174,700.[20] The African experience of Atlantic slavery is captured by Olaudah Equiano, an Igbo enslaved as an 11-year-old and transported to the West Indies and thence to Virginia. In 1789 he published an 'interesting narrative' of his life, in which he handsomely conveyed the suffering of slaves, herded like sheep, tortured and raped. Equiano's book contains what seems to be our first sighting of *wrecker*, a ship used to salvage sunk or stranded vessels – or, as in Daphne du Maurier's novel *Jamaica Inn*, lure them in for looting. The word stands as a symbol of the deviousness of a whole brotherhood of coastal parasites.

The power of Spain, so majestic during the sixteenth century, diminished sharply in the seventeenth. The so-called Revolt of the Netherlands drained Spanish resources, and the vast imports of gold and silver from the Americas triggered crazy inflation. Spanish cargoes were increasingly ferried on foreign vessels, and territories overseas needed constant, expensive protection from the sniping attacks of enemies. The Anglo-Spanish Treaty of Madrid in 1670 confirmed the withering of Iberian power. 'If Spain in the sixteenth century had furnished the model to be followed,' writes the historian J. H. Elliott, 'now in the later seventeenth it was the model to be shunned.' Spain conceded English ownership of its colonies and dominions in the Caribbean and North America, and, for all that it managed to hang on to its possessions on the American mainland, 'there was a widespread impression that Spain itself was in terminal decline.'[21]

Meanwhile English mastery of the seas strengthened. As it did so, the intrepid Englishman became a stock character. A perfect embodiment of the type was the buccaneering William Dampier, who circumnavigated the globe three times and would be characterized by Coleridge in his *Table Talk* as 'a rough sailor, but a man of exquisite mind'. An observer rather than an analyst, he wrote accurately of his experiences; his *A New Voyage Round the World* (1697) is an idiosyncratic, evocative account of a series of journeys made between 1679 and 1691. The journeys take in places as far apart as China and Haiti, Chile and Indonesia. Reading Dampier is a bit like immersing oneself in a Patrick O'Brian novel, but there are long passages of assiduous note-taking. Thus 'The Guava Fruit grows on a hard scrubbed Shrub, whose Bark is smooth and whitish, the branches pretty long and small, the leaf somewhat like the leaf of a Hazel, the fruit much like a Pear, with a thin rind'; and, of the people of New Holland (i.e. Australia), 'Setting aside their humane shape, they differ but little from Brutes. They are tall, strait bodied, and thin, with small long Limbs. They have great Heads, round Foreheads, and great Brows. Their Eye-lids are always half closed, to keep the Flies out of their Eyes . . . and therefore they cannot see far.'[22]

It is in Dampier that we find the first records of several of the phenomena mentioned above, such as avocados and cashews; he is also the first English author we know to provide a proper account of those little sheaths which Willem Piso labelled vanilla, the pods of which he saw being dried in Mexico. He introduced English audiences to the Tamil *catamaran*, the swift craft he saw off the Coromandel coast, and the *barbecue*, which derives from the Haitian Taino word *barbacoa*. Dr Johnson would explain the latter in his *Dictionary* as 'a term used in the West Indies for dressing a hog whole; which, being split to the backbone, is laid flat upon a large gridiron, raised about two foot above a charcoal fire, with which it is surrounded'. The process sounds not unlike torture, yet the sacred fire pit was a sign of the Taino culture's ceremonial relationship with foodstuffs. The process of smoking meat – and the attendant pleasure of sitting back and watching it smoke – was known to Europeans long before they voyaged to the New World, but the adoption of this particular word signals a fresh appreciation of the way in which sharing food fosters community.

It was Johnson, too, who wrote in the preface to his *Dictionary*, more than 150 years after Samuel Daniel's prescient words, that

> Commerce, however necessary, however lucrative, as it depraves the manners, corrupts the language; they that have frequent intercourse with strangers, to whom they endeavour to accommodate themselves, must in time learn a mingled dialect, like the jargon which serves the traffickers on the Mediterranean and Indian coasts. This will not always be confined to the exchange, the warehouse, or the port, but

will be communicated by degrees to other ranks of the people, and be at last incorporated with the current speech.

We may demur at Johnson's talk of corrupt language and depraved manners, but he neatly limns the essential business of the English abroad. Without other people's resources, their little island could not wield much power. It was forever stretching for more: more land, more goods, more connections, more words. As England became Britain, and as Britain's possessions overseas increased, so its society was 'caught up in, transformed, and sometimes traumatised by the business of empire'.[23] Empire was not something scrupulously planned: the process of its growth was littered with accidents, both happy and unhappy. The people's experience of it was richly various. And as they absorbed this experience, they taught those they governed the chief features of their own society. According to the historian Niall Ferguson, the most impressive of these were

1. The English language
2. English forms of land tenure
3. Scottish and English banking
4. The Common Law
5. Protestantism
6. Team sports
7. The limited or 'night watchman' state
8. Representative assemblies
9. The idea of liberty.[24]

It is fitting that language heads the list, for there is no clearer legacy of empire than the international prevalence of English, and at the same time the English word-stock is, we can see, strongly marked by imperial rivalries and the variety of imperial treasures.

6. Genius

Natural ability and special endowments; the prevailing character (of an institution, place or language); the tutelary god assigned to a person at birth, which shapes his or her fortunes and character

From the Latin, and ultimately from the Greek verb for 'to be born' or 'to come into being'

While adventurers conveyed the 'treasure' of English to strange shores and returned with impressive cargoes, on the home front England repeatedly had to brace itself for invasion. Even though no foreign troops broke the English defences, foreign words burst into the consciousness of a nation at once politically unsettled and culturally exuberant. 'The Spanish are coming!' exclaimed a character in John Marston's *Histriomastix* (1599) – a line that was surely meant to get a laugh.[1] But there were other incursions – real and imagined, novel and unfamiliar – that seemed to pose more subtle challenges to the state, the people and their language.

In 1605 a volume with the swanky title *A Restitution of Decayed Intelligence* was published in Antwerp. It was the work of an Oxford-educated man called Richard Rowlands, whose passion for all things Teutonic was so strong that it had led him to reclaim his ancestral surname, Verstegan. This same enthusiasm was clear in the *Restitution*, where Rowlands vigorously promoted Anglo-Saxon words and customs, and complained that his countrymen had lately borrowed so many terms from Latin, French and other tongues that English was 'of itself no language at all, but the scum of many languages'. We might just as soon, he claimed, 'fetch words fro[m] the Ethiopians, or East or West Indians, and thrust them into our language and baptise all by the name of English, as those which wee daily take from the Latin, or languages thereon depending'. In illustration of the problems facing English-speakers, he told the story of a London courtier writing to 'a personage of authoritie in the north partes, touching the training of men and providing furniture for warre'. The courtier 'willed him among other things to *equippe* his horses': the letter's recipient was stumped by this word, wondered if it was another way of talking about 'quipping' or, more plausibly, 'whipping', and in the end sent a messenger back to London 'to learne the meaning thereof'.[2]

As you may already have noticed, Verstegan is not wholly innocent of the crime he deplores. After all, the title of his book is hardly a model of Germanic simplicity. Moreover, according to the *OED*, he is the first to use the difficult words *conjuncture, obiterly* and *confederated*, among others, and he introduces *blood royal*, a calque of *sang royal*. For the indignant Verstegan things would get worse before they got better: the peak period of borrowing from Latin was around 1615. Nevertheless, he spoke for a generation who found their language both exciting and mystifying – and who debated its rights and wrongs in moral terms.

This was a period of dramatic change in English vocabulary. Of particular concern was the flood of new words that had poured into the language in the previous hundred years. And there really had been a huge number: a third of all the English words with Latin etymologies were first used in the 140 years between the arrival of printing and the death of Shakespeare. The position Rowlands took in *A Restitution of Decayed Intelligence* was essentially conservative, a rebuff to the wilful innovators who had puffed up the nation's lexis. The sort of people its author was thinking of were the humanists Sir Thomas Elyot and Sir Thomas More.

Elyot, a diplomat and scholar, had been especially influential. His *The Boke Named the Governour* (1531) was at once a treatise on political education and a celebration of English and of verbal innovation. Elyot's decision to write in English what was essentially a manual of upper-class instruction was itself a radical departure from received practice, and demonstrated a commitment to a new, popularizing, ideal of education. His solution to the commonly perceived deficiencies of the language was to bring in a large number of loanwords. Some of these have stood the test of time – Elyot is the earliest known user of *encyclopedia, entertainment, modesty* and *hostility* – but we may balk at *concinnity* and *ingurgi-*

tation, the latter being an appropriately mouth-filling term for excessive guzzling.

Sir Thomas Elyot's lexically voracious work was acclaimed by Henry VIII and went through eight editions in half a century. Yet, as one Victorian commentator could later observe, Elyot 'endured the sneer of . . . cavillers, for his attempt to inlay our unpolished English with Latin terms'.[3] Elyot's contemporary Roger Ascham, who served as private tutor to Princess Elizabeth (teaching her Greek in the morning and Latin in the afternoon), worried that Elyot's novelties were obstructive – that borrowings 'make all things darke and harde'. Ascham argued the need for 'propriety' and plainness. Elyot and Ascham represented the opposing camps in what was little short of a war over the vernacular, its uses and its integrity. The plasticity of English – its capacity for adventure – was fiercely contested. A porous national language was interpreted, correctly, as a sign of the increasingly porous structure of society as a whole.

The influx of new language – new words, and new meanings – reflected a massive intellectual upheaval, which we now of course call the Renaissance. In fact the word *Renaissance* (or *Renascence*, as Matthew Arnold was apt to insist) did not find favour until the Victorian era, when it was given currency by two very different historians, Jules Michelet and Jacob Burckhardt: I use it here in the interests of convenience. Although the wholesale rediscovery of classical form – sometimes termed a *rinascita* – began in Italy in the fourteenth century, its effects were most urgently felt in England some 200 years later, in a period of intellectual and artistic rejuvenation. This cultural ferment teemed with new attitudes, ideas and concepts, as well as reintegrating old ones. Knowledge of the world was expanding fast, and a great deal of the language borrowed during the period reflects the need to equip English with a more sophisticated range of terms for dealing with abstract matters.

In theology, medicine, anatomy, and the study and naming of plant and animal life, new specialist understanding called for new, exact words. Writing in 1573, more than forty years after Elyot's tsunami of strange terms, the logician Ralph Lever could still acknowledge that there were 'moe things, then there are words to expresse things by'.[4] But the words were catching up. Understandably, nouns headed the field, and many of them were abstract. The Greek *pathos* was first used in 1579, while *chaos* began to be used figuratively at this time; the Latin *species* is found in 1551, with *specimen* and *spectrum* in 1610 and 1611. There is at this time an emerging technical vocabulary, comprising words such as *series*, *apparatus* and *complex*. Furthermore, we can date *genius* to the early years of the sixteenth century, *acumen* to Elyot's *The Boke Named the Governour*, and *decorum* to Ascham's *The Scholemaster* (1570): these are examples of words adopted to denote not brand-new concepts, but brand-new ways of voicing those concepts and, beyond that, in response to an urge to dignify intellectual and personal accomplishments with fine, unsullied terms. Latin was favoured for inscriptions, because it seemed sacred and incorruptible, and bringing Latin into English seemed a way of endowing the vernacular with these qualities.

Some of the new words came directly from Latin, like *dexterity*, *gratis* and *factotum*; others, like *tonic, cosmos, idiosyncrasy, misogyny* and *autodidact*, came straight from Greek. Some were closely modelled on Greek, like *anthropology*, and yet others, such as *dogma, atmosphere* and *enigma*, came from Greek via Latin. At the same time, vocabulary of a different kind was drawn from French; while French could often be a 'relay' language for borrowings from Latin and Greek, its direct contributions tended to be concerned with the social arts. John Palsgrave in his *Lesclarcissement de la langue francoyse* (1530) noted recent changes in both English and French, and among these he highlighted borrowings such as the verb *to surmount*, although he could in fact have found it in *Troilus and Criseyde*. French imports of the years immediately following Palsgrave's work included *maître d'hotel* and *perfume*; a little later came *portrait, rendezvous* and *masquerade*, along with a crop of words of recoil – *mediocre, naïf, grotesque* and *obscene*.

The critic F. W. Bateson once analysed a substantial section of the *Shorter Oxford Dictionary* and found that 'of every 100 words in use in 1600, 39 were introduced between 1500 and 1600.'[5] In fact the most rapid growth seems to have spanned a period of approximately eighty years, running from around 1550 to 1630. As Seth Lerer observes, this is 'about more than numbers. It is about the idea of numbers: about a rhetorical and social ideal of amplification, about a new fascination with the copiousness of worldly things, and about a new faith in the imagination to coin terms for unimagined concepts.'[6] Heatedly – excitedly, or furiously – the Elizabethans recognized that their language was in flux. They thought of it as a stream, forever carrying items away from them and washing new ones into view.

One of the cardinal features of the period was the increase in the numbers of books published, and in the audiences they reached. While literacy levels were not high – as late as 1640 no more than a fifth of women and two-fifths of men were able to sign official documents, rather than just using a mark – there was an emergent popular culture, a demand for printed material among the yeoman and tradesman class, and a capacity among these groups for reflecting on what they read. Books disseminated every kind of English, from high-flown rhetoric drenched in Latin to the cant of the criminal underworld. In between, there was the lucid prose of the Authorized Version of the Bible and the Book of Common Prayer, volumes that were instrumental in solidifying the status of English as the new language of authority. Two hundred and ninety editions of the Book of Common Prayer were produced between 1549 and 1642, and more than 500,000 copies were in circulation by the end of that period. The King James Bible built on the example of Tyndale; its linguistic temper is conservative. The Book of Common Prayer incorporates this same language in its liturgy. Neither ushered in many new words, although both would give lasting dignity to a wealth of expressions. To give just a couple of examples from the former: 'the spirit . . . is willing, but the flesh is weak', and 'no man can serve two masters.'

There was plenty of other reading material to choose from: printed songs and ballads, pamphlets, copies of plays, expensive legal texts, and freshly minted verse at what were often wicked prices, as well as impressive manuscript collections of poetry.[7] A wealth of new literary terminology reflected the increasingly rich culture of English letters. The English Renaissance, while offering many visual stimuli, conveyed its excitement chiefly through the written word. It was at this time that one began to refer to the distinct category of *fiction*, the role of the *critic*, *juvenilia*, and the *lyric* and *dramatic* classes of literature, and began as well to distinguish explicitly between forms such as the *adage* and the *epigram*. Moreover, against the background of these generic distinctions, there was fresh scope for eclecticism. The bright new terminology marked the emergence of a proudly national literature in the late sixteenth century – though the formula 'English literature' would not achieve currency until 200 years later. This national literature comprised works such as Shakespeare's history plays, William Camden's wide-ranging survey entitled *Britannia*, Sir Philip Sidney's *Arcadia*, Edmund Spenser's *The Faerie Queene*, and Michael Drayton's celebration of England's variety, *Poly-Olbion*. (The last of these affords our first sighting of *nymphet*, a noun given a scandalous twist some 350 years later by Vladimir Nabokov in *Lolita*.) One contemporary borrowing was the Greek *chorography*, a term to denote a map that was also a repository of proper names, such as those of places and people. Elizabethan chorographies drew attention to the pedigree of the nation and its inhabitants.[8] The new form represented the anatomy of England; national identity was embodied in the land and in the language which flowed through its arteries.

Another new form was the *essay*, introduced into English by Francis Bacon in 1597. Persuasive, imaginative and eloquent, Bacon's *Essays* were modelled on the writings of the Frenchman Michel de Montaigne.[9] More concise than Montaigne, Bacon was also less intimate; his writing thrives on images that are powerful, colloquial and oddly remote ('All rising to great place is by a winding stair'; 'Suspicions amongst thoughts are like bats among birds'). Like most writers with a gift for aphorism, he was concerned more with common truths than with the subtle varieties of human experience. Many of his images exploit simultaneously the literal meaning of a word and its figurative meaning. His style can be oracular, but one of his central beliefs is that a philosophical writer must achieve 'quiet entry' into the minds of his audience. Thus he combines strict reason with sensuous poetry, and his writing is full of new terms. A few seem over-egged (*conglutinant*, *obtenebration*), but others have endured impressively.

Bacon has a particular way with adjectives, and in his writings we can spy the first appearances of *versatile*, *prescient*, *ignoble*, *acoustic* and *juvenile*. Items of this kind testify to his deep knowledge of Latin and Greek, yet his use of classical words is disciplined and seems always to be conditioned by a desire to express himself concisely rather than by the urge to flaunt his erudition. As Geoffrey Hughes puts it, 'he realizes the potent capacity for dignified abstraction in the classical register and uses it to great effect.'[10] Shelley thought that Bacon's style was powerful enough to burst the circumference of the reader's mind. But actually this wasn't what Bacon wanted. He was sensitive to the intellectual frailty of a large part of his audience, and felt he had to create a new form of rhetoric that would imprint itself on both their reason and their imagination. He was, appropriately enough, the first to distinguish overtly between the ancients and the moderns, and it is to him that we owe the word *progressive*.

The educationalist Richard Mulcaster, one of whose more illustrious pupils was Edmund Spenser, promoted English as a medium for serious works, and felt it was a mark of English intelligence that borrowings from other languages were so frequent. 'Our tung doth serve to so manie uses,' he argued, 'because it is conversant with so manie people, and so well acquainted with so manie manners, in so sundrie kindes of dealing.' He pointed out that 'it is not for foulls to be so well learnt.'[11] Borrowing was done either out of necessity – to describe or explain new practices and new phenomena – or to garnish high-minded writing and thinking. A society without borrowing would, he saw, be poorer both materially and intellectually.

Yet anxiety about new coinages, around half of which were sourced from Latin, gnawed away at patriotic consciences. The result was an outpouring of public condemnation, which has come to be known as the 'Inkhorn controversy'. Inkhorns were small vessels used for carrying ink, and the image summoned up by the controversialists was of writers spurting out horrid polysyllables, almost as if intent on wasting their materials. Such addicts of exotic terms would rarely use a short word where a long alternative could be found. Their innovations were seen not as a mark of skill, but as evidence of a deranged pomposity. In fact the very word *innovator* was damning: in John Florio's *A Worlde of Wordes* (1598), which glossed more than 40,000 Italian terms, it is deemed synonymous with 'disturber'. The enraged purists argued that novel, imported terms weakened not just the English language, but the whole English character. The friends of the polysyllable were an enemy within. In one camp stood George Gascoigne, sometime Member of Parliament for Bedford and Midhurst, who equated a taste for verbal ornament with a betrayal of English values, and told aspiring poets to 'thrust as few words of many syllables into your verse as may be': in the other was George Chapman, who, despite a similar suspicion of the 'many syllables in harsh collision' found in French and Italian, insisted that poetry should be difficult and recondite, and spent eighteen years producing a rather loose translation of Homer that was later cherished by John Keats.

The debate was strenuous, and widely taken up. Thomas Wilson's *The Arte of Rhetorique* (1553), which voiced suspicion of 'oversea language' and 'Englishe Italianated', was reprinted seven times by three different printers. Another strongly argued contribution came from the Cambridge scholar Sir John Cheke, an advocate of simplified spelling, who spoke for all reformists when he pronounced, 'I am of this opinion that our own tung shold be written cleane and pure, unmixt and unmangeled with borrowings of other tunges, wherein if we take not heed . . . ever borrowing and never paying, she shall be fain to keep her house as bankrupt.' His words, with their strikingly commercial metaphor (and their debt, in *unmixt* and *unmangeled*, to French), would become part of the preface to Sir Thomas Hoby's 1561 translation of Baldassare Castiglione's hugely influential *Il Libro del Cortegiano*. Castiglione's book proposed an ideal of gentlemanly conduct, and Cheke was adamant that such a work should allow 'no counterfeitness of other tunges', serving instead as an advertisement for elegant, plain English. It was with this in mind that Hoby translated Castiglione's *sprezzatura* – a studied carelessness that was the essence of courtly refinement – as the less glamorous-sounding 'recklessness'. Yet, as it happened, Castiglione had been quick to spot that meetings between different cultures resulted, inevitably, in the exchange of words, and he likened these words to 'articles of trade'.

It was within this context of nonchalant self-promotion that *conceit*, once an innocent word for a thought, became irretrievably associated with stylistic posturing. *Concettismo* was the Italian term for extravagantly metaphorical poetry; John Donne was the form's master in English. As *conceit* grew to be more and more closely associated with trickery, with the sinuous performances of wit, and with fanciful expression, it became a word of contempt − for what the *OED* defines as 'an overweening opinion of oneself' − and, as Owen Barfield notes, its degradation meant that its ancestor, the non-judgemental Latin word *conceptus*, was borrowed afresh, this time as *concept*.[12] *Conceit* had originally been conveyed into English by French. For two other striking examples of pairs of words that have the same Latin source but have come by different routes − one straight from Latin, the other via French − think of *fact* and *feat*, and of *secure* and *sure*. In each case the French word conveys an impression of specious certainty. Do I believe in feats, conceits and what you say is 'sure'? Maybe. But they are less solid than facts, concepts and the promise that something is secure.

This was a period in which people asserted their individuality with electrifying vehemence. Thus a poet might be introspective, but his introspection was something to put on show. The classic example is Donne, whose many poems addressed to women seem always to be addressed at least as much to himself. Personal identity was nervously examined, and the image of selfhood was achieved through language − first through imitation, and then through invention. Words have always been read as indices of character and class, but in the Renaissance period this kind of interpretation was especially sensitive. In the first part of *Henry IV*, Hotspur criticizes his wife, Kate, for using the expression 'in good sooth'. 'You swear like a comfit-maker's wife,' he tells her, adding that she should leave 'such protest of pepper-gingerbread, / To velvet-guards, and Sunday-citizens'. What he wants is for her to come out with 'a good mouth-filling oath'. Hotspur voices a snobbery that is, in truth, a trope of the Renaissance in England. Its object is the primness of the middle classes; writers frequently sent up the quaint middle-class avoidance of religious oaths and the Puritan mannerisms of their speech. Hostpur mocks Kate for carrying on like the wife of some gauche little citizen − a woman stifled by tweeness. Any jokey antipathy specifically aimed here at comfit-makers may have been related to the popularity of a type of comfit containing caraway seeds, which was consumed to prevent flatulence. English-speakers of the period divided into those who were quite at ease with windy utterances and those who squeamishly avoided them.

Where there was opulence of language, it reflected the opulence of society. Erasmus's *De Copia* (1512) circulated the idea that one should assemble personal treasuries of words and expressions for use in future speeches and letters, and the principle that abundance was excellent soon came to be applied in other areas. Consumption was overt and often outrageous – symbolic rather than instrumental, a modern economist might say. In his *A Survey of London* (1598) John Stow, a prolific collector, whose career had included a stint as a surveyor of alehouses, describes a feast of a couple of generations before, which included 100 'fat muttons', 91 pigs, 444 pigeons, 168 swans, and an especially staggering 4,080 larks.[13] It's not quite clear how many people sat down to this repast, but it barely seems to matter. It is tempting to call this a *banquet*, but at that time the word could simply denote a dessert or a snack. What Stow depicts is a full-flavoured sort of gourmandise, and feasting on this scale was still known when he produced his portrait of the city and its suburbs. Possessions were displayed with pride. Portraits of the period emphasize their sitters' material wealth. But sophistication did not preclude a taste for base entertainment. Elizabethan hedonists could watch cockfights, or see bulls and bears baited within the 'bastard sanctuary' of the Paris Garden in Southwark. The noun *cornucopia*, first adopted by the dramatist, poet and self-anointed celebrity Robert Greene (on whom Shakespeare's Falstaff was loosely modelled), was a symbolic buzzword of the moment.[14] The horn of plenty promised both flowers and filth.

Contemporary accounts displayed unabashedly the manners and habits of the people. William Harrison's *The Description of England*, composed mainly during the 1570s, is a sprawling chronicle which tells us what Elizabethans ate, what sort of pets they kept, and what they did to their criminals. Harrison's vision is sharp-eyed: on the nobleman's table there are glasses from Murano, and there is a choice of 'about fifty-six sorts' of table wine to put in them. Women's doublets have pendant codpieces, and the colours of their garments have fanciful names like 'popinjay blue'. Far more, he frets, is spent on bodies than on souls. Harrison mentions trade with Norway, Iceland, Portugal, Russia and China, among others. He also notes the corruption of English with foreign terms of eloquence, the skill of his countrymen in learning other tongues, the persistence of Cornish and of Gothic speech in Orkney, and the roiling argot of the street and the tavern. Another vigorous account is that of Philip Stubbes, whose *The Anatomie of Abuses* (1583) is a diatribe against the excesses of fashion, documenting the 'notable vices and imperfections' of the world – and of his own country in particular. He sounds a bit like a Grumpy Old Man, railing against the wearing of earrings and silly hats, ridiculous footwear and make-up, as well as at the impudence of poor men's daughters, the appalling antics of drunks, the greed of fat-cat lawyers, and the savagery of football players. He identifies 'newfanglednesse' as a symptom of the worst kind of pride.

Stubbes, whose idea of pleasure was a tour on horseback of schools and almshouses, would have been appalled by the inventory that was taken of the wardrobe of Henry VIII after his death: it showed that he had owned 196 cloaks. Surprisingly, only 29 of them were furred. In the early part of his reign he had acquired a number of magnificent fur gowns – one, purchased in 1537, required the pelts of 350 sables. But later his taste was for rich fabrics. Whereas his father had insisted on an ermine coverlet for his bed, Henry liked linen quilts stuffed with wool. The rich men and women of the period took pleasure in silks, jewelled *brocade* (a fabric first mentioned by Hakluyt, and taking its name from the Italian *broccato*, 'embossed'), sparkling *tinsel* (which can be traced to the Latin *scintilla*, 'a spark') and shimmering damask. It seems likely that improvements in heating methods, along with the wider use of glass windows, made warm clothes much less necessary indoors.[15] When Shakespeare's Lear berates his rebellious daughters Goneril and Regan, he points out that their 'gorgeous' apparel 'scarcely keeps thee warm': their modern counterparts are the young women who wear more in bed than they do to a nightclub. Floating, superfine clothes are feats of magic more than of engineering, like the mythical knickers which, tossed into the air, never return. Words too can be flyaway – delicate, temporary, brief fireworks of erudition – and amid all this period's finery there was an extraordinary efflorescence of language. The figures and flowers of rhetoric could be like the filmiest of fine garments.

We see this in a good deal of Elizabethan poetry, which is marked by self-consciousness. Sir Thomas Wyatt and the Earl of Surrey forged a style rich in literary devices and effects. Their poems were like exercises – experiments in introspection, at once virile and psychologically acute. What was more, their craft had practical uses. George Puttenham's popular *The Arte of English Poesie* (1589) praised their polished diction and their taste for the sweet stateliness of Italian. (He was also one of the growing number of commentators who thought that the speech of London and the counties bordering it was the best kind of English.) Puttenham presented poetry as a courtly accomplishment, and emphasized that the rhetorical dexterity of the poet could be exercised in the political arena as well. Furthermore, he characterized the language of poetry in strikingly physical terms: one kind of device was a 'privie nippe', another a 'rebound', and a third a 'changeling' – images out of a story of political or romantic intrigue, we might think, rather than from an account of different types of metaphor.

Less an aesthetic manifesto than an ideological primer, Puttenham's urbane volume highlights the power of language as an instrument of persuasion and imagines the many devices of rhetoric as political tools – capable of being used to Machiavellian ends. No mere theorist, Puttenham knew the pitfalls of public life from the inside; he was imprisoned for allegedly inciting the murder of a bishop, was excommunicated from the Church of England for failing to pay alimony to his estranged wife, and had to sue his wife's family after they arranged for his London lodgings to be ransacked. *The Arte of English Poesie* was published anonymously, yet its cavalcade of rhetorical skills was unmistakably the work of a man characterized by his peers as a master of eloquent mischief. It is for us to decide whether Puttenham is being mischievous, patriotic or equivocal when, in his extensive gloss of Latin and Greek rhetorical terminology, he mentions what seem to be equally useful English equivalents. What should we think, for instance, of his talking up *decorum* by drawing attention to the word's existing alternatives: *decencie, seemelynesse, comelynesse* and *pleasant approche*?

It was against this background that Robert Cawdrey, a school-master, published the first monolingual English dictionary in 1604.[16] This somewhat limited work, entitled *A Table Alphabeticall*, was intended 'for the benefit & helpe of Ladies, Gentlewomen, or any other unskilfull persons'. It advocated the avoidance of 'strange ynckhorne termes', 'affected Rhetorique' and anything 'unusually' difficult. At the same time, it helped readers grasp the meanings of obscure, technical or foreign terms. So, for instance, Cawdrey glossed *apocrypha* as 'not of authoritie, a thing hidden', *planet* as 'wandring starre' and *circumcise* as 'to cut the privie skin'.

Further dictionaries built on Cawdrey's example. John Cowell's *The Interpreter* (1607) dealt with the terms of law, which came mainly from French and Latin, with a handful from German and Greek. For example, *curfew* 'commeth of two French words' – *couvrir* and *feu* – and 'We use it for an evening peale, by the which the Conquerour willed every man to take warning for the raking up of his fire, and the putting out of his light.' Henry Cockeram's *The English Dictionary* (1623) targeted among others 'young Schollers, Clarkes, Merchants, as also Strangers of any Nation', and boasted that it contained 'some thousands words never published by any heretofore'. Another legal man, Thomas Blount, produced a volume entitled *Glossographia* (1656), which was a compendium of 'hard' terms – 'whether Hebrew, Greek, Latin, Italian, Spanish, French, Teutonick, Belgick, British or Saxon, as are now used in our refined English Tongue'. Thus *comma*, from the Greek, is 'the least note of distinction, or a point in the part of a Sentence without perfect sense', and *sherbet* is either a Persian term for 'a kinde of drink . . . compounded of juyce of Lemons, Sugar, Amber, and other ingredients . . . [or] of Violets, Honey, juyce of Raisons, and the like' or an Arabic one that 'signifies drink in general'. Readers may have found some of the explanations puzzling: we are likely to be unhappy with the information that *lurid* can mean 'pale, wan, black, and blew', and may be startled to read that a *colon* is 'a mark . . . made with two pricks'. Certainly, works of this kind were unable to impose standards, and tended only rather ineffectually to unpack the mysteries of modish diction.

As all this suggests, the Elizabethans and Jacobeans loved language: they made abundant use of loanwords, and were creative with the linguistic resources that already existed. Rejoicing in the vertiginous possibilities of self-expression, they were mostly opportunists, plucking fresh terms from exotic sources. One of the most arresting features of the period is the way in which lofty words cohabit on the page with plain ones. Shakespeare exemplifies this nicely. Hamlet can accuse his mother of 'honeying and making love / Over the nasty sty' with his uncle (a 'mildew'd ear'), yet can speak of the earth as a 'sterile promontory' and of the sky as 'this brave o'erhanging firmament, this majestical roof fretted with golden fire'; he refers to Hyperion and Hercules, and employs words as unwieldy as *cerements*, *suspiration* and *malefaction*, but can spit 'buzz buzz' at Polonius and can later say of the courtier's corpse, 'I'll lug the guts into the neighbour room.'

The fondness for wordplay which characterizes so much Elizabethan drama was a practical necessity. The influence of the Master of the Revels, a royally appointed official who had licence to carry out censorship and exact hefty fines, meant that playwrights needed to find ways of dealing obliquely with delicate matters – be they sacred or profane. Shakespeare is a master of delicate periphrasis, as of riddling puns. His more suggestive puns – Hamlet's talk of 'country matters', for instance – were the main reason Thomas Bowdler found it necessary to produce for nineteenth-century readers his *Family Shakespeare*. Dr Johnson pronounced that the art of the pun 'was to Shakespeare the fatal Cleopatra, for which he was prepared to give away the world'. It is a typically eighteenth-century attitude: Johnson and his peers admired Shakespeare almost in spite of his language. Yet it was not the playwright's instinct to be difficult. The reason we can still read Shakespeare quite comfortably, while struggling with many of his contemporaries, is that his language has a comparatively low level of 'surface difficulty'.[17] In his plays the ability to speak English is usually esteemed a virtue; characters who do otherwise, like Cardinal Wolsey effortlessly mouthing Latin in *Henry VIII*, are being marked out as villains.

Nonetheless, Shakespeare, drolly convicted by Ben Jonson of possessing 'small Latine and lesse Greeke', takes pleasure in exploiting the root Latin and Greek meanings of English words. Moreover, he crafts phrases that have become staples of English idiom: 'brevity is the soul of wit', 'pomp and circumstance', 'green-eyed jealousy', 'more sinned against than sinning', and so on. His works contain our first sightings of some 1,700 words. These include, just to give a few of his adjectives, *lacklustre* and *priceless*, *eventful* and *frugal*, *sanctimonious* and *fashionable*. Among the previously unrecorded words that appear in *Hamlet* are *compulsive, excitement, proposer, unpolluted, to sate, to commingle* and *to besmirch*. Hamlet's education – at the university of Wittenberg – makes him the ideal vehicle for Shakespeare's linguistic daring. Yet he can also make use of a term from the game of bowls ('Ay, there's the rub') and can say with consummate colloquialism that the fawning Osric has 'got the tune of the time' – the pop-song sensibilities of a 'drossy age'.[18] The dramatist was happy to put the Warwickshire dialect of his youth in the mouths of his characters – as when Hal, pretending to be his father, refers to Falstaff as a 'boulting-hutch of beastliness', or in the use of *keech* ('a cake of wax') as a term of abuse.[19] Stephen Greenblatt identifies among the dramatist's talents the 'uncanny ability to absorb vocabulary from a wide range of pursuits' and his 'lightning transformation of technical terms into the intimate registers of thoughts and feelings'.[20]

It is possible, of course, to exaggerate a writer's innovations. When we find in *Pericles* the first recorded reference to *pageantry*, or in *Cymbeline* and *The Tempest* the earliest mentions of a *mountaineer*, we may reasonably pause to ask if the novelty is Shakespeare's or if he is merely registering the usage of his day. It is hard to be sure, but any historical account of a language will depend on the tangible documentary evidence of the written word, rather than on alluring hearsay or wispy speculation. Perhaps some contemporaries of Chaucer or Skelton spoke of *pageantry*, but we have no evidence that they did, and in its absence we are safest to assume they did not. There are, in any case, other reasons for emphasizing the role of literature. To quote one recent history, 'The recorded text is the currency of the expansion of cultural markets. Texts can be sold at any time, while oral culture can only be sold at the moment of performance.'[21] A literary language – recorded, sold, resold – can be taught and preserved. By looking at written works, and especially at those that have been highly valued, we can take the temperature of the society in which they were produced.

Not surprisingly, Shakespeare touches on the Inkhorn debate. In his plays there are several characters whose polysyllabic effusions are clearly meant to be ridiculous. Some, like Dogberry in *Much Ado about Nothing* ('Comparisons are odorous'), are guilty of what we would now call malapropisms – a common enough thing when fancy new language is being juggled. In *Hamlet*, Polonius says he is 'brief', but his rhetorical figures ("Tis true 'tis pity, / And pity 'tis 'tis true') are laughably vacuous, and Hamlet himself mocks the unctuous Osric and what Horatio calls his 'golden words', while the showy abuse of the Latin adverb *ergo* is guyed when the first gravedigger comically mispronounces it *argal*, and the Latinate pomposity of Hamlet's usurping uncle Claudius is a courtly mask through which audiences can see. Holofernes in *Love's Labour's Lost* is a linguistic fusspot: besides being a snob about spelling, he relishes piling up synonyms and uses fine words to set himself apart from those who are less educated. Shakespeare used the very new word *pedant* to describe him; also used by Christopher Marlowe in *Edward II* and by Sidney in *Arcadia*, it derives from the Italian *pedantaggine*, which is defined in John Florio's dictionary as 'one that would fain seem wise and learnt, and is but a fool and an ignorant self-conceited gull'. The character who attaches this word to Holofernes is Berowne, who elsewhere in the play disavows the 'taffeta phrases' and 'figures pedantical' so frequently used for wooing. Another character, Don Adriano de Armado, may have been modelled on Philip II's secretary of state Antonio Pérez; he is an amalgam of Continental pretensions, and his rhetoric burlesques the style of Perez's writings.[22] We are told he is 'a refined traveller of Spain', 'hath a mint of phrases in his brain' and exhibits a particular taste for 'fire-new words' – for glittering novelties still hot from the forge.

It is in Ben Jonson's *The Poetaster* (1601), though, that the tooth-breaking awkwardness of the new words is most graphically satirized, when the bad poet Crispinus is obliged to spew up some of his half-digested novelties. His vomit of 'terrible, windy' polysyllables, caught in a basin by the poet Horace, includes some indigestible items – in one retch he brings up both *turgidous* and *ventositous* – but also some lasting ones, like *strenuous*, *retrograde* and *defunct*.

Jonson was one of those who envisioned a lucid path through

this forest of verbiage. His *The English Grammar* – written before 1623, though not published until after his death, in 1640 – was created 'for the benefit of all Strangers', and attempted to organize English grammar on the model of Latin. Drama was a contentious arena, and its linguistic fashions were especially contentious. Jonson argued for restraint. In his view, the cream of language comprised the oldest parts of present usage and the newest of the past. Novelties were, at best, acceptable; at worst, they were to be scorned. 'Custom is the most certain mistresse of language,' he wrote in *Timber, or Discoveries* (also published in 1640), 'as the public stamp makes the current money.' The title of this volume is apposite: the literary and linguistic 'discoveries' of the Renaissance, like the discoveries of colonialists and explorers, posed problems both practical and ethical. 'Language most shows a man,' writes Jonson. 'Speak that I may see thee.' Yet confusion reigned. In his play *Bartholomew Fair* (1614) he presents language as a kind of chaotic game: its words are irregular, and when they are given some sort of order it is in a spirit of festive self-regard.[23]

Modish words were sometimes the object of self-conscious reference. In John Webster's *The Duchess of Malfi*, first performed in 1614, the Calabrian duke, Ferdinand, is flummoxed by the Greek word *lycanthropia* – a popular new term for an obscure yet commonly imagined malady – and remarks, 'I need a dictionary to't.' His frank admission of ignorance struck a chord with contemporary theatregoers, for whom such novelties were sometimes exciting yet often troublesome. In 1612 the playwright Thomas Heywood published *An Apology for Actors*, in which he defended the theatre against Puritan invective and argued that the language of drama represented the very best of English, but a few years later John Green, in a refutation of Heywood, disparaged the linguistic 'mingle-mangle' of English drama. According to Green, 'before the Conquest by Bastard *William* that the French came in, our English tongue was most perfect,' but in the centuries since then it had been depraved, and 'a plaine man can scarce utter his mind, for want of Phrases . . . according to the fashion.'[24]

'Bastard William', not 'William the Conqueror': the choice of words is telling. In the last years of the sixteenth century we come across the verb *to Frenchify*, coined by Robert Greene; another early user is Richard Rowlands. Its thrust is pejorative: Greene pokes fun at a 'Frenchefied' man whose hair laps over his shoulders. Suspicion of foreigners and foreign ways was reflected in the language of the street – and above all in the language of sex. The French were the principal target: someone infected with syphilis was said to have 'learnt French', and syphilis itself was known as the 'French disease', 'French pox', 'French measles', and even 'the French razor', on account of its causing victims to lose their hair. But others were similarly attacked. 'Spanish buttons' was slang for the buboes that ravaged the body of anyone infected with venereal disease, while 'Spanish water' referred to infected semen. 'Italian tricks' was slang for buggery, as was 'Italian sin', and the jobbing playwright Thomas Dekker, though happy to adopt Italian vocabulary, referred to 'back-door Italians'.[25]

Soldiers, diplomats, merchants and intellectuals, who travelled in all three countries, were able to correct crude stereotypes, although often they buttressed them, complaining of brawling, duelling Parisians, of the moral laxity of Venice, of the assassins and poisoners of Rome, and of the sheer difficulty and costliness of travelling in Spain.[26] Travel itself was viewed with suspicion, as it exposed pliable minds to Catholicism. This suspicion increased in the later years of Elizabeth's reign, when those venturing 'across seas' were assumed to be at risk of kidnapping by Spaniards. While travel developed character, it also created artificial challenges. The pejorative word *gesticulate*, adopted around 1600, grew out of English tourists' distaste for the excessive gestures of Italians, French and others.[27] The English, by contrast, made little use of gestures.

In this area, too, Shakespeare is a good source of up-to-date adoptions. Most of his French appears in *Henry V*. Near the end of the play, the eponymous hero suggests to his French princess that between them they can 'compound a boy, half French, half English, that shall go to Constantinople and take the Turk by the beard'. The lines are a reminder that, even amid the religious ructions of the period, there were ill feelings of a higher pitch than those between England and France. In a different spirit are the princess's attempts to learn English words. 'Comment appelez-vous les pieds et la robe?' she asks. Her tutor answers, '*De foot*, madame, et *de cown*.' Instead of hearing *feet* and *gown*, she hears in his mispronunciation the French *foutre* and *con*, which understandably alarms her. The words, she exclaims, are 'de son mauvais, corruptible, gros, et impudique'. Her conclusion? 'De tongues of de mans is be full of deceits' – a nice summary of the imbroglios of human communication. There are dashes of French elsewhere – as when Sir Toby Belch in *Twelfth Night* corruptly renders *quelque chose* as *kickshaw*. Shakespeare's Spanish words include *hurricano*, *ambuscado* and *barricado*. In *The Winter's Tale* the pranksome Autolycus mentions a ballad in which a woman 'longed to eat adders' heads and / Toads carbonadoed' – a preposterous exaggeration of the perversions of the Continental diet. By contrast, Falstaff is warmly receptive to foreign food and drink. When he refers to 'sherris sack', meaning the dry wine from Jerez, this is of course *sherry*. He relishes its 'twofold operation', conveniently believing that it warms the blood and stirs the brain, whereas we may think of other, less helpful, effects of heavy drinking.

When it comes to Italian, we should take a step back to review the terrain in all its breadth. Today it is a language commonly associated with three *f*s – food, fashion and football. Whether or not we can really speak any Italian, we all have a little of it at our disposal. Ordering an espresso, or intoning the names of Italian cars and fashion designers, or rolling one's tongue around the titles of the dishes on an Italian menu, one savours the language's apparent opulence. *Carpaccio di manzo. Salvatore Ferragamo. Saltimbocca* – the dish that, taken literally, jumps into one's mouth – and *tiramisu* – a 'pick me up', though its effect is nothing of the sort, as Tony Soprano could confirm. Terms of art, too: *replica*, *impasto*, *chiaroscuro*. The textures of the words are, to me at least, luscious. They suggest a more romantic world. (Such feelings are not academically respectable: they smack of deep-seated prejudice or of pride, as in Anatole France's claim, 'La langue française est une femme . . . si belle . . . si noble . . . si sage.') We have borrowed from Italian *la dolce vita*, *Cosa Nostra* and *mamma mia*, and each hints at the places where Italian culture and society have touched the lives of English-speakers.

Over the past seven centuries, the busiest areas of borrowing have been art, music and food, and the busiest periods have been between 1550 and 1650 and in the nineteenth century. Laura Pinnavaia, who has researched the Italian element in English, explains that in the period between 1550 and 1600 'the majority of Italian borrowings seem to deal with plants, man's physical appearance and state, sensations and perceptions, actions, social groups, behaviour, war, weaponry, fortifications, armed forces, crime, linguistic expressions, poetry, geometry, mathematics, the textile industry, commerce and sports.' If that sounds a broad range, compare the period from 1600 to 1650, where there is a particular concern with 'physical geography and the weather'. In the second half of the seventeenth century most Italian loanwords in English regard 'state, religion, theatre, education and finances'. Then from 1700 to 1750 'musical terms predominate' – we are likely to think of *opera* and *piano*, and maybe also of more specialized words such as *intermezzo* and *pizzicato*. In the next half-century opera is to the fore, and so is geology. From 1800 to 1850 'one sole semantic field dominates: that of entertainment,' and in the half-century that followed the key domains included sculpture, ceramics and the Church.[28] A few concrete examples may cement our impressions. *Carnival* is sighted in 1549, *fresco* in 1598, and *umbrella* in 1609 in a letter by John Donne, although the first Briton to carry an umbrella was Jonas Hanway more than 150 years later (and he was ridiculed for doing so). *Gusto* makes an appearance in 1629, though it took almost two centuries for it to catch on. *Gambit*, which comes from an Italian term for tripping one's opponent while wrestling, appears in a book about chess in 1656.[29] Other Tudor imports from Italian included *cameo*, *madrigal*, *motto* and *stucco*, while *violin* – from *violino* – appears in the works of Jonson and Spenser.

The inspirations here are not obscure. The Renaissance engendered a mania for all things Italian. Traders exploited this, but relations with Italy cooled with the accession of Charles I. In the second half of the seventeenth century a fresh influx of Italian words had much to do with the waning of Puritanism and the religious tolerance of Charles II. The phenomenon of the Grand Tour and the Romantic poets' enthusiasm for Italian literature inspired later borrowings, which revolved around leisure more than commerce.

For Elizabethans, however, Italians' skills in trade and the conduct of state affairs were as compelling as their artistic prowess. Political thought was influenced by Niccolò Machiavelli's *Il principe* (published in 1532), which argued that proper government calls for real strength but only feigned morals. Machiavelli's name became a sort of denotative cliché for the sinister extremes of statecraft. Moreover, Machiavelli's promotion of *virtù* – a combination of shrewdness, vigour, skill and effort – skewed the meaning of the English word *virtue*. For what *virtù* certainly didn't mean was 'goodness', and his English readers, even if they were aware of the gap between *virtù* and *virtue*, couldn't help conflating the two. Peggy Knapp has argued that 'The influence of the *Prince* impeded the bond between power and goodness from becoming an automatic and ordinary usage in early Modern English, by treating . . . manly action . . . as working best . . . when it is a . . . charade.' Ultimately, the adoption of what we may anachronistically call *realpolitik* 'allowed some relaxation of private moral strictures in governing the nation'.[30] Not insignificantly, from the time of its first adoption in the 1560s, the adjective *Machiavellian* has been used disparagingly.

In the drama of the period, Italy was associated with criminality and splendour – with court intrigue, wicked poisonings, and pageantry. Playwrights were impressed by the Italian touring companies and their gory interpretations of Seneca. Stephen Gosson's *Playes Confuted in Five Actions* (1582) mentions the popularity in London of spectacles staged in Italian. Webster's dramas are crammed with ostentatious Italianism. His characters describe in detail the use of a *stiletto* as a murder weapon and say things like 'Me thinks, being an Italian, I trust you.' We find the same rather fanciful local colour in John Marston's *The Insatiate Countess* (published in 1613) and Philip Massinger's *The Unnatural Combat* (*c.*1624). John Ford includes snatches of Italian song in *'Tis Pity She's A Whore* (1633). Thomas Middleton's *Women Beware Women* (*c.*1621) is set in sixteenth-century Florence among members of the Medici family. Jonson's *Volpone* is more authentic, and in his detailed presentation of Venetian quackery the playwright, perhaps drawing on the knowledge of his friend Florio, includes such words as *ciarlatani*, *piazza*, *vertigine* and *ampulla*. In the same play Proteus makes mention of a 'Lombard proverb' to do with financial necessity: here is our first imperfect sighting of the enduring calque *cold feet*.

While many of the Italian contributions to English have come via French, in the sixteenth century numerous words came from Italian directly. Trade connections were important in this, and are evident in such Italian loans as *contraband, traffic, frigate* and *mercantile*. At the same time the promise of art, music, luxury and romance inspired travellers to visit Italy, and they returned with samples and tokens of them all. William Thomas's *Principal Rules of the Italian Grammar* (1550) was the first concerted attempt to help English-speakers learn Italian.[31] Half a century later, Giovanni Botero's *Relationi Universali* was phenomenally successful in a translation by Robert Johnson, which expanded Botero's treatment of his country and countrymen.[32]

The riches of Italy at this time are suggested in the paintings of Titian, Raphael and Michelangelo and the architecture of Palladio and Giulio Romano. Thomas Coryat's *Crudities* (1611), a digest of bits and pieces 'hastily gobled up' during five months' travel on the Continent, affords a distinctively English and rhapsodic view of Italy: of the 'very prety' hats of women in Piedmont; of Padua, a city 'as sweetly seated as any place of the whole world'; of Venice and 'the resplendent rayes of her unparalleled beauty'; of 'very delectable' Verona and the 'goodly vineyards' between Brescia and Bergamo.[33] Coryat is a faintly absurd character, who can tell us little of Turin because 'I found so great a distemperature in my body, by drinking the sweete wines of Piemont, that caused a grievous inflammation in my face and hands . . . that I had but a smal desire to walke much.'[34] He records what were at that time positively bizarre items like forks, and mentions the 'place where the whole fraternity of the Jews dwelleth together, which is called the Ghetto'.[35] This may come from *getto*, the Italian word for a foundry – the first such community in Venice was established in 1516 on a site where there had previously been a foundry – or from *borghetto*, a word for a small settlement outside city walls, which now seems to be a favourite name for places offering *agriturismo* to people who have overdosed on *Under the Tuscan Sun*.

Other nouns that came in at this time were *regatta, gondola* and *lottery*, as well as *tarot* and *carnival*. The last of these was reckoned by Florio to derive from a Latin expression meaning 'farewell to flesh'; the word *carnival* was properly applied to Ash Wednesday, the day of penitence that preceded the Lent fast. Besides festive terms, there was the usual influx of foodstuffs (*macaroni, rocket*), but it was in the language of manners and courtliness that Italian proved especially influential. It is to Italian that we owe such terms as the already mentioned *gusto* and – less obviously – *gambol* and *disgrace*. A few borrowings were even more heavily anglicized; *bankrupt* renders the Italian *banca rotta*, 'broken bench', which recalls the stipulation that insolvent Venetian money-lenders destroy the counters from which they traded.

The embrace of Italians' architectural style and enthusiasm for fine gardens is reflected in the imports *cupola*, *pergola* and *grotto*. These kept their pleasing Italian appearance, while words like *pilaster* and *pedestal* assumed less obviously exotic forms. Another architectural addition was *balcony*. Based on the Italian word for a scaffold, it was unsatisfactorily defined by Florio as 'a windowe, a bay-windowe, a bulke, a stall of a shop', and its novelty was sufficient for Milton to use it only tentatively in *Areopagitica* half a century later.[36]

A final symptom of the vogue for the Italian was the enthusiasm for names like Orlando, Bianca and Juliet, all of which were popularized by Shakespeare. The dramatist had a sketchy knowledge of Italian, yet was keen to show off what he did know. His plays often have Italian settings: the names of *The Merchant of Venice* and *The Two Gentlemen of Verona* reveal their locations, and we travel to Messina in *Much Ado About Nothing*, to Verona and Mantua in *Romeo and Juliet*, and to Padua in *The Taming of the Shrew*, while *The Tempest* features the ruling families of Milan and Naples. In truth, his knowledge of Italian geography and customs was not impeccable – he locates Padua in Lombardy, for example, and imagines characters from Verona sailing right around the Italian coastline to reach Milan, even though Milan was less than 100 miles away overland.

This hardly mattered, though, when the romance of Italy and Italian was in the air. Shakespeare uses several dozen Italian words, including *magnifico*, *ben trovato*, *coragio*, *ben venuto*, *Diablo*, *perdonato* and *signor*. In *Love's Labour's Lost* he introduces the Italian *stanza* and *fantasim* – the latter a very strange word employed by him alone, to signify a fantastic being. In the same play he uses *zany*, a word for a clown, which is a corruption of Giovanni, the stock name for clownish servants in *commedia dell'arte*. In the second part of *Henry IV* Pistol speaks bad Italian – no coincidence, for his name may suggest not just the obvious link with an erratic little weapon, but also connections with the Tuscan town Pistoia (which was known for its well-made daggers) and with the Italian *pistolfo*, a successful sort of rogue or beggar. In *Pericles* Thaisa quotes a motto which she believes to be Spanish although it is much closer to Italian. Falstaff derides 'mad Mustachio-purple-hu'd-Maltwormes', and his word *mustachio* blends the Spanish *mostazo* and the Italian *mostaccio* (meaning 'face') – both of them linked at once to the Latin *mustaceus*, a rhombus-shaped pastry doused in new wine and handed out at wedding feasts, and to the Greek *mystax*, meaning the upper lip. *Bandit* first appears in the second part of *Henry VI*. In other plays we come across *capriccio*, *varletto*, *cubiculo* and *basta*.

Italian verbiage is often the mark of a character who has ideas above his station, or a way of mocking such a person. In *Romeo and Juliet*, the effeminate and foppish manners of Tybalt call forth a volley of scorn from Mercutio, who, describing him to Benvolio, sneers at 'antic, lisping, affecting fantasticoes' and 'new tuners of accents' – in other words, people like Tybalt who put on foreign manners and accents, or who use imported terms to make themselves sound modish or clever. Mercutio laughs, in particular, at Tybalt's fancy fencing jargon. 'Ah, the immortal passado! the punto reverso! the hai!' he exclaims. 'The what?' blurts Benvolio, suggesting that Shakespeare expected his audience to find these Italian terms bemusingly absurd.

We see something similar in Ben Jonson's play *Every Man in his Humour*, where the preposterous Bobadill is showing off about his swordsmanship. Imagining a lunge being made at him, he proudly explains that 'The best-practised gallants of the time name it the passada: a most desperate thrust, believe it!' The most desperate thrusts, though, are the verbal ones executed by these fashionable fools; their braggadocio is a bit like the fighting talk of modern schoolboys who have overdosed on martial-arts films and the pedantic belligerence of hip-hop. Indeed, before *braggadocio* became a word for emptily boastful talk, it was used of the playground swaggerers who gave it breath. It too is a word of Italian origin, first used by Spenser as the name of a cocky character in *The Faerie Queene*.

Shakespeare, we should be clear, was not alone in his appetite for Italian terms. *Miniature*, from *miniatura*, is first used by the exceptionally well-travelled Sir Philip Sidney in his pastoral romance *Arcadia*. He took the title of that work from the Neapolitan poet Jacopo Sannazzaro, and played a large part in popularizing the Italian sonnet form. Sidney had lived in Venice, where he had known the painter Tintoretto, and had studied at Padua. In his writings, he advocated adventure, professing that the limit of what a poet could achieve was determined by 'the zodiac of his own wit'. Moreover, his circle included the lexicographer John Florio. But back to *miniature*: Sidney describes women playing in water, the bubbles of which 'set forth the miniature of them'. In Italian *miniatura* had at first been used exclusively of the little images used by scribes to decorate the initial letters of their manuscript chapters. It then broadened to signify any small portrait. It took about a hundred years for the meaning to extend to include anything on a small scale. In *Gulliver's Travels* (1726) the Queen of Brobdingnag plops a giant steak on Gulliver's plate – 'her diversion was to see me eat in miniature.'

Sidney's works include many other first sightings. He was a modernizer, keen on experiment and on pushing language to its limits. Some of those first sightings are of words in common use today – *bugbear*, *hazardous*, *loneliness*, *pathology* – though others are more recondite – such as *sdrucciola*, for instance, which is a technical term to do with poetry, again borrowed from the Italian. In his manifesto *An Apology for Poetry* (published posthumously in 1595) he contrasts the 'rude stile' of traditional ballads with the 'gorgious eloquence' of a Greek ode. His appetite for finely trimmed poetry means he rejoices in Italian eloquence. He salutes the 'fertileness' of Italian wit, and in his opening paragraph he uses the word *pedanteria*; he brings in not just Sannazzaro, but also Ariosto, Boccaccio, the Florentine humanist Cristoforo Landino, and the troupes of Italian actors he has seen on a trip to Venice. Classical references outweigh contemporary ones – and he constructs his argument in the seven-part form of a Latin oration – but Sidney is visibly engaged with the literary culture of the Continent. Spanish was spoken in his circle; his uncle was the patron of Thomas d'Oylie, who compiled a valuable Spanish grammar and dictionary, and the *Arcadia* is indebted to Jorge de Montemayor's pastoral romance *Diana*. In 1578 he had considered a voyage to America, and in 1585 the plan resurfaced. But, ordered back from Plymouth by the Queen, he was created governor of Flushing in the Netherlands, and it was there that he died a year later, of a thigh wound sustained in battle. In the final stages of his life he was busy translating the work of a French Huguenot poet, Salluste du Bartas.

The Italian connection is at least as clear in the works of Edmund Spenser, whose friend Gabriel Harvey claimed that as a young man the poet had the look of an 'Italianate signior'. Spenser had drunk deeply of Ariosto and Tasso, and was the first English poet to give the name *canto* to the sections of his work. Yet his relationship with foreign terms was equivocal. Whereas his contemporaries tended to be either purists or addicts of neologism, Spenser advertised a third way – the embrace of archaism. His verse is formulaic and steeped in the antique. Perhaps the last major English author to be significantly influenced by Chaucer, he breathed new life into old words and outmoded forms: items like *eftsoons* and *glitterand, beautifullest* and *ribaudry*. When Hamlet questioned the use of the strange word *mobled* (an old Warwickshire term), a Shakespearean audience familiar with Spenser might have discerned a small joke at the expense of such revivals. In the dedicatory letter prefixed to *The Shepheardes Calender* (1579), which may have been penned by Spenser or by his Cambridge contemporary Edward Kirke, the author complains that English writers have tried to compensate for the deficiencies of their tongue and have 'patched up the holes with peces and rags of other languages, borrowing here of the French, there of the Italian, every where of the Latine'. As a result, the English of the day was 'a gallimaufray or hodgepodge of al other speeches'. 'Gallimaufray or hodgepodge', intended as an ironic coupling of modish French and plain English, was fraught with more irony than Spenser realized: while the first signified a French dish made by mashing together an assortment of kitchen leftovers, the latter was, as we saw earlier, an old corruption of *hochepot*, also French.

Spenser's values are demonstrated in *The Faerie Queene*, which is one of those daunting works that tend to be read only by fierce academics and reluctant undergraduates. His goal was to reproduce both the colour of the medieval world and its chivalric values: to this end the poem is 'clowdily enwrapped in Allegoricall devices', designed to 'fashion a gentleman or noble person in vertuous and gentle discipline'. Spenser was fond of 'good and naturall English words, as have ben long time out of use and almost cleane disinherited', and recovered some so musty (*gride, forswatt*) they looked unfamiliar enough for readers to think them brand new. But many of the words in *The Faerie Queene* that appear venerable are his own coinages. One lasting example is the adjective *blatant*, beloved today of football commentators ('a blatant foul') and teenagers (especially when turned into an adverb – 'he was blatantly cheating'). He also coined *derring-do*, a term at which he arrived only as a result of misreading a passage in Lydgate.

A different perspective had been presented by Joachim du Bellay in his *Defence et illustration de la langue française* (1549). Du Bellay, whose poems Spenser had translated in childhood as an intellectual exercise, had the same sort of interest in the vernacular that Spenser developed, but argued that French could be valuably augmented by new words drawn from Latin – and used in support of this the image of a branch being grafted on to a healthy tree. Du Bellay was keenly aware that language was mutable, and that it could be improved only through what he called the 'artifice and industry of men'. He and his contemporaries believed the Bible story of the Tower of Babel, and felt that ever since Babel there had been a fierce competition between languages. The only solutions were pragmatic. The purists, he claimed, were like fastidious antiquarians who saw the past as if through a pane of glass; they treated Latin and Greek like precious relics, and were incapable of exploiting other cultures to enrich their own. The virtues of language were achieved through choice and free will, not through squeamishness. Many of his peers believed that to ennoble one's language one had to seize on the ornaments and excellence of other languages. Du Bellay noted this tendency ('Nous favorisons toujours les étrangers') but insisted on a greater degree of autonomy for French. Yet even as French was to be embellished from within, discreet borrowing was prudently to be continued.

By the time Richard Rowlands entered the fray, the arguments had curdled, and many commentators who would once have fretted about linguistic flux were determined to find in it at least the germ of progress. One of those to put forward the idea of English as an organic being was the Cornishman Richard Carew. In his 'Epistle on the Excellency of the English Tongue', published in 1614 but written around 1595, this bee-keeping etymologist applauds the habit of borrowing. Relishing 'our tongue[']s copiousness', he playfully refers to the 'thefte of woordes' from other languages, and commends the 'sweetnes of our tongue', which contrasts with Italian ('pleasante but without synewes'), French ('delicate but over nice'), Spanish ('majesticall, but fullsome') and Dutch ('manlike, but . . . very harshe'). He concludes excitedly that 'the most renowned of other nations have . . . entrusted . . . [England] with the rarest Jewelles of their lipps perfections.'[37] Carew makes the claim – surprising to most readers of this book, I suspect – that English-speakers are extraordinarily adept at learning other tongues. Less worryingly, whereas many of his contemporaries argued that the majesty of Latin and Greek was the result of their purity, he points out that plenty of Latin and Greek authors had no qualms about borrowing words from other languages.

Carew's *Survey of Cornwall* (1602) offers a different slant on the state of English. He explains that the dominance of the national language has forced Cornish 'into the uttermost skirts of the shire': whereas, half a century before, Andrew Borde had claimed that many Cornish folk knew not one word of English, Carew suggests that now very few lack competence in the language and most can speak not even a tiny amount of Cornish. At a time when regional accents and the language of the 'common people' are typically derided or overlooked, Carew argues that the language spoken in the south-west is ancient and correct. Carew's enjoyable chorography, which pauses to consider sign language and the distinctive dancing style of Cornish rats, is yet another strand in the tangled purple of Renaissance arguments about language.

As we have seen, those involved in these arguments traded anxieties about the resources that English-speakers had at their disposal. Did they need to be supplemented, or were they instead to be regulated? In the four centuries since the Inkhorn controversy, the question has frequently returned. During the last few hundred years governments in France, Russia, Germany and Slovakia have mounted campaigns for withstanding foreign influence on their languages. One notable example was the attempt by the Fascist government in Italy to eradicate French and English borrowings, which achieved at least one success in replacing the commonly used *chauffeur* with the newly invented and nicely Italian-sounding *autista*.[38] By contrast, English has as at no point been subject to a government-endorsed stand against loanwords. The history of the language is in fact remarkable for being free from this kind of intervention. Many of the acquisitions and coinages of the Renaissance were later abandoned as their lustre faded – much of what glitters is little more than trash – but the coextensiveness of innovation and insecurity was now established.

7. Powwow

A shaman or healer; a council or conference of North American Indians; a meeting of powerful people

From the Naragansett *powwaw*, and ultimately from the proto-Algonquian *pawewa*, 'he who dreams'

Potato. Tobacco. No words hint more tantalizingly at the early English experience of the New World, and they serve perfectly to introduce the language's North American acquisitions. English adventurers crossed the Atlantic in search of gold; they returned with bounty less glamorous but more rich. Potatoes, ferried eastward from Chile and Peru, and intercepted during the Spanish armadas, would become a staple of the English and Irish diet. Tobacco would be the nub of a national mania. Both these words – ordinary to us, but glistening then with possibility – were encountered in the talk of Spanish seamen. Yet we can trace deeper roots: the ancestry of *tobacco* has been credibly identified as Taino, while *potato* was a mutation by Spanish-speakers of the Carib *batata*.

One of the main players in spreading word of the discovery of tobacco in the New World was Jean Nicot, the French ambassador in Lisbon. In 1561 he sent a powdered sample to Catherine de' Medici to help alleviate a migraine. His name is eternally and somewhat ignominiously preserved in the word *nicotine*. The leaf was first ferried back to England four years later. The man who brought it – to the Cornish port of Padstow – was John Hawkins. We have met this eminent shipbuilder already, transporting Cephalonian currants; he was also an early pillar of the slave trade, who achieved notoriety by selling Africans to the Spanish. Hawkins brought two other things of value: a favourable report of Florida's potential for settlement, and the sweet potato. In that year Hawkins could write, 'These potatoes be the most delicate rootes that may be eaten, and doe far exceede our passeneps or carets.' But this was *Ipomoea batatas*, the supposedly aphrodisiac root mentioned by Shakespeare's Falstaff, not the starchy *Solanum tuberosum*. And, understandably, Hawkins was more excited by the commercial possibilities of the tobacco leaf: he had seen it smoked by Timucuan Indians and French settlers, and had noted its sedative effects.

Hawkins's involvement notwithstanding, the first known reference in English to *tobacco* appears in John Frampton's 1577 translation of a work by Nicolas Monardes, offering 'joyfull newes out of the newe founde worlde'. Monardes, a doctor practising in Seville, had cultivated tobacco and claimed that it could remedy more than twenty different medical complaints. It could destroy worms, dissolve swellings, and alleviate the 'naughtie breathyng' of children. These and other allegedly therapeutic qualities were eagerly publicized. Tobacco offered a taste of America, a draught of New World novelty, the opportunity – as it was put by Henry Buttes in a cookbook published in 1599 – to 'breathe Indianly'. Sir Walter Raleigh converted many in his circle to the addictive rewards of smoking, and may even have taught Queen Elizabeth the correct way to smoke a pipe. The use of the verb *smoke* in this context can be traced to the early years of the seventeenth century: the *OED*'s first citation is from Richard Brathwait's *The Smoaking Age* (1617), the frontispiece of which offers what may well be the first picture of a tobacco shop. *Cigar* is another loan from Spanish; its root is *cigarra*, 'cicada', and the connection is visual, as the cured tobacco leaf resembles that insect's long papery wings.

Cultivation of the tobacco plant was begun by the English settlers (or planters, as they were known at first) in 1612.[1] In the vanguard of this was the pious yet commercially sensitive John Rolfe, who in 1613 established the first truly successful plantation. The first consignment of Rolfe's fine Virginia tobacco was shipped to England the following year. Thereafter the trade burgeoned. In 1618, 41,000 lb of tobacco was exported from Virginia; by 1629 the figure was 1,500,000 lb. Public attitudes to smoking were hardly complacent. In 1604 no less a figure than King James, the one-time importer of *skol*, wrote 'A Counterblaste to Tobacco', decrying the habit as harmful to the nose, the eye, the brain and the lungs. 'What honour or policie can move us', he wondered, 'to imitate the barbarous and beastly manners of the wilde, godlesse, and slavish *Indians* . . . in so vile and stinking a custome?'[2] Nevertheless, the growth of the colony was accelerated by the demand for this 'golden weed'. Fertile, untouched land was needed, and plantations began to appear at intervals, extending far up the James River – a bitter-sweet detail. The planters had no tradition of expertise to draw on; their work proceeded by trial and error. The business was obsessional, and they became so absorbed in producing tobacco that they gave the 'Indians' firearms and employed them as hunters.

But we need to step back for a moment: the establishment of English outposts in North America sowed the language in what would eventually become the world's greatest economic power; yet the settlers' success was no overnight achievement – it marked the end of a string of failures. *Virginia* was the name the settlers gave to the territory where they established their first truly solid redoubt. They named it for the queen who had encouraged its discovery (and who was 'virgin' on account of never having married). The name has endured, and, like the names of so many features of the American landscape, it embodies idealism, a Christian vision of the land's sanctity. The name is also a sigh of relief on the part of a nation that had struggled to impress itself on a land 3,000 miles away.

We often define ourselves in relation to what we are not. Elizabethan England expressed its essence through its relationship with foreign parts, and strange cultural artefacts acquired abroad became vital images of the triumph of Elizabeth and her court. England's navy, for which the coal trade served as a nursery, was strong. Yet the English were not the first to try to settle in North America. Indeed, they were slow to get in on the act. Bartholomew Columbus had sought English funding for his brother Christopher's transatlantic expedition as long ago as 1488, but Henry VII had been more concerned with making good his position in a country he had only recently seized, and when the Columbus brothers did secure funding it was from Ferdinand and Isabella of Spain.

It took a hundred years for the English to recognize this as a missed opportunity. In the meantime, others made significant advances: the Spanish, besides their extensive claims in South and Central America and in the Caribbean, had penetrated the southern regions of North America, including Arizona and Florida, while the French had closely explored the east coast of America, finally establishing a colony at Acadia. The evidence of their early successes is still manifest in a host of American place names: we can see that Colorado, Nevada, Montana, California and Florida all come from Spanish, while the names of Maine and Vermont testify to the French presence in the early seventeenth century.[3] Ironically, neither the eternally famous Columbus nor Amerigo Vespucci, the Florentine from whom the continent probably takes its name, seems actually to have set foot on American soil, although half a millennium before them the Icelandic explorer Leif Eriksson may have done so. But Columbus opened up the idea of America, and those who followed him and did investigate the land saw its promise.

Among the legacies of Columbus's discovery were, according to one powerful account, 'the very structures of what we know as modern civilization', the 'Westernizing [of] the great bulk of humanity', 'the vast redistribution of life-forms . . . in effect rejoining the continents', and a dramatic transformation of 'the products and processes of the environment' that has enabled mankind to 'dominate the earth as no single species ever has'.[4] From a Western perspective, Columbus's exploits can be seen as the beginning of Modernity and of a Golden Age. Christopher Marlowe's Dr Faustus is the quintessential post-Columbian, exclaiming, 'O what a world of profit and delight' and boasting, 'All things that move between the quiet poles / Shall be at my command.' Not insignificantly, in the late sixteenth century *Columbus* became a general term in English for a successful, ambitious explorer.

In England, the fifteenth century and the first half of the sixteenth were a period of qualified prosperity; there was no compelling reason to look for opportunities abroad. But in the later stages of the sixteenth century, as population rose and agricultural production faltered, this changed. One harvest in six failed completely, and food was often in short supply. The motives for heading overseas were clear. Some imagined exploiting the raw materials of far-flung places; others sought to glorify their country, their God or themselves; still others set off with moral tutelage on their minds, dreaming of converting exotic infidels; and then there were those who craved the excitement of discovery – perhaps with a little piracy or pillage on the side. It would become almost a cliché of the period that Virginia was a delicate, fragrant creature, which had to be saved by English husbandry from the depraved extremes of Spanish lust. Later, the Native Americans would be characterized as children in need of the settlers' parental guidance. Yet there were some very different stereotypes in circulation: either the colonists were the dregs of society, roguish hedonists and thieves making the most of a voluptuous paradise, or the land to which they were headed was barren and unhealthy, and only the most robust adventurers could survive there.

Certainly the entire rhetoric surrounding colonialism was factious. One constant theme, though, was that England stood to benefit from opening up this new vista. Some insisted that the Americans, converted to Christianity, could buttress Protestant resistance to the march of Spanish Catholicism. At the same time, it was clear that people unwelcome in England – for reasons of religious conviction or social maladjustment – could be conveniently deported to the new colony. American bases could be used by privateers to launch attacks on vessels that became detached from the Spanish fleet. Furthermore, the Americas had the potential to be a substantial market for English goods, while goods imported from America would reduce the need for trade with England's Continental rivals.

There were hazards, of course, and these were evident from the outset. The word *cannibal*, derived from Arawak, first appears in Richard Eden's 1553 translation of a part of Sebastian Münster's *Cosmographia* about 'the newe India', which records Columbus's encounter with cannibals – people he assumed to be devourers of human flesh – in a Caribbean village. The account is probably erroneous, but it suggests the background of anxiety against which transatlantic voyages were made. In the 1560s the accounts of Davy Ingrams, who claimed to have walked the length of America's Atlantic coastline after being shipwrecked, offered a startling description of the region's man-eaters and savages, who sheathed their genitals in gourds and drank the blood of their infirm elders.

Before the word *Indian* came into regular use as a name for the native peoples of India, it was frequently used of the aboriginal peoples of America and the Caribbean. *India* was happily applied to America, too, after the example of the Spanish and the Portuguese. Richard Eden's reference to 'the newe India' makes it clear that he is distinguishing the Americas from the 'old' India (a land of which King Alfred in the ninth century had been at least dimly aware, and which he had called by that name). But Samuel Purchas could declare that 'The name of India, is now applied to all farre-distant Countries' – and could blame Columbus for this common error.[5] Only with the rise of British interests in India proper would this confusing usage come to an end.

The risks indicated – and fantasized – by writers such as Richard Eden could best be justified on financial grounds. One of the possibilities most keenly envisaged by those who funded voyages was the discovery of a north-west passage, first mentioned in 1576. A commercial sea route around the Americas could facilitate trade with China. Early attempts to locate it included those of Francisco de Ulloa, who was commissioned by Hernan Cortés to find the mythical Strait of Anian, and of Martin Frobisher, the admirer of Sir John Mandeville, who spent fifteen years drumming up funding for his ambitious quest. Frobisher returned from his first voyage with 'black earth' rumoured to contain gold; his second voyage yielded further samples of ore; and his third, which resulted in a further shipment of rock, included an inadvertent 60-mile spurt up the Hudson.

English interest in the Americas was most vigorously promoted by tobacco's champion, Sir Walter Raleigh. With his broad Devonian accent, expensive clothes, perfumed locks and ferocious energy, Raleigh cut a memorable figure in the world of the court. He was inspired by the example of his half-brother Humphrey Gilbert, who in 1583 planted the beginnings of a colony at what is now St John's in Newfoundland: the Queen's coat of arms was displayed, an enticing vein of silver was discovered, and his ships were loaded with fresh lobster. Even before leaving, Gilbert had sold a 'paper empire of twenty million acres he had never seen'.[6] Although he died during the return voyage to England, and his charts were lost with him, the expedition hinted at the rewards of settlement. 'O my America! my new-found-land,' John Donne could write around the turn of the century in his poem 'To his Mistress Going to Bed', applying to one of his seductions the fashionable metaphor of discovery. 'My mine of precious stones, my empery, / How blest am I in this discovering thee,' he exclaimed – *empery* being a now disused word for an imperial dominion. (*Imperialism* does not turn up till the nineteenth century, but *imperial* is found in the age of Chaucer, and *imperialist* is seventeenth-century.) Donne's erotic, arrogant lines articulate the colonial dream that inspired Raleigh and his successors. But, as they found out, there were many different Americas, and settlement proceeded haphazardly, rather than to the steady rhythm of triumph.

From the first, and despite a certain amount of public indifference, there were visionaries and business-minded explorers back in England who craved information about the New World settlements. Many of the stories that made their way across the Atlantic were gossip – and gossip always travels faster than official accounts. But serious books about the New World were devoured by readers. Their hyperbole was sometimes satirized, as by Jonson, Marston and Chapman in the play *Eastward Ho* (1605), which poked fun at adventurers who gave up 'competent certainties' in order to pursue 'excellent uncertainties'. The play succeeded thanks to excitement about Virginia. There was a groundswell of political and intellectual argument for expansionism, and the literature that supported it was eloquent. One valuable point of reference was Theodore de Bry's collection of travel accounts. Published in thirteen parts, beginning in 1590, its detailed narratives and fine engravings informed the European picture of the New World for at least a hundred years.

In England, the passion for discovery was given public voice by Richard Hakluyt, a keen student of voyages, maps and discoveries, who also happened to be another fan of Mandeville. He was the armchair traveller *par excellence*, quick to absorb the pet terms of cultures he had never directly experienced. (The furthest he ever ventured was Paris.) Hakluyt incorporated in one large body of work the scattered fragments of a whole history of travel narratives. His evangelism inspired fresh interest in the possibilities of 'abroad'.

Hakluyt's *Principall Navigations, Voiages and Discoveries of the English Nation* was set before the public in 1589. When the three volumes of its enlarged second edition began to appear nine years later, the title included the word *Traffiques*, a term that had only lately come to be used of trading expeditions. Hakluyt was confident that England would soon compete on equal terms with Spain and Portugal in carving up the spoils of adventure, and he was thus an invaluable propagandist for Raleigh's ambitions. So was his friend Michael Drayton, Herculean author of the huge *Poly-Olbion*. Drayton's ode 'To the Virginian Voyage' suggested that reading Hakluyt 'shall enflame / Men to seek fame':

> And cheerfully at sea
>   Success you still entice
>   To get the pearl and gold,
>   And ours to hold
> *Virginia*,
>   Earth's only paradise.

In fact Hakluyt saw colonial projects as 'the necessary cure for the nation's ills', where 'even miscreants could play a crucial role in economic development'.[7] But he was careful to praise the heroic endeavours of travellers and to emphasize the abundance of gold, silver and pearls.

Raleigh's quest for this paradise was carried out only in fits and starts. In March 1584 Queen Elizabeth endorsed his wish to explore the uncharted territories beyond what Hakluyt called the 'gruesome waters' of the Atlantic. She granted him 'free liberty and license from time to time to discover, search, find out and view such remote, heathen and barbarous lands, countries and territories not actually possessed by any Christian prince nor inhabited by Christian people'. Moreover, she assigned him the right 'to have, hold, occupy and enjoy . . . [them] forever'.[8] Raleigh sent two ships out a few weeks later, under the command of Philip Amadas and Arthur Barlowe. They arrived in the Canaries in early May, in the West Indies a month later, and on the North American coast at the beginning of July.

The early expeditions to America were amply documented, and the documents are evidence of the wonder the voyagers felt. After his return Barlowe wrote a glowing account. 'I thinke in all the world the like aboundance is not to be founde,' he enthused. The land was rich and apparently undisturbed: the valleys were 'replenished with goodly Cedar trees', and the woods were 'full of Deere, Conies, Hares, and Fowle . . . in incredible aboundance'. 'The soile is the most plentifull, sweete, fruitfull, and wholesome of all the world,' he could note. He and his party were provided by the native inhabitants with 'divers kinds of fruites, Melons, Walnuts, Cucumbers, Gourdes, Pease, and divers rootes, and fruites very excellent good, and . . . corne, which is very white, faire, and well tasted, and groweth three times in five moneths'. They found themselves in a place that 'smelt so sweetely . . . as if we had bene in the midst of some delicate garden, abounding with all kinde of odoriferous flowers, by which we were allured'. The scented woodland was thick with wild muscadines and their plump bronze grapes, and with the spicy reek of cedar.[9]

Barlowe's account may have been intended as a puff to boost support for Raleigh's proposed settlement. Later, conflicting reports filtered back to England. But his prose oozes with an excitement that is unfeigned. To the explorer in a new land, everything appears as though in italics. At the same time, the literature of exploration is one of self-legitimation. Typically, others' claims are dismissed, and the virtue of the explorer's own project is underscored. Thus Barlowe's insistence on his amazement: 'My selfe having seene those partes of Europe that most abound, finde such difference, as were incredible to be written.' In other words, 'Believe me. This place is *something else.*' The ships returned with spoils sufficient to suggest the opportunities available in this new land: samples of the local plant and animal life, along with two 'lusty' native men, Manteo and Wanchese, who ended up staying in England for a year. Their appearance and conduct shaped English perceptions of what lay across the Atlantic.

Manteo and Wanchese were taught English by another early visitor, Thomas Harriot, a gifted Oxford mathematician with interests in algebra and astronomy. The monkish Harriot was at once scholarly and practical – among his achievements was an analysis of the best way to stack cannonballs – and Raleigh involved him closely in designing his ships, as well as drawing on his expert understanding of navigation. In April 1585 Harriot crossed the Atlantic on a ship commanded by Sir Richard Grenville, his designated role being that of 'geographer'. He spent a year in America, and his *Briefe and True Report of the New Found Land of Virginia* (1588) tells of his contact with the natives. Sympathetic to their customs, it contains details of the local languages, and there are copious references to the many striking plants and animals he came across. Where no existing English word will do the job, he gamely transcribes the local Algonquian form, noting the names for several types of acorn and mentioning the novelties *cassava* and *maize* in addition to items less well known to us: the wholesome berries called *sacquenummener*, two types of beetle, the *saquenuckot* and *maquowoc*, and the *seekanauk*, a crusty shellfish good to eat. At pains to make the land sound as rich as possible, he itemizes the different foods it can provide – from partridges and geese to swans and 'wolvish dogges'. To Harriot, of course, it was far from obvious that, while *tobacco* and *canoe* would survive, most of these words would perish.

Grenville's party established the first English settlement in America. This was at Roanoke in Virginia. The settlement was not self-sufficient, relying on provisions from back home. The newcomers explored the hinterland, hoping to find gems and gold, but they did not venture far. Relations with the native inhabitants were awkward; efforts at diplomacy were unsuccessful, perhaps in part because Wanchese, who was one of the guides, had during his time in England formed a low opinion of English values. (Among other things, he had been obliged to wear a silly outfit made of brown taffeta.) The natives were puzzled by the newcomers. Were they perhaps the reincarnated spirits of their ancestors? Were they deities? Or were they just interlopers?

The last of these suspicions seems to have crystallized, especially when the English spread smallpox and measles. Under the thuggish management of Ralph Lane, the colony became a magnet for the natives' malice. Left to fend for themselves, the settlers struggled. They lacked proper fishing equipment, and were poor hunters. If we believe Lane's claims in a letter to that most polished of courtiers

Sir Philip Sidney, some turned savage.[10] As prospects soured, Lane returned to England with Francis Drake, and a relief ship found no one to supply.

Raleigh dispatched a second party in April 1587. Their leader, John White, made drawings of the plants and creatures encountered both during the voyage out and in Virginia itself. Those from the journey include hermit crabs, scorpions, West Indian iguanas, fireflies, a pineapple, a flamingo (the name of which is the Portuguese for 'belonging to flame'), bananas, a dolphin and flying fish. In Virginia he found time to draw a vast range of birds, including a brown pelican (an 'alcatrassa' we're pleased to see him call it), a bald eagle and three different kinds of woodpecker, as well as many types of fish (striped bass, catfish, grey mullet), a turtle and a diamondback terrapin (which he gave the wrong number of toes), a Scarlet King-snake 'which the Salvages . . . doe eate', a cicada – its shrill chirping no doubt an irritation – and a 'dangerous byting flye' which appears to be a gadfly.[11] White was less effective as governor of the colony. The natural abundance of the land was intimidating and exciting, the settlers' existence precarious. On 18 August White's daughter Eleanor gave birth to a daughter, the first English child to have been born in America, and she and her husband Ananias Dare named the child Virginia. The birth of Virginia Dare seemed a symbolic moment – evidence of the colony's potential for growth.

However, supplies were again a problem. White returned to England to gather fresh provisions, but the Spanish Armada of 1588 disrupted his return; its menace – 130 ships and 25,000 men – was exceptional, terrifying, enough to quell thoughts of all other business. By the time he made it back to Roanoke, in August 1590, the colony had been wiped out. It appeared that the settlers (including his own daughter and granddaughter) had been exterminated. But there is a lasting suspicion that the colonists, although magnificently underprepared for the hardships they would face, were ultimately the victims of political skulduggery – though they would not have used that word, an eighteenth-century American coinage originally used to suggest illicit sex.

The fascination with the possibilities of the West was not snuffed out by Roanoke's tragic end. Grenville had been able to produce hard evidence of the land's fertility, and wagging tongues suggested he had understated his cargo in order to keep to himself the profits of his trip. In 1592 a Portuguese craft was seized by the English off the Azores: it was laden with carpets, drugs, silks and pearls, and, best of all, among its contents was a map that showed the geography of Portuguese trade. As Jerry Brotton points out, this map was precious for commercial reasons as well as navigational ones, and 'was even more prized for its promise of offering the English . . . access to territories which would yield such fabulous commodities'. It was a perfect illustration of the ways in which charts, maps and globes stirred the imagination. Possession of such a document conferred authority and power on the owner, and viewing someone else's hinted tantalizingly at a world of 'expanding intellectual, political and commercial horizons', providing a key to 'arcane information and esoteric learning, . . . trade routes, market-places and commodities'.[12]

The key did not immediately unlock the New World, but it was another in a succession of encouragements. In 1595 Raleigh, by then a man of forty, set off in search of El Dorado, the golden city rumoured to be located somewhere in the jungle of South America. Although he had urged forward others' adventures, this was his first trip to the Americas. It would be a couple of hundred years before people began to be speak figuratively of El Dorado – as in Fenimore Cooper's *The Prairie* (1827), where we read of 'A band of emigrants seeking for the Eldorado of their desires' – but in truth its status was always emblematic, since, while the yearning for this gilded city was all too real, its object existed only in the imagination. When Raleigh failed to return with the spoils the government craved, his punishment was at first derision, and then, after further misadventures and the death of Elizabeth, a long stretch in prison and a brutal execution.

Other, more immediately commercial, openings were targeted. In 1603 a consortium of Bristol merchants, excited by the possibilities of importing the bark and roots of the sassafras tree, sent two ships to trade with the Native Americans. *Sassafras* was a Spanish word, possibly adopted from an American language. It had first been mentioned in Frampton's translation of Monardes, and it was there that its powers as a cure for syphilis were first vaunted. The enterprise was risky, calling for the audacity of youth, and the two ships were commanded by Martin Pring, a man of just twenty-three. Pring took with him merchandise including pickaxes, shovels, thimbles, mirrors, scissors, shoes and fish-hooks. He also took two vicious-looking mastiffs and – a delightful contrast – a boy skilled in playing a stringed instrument called the gittern. One way or the other, Pring meant to subdue the Native Americans. He sampled the cherries of Martha's Vineyard, assembled a sizeable cargo of sassafras, and returned with an optimistic view of the possibilities for trade and settlement.

More such missions followed. In the course of two voyages, George Waymouth reached Baffin Island, as Frobisher had done before him, and explored the coast of Maine. An account of the second of these trips, James Rosier's *A True Relation of the most prosperous voyage*, attracted a good deal of attention. It mentions 'many fruit trees, which we knew not' together with unfamiliar dogs ('some like Wolves, some like Spaniels') and, unsurprisingly, the abundance of tobacco – 'excellent sweet and strong'.[13] Rosier was much concerned with the 'profits' the land afforded, and he was alert to its diversity. He was intrigued by the different kinds of woodland he saw, and made notes about these and other findings. Samuel Purchas abridged Rosier's short book, and usefully appended a list of Eastern Abenaki vocabulary collected but not published by Rosier. The list mentions *coribo* (caribou), *moosurr* (moose) and a kind of axe called a *tomaheegon* (tomahawk).[14]

The next voyage would be a more enduring success, for it established what was to prove the first permanent English settlement in North America. In the winter of 1606 the London Company's three ships set sail. The flagship, *Susan Constant*, was a vessel of 120 tons, and was accompanied by the 40-ton *Godspeed* and the 20-ton *Discovery*. These were small craft: the biggest was less than 80 feet and the smallest just 38 feet at the waterline. There were about a hundred would-be settlers on board. Inevitably, the party was heavily male. While it included a number of 'gentlemen', the hard practicalities of planting a colony had been recognized, and with the gentlemen there travelled an assortment of labourers, as well as a blacksmith, a tailor, a couple of bricklayers and a barber. They sailed via Martinique and Nevis – in the latter they caught and ate an alligator – and made landfall in April the following year, naming the site Jamestown after their king. Soon after, they were joined by two further parties, many of them craftsmen with skills valuable to the settlers. Among them was Robert Cotton, a maker of tobacco pipes, and archaeologists have found well-preserved examples of his distinctive squared-off pipes, made of red Virginia clay. Other archaeological discoveries are a mix of the expected, including daggers and armour, and oddities such as a finely tooled silver device for excavating wax from ears.

The London Company's shareholders expected to get rich. They hoped that gold and diamonds would be found. But fresh waters and tall trees could be guaranteed, and these helped ensure the agricultural basis of the new colony. Swathes of land were granted to all who signed up for the voyage. Unlike at home, they could have good houses, orchards and vegetable gardens. The response was optimistic. There has long been an enthusiasm among the English for securing individual holdings and investing each with its own character and family culture. Those who settled abroad would always glance nostalgically back to the mother country, especially as they struggled with the many unadvertised hardships of life in Virginia. But the choice between a small patch of territory within the British Isles and a more substantial holding abroad was straightforward. In England, food supplies were erratic and shortages were a common problem: in Virginia they were not. Reassuringly, contemporary illustrations showed the natives as tall, broad people, healthy and well nourished. They had clearly reaped the benefits of their land's bounty, as the English were to now.

The encounter between two communities who speak different languages can have fatal implications. Indeed, the different languages of the colonists and natives were keys into their different sensory worlds. The Native Americans experienced all the senses together, fully integrated; the settlers trusted sight above all other senses.[15] The two peoples' systems of judgement and perception were fundamentally at odds. Yet relations with the native people were friendly at first. The English were allowed into their villages, where they made presents of beads and glass. They found mulberries, raisins and sugar canes, vines, olives, hemp and crabs. The progress of English was informal, as it has been generally. A teenage boy, Thomas Savage, was chosen to serve the chief of the Powhatans, in order to learn how to channel information between the two mutually unintelligible groups. Not for the settlers a systematic programme of linguistic re-education: theirs was a more pragmatic and spontaneous approach. Only in time, as increasing volumes of settlers outnumbered the comparatively static indigenous population, did European languages become dominant.

Soon, however, differences in the ways the Native Americans and Europeans used their senses caused friction. To the Native Americans their encounters felt unequal, and the equilibrium of their culture was disturbed by the newcomers' insensitivity and their fussiness about boundaries and borders. As the settlers developed policies regarding contact, so exchanges became increasingly restricted. Encounters were supervised and sterile. The native people who were endued with English 'godliness' got haircuts, cobbled shoes, solid-framed houses and written laws, as well as new words.[16] But the settlers' property titles usurped the natives' long-established sense of ownership as a divine gift. In *The Tempest* Shakespeare offers an imaginative portrait of the indigenous peoples' response, as Caliban complains:

This island's mine, by Sycorax my mother,
Which thou tak'st from me. When thou cam'st first
Thou strok'st me and made much of me, wouldst give me
Water with berries in't, and teach me how
To name the bigger light, and how the less,
That burn by day and night; and then I loved thee,
And showed thee all the qualities o'th' isle,
The fresh springs, brine-pits, barren place and fertile –
Cursed be I that did so! . . .
For I am all the subjects that you have,
Which first was mine own king.

In the same play, Gonzalo's ideal commonwealth – a place without traffic, letters, vineyards, sovereignty – is the reverse image of the same situation. We see here the discrepancy between two sets of ideals, two understandings of ownership, two ways of knowing the world.

Assessing conventional accounts of the relationship, Richard White has written that 'Indians are the rock, European peoples are the sea' and 'The sea wears down and dissolves the rock; or the sea erodes the rock but cannot finally absorb its battered remnant, which endures.' As White explains, in the Great Lakes region that the French called the *pays d'en haut*, the Indians and the Europeans reached an accommodation – a middle ground between the two inimical cultures. The reason was simple: 'whites could neither dictate to Indians nor ignore them,' and needed them 'as allies, as partners in exchange, as sexual partners, as friendly neighbours'.[17] Eventually, the American republic would succeed where the English and the French failed – in dictating the perimeters, both literal and metaphorical, of this middle ground. But, before this could be achieved, there were to be many traumas and misunderstandings.

This clash of cultures is epitomized in the experience of the adventurer Captain John Smith, who was critical in establishing the English presence. A man of action, he had fought in France and the Netherlands, and in his youth he had travelled to Morocco to serve as a mercenary. Memorably, during the siege of a Turkish stronghold in Transylvania he beheaded three men he had defeated in duels. Smith's first attempt to grapple with the alien zone of America was his *True Relation of such occurrences and accidents of noate as hath hapned in Virginia* (1608). There he refers to the chieftain of the Powhatans having a rich coverlet made of 'Rahaughcums'.[18] This is a *racoon*, although our modern spelling did not appear until more than sixty years later. In the local Algonquian language the word was equivalent to 'he scratches with his hands': raccoons like to dig for crabs and eggs with their clawed yet sensitive front paws. The spelling must have unnerved Smith's readers; his London printer apologized to them for what were doubtless faults in the names of places and objects, so many of them 'somewhat strange'.

Smith travelled with the first fleet bound for Virginia in 1607. Famously, during a winter foray up the Chickahominy River he was seized by Native Americans and brought before the area's tribal overlord. He was – at least as far as he could make out – saved from death only through the intervention of Matoaka, the 11-year-old daughter of a powerful chieftain called Wahunsenacawh. To posterity this remarkable young woman is known as Pocahontas (her childhood nickname, meaning 'little wanton'). Vigorous and free-spirited, she would turn cartwheels naked for the delight of the male colonists. Her efforts on Smith's behalf may have been theatre more than a real and spontaneous act; read literally, though, they can be seen as a defining moment in the 'Englishing' of America. Without her stepping in, Smith would very likely have been killed, and would not have had the opportunity to become a promoter of colonization – or of a theory of where settlements should be planted and how they should be underpinned. Smith described Pocahontas as a 'nonpareil', and claimed that her help was second only to that of God in preserving the colony from 'utter confusion'. Her marriage to John Rolfe at Jamestown in 1614, her renunciation of idolatry and embrace of Christianity, and her subsequent life at Brentford in Middlesex – where she was plain Rebecca Rolfe – were interpreted as symbols of a promising Anglo-Indian entente. Such interpretation now seems hyperbolic, but visitors to the Unites States Capitol are treated to John Gadsby Chapman's painting of her baptism and Antonio Capellano's bas-relief of her saving Smith from execution – seminal episodes in the nation's myth of its identity.

In the autumn of 1609 Smith returned to England. Having already been paralysed by a stingray's venom, he was burnt when a spark from a flintlock ignited the pouch of gunpowder he kept fastened to his waist. He sailed to London for treatment, never to return. But his time in Virginia resulted in significant publications; he took pains to document what he had encountered on his travels, and communicated a fantasy of a land where people of 'great spirits and small meanes' could become rich. As his biographers Dorothy and Thomas Hoobler put it, 'Smith founded more than a colony. He gave birth to the American dream.'[19] First, he drew a map of Virginia, which was published in 1612 and promised a description 'of the Country, the Commodities, People, Government and Religion'. It symbolized, as maps so often do, the colonist's control over the landscape, but it also reflected his passion for cataloguing and collecting, on top of an instinctive desire to index his experiences. In the accompanying text he refers to *putchamins*, which are persimmons, and *tomahacks*, which are a little easier to recognize. He mentions *mockasins*, too, and various kinds of root useful in medicine, as well as the *maracock*, a passion flower deemed good to eat.

A Description of New England followed four years later, its title a badge of Smith's proprietorial attitude. Its pages are luxuriant with descriptions of the local trees and fruit, birds and fish; he mentions seeing moose, whales and wildcats. His writings contain what may be the first references to the rattlesnake, the stingray and the cockroach; the last of these, from the Spanish *cucaracha*, is in his version a *cacarootch*, a spelling that takes us into the insect's dung-rootling world. Mainly, though, the land's bounty is his theme. When he travelled up the Potomac, he found sand glistening with golden flecks. Once assayed, it turned out to be little more than gilded dirt. But there were other resources that seemed as precious as the ones for which Smith had originally hoped. He records eating an assortment of 'fat' wild beasts; there were beavers, otters, martins, mink and bears. The rivers were a particularly rich source of food, covered as they were with swans, ducks, geese and cranes, and the water was so glutted with fish that it seemed possible to scoop them out with a frying pan.

As a writer, Smith was intent on promoting the idea that England should have colonies, and his language conveys the excitement of the New World. The first English author to talk of *terra incognita*, he peppers his pages with a host of other new words: *prickly pear, awning, adrift, roomy*, plus some real oddities, like *jubartes*, the name of the New England fin whale, and, from the Dutch, *lopeskonce*, an 'entrenchment'. These terms reveal the spacious wonder of encounter. Smith's surroundings bristled with oddity. Even now, the Native American language of the natural world can sound stunningly seductive. There are the flora: mockernut hickories and chinquapin oaks, or pipsissewa and blue cohosh and hoary puccoon. And then there are the fierce-sounding fauna: the Catahoula hog dog, the tautog, the muskellunge and the squeteague. Of the words heard by the settlers, the ones that caught on were those for which there was no immediate alternative. For a time, *netop*, a word for a close friend, enjoyed some use among English-speakers in America, but it died away. On the other hand *hickory*, which could be expressed no other way, lived on.

Hickory was in fact a shortened and adapted form of *pawcohiccora*, the native Virginian name for that particular species of tree, known for its tough, flexible wood. Hickory is an excellent material for burning, as well as for bows and tool handles; John Wesley may have complained that it bore 'a bad kind of walnut' – a pecan – but the settlers valued it highly. The Indian world view is reflected in calques such as *happy hunting ground*, *peace pipe* and the expression *bury the hatchet*. *Firewater* is another likely calque, based on the Algonquian *scoutiouabou*. In time, terms reckoned (not always correctly) to show Indian influence were sometimes known as *wigwam words*.

The more evocative of them captivated a succession of settlers. In 1613 Alexander Whitaker, a 28-year-old minister at the settlement of Henrico on the James River, writes of catching pike, carp, eels, crayfish and *terrapins* (from the Abenaki, *turepe*). He is astonished by the flying squirrel and 'the female Possowne, which will let forth her yong out of her belly, and take them up into her belly againe at her pleasure without hurt to her selfe'.[20] This is the *opossum* – Smith says it 'hath an head like a Swine, and a taile like a Rat, and is of the bignes of a Cat'.[21] It sounds like an image out of Marco Polo or Mandeville. The creature's local name literally meant 'white dog'; it is easy enough to see why, as the Virginia opossum has a thin-lipped white face, but it is best known for its distinctly un-doggy habit of feigning death when threatened by predators.

Papoose, from the Algonquian, makes its first appearance in William Wood's *New England's Prospect* (1634) – a book later devoured by Henry David Thoreau, who could not fail to be impressed by how 'emasculated' his country seemed alongside the one Wood had described. *New England's Prospect* was the fruit of four years spent in Massachusetts, which Wood insisted was preferable to Surrey and Middlesex. As if to undermine his claim, he introduces *skunk*, which he spells 'squunck'; it derives from the Abenaki *segongw*, which approximates to 'one who squirts'.

The corruption of these words as they have been absorbed means that their origins are obscured. Take, for example, the noun *woodchuck*.

If you have ever been caught up in the well-known tongue-twister about this burrowing rodent, you may casually assume that its name is no more than a cute description of its favourite activities. But actually it is a corruption of the Cree *wuchak*, meaning 'a fisher' – odd, since the woodchuck's diet consists mainly of grasses and grubs.

The Eastern Abenaki *wigwam* first appears in 1628, whereas the *tepee* favoured by tribes such as the Cheyenne and the Lakota makes no appearance until 1743. *Totem* comes from Ojibwa, and appears in French as early as 1609, though it cannot be found in an English text until the eighteenth century. *Squash* is a shortened form of the Narragansett *askutasquash*, which literally means 'vegetables eaten while green'. Later accessions include *pecan* from one of the Algonquian languages, *pemmican* from Cree, and, from Massachusett, that appealingly strange word *mugwump*, which was a term of respect before it became a jocular word for a political independent or someone swollen with self-importance.

The more intellectually curious settlers, like Alexander Whitaker, were intrigued by the indigenous culture. Native phenomena and customs were observed with minute curiosity. And, understandably, they omitted the more brutal moments of conquest and mastery from their accounts. A significant document for our understanding of the settlers' programme of change is the translation of Ovid's *Metamorphoses* by George Sandys, who in 1621 had sailed to Virginia with his relative Edwin Wyatt. Sandys's translation, crafted during the long evenings, frequently sanitizes the violence of Ovid's original. His vision of imperial Rome and its cultural fruits was not so much an evasion of his own imperial experience as a corollary to it. The revised, annotated and illustrated second edition of 1632, complete with ornate homage to Charles I, hints at his sense of the work's relevance to the colonial project. For instance, his translation at one point reads:

> Where once was solid land, Seas have I seene,
> And solid land, where once deepe Seas have beene.
> Shels, far from Seas, like quarries in the ground;
> And anchors have on mountaine tops been found.

In the margin, Sandys adds, 'Such have I seene in *America*.'[22] The personal note is a reminder of Virginia's capacity to fire the imagination; the bigger picture is, tellingly, less frank.

The agricultural and intellectual opportunities the colony afforded were not the only motives for emigrating there. The religious conflict at home prompted many Puritans to seek a better life abroad. The New World would become a safe harbour for religious malcontents; among the many who thought about relocating there was Oliver Cromwell. The most famous of these migrants were the Pilgrim Fathers, who mostly came from Nottinghamshire and left Plymouth in September 1620 aboard the *Mayflower*. The party consisted of families, a number of servants, a few hired hands – 104 people in all, two of them born en route – plus a mastiff and a springer spaniel. Sixty-five days after setting sail they made landfall at Cape Cod, although it was several more weeks before they were able to leave their cramped berths. It is an indication of the religious temperament of the passengers that one of them, William Brewster, had with him a son called Wrestling, whose name was short for 'Wrestling with God', while a second, William White, had a son called Resolved.

It was yet another William, a polyglot Yorkshireman surnamed Bradford, who dubbed the emigrants Pilgrims – more often at the time they called themselves Strangers. Their mission was to introduce the Christian gospel to the Native Americans, and they made a promising start. Soon after their arrival the Strangers had been greeted by an Indian, Samoset, with the single word 'Welcome!' which he had learnt from English fishermen he had come across up the coast in Maine. The snippets of English he had picked up were a small yet significant help to the newcomers, enabling basic communication.

In his account of the Plymouth plantation, Bradford could refer to a native chief by his traditional title of *sachem* – his use of the word casual and comfortable. In dealing with the tribal leaders, the Strangers had as their intermediary a Patuxet tribesman called Tisquantum, who had twice been kidnapped by the English and had experience of working for the London merchant John Slany. Tisquantum served as both interpreter and guide. Seen as a traitor by his people, he proved invaluable to the colonists, showing them where to find good fish and where best to plant their corn. Although he died in the winter of 1622, the contact he facilitated between the Strangers and the native inhabitants was close. It grew through gift-giving and polite mimicry, and was reflected in treaties between them and the exchange of key elements of their languages.

The mood is captured by Edward Winslow, one of the settlers who travelled aboard the *Mayflower*. His *Good Newes from New England* (1624), ostensibly promotional, contains gruffly delivered advice for anyone contemplating the trip to America, yet also refers to the 'ingenious and observative' natives, their 'very copious' language and the 'friendly entertainment' offered by an Indian chief's *Squa-sachim*. This word became *squaw*, which is now most often found in place names (almost 800 of them). It has increasingly been demonized, partly on account of a spurious claim that its Algonquian meaning is 'vagina', and there have been moves by activists to efface it from maps: for instance, Minnesota's Lone Squaw Island has become Nokomis Island, while Oregon, South Dakota and Maine are among the other states that have passed laws to sanitize their toponyms.[23] Naming is a means of imposing yourself on others – one of the more immediate ways of exercising power. Winslow also alludes to the 'office and dutie of the *Powah*' – an individual 'eager and free in speech' whose services are enlisted in extreme circumstances.[24] Here is the first sighting of the Narragansett word that heads this chapter, *powwow*, which was at first understood to mean a medicine man rather than the conference where he officiated, and which came to be used in a less ceremonial sense in the nineteenth century.

For the Strangers, there were hazards aplenty: the hostile natives, errant livestock, wolves, and, from 1630, John Winthrop's rival Massachusetts Bay Colony. It hardly seems a coincidence that Bradford may well have been the first person ever to commit to the page the phrase 'out of kilter'. The Strangers saw themselves as counterparts to the Israelites making their exodus out of Egypt, menaced by a race of free-livers who threatened to pollute them with their degeneracy.[25] Meanwhile, the pious Winthrop told the members of the Massachusetts colony that 'the eyes of all people are upon us,' and assured them, 'we shall be made a story and a byword throughout the world.' (Alert to the importance of commerce, Winthrop is also the first author to mention the beads known as *wampum* – an abbreviation of the Massachusett *wampumpeag* – which were used as currency.) Far from their roots, which tended to be in the east of England, his followers had the opportunity to forge a new paradise. Profanity had no place there, and it is the old Puritan prohibition of swearing that lies behind the enduring American repertoire of muted profanities: *doggone, gee whiz, drat* and the like.

In all, 21,000 English migrants moved to Massachusetts between 1629 and 1640. By 1700 their numbers had swollen to 100,000; by 1800 to over a million, and by 1900 to around 6 million. Later, as they spread far beyond the Massachusetts borders, they laid the foundations of Chicago (the name of which comes from an Algonquian word for a field of garlic), Cleveland, Denver and Seattle. Starting in 1634, Roman Catholics emigrated to Maryland. Three other groups followed: a party of distressed Cavaliers and their servants moved to Virginia in the middle of the seventeenth century; the Delaware valley absorbed many Quaker immigrants from the north Midlands and Wales between 1675 and 1725; and in the eighteenth century there was a significant influx of Irish, as well as of borderers from Scotland and the north of England, into the Appalachian backcountry of the Shawnee and the Cherokee.[26] From the Shawnee they would learn *wapiti*, the name of the white-rumped elk; from the Cherokee, *sequoia* – the word a tribute to a native man who developed a type of spelling-book for his language. The effects of the huge influx were profound. The native culture of the eastern seaboard had existed, largely undisturbed, for half a millennium. Yet within fifty years of the English settlers' arrival – with guns and disease – the indigenous culture had been devastated.

This happened despite repeated attempts at enriching links between the settlers and the natives. One of the key players here was the missionary John Eliot, who arrived in Boston in the winter of 1631, accompanied by twenty-three barrels of books. Convinced that the natives were the descendants of the ten Lost Tribes of Israel, Eliot sought to return them to the fold. During the 1640s, 'the absorption of the English in their own affairs . . . gave the colonies even more scope than they had previously enjoyed to go their own way.'[27] For Eliot, this freedom was invaluable. His *Indian Dialogues*, published in 1671, fictionalize his sustained efforts to convert the local people, which included making a Massachusett translation of the New Testament and later a Massachusett version of the whole Bible – the first Bible to be printed in North America.

Another passionate attempt to understand Native American culture from the inside was *A Key into the Language of America*, published in 1643 by Roger Williams, who was the founder of Providence, Rhode Island. The volume's subtitle was 'An help to the Language of the Natives in that part of America, called New England', and it included 'briefe Observations of the Customes, Manners and Worships . . . of the aforesaid Natives, in Peace and Warre, in Life and Death'. Williams was a sympathetic observer and enjoyed amicable relations with his Native American neighbours, partly thanks to his sensitivity to their property rights. Looking over the *Key*, it's hard not to notice the onomatopoeic quality of words like *honckock* (geese) or *quequecum-mauog* (ducks), and hard not to be impressed by the sharp fruits known as *wuchipoquameneash* (of which a noted English doctor exclaimed, 'God never did make a better Berry').[28] But the words that Williams recorded have made little impression on English, even if on Rhode Island menus – and in the animated comedy *Family Guy* – you can still find the *quahog*, a type of clam for which, Williams reported, 'the Indians wade deepe and dive.' Williams hoped his book would 'open a Doore; yea, Doors of unknowne Mercies to Us and Them'.[29] His valuable connections with the Narragansett tribal leaders were overshadowed, however, by disputes over land within the Rhode Island community.

Many Europeans, most of whom had neither Williams's patience nor his ear, used pidgin languages to communicate with the Native Americans. One example was Pidgin Delaware, a form of Unami, which originated through contact between Dutch traders and Unami-speakers on the Delaware River in the 1620s. It came to be used by English and Swedish settlers, too, in their dealings with the natives of Delaware.[30] These languages helped develop links between communities; their reduced, transparent vocabulary bridged divides. Yet the overall effect was one of massive acoustic and lexical confluence. As Edward Finegan observes, 'colonial English swam in the polyglot tides around it, not only local Indians, but Dutch in New Amsterdam, French in Louisiana and Canada, and Spanish in New Spain'. In the Delaware valley the English settlers encountered Swedes and Finns. By 1644 there were speakers of sixteen languages in Manhattan, and the Native Americans the settlers met spoke as many as 221 different tongues.[31]

Exploration of other frontiers would lead to contact with still other languages. Thus Micmac, spoken in Newfoundland, provided *toboggan*, and the Eskimo–Aleut languages spoken by Inuits at America's Arctic fringes would also supply a small number of words, the best-known of these being *kayak* and *igloo*. *Mukluk*, the name of a high winter boot that has recently enjoyed unexpected cult status, derives from the central-Alaskan Yupik name for a bearded seal: traditionally, the boot's sole has been made from the skin of seal or caribou. A further recent addition is *tiktaalik*, the Inuktitut given name of the creature which is considered the vital evolutionary link between fish life and land animals. *Anorak* is from Greenland Eskimo, although it is fair to say the word is now used more often of studious people than of the garment they were once reckoned to hold so dear. (Its friend *parka* is of Russian origin, learnt from the nomadic Nenets herdsmen of Siberia.) The culture of the Inuits has frequently been misunderstood. In a pamphlet published in 1825, we read, 'The Esquimaux dwell in caves under ground, and do not seem sensible of their desolate existence.'[32] The accompanying list of vocabulary includes what is certainly the first sighting in an English-language publication of *inuk*, the name for an Inuit man. We are likely to find this picture risibly limited, but then a brief encounter with Inuit legend may suggest why so little has been learnt from and about the Inuit culture. In translation, this sample sentence is perhaps mildly disturbing: 'In the old days when the aged were too old to travel, they were left alone in a snowhouse to perish.' But what of the original? 'Akunialuk ningiungunitsait aulagunnasiangimut KimatauKattalauttut illuvigammi.'[33]

It seems fair to say, overall, that very little of the cultures upon which the Europeans intruded has survived to the present. Certainly there is not much outside the tribal reservations that persists in pristine form. As the historian Francis Jennings commented more than thirty years ago,

> The identifiably Indian cultural traits still with us have been assimilated into Euramerican culture and adapted and conformed to structures of European institutions and ideas. Our culture has consumed Indian traits the way our language has gobbled up words: . . . canoes have been adopted without displacing sails or oceanic navigation.[34]

The main image this conjures is of the language's insouciance: of English as a machine, hammering through anything that looks like an obstacle, and harvesting anything that could be an asset.

Today, the controversy surrounding the terminology we should use of these peoples is the thing most widely known about them. Are they Native Americans, American Indians, Amerindians, Aboriginal Americans or Original Americans, the First Nations, the Indigenous Peoples of America, or the Peoples of Abya Yala? The debate, which shows little sign of letting up, treats them as a single unit, rather than a complex group. Furthermore, it is an expedient way of sidestepping the real issue: the obliteration of the culture of the New World by immigrants from the Old.

8. Bonsai

A small Japanese tree, intentionally dwarfed; the philosophy or aesthetics of miniaturization

From the Japanese word for a potted plant, which is related to the Chinese *penjing*, meaning 'tray landscape'

At the same time as ambitious and sometimes desperate migrants were venturing west, a small number were heading in the opposite direction. One destination, about which I shall say more in due course, was India. Another was Japan, and it is there, like Jonathan Swift's Gulliver, that we now briefly venture.

There is a long-standing, clichéd image of Japan as an insular, impenetrably exotic land. To a contemporary audience, it is a place where modernity and tradition awkwardly coexist – Hello Kitty and *manga* alongside tea ceremonies and Kabuki theatre – and where you can buy schoolgirls' soiled knickers out of vending machines. From the beginning of the fourteenth century it was known to Europeans from the writings of Marco Polo, who claimed its earth was sown with gold. There could be few greater seductions for adventurers, and it was with the object of finding a sea route to this ore-rich land and its equally fabled neighbour China that Columbus set off from the Spanish port of Palos in 1492. As we know, Columbus ended up elsewhere, and the first Europeans to establish trade with the Japanese were the Portuguese. Their missionaries began to proselytize in Japan in 1549, and sixty years later a group of Jesuits produced the first Japanese–Portuguese dictionary. This volume attempted to unravel the mysteries of a tongue that, notwithstanding the large cultural influence of Chinese, had no link to any other known language. Four hundred years later, and despite attempts to find a connection with that contested group the Altaic family of languages, the genetic affiliations of Japanese are still a puzzle.

Convincing insights into Japanese life were rare. Sixteenth-century maps represented Japan as an edible-looking little squiggle, remote and prawn-like. Only tiny slivers of the Japanese language found their way back to Europe. In the 1550s Richard Eden translated some travel narratives, and in 1577 a fresh edition of these appeared, jazzily entitled *The History of Travayle in the West and East Indies, and other countreys lying eyther way, towardes the fruitfull and ryche Moluccaes . . . with a discourse of the Northwest passage.* The text was augmented by Richard Willes, who had until recently been a professor of rhetoric at Perugia, and who now tried to give coherent shape to Eden's sometimes chaotic words. In the revised work, readers were treated to the information that Japan was often snowbound; its inhabitants were melancholy and violent, yet also courteous. Here, too, were the first appearances of *Mogul* and – perhaps more impressively – *Chinese*, and the text described *hara-kiri*, albeit without giving it that name. There was also a reference to the *Bonzii* who gave sermons, resided in abbeys and were 'chast[e] by commaundement'.[1] This term for a Buddhist cleric, the singular of which is *bonze*, is generally reckoned the first Japanese word borrowed by English.

The earliest English accounts of Japan are in letters and diaries written by travellers in the early part of the seventeenth century. In the summer of 1598 the shipbuilder William Adams set sail for the East Indies, with the goal of procuring spices. After nineteen months of arduous misadventure, he and his sickly crew of twenty-four landed in Japan, hoping to be able to sell their cargo of cloth there. Adams was the hardiest of Elizabethan seafarers, prepared to gnaw on a raw penguin when there was nothing else to eat. He was also a skilled pilot and, once settled, a perceptive observer, who became a counsellor to the first *shogun*. This is one of the unfamiliar words contained in his logbook; another is *miso*.

One of Adams's deputies was a Coventry man, Richard Cocks, who kept a diary of his experiences in Japan between 1615 and 1622. Cocks meticulously recorded his daily life, noting the details of every transaction in which he was involved. Sometimes his diary is tedious, but there are moments of startling freshness: he echoes Richard Eden's description of *hara-kiri*, again without giving it that name, indicates the brutality of Japanese law (a teenage boy is cut to pieces for stealing a small boat), notes the Japanese people's pleasure in drinking and gift-giving, and observes the rapidity with which they acquire the habit of smoking tobacco. Cocks also provides first sightings of the word *furo* for a bathhouse, along with *Korean*, *watermelon* and the Chinese boat called a *sampan*. In November 1616 he provides a savoury image of his time in Japan, as he writes, in his usual tangled script, of being given 'a present of a *bento* or box for 5 persons to eate in'.[2] That same year he also mentions seeing a *cummerbund*; the word is Persian, and would become better known in British India.

Overall, the impression Cocks affords of Anglo-Japanese relations is one of slightly stiff cordiality. Despite sustained efforts, the English were unable to persuade the Japanese to grant them trading rights, and this led them in 1623 to abandon their base on the island of Hirado. Not long afterwards the entire Spanish community was deported, and in 1638, appalled by the continuing and successful intrusions of the Christian missionaries, the Japanese chose to break off contact with all outsiders save the Dutch, whose sole focus was trade. Japanese nationals were forbidden to venture abroad. Moreover, foreign books were banned – an interdiction that was lifted only in 1720.

Thereafter information was for a long time scarce. *Soy* is first mentioned in a travel book published in 1679; the alcoholic rice drink *sake* appears in another travelogue eight years later. But for an illuminating insight into the culture of the region English-speaking readers had to wait for Engelbert Kaempfer's *History of Japan*, the manuscript of which was acquired by Sir Hans Sloane and published in an English translation by John Gasper Scheuchzer in 1727. Kaempfer, who had worked as a doctor near Nagasaki, was the first Western writer to describe *Ginkgo biloba*, and the *History* contains a wealth of other such words that would have looked gleamingly new to contemporary readers. Among these are *samurai*, the festival known as *matsuri*, *Zen*, the *Shinto* religion and *mikado*, the archaic name for the emperor, literally meaning 'exalted gate'.

The year before Kaempfer's account appeared, Japan was mentioned for the first time in a work of Western fiction. Jonathan

Swift was impressed by what he learnt from Scheuchzer's translation of Kaempfer, which had circulated in manuscript among his well-connected friends within the Royal Society. Right at the end of the third section of *Gulliver's Travels*, Gulliver arrives in a port he identifies as Xamoschi, where he passes himself off as a Dutch merchant, and from there he proceeds to Nagasaki. His stay is not long, and he concludes, 'Nothing happened worth mentioning in this Voyage,' but this is deliberately disingenuous of Swift, for the language machine devised by one of the scholars whom Gulliver meets at Lagado is modelled on a contraption described by Kaempfer, and, in a moment of pointed satire, the civilized and ceremonial Japanese are sharply contrasted with the jabbering Dutch. Swift suggests that the European traders, rather than being superior to the foreigners with whom they trafficked, were actually the less dignified of the two parties. Simultaneously, he hints at the elusive mystery of this faraway, little-known land.

It would remain mysterious for more than another hundred years; only in the summer of 1853 was Japan coerced into reopening. An American naval detachment under Commodore Matthew Perry dropped anchor off the coast of Tokyo (then called Edo) and refused to budge until the Japanese signed treaties to safeguard American victims of shipwreck and facilitate trade. The arrival of Perry's black-hulled frigates was unwelcome, but Perry had sixty-one guns at his command: resistance would have been suicidal. The menace of the black ships led to the Treaty of Kanagawa, which ended Japan's deliberate slumber. The short-term rewards included a breeding pair of Japanese Chins, which were given to Queen Victoria. In the longer term, the Americans' arrival forced Japan into the modern world – with political and later industrial consequences that Congress could never have anticipated when they appointed Commodore Perry to lead the expedition.

Of the words to make the journey back, the most eagerly embraced was *tycoon*. The Americans had employed the honorific *taikun* when addressing the shogun, and John Hay, then a clerk in the Interior Department, picked up on this term, using it of Abraham Lincoln.[3] In Britain the word was emblazoned on the spine of a new book aimed at readers interested in digging a little deeper into Japanese culture, Sir Rutherford Alcock's *The Capital of the Tycoon: A Narrative of a Three Years' Residence in Japan* (1863). Alcock had from 1858 been the head of the fledgling British diplomatic mission in Japan, and his two volumes exposed the workings of Japanese diplomacy, manners, government and religion, though they also earned him a parliamentary rebuke for insensitivity to Japanese religious feeling.

The overthrow of the last of the Tokugawa shoguns in 1868 ushered in a new period of political turbulence, to which outsiders were largely indifferent. More excitingly, the new Meiji government promised a programme of 'Civilization and Enlightenment'. European ideas were slowly absorbed, and traces of Japanese culture percolated westward. To the decade following Alcock's book we can date the first references to a *futon*, *shiitake* mushrooms, *ju-jitsu* and the Japanese masked drama called *Noh*. Since then there has been a fairly steady flow of words from Japanese. *Geisha* first appears in 1887; *sushi*, which we are likely to associate with late-twentieth-century sophistication, as far back as 1893; and *tsunami*, which literally meant 'harbour waves', in 1897. *Bonsai* became known around the turn of the century, and the dwarf trees were first exhibited in London in 1909. To the same period we can date the adoption of *pillow book*, a calque that captures the sense of the Japanese *makura no soshi* (literally, 'narrative scroll of the pillow'). This was the title of a translation of a celebrated work by Sei Shonagon, a lady-in-waiting at the imperial court in the tenth century. Previous translations had appeared under the less compelling titles *Pillow Miscellany* and *Pillow Sketches*. This notebook of intimate thoughts, composed at night, comprised opinions, details of happenings at court, and scrupulous records of things found agreeable and disagreeable. It also blossomed with lists. To many modern observers, the pillow book seems quintessentially Japanese – artful and formal even in its own privacy, yet touchingly personal in its anecdotes and erotic phrases.

None of these words was quickly adopted into everyday speech. But in the past sixty years borrowing from Japanese has grown, and so has acceptance of words first noted in the nineteenth century, in step with Japan's emergence as the world's second largest economic power. More recent imports from Japanese have tended to be concentrated in the spheres of food and drink, martial arts and pop culture. *Teriyaki*, *aikido* and *karaoke* (literally 'empty orchestra') are conspicuous examples. The art of *origami*, dating at least from the twelfth century, was popularized in the 1950s and '60s, notably in Britain by Robert Harbin, whose *Paper Magic*, with illustrations by the entertainer Rolf Harris, appeared in 1956. The Japanese skill in consumer electronics has been influential (think, for example, of *Nintendo* and *Tamagotchi*), and the cult status of Japanese cartoons and comics, which has given us both *manga* and *anime*, promises in the near future to introduce new terms. *Ninja*, literally 'one skilled in stealth', seems to have been borrowed in 1964, the year Tokyo staged the Olympics – a fitting moment, since the word, once sinister, has increasingly approached a sort of endearing cuteness, and the Olympics allowed Japan, after the disgrace of defeat in the Second World War, to show the world its economic revival. Out had gone the alleged 'feudalism' of Japanese culture, and in had come a new spirit of *demokurashii*.

This last word, instantly recognizable as *democracy*, is a symptom of the Japanese adoption, since the war, of many foreign items. These have mainly come from English (there may be as many as 50,000), and those that are not from English have been treated as if they are. For instance, the source of *arubaito*, which means 'part-time job', is the German *Arbeit*, but a Japanese speaker of English may well say 'I have an arbeit.' Words taken from English include *kurisumasu* (Christmas), *moningusabisu* ('morning service', i.e. a set breakfast), *engejiringu* (engagement ring) and *depato* (department store).[4] One of the features of these words is that they cluster consonants less closely than English does, as the Japanese find clusters of consonants hard to articulate. Thus in baseball the term *strike* becomes *sutoraiku*. English *technology* has become *tekunorojii* and from there has been clipped down to size as *teku*. The embrace of such terminology shows that the Japanese, while not especially confident in their use of English, have become obviously Westernized. Meanwhile, the once ubiquitous *pokemon*, the name of the toy devised by Satoshi Tajiri in the mid-1990s, is an example of a word that has its source in English ('pocket monster') but was borrowed back into English.

Japanese technological mastery and the nation's distinctive fashions mean that borrowing from this source is likely to continue apace. Of late we have quickly embraced *sudoku* – a sign of its acceptance is the emergence of the noun *sudokist* to denote one of its enthusiasts. Maybe another puzzle, *kakuro*, will supplant it: in 2005 the *Guardian* became the first British newspaper to feature this numerical equivalent of the common crossword, reflecting an understandable appetite for second-guessing which Japanese fad will be the next to go global.

Other borrowings from Japanese remain to a large degree localized. In Hawaii, where there is a considerable Japanese population, one may hear flip-flops called *zori*, or the word *bocha* used of taking a bath. These terms will probably be meaningless to a native of San Francisco, let alone to an English-speaker in Manchester or Mumbai. Some of the localization has to do with taste rather than geography. Connoisseurs of pornography and sex games may be familiar with the practice known as *bukkake*, but to most people the word is as baffling as the thing it signifies. Perhaps the next Japanese word to achieve critical mass in our increasingly atomized society will be *hikikomori*, which denotes a phenomenon in which teenagers and young adults deliberately withdraw from everyday life and isolate themselves. Japan does not have a monopoly on such oddities, but still, to a majority of English-speakers, its culture and language appear to convey an air of both the eagerly modern and the austerely antique.

9. Onslaught

A fierce or destructive attack; a flood or deluge; a large quantity of people or things that proves difficult to cope with

From the old Dutch word *aanslag*, which in modern Dutch usage has the specific sense 'assassination attempt'. It is related to the Old High German *anaslaht*, 'a rain shower'.

The native languages of America and Japan were, for those adventurous English who encountered them in the seventeenth century, realms of wonder. I have spoken about language as an affront to the senses – the Vikings' 'acoustic onslaught' – but when we travel it is possible to experience something different: to be pleasantly enveloped in the unfamiliar sounds that hover all around. Roland Barthes has written about this, specifically with Japan in mind: 'Here I am protected against stupidity, vulgarity, vanity, worldliness, nationality, normality. The unknown language, of which I nonetheless grasp the respiration, the emotive aeration, in a word the pure significance, forms around me, as I move, a faint vertigo.'[1] *Vertigo*: a turning or whirling around, a feeling of giddiness. It is a Renaissance borrowing into English, from Latin – perfect for summing up the feelings of a stranger in a strange land, a Richard Cocks or a Thomas Harriot. But even on terra firma this feeling was possible. For many seventeenth-century speakers of English, their own language was an object of infatuation. Studies of language proliferated. To most writers of the period, modern languages seemed unstable, and contemporary works of commentary and analysis tended to convey an unhappy image of English. Their mission was to prune the language or endow it with new logic, to create what we might now label a 'science of rhetoric'.

Examples of this scientific tendency include John Wilkins's reformist proposal for 'a philosophical language', John Locke's examination of the relationship between language and thought (central to which was the recognition that the connection between words and the things they denote is arbitrary), John Dryden's theory of the nature of literary language, and the stylistic prescriptions of Thomas Sprat. In private, and often in obscurity, countless others distilled the essence of their lives' experiences as teachers or readers. The books they wrote were sometimes ponderous, sometimes sophisticated, and often a little mad. Their names are mostly forgotten. Who now remembers Cave Beck, an Ipswich schoolmaster, whose *The Universal Character* (1657) attempted to use numerals to make language more systematic? ('Honour thy father and mother' became, in Beck's scheme, 'leb2314 p2477 and pf2477.') Who, for that matter, knows much of Owen Price, author of *The Vocal Organ* (1665), which proposed a physiology of sound that has its modern counterpart in phonics, an effective yet controversial method of teaching people to read? Schemes of this kind were mocked by Swift in *Gulliver's Travels*: in the grand academy at Lagado, projects to trim language were pursued, because 'every word we speak is, in some degree, a diminution of our lung by corrosion, and, consequently, contributes to the shortening of our lives.'

The period's anxieties were manifold, and shuddered right across Europe. In England, they would eventually bear rich fruit: the land of Newton, Milton, Hobbes and Locke would become the first great imperial power to be buttressed by industrial achievement and governed by a representative political assembly. But first there were convulsions, and everyone felt them. The subject is explored deftly by Owen Barfield in his classic *History in English Words*. It is in this period that a new language of doubt begins to emerge: words like *dubiousness* and *sceptical*, along with the more recondite *dubitable* and *scepticity*. There is, too, a special vocabulary of religious doubt – of scepticism, that is, about others' religious values or inclinations. Thus *popery* and *libertine*, *reprobate* and *monkish*. Furthermore, a new language of self-scrutiny is apparent in a growing list of words such as *self-confidence*, *self-esteem*, *self-knowledge* and *self-pity*. John Locke stamps the word *self-consciousness* with what we now regard as its usual meaning in *An Essay Concerning Human Understanding* (1690).[2]

Locke's influence on the century that followed his *Essay* was immense. His terminology was widely adopted. To Locke we owe the notion that the mind is a blank slate or a dark chamber. We also owe to him some of the enduring implications of words such as *property* and *conception*, and our uncomfortable addiction to that little word *idea*. Moreover, Locke's emphasis on the need to use judgement to supplement our knowledge has influenced the English-speaker's striking habit of very frequently using, almost as though in parentheses, 'epistemic' verbal phrases – 'I think', 'I gather', 'I guess', 'I take it', 'I suppose'.[3]

The background of Locke's philosophy was the Civil War. Out of its pressures came insight into not just rights, liberties and government, but also the boundaries of knowledge. As the historian Jonathan Scott has pointed out, 'England's was the first experience of Europe's religious troubles to be accompanied by a highly developed culture of the vernacular printed word,' yet the nation's culture remained chiefly oral.[4] Performance was central to the politics of the period, but there was a persistent sense that the words did not exist to do justice to either the extremes of political violence or the extremes of religious experience. As political and religious institutions tottered, the imagination and intellect had startling opportunities for inventive expression. More about this in a moment: for now, my focus is the turmoil out of which the philosophical and investigative genius of the later seventeenth century – most clearly embodied in the works of Locke and Isaac Newton – at first tentatively and then impressively emerged.

Religious tensions were high. Under Charles I, who succeeded his father, James, in 1625, religion was an instrument of government. But there were plenty whose faith did not fortify the policies of the king and his ministers. His marriage that year to Henriette-Marie of France precipitated a wave of conversion back to Catholicism. His vision of a 'high' Anglican Church with a new emphasis on ceremony was inspired and then effected by William Laud, whom we have already met as a promoter of Arabic scholarship. Laud's reforms antagonized Puritans. For a decade Charles tried to rule the country without a parliament, and when a new one was established in 1640 it passed laws that undermined his authority. Conflict was inevitable. The civil wars that began in 1642 culminated in victory for the bourgeoisie: Charles was beheaded, and Oliver Cromwell, the so-called Lord Protector, wielded power pragmatically and with scant respect for democracy. Cromwell stamped out once and for all the Crown's interference in the economy; he established that foreign policy was a matter for Parliament; he curbed the rule of the Church and the religious intolerance that arose from it; and, less appealingly but no less importantly, he raised to an art form the exploitation of English colonial outposts. His achievements sharpened the consciousness of being a nation, enhancing ordinary people's awareness of their common national identity. Testimony to his influence is the assortment of words bearing his name, usually found in historical and political writings, all of them reeking of fear and awe: *Cromwellian*, *Cromwellite*, *Cromwellism*, *Cromwellized* and even, later, *Cromwelliad*. In his lifetime Cromwell was presented as prince, pilot and physician: after the Restoration his corpse was dug up and burnt, save for his head, which was put on public display. The busy conversion of his name into other nouns as well as adjectives and verbs is symptomatic of the period's edgy verbal inventiveness.

Even while Thomas Hobbes can write of the *spontaneous* quality of 'voluntary actions', coining a new word for man's natural impulses, we can see a wider cautiousness and nervousness of disposition, a habit of self-flagellating introspection. Confessional writing abounds, and so does the kind of literature that, even at its most combative, seems to apologize for its own existence. Hobbes identifies as one of the laws of nature that a man 'strive to accommodate himselfe to the rest', and he calls such behaviour *compleasance* (which we now spell *complaisance* and associate with a kind of obliging conduct that is rather more uncomfortable than its debonair name suggests). To be complaisant is to be yielding, to comply in the interests of self-preservation or saving face. Charles Barber makes the point that in the seventeenth century the meaning of *honour* alters: 'there is an increase . . . in usages which are defensive in attitude ("good name") at the expense of ones which are expansive in attitude ("glory"): negative reputation becomes more important than positive reputation.'[5] Rationality, all the while, was fighting down occult and obscure beliefs; dissenters, partisans and 'enthusiasts' were in thick supply, and the vocabulary of right-mindedness tended to extremes of either floridly repudiative classicism or prosaic modesty.

Matters of fact began at this time to be distinguished from matters of opinion. Hence the rise of the expression *a matter of fact*, sometimes found in the plural. The distinction suggests not certainty, but rather a culture where dispute is the norm and areas immune from it – or apparently immune from it – need to be marked off, as if with a groundsman's white lines. Contemporary styles of argument differ greatly, but all feel combative. On the one hand we find the crude and even hysterical rhetoric of the radical preacher Abiezer Coppe; on the other the ruthless clear-sightedness of Thomas Hobbes, whose arguments proceed with geometric precision. Especially active in this domain were the reformist Puritans, who objected to the ornate language of the elite. Pompous phrases and abstruse vocabulary alienated ordinary people. Puritans were distinguished, it was believed, by a language replete with terms like *discipline* and *abomination*. Another word they favoured was *godly*. Godliness was made manifest through *zeal*. They used the word *saint* to signify the elect, and had their own scathing language to express their disgust for the doctrine of the Real Presence in the Eucharist and the whole idolatrous business of the Mass – the priest with his rosary was a *beadmaster*, for instance, and the bread that denoted the body of Christ was nothing more to them than a *breaden god*.

The dissenting Quakers saw the world around them as a corrupt place where the flesh and its pleasures were wrongly exalted and obstructed God's spiritual presence. They strove for an unadorned speech and, in a period when the language of courtesy was staggeringly artificial, dispensed with the crouchings and cringings of compliment and the effortful language of deference. They used the familiar *thou* with all to whom they spoke, regardless of what custom dictated, even though it often resulted in their being labelled rude or uncivil. Additionally, they had their own special words, such as *steeple-house* instead of *church*, and abandoned the familiar names for the days of the week, speaking instead of the 'first day' (Sunday), the 'second day' and so on.

At the same time as the Quakers were discarding the language of religious ceremony, other areas of language were registering the plight of orthodox religion. The word *charity* became detached from its theological moorings. Popular words like *goodbye* (literally 'God be with you') and *gossip* ('relation in God') are evidence of the way religion is all but invisibly embedded in our language. *Goodbye* is not found until the second half of the sixteenth century. *Gossip* is a word of much greater age, but its meaning has altered dramatically: once the usual term for a godfather or godmother, it from the fourteenth century denoted any close friend, and only from the sixteenth century was it used of idle talkers and people bent on spreading rumour; two centuries later it began to signify not just the folk who indulged in this sort of tittle-tattle, but also the tittle-tattle itself. As Geoffrey Hughes says, these words exemplify 'phonetic erosion' and 'reflect in the secularisation of their meanings the eclipse of the influence of the Church'.[6]

Many words that now seem secular in flavour have religious origins: salient examples include *holiday*, *anathema*, *passion* and *propaganda*. Originally *propaganda* was a special term for the promotion of Christian faith; its use of any systematic spreading of a doctrine grew up in the eighteenth century, and for at least a century now it has been used scathingly of the means used by one cause to discredit others. Where once the word was automatically associated with the Congregation of the Propaganda set up in 1622 by Pope Gregory XV, by the twentieth century its debasement made this use problematic, and in 1967 the committee of cardinals responsible for foreign missions was rechristened, becoming the Congregation for the Evangelization of Peoples.

Another such word whose origins are long forgotten is *hocus-pocus*. This has been taken for a savage seventeenth-century corruption of the Latin *hoc est corpus*, a phrase pronounced during Communion. According to this view, its childish syllables mocked what some saw as the knavish trickery of claiming that the bread and wine of the Eucharist were the body and blood of Christ. But the link between *hocus-pocus* and the Latin Mass was not made until the 1690s, seventy years after the word's first recorded use. Whatever its etymology, the appeal of *hocus-pocus* was straightforward: its sound brought to mind a juggler's sleight of hand, while also conveying an illusion of Latin gravity. It was a word, quite simply, to conjure with.

Hocus-pocus belongs to a class of esoteric language that appeals to people who identify themselves as word-lovers. Greek is an especially rich source. A *deipnosophist* is a person skilled in making talk at the dinner table. Someone described as *callipygous* has pretty buttocks. One author who especially favoured words borrowed from Greek was the politician Hamon L'Estrange, whose *The Reign of King Charles* (1656) was censured for its polysyllabic excesses. A critic punned that his high style was difficult to climb over. L'Estrange was quick to counter this wooden conceit: 'I declare to all the world . . . that having conversed with Authors of the Noblest and cheif Remarque in several languages . . . their words . . . became at length so familiar with me, as when I apply'd my self to that present work, I found it very difficult to renounce my former acquaintance with them.' He goes on to argue, 'Our language had of late already admitted very neer all of them into so frequent use in ordinary discourse, as almost amounted to a Naturalization of them.'[7] 'Infelicitous pedantry' is the nineteenth-century judgement of Isaac D'Israeli, who notes that L'Estrange had 'opened on us a floodgate of Latinisms'.[8] Especially distrusted were popular new tags such as *ad hoc, ad hominem, ad infinitum* and *ad nauseam.* The fondness for trite appendages encouraged sloppiness in students. In the preface to a 1672 book intended to help children master Latin, the Grantham schoolmaster William Walker complains 'What Need there is of all the Helps of this Nature, that can be had, to deliver young Latine-makers from Barbarity in their making of Latin'.[9] Bizarrely, he goes on to show readers the correct Latin rendering of such English expressions as 'Handicrafts men are exercised in sordid arts' and 'The blood of innocents maketh *satisfaction* for one[']s lust.'[10]

The flood of Latinisms may have abated, but we hear and see Latin all the time. There are, for instance, most of those words that end *-us* or *-um*: it would be easy to provide a vast list, but if we choose arbitrarily from among the *f*s we have *focus, fungus, factotum, forum* and *fulcrum.* (*Hokum* and *tantrum* are false friends, not Latin at all.) The word *factotum* is one of a large number partly rooted in the everyday verb *facere,* 'to make' or 'to do'; others are *facile* and *effect, facsimile* and *fact,* and even, somewhat indirectly, *fetish.* While many words borrowed from Latin have been altered – their endings clipped away or adjusted – plenty have kept their Latin form: *abdomen, alibi, benefactor, cervix, lumbago, minus, patina* and *delirium* suggest something of their variety. Latin prefixes and suffixes have long been used to build new words on the foundations of existing ones. Again, an adequate survey would be huge, but think of all the things we can do with the prefix *extra-,* meaning 'beyond' or 'outside'. *Extraordinary* has become everyday, but what about *extrapolate, extramural, extratemporal* or *extracathedral?* If we are deranged, we may have *extraterrestrial* encounters; if disinclined to keep our wedding vows, *extramarital* relations. *Extravagant* is first used in the sense in which we now know it in the early eighteenth century, but before that it meant 'roving' or 'vagrant': the 'extravagant' ghost in *Hamlet* is so called because he strays out of bounds, not because he is a big spender. Darwin referred to *extra-stomachal* digestion, and T. S. Eliot, as if with a nod to his ancestor Sir Thomas Elyot, speaks of *extra-academic* honours. This is to say nothing of the much more common prefix *ex-,* which we find in so many energetic verbs: *excel, explode, exclude, express, extort, extend, expostulate, expunge.* Latin is responsible for many of the long-tailed beasts that roam the jungle of print.

A very different source of seventeenth-century lexis was Hebrew. The Reformation had stimulated the study of this liturgical language: the religious haggling of the period urged a return to the Hebrew Bible, Henry VIII's matrimonial entanglements were scrutinized by Hebrew scholars of theology, and the breach between England and Rome encouraged interest in Hebrew as a specially Protestant language of prayer. The creation of the Authorized Version of the Bible under James I involved no Jews, but was informed by Jewish scholarship, and in the 1640s and '50s the study of Hebrew increased – a preparation for the Second Coming, which many anticipated earnestly. It was widely believed that embedded in the Hebrew language were numerous occult truths, and Hebrew patterns of diction were adopted by sectarian writers keen to lend their rhetoric an air of holy mystery. At Oxford and Cambridge, Hebrew scholarship was improved by a Polish immigrant, Victorinus Bythner.

Hebrew words had been borrowed before: *hosanna, Satan, behemoth, mammon,* and the two calques *Passover* and *Adam's apple,* which were introduced by Tyndale and Hakluyt respectively. Now more loans were taken up. Among them were *matzo, mezuzah,* the incantation *abracadabra* (possibly Aramaic) and *Selah.* The last of these was a word found in the psalter, signifying the need for a pause at the end of a verse – and was later adopted by the poets e. e. cummings and Wallace Stevens. Another potent word of Hebrew origin, *Messiah,* had been used in Old English translations of the Gospels, but it was only in the King James Bible that it was given its proper Hebraic spelling. Even a comparatively familiar word of Hebrew origin, such as *jubilee,* has a deep history of religious significance. Originally it denoted a year of rest taken after seven cycles of seven years: debts were cancelled, and a trumpet crafted from a ram's horn sounded the call to communal rejoicing. Chaucer is one of the first to use it without a religious context, and in the sixteenth century, despite a renewed awareness of its Hebrew meaning, its secular force increased.

Even as the Authorized Version – 'drenched with the splendour of a divinely sanctioned authority'[11] – established itself in the public consciousness as the most exact and atmospheric rendering of the scriptures, there was a nagging perception that the Bible was no more than an abridgement of the ancient records of Christianity. Radical figures set out to supplement the scriptures. While the Somerset Puritan John Traske was so concerned with eking out the literal truth of the Old Testament that he was thrown in jail for 'Judaizing', his disciple John Robins took a different approach. Acclaimed by another visionary, Joshua Garment, as the reincarnation of God, Robins spoke sensational prophecies in tongues – assuring all who cared to listen that 'my *Hebrew, Greek,* and *Latine,* comes by inspiration.'[12]

It is significant that the verb *to Hebraize* ('to use a Hebrew idiom or manner of speech') makes its first appearance in 1645, in a work by the period's most important creative writer, John Milton. The fusion of classical and biblical language is limpid in Milton's works. He considered writing his masterpiece *Paradise Lost* in Latin, but ultimately decided to compose an English epic to rival its classical forebears and trumpet the integrity of

Protestantism – and chose for it a language imbued with classical resonance and allusion. Milton's sonorous style was in part the consequence of his blindness: having lost his sight in his early forties, he dictated the poem to his daughters and other amanuenses; its acoustic subtlety reflects his oral method of composition. Milton's command of ten languages is frequently evident: he wrote poems in Latin, Greek and Italian, as well as producing several important prose works in Latin, and the rhymeless verse of *Paradise Lost* combines the gravitas of Latinism with flightier borrowings. One of the reasons for his use of what can seem very indirect Latin expressions was a concern to dignify a well-worn story; Satan refers to 'the apple', but Milton, avoiding the trivializing effect of repetition, calls it 'the fruit of that forbidden tree' and 'that defended Fruit'. Milton's diction perfectly shows how the Latinate resources of English can be used to add scientific and moral resonance to everyday objects and experiences.

The scope of English as a scientific language was topical. The founding of the Royal Society in 1660 created an institutional standard for scientific writing. Its motto, 'Nullius in verba' (literally, 'On the words of no one'), was a necessary defence against the verbal wranglings of sectarianism, but it highlighted a philosophical creed that put actions before words: experiments counted for more than theories. The cardinal example of this is Robert Hooke's *Micrographia* (1665), which spoke 'ad oculum': its statements were made in the form of brilliant graphics, not brilliant prose. Where prose was needed, it was to be lean. The stylistic economy preached by the Society's historian, Thomas Sprat, was the antithesis of the sort of learned amateurism practised by Robert Burton or Sir Thomas Browne. (Sprat, like his nursery rhyme namesake, could take no fat: Browne no lean.) Burton's *The Anatomy of Melancholy* affords first sightings of *meteorologist, feral, hirsute* and *literati*, while the colourful Browne, who had studied at Montpellier, Padua and Leiden, was a prolific coiner of new words, responsible for *electricity, therapeutic* and *literary* as well as for the altogether more odd-looking but self-explanatory *retrocopulation* and *masculo-feminine*. Sprat recoiled from the 'vicious abundance' of such phrasing, from 'volubility', and from all the tricksy vanity that 'makes so great a noise in the World'. 'Primitive purity' and 'shortness' of expression were the order of the day. Sprat's colleagues in the Royal Society borrowed words, but far more often used prefixes and suffixes to extend the reach of existing vocabulary.[13] Sprat was not the first to insist on primitive purity, and he would not be the last. Nor did the Royal Society have a monopoly on science. But the period's move toward institutionalizing knowledge promoted a new attitude to the national language.

In universities, teaching was done in Latin. However, those looking to a wider audience needed to untangle the prolixities of Latin diction and find, where they could, equivalents for its cumbrous polysyllables. Interest in Descartes's philosophy spawned English equivalents for Cartesian terms: *subtle matter, moral certainty*, and specialized senses of *concept* and *idea*. But scientific thinking called for precise language, in which words meant one thing and one thing only. Sometimes polysyllables seemed more exact. Greek was especially useful, given its capacity for fashioning compound and derivative terms. This process of building words using prefixes and suffixes is responsible for the very large number of English words which have at least part of their roots in ancient Greek. This is in fact greater than the total number of ancient Greek words known actually to have existed: speakers and writers of English have imaginatively confected Greek compounds and hybrids far removed from anything that would have passed the lips of an Athenian orator.

I have mentioned Greek in passing several times already. Nicholas Ostler writes, appealingly, 'This is the language of the people who brought wine, olive oil and literacy to the Mediterranean world, who invented logic, tragic drama and elective government.' 'All of Europe', he suggests, 'became . . . their students.' Yet Greek was spread not just by culture, but also by 'speculative commerce' and 'naked imperialism'.[14] Behind the intellectual refinement of Greek lay a powerful military confidence. Ancient Greece was united by conflict, by the need to show unity in the face of opposition. The word *barbarian* has its roots in Greek disdain for outsiders: the rest of the world, ripe for conquest, bleated what sounded like *bar-bar* (compare the modern *blah blah* or *rhubarb*), a pathetically emasculated noise. The Greeks' language developed as an instrument of persuasion, a sophisticated rhetorical weapon in their bids to colonize the Black Sea, the Mediterranean and the urban centres of Persia. Later, the triumph of Rome reinforced the position of Greek culture: the Romans were seduced by a heritage that combined political and cerebral muscle with unbridled *hedonism* (a word rooted in the Greek for 'sweet').

In English, Greek words, many of them filtered through Latin, have always conveyed prestige. Greek enjoyed a second wave of influence because of its scientific uses in the eighteenth and nine-teenth centuries – we might think of this as a 'late' influence – but its force has since declined with the decline in general knowledge of Greek. Words adopted from Greek have tended at first to be used in technical or scientific contexts, yet many – *ecstasy, pathos, method, idea, kudos, phenomenon, hubris, problem* – have long since broadened their scope. The strict etymological senses of such words are obscure now to all but a few, and to insist on them is overfastidious. Often, however, we have lost the inherent poetry of a word. *Comet* derives from *kometes*, the Greek for 'long-haired': the Greeks referred to what we call a comet as an *aster kometes*, meaning 'long-haired star'. A comet leaves a trail behind it; the trail is dust, but ever since Aristotle pictured comets as stars with hair, these small celestial bodies have been doomily romanticized, as in the opening scene of Shakespeare's *Henry VI*, where comets 'brandish . . . crystal tresses in the sky'.

It is from Greek that we get the august *philosophy, logic* and *math-ematics* as well as the less rarefied *grammar*. The same source accounts for the more specialized *anatomy, astronomy, archaeology* and *pharmacy*. Greek prefixes are continuingly prolific: *meta-* and *micro-* are obvious examples, with the latter found in hundreds of words, from *micro-analysis* to *microzoon* via the comparatively ordinary *microphone* and the unfortunate *micropenis*. We find the suffix *-cracy*, indicating influ-ence or rule, not only in words of plainly Greek origin (*aristocracy, democracy*), but also in confections like *bureaucracy* and *meritocracy* – and in *logocracy*, a word Washington Irving used to characterized the wordy cultural politics of nineteenth-century America. *Orthography* and *ethnog-raphy* are words sourced in Greek, but *discography* and *radiography* are hybrids. A couple of other key prefixes from Greek are *poly-* and *hyper-* (as in *polygamy* and *polythene, hypersensitive* and *hyperspace*), while some other fecund suffixes include *-scope*, *-metry* and *-path* – think for instance of *periscope*, *symmetry* and *sociopath*. There is something hard and self-secure about these words. They seem, paradoxically, both real and remote.

During the Renaissance, many new terms for parts of the body were introduced from Latin and Greek. These included *penis, clitoris, uterus, scrotum* and *anus*, along with the less intimate *skeleton, cranium* and *pancreas* (the last of these the Greek word for a sweetbread). Edward Gibbon would later acclaim the 'decent obscurity of a learned language': classical terms were not smutted with the grease of everyday use. The Greek names of certain medical complaints have nevertheless been cut down to size by speakers who have struggled to pronounce them: *hydropsis* became *dropsy*, and *paralysis* shortens to *palsy*. The source of *migraine* is the Greek *hemikrania*, meaning 'half the skull'. Intriguingly, in the medical profession, many of the more lucrative specialisms have names derived from Greek: *gynaecologist, paediatrician, psychiatrist*. Compare with these the distinctly Anglo-Saxon and more modestly remunerated *midwife*. You're never going to make as much as a *toothpuller* as you will by being an *orthodontist*.

The taste for hard words persisted through the seventeenth century. If we look at a highly technical work like Nicholas Culpeper's 1653 translation of Johann Vesling's *The Anatomy of the Body of Man*, we find a host of daunting words. For example, in his description of 'the Instruments of Generation in Man', Culpeper writes in a short space of *epididymides, pampiniformia*, 'the plexure of the *Mesenterium*', a membrane called the *albuginea, cremasters* and *erythroides*.[15] 'I wish this poor *Nation* much good by this Work,' writes Culpeper in his address to the reader, 'that the Lord would open their eyes, that they might see the truth and themselves.' One wonders how many of Culpeper's contemporaries would have been at ease with his armour-plated language. It seems fitting that a standard work of the period, Richard Wiseman's *Severall Chirurgicall Treatises* (1676), was usually known by the blackly humorous title 'Wiseman's Book of Martyrs'.[16] The adjective *chirurgicall* must have seemed evasive; the sort of interventions Wiseman had in mind could kill you.

Ultimately, the works to achieve lasting popularity were those that used vernacular syntax and straightforward language rather than

Latin structures and baffling verbiage. But, ironically, the seventeenth century was the last in which natural language could girdle all of human experience; since then large areas of thought have become the province of artificial languages comprising formulae, mathematical notation and symbols. Our knowledge of the world, and the images we have of it, increasingly defies expression in words.[17] Reviewing the seventeenth century's grapplings with science, we can see them as a logorrhoeic orgy, yet also, conversely, as a last attempt to encompass experience in terms accessible to the non-specialist.

In June 1665 John Evelyn, a man of encyclopedic interests that included mechanics, forestry and London's sewers, wrote to Peter Wyche, who was chairing an inquiry by the Royal Society into the improvement of English, pointing out the need for imported words when there were no available equivalents. The 'corruption' of the language had resulted from 'Victories, Plantations, Frontieres, Staples of Com'erce, pedantry of Schooles, Affectation of Travellers, Translations, Fancy and style of Court, . . . mincing of Citizens' and several other things besides.[18] Evelyn noted that there was no adequate substitute in English for *ennui, bizarre, concert, emotion* or *naïveté*. He was a ready user of such terms. *Naïveté* was in fact warmly embraced. It proved a useful alternative to describing an action or statement as *ingenuous*, an adjective which contemporary users were apt to confuse with *ingenious*.[19] Other words looked more parlous: Evelyn feels able to call a village a *dorp* and a wine-grower a *vigneron*, and denotes the afternoon as *pomerid* after the Latin *pomeridianus*. In 1644 he writes of going to a *museum* – the term derived via Latin from the Greek *mouseion*, a place sacred to the Muses. And, recalling 1666, the year of the Great Fire of London (which he terms an *incendium*), he is the first to write in an English sentence of an *annus mirabilis*.

French influence was reinvigorated in 1660 when, at the invitation of Parliament, Charles II returned from the Continent. In exile, Charles had shuttled between Brussels and Bruges, Cologne and Paris. Now he entered London jubilantly. Even though support for his return was not emphatic, he soon established a new culture at court, bringing in a gossipy, competitive, salacious temper. He cut a surprising figure: tall, cynical, even vinegary, yet also approach-able. Charles and his favourites introduced new amusements. The card game *basset*, played by Charles's followers, takes its name from Italian. Yet, on the whole, fashions were French, and so were manners. 'He brought the spirit of mockery with him,' observes Logan Pearsall Smith, and brought as well 'a reaction against the austerity and zeal of the pious Puritans'. Hence, it would seem, such new terms as the verbs *burlesque* and *ridicule*, along with the adjective *jocose* and the nouns *badinage* and *travesty*.[20] *Clique* and *manoeuvre* are new words of the period that suggest its delicate social tactics. Both retained their original spelling, and the former kept its French pronunciation. *Caprice* is first sighted in 1667; *shabby* in 1669; *bigotry* in 1674; *nonchalance* in 1678. *Faux pas* first appears in Wycherley's *The Plain Dealer* in 1676. *Chagrin*, which is one of the 'hard words' explained in Thomas Blount's *Glossographia*, can be traced via French to a Turkish word for coarse untanned leather; the connection is that things apt to trouble the mind are bristly and chafe one's sensibilities. And in George Etherege's *The Man of Mode* (1676) – a play where we find talk of *belles assem-blées*, *bel air* and an *embarrass* of coaches – Sir Fopling Flutter, eager to be the centre of attention, declares when congratulated on his gloves, 'I was always eminent for being *bien ganté*.'

Banter is another new word of this period, its etymology uncer-tain, and it captures the spirit of mockery nicely. Swift disapproved of it and claimed in *The Tatler* that after a short time in vogue it had 'at last retired', but we know otherwise. One of his satiric fore-runners, the sadly forgotten Robert Gould, in 1687 wrote that English 'will fail, / As th'Inundation of *French* Words prevail'. He proposed as the standard for contemporary usage the poet Edmund Waller – 'all beyond, / Tho' spoke at Court, is Foppery and fond.'[21] Gould might have been expected to characterize the language of the court using words borrowed from French, but in fact *foppery* looks to have German origins, while *fond*, still then commonly used as a somewhat poetic equivalent for 'silly', may be from the Norse, related for instance to the modern Icelandic *fáni*, which means someone who emptily swaggers.

Another source of French – different in route and in mood – was the influx of Huguenots following the decision by Louis XIV to revoke the Edict of Nantes in 1685 and outlaw Protestantism. The exodus brought French talent to England. For instance, many Protestant seamen fled France's Atlantic ports, depleting the French naval reserves. These people came to be known as *refugees*, a borrowing from French, where the verb *réfugier* means 'to take shelter'. For a long time, a refugee had by definition to be a Huguenot; although today the term is more loosely applied, its emotive force is un-diminished. Then as now, refugees adapted to their place of refuge while preserving their own traditions. Londoners who wanted to learn the language of Pascal and Molière could attend services at the French Church in Threadneedle Street, where they heard the eloquent preaching of ministers like Charles Bertheau.

Yet, at the same time as Louis XIV was tarnishing his political reputation, his opulent court at Versailles was adding fresh lustre to the image of his country, and, even if some of the contexts in which the language was encountered were sober, the new borrowings from French tended to relate not to life's necessities, but to the frippery around its edges. When they kept their French pronunciation – as in the case of *naïveté*, for instance – it was as though they were at all times to be placed within inverted commas. The playful, self-conscious deployment of French tags is one we can still recognize. The effervescence of French culture apppears to be summed up in the word *champagne*, which first appears in Samuel Butler's *Hudibras* (completed in 1664). In *The Man of Mode* the characters sing of 'the joys of good wine' and in particular of 'sparkling champagne', which 'recovers / Poor languishing lovers' and 'drowns all our sorrow' – at least until the hangover kicks in on the morrow. The reference to 'sparkling champagne' is striking, because at that time the pref-erence in France was for the region's still wines. It was in England that the drink we now automatically call champagne first achieved real popularity, and it only achieved its mythic status in the years after the French Revolution.

Champagne is a sensuous whisper of a word. We hear it and we think of popping corks and winking bubbles, of the gentle ticking of pleasure. In the age of Butler and Etherege it was widely felt that if a word sounded attractive it was fit for adoption. Dryden favoured bringing in foreign words if they were 'sounding' (that is, sonorous, like his adoption *hoi polloi*), and boasted that 'I trade both with the living and the dead, for the enrichment of our native language.' In his view, poetry needed ornamental language, and it was often to be found abroad. Yet he argued that innovation ought to be carefully managed, 'for if too many foreign words are poured in upon us, it looks as if they were designed not to assist the natives, but to conquer them'.[22] His sensitivity was born of the awareness that people were by inclination 'censorious' and 'detracting'; here was a writer who knew the taut politics of usage, and who was apt to nod to the demands of Hobbes's *compleasance*.

All the same, Dryden could use a word like *double-entendre*, which first makes an appearance in his *Marriage à la Mode* (1673), and he appears to have been the first author to use *à propos* and *carte blanche*.[23] *A propos* was still causing concern a hundred years later, when a critic styling himself Peter Pikestaff chose to defend it in a catalogue of scandalous Gallicisms in *Town and Country Magazine*. Dr Johnson would later suggest that Dryden's employment of this type of vocabulary stemmed from 'a vanity . . . to show . . . the rank of the company with whom he lived'. Citing Dryden's use of *fraicheur* where he would prefer *coolness*, Johnson pronounces, not a little pompously, that the poet's affectations 'continue only where they stood first, perpetual warnings to future innovators'.[24] Of course, Dryden was apt to satirize social aspirations, and affected talk was one of their most obvious markers, so readers should be wary of viewing Dryden's snippets of French as symptoms of pretentiousness on his part. In *Marriage à la Mode*, the coquette Melantha changes her allegiances as often as her clothes, and her alertness to the fashion at court for all things French manifests itself in talk of *malheur, esprit, douceur* and *naïveté* – words she has written down in a notebook, hoping to make a big impression by using them. The courtier Palamede, whose favour she has been seeking, has to fan himself with his hat after her torrent of Gallicisms, and, left alone on the stage, muses, 'I never thought before that wooing was so laborious an exercise' – a line that is sure to strike a chord with anyone who has ever thought that the 'language of love' involved just a little too much bowing and scraping.

Appropriately, a new word of this period is *romantic*. It first appears in a couple of entries in John Evelyn's diary for 1654. Evelyn's diaries were not published until much later, and he revised them late in life in the 1680s, so his adoption of the word cannot be confidently dated to that year. The first instance recorded in the *OED* is in 1659. The word meant something along the lines of 'exhibiting the qualities of romances', the romances in question being works relating acts of gallantry and chivalry, popular with female readers and with satirists looking for easy targets. The defining quality of these works was their essential unreality: they were full of flying steeds and men of iron, magic armour and ivy-clad castles. This unreality was keenly felt by those who, in the seventeenth century, were beginning to embrace a new rationalism. The emergence of the word *romantic* testifies to such people's awareness of the gulf between rationalism and romance. Many regarded with contempt the purely fictitious nature of romance, and at first the word had pejorative overtones (as if to say, 'How absurd!'). Only in the second half of the eighteenth century did 'romantic' sensibility – in particular, a romantic sense of landscape – catch on. Crucially, it said more about our response to things than about the things themselves. And it was a response steeped in the colours of literature.

The sparkle of contemporary life was broadcast in the theatres. Closed during the Civil War, they reopened in 1660. Drama of the period tends to be complicatedly witty, and sexual references are teasingly indirect. When Swift complained, in the 1720s, that the theatre was a wellspring of affectation, he was reviewing some sixty years of highly perishable theatrical usage. One author notable for depicting amorous intrigue from a pointedly female perspective was Aphra Behn, who, having apparently worked as a colonial spy in Surinam, was nicely placed to expose the subtle interplay of politics and gender in her fiction, poetry and works for the stage. Among the terms Behn adopts is, from the Italian, *novella*, which has a conveniently feminine look about it; another is (as a verb) *masquerade*, a perfect embodiment of the motley artifice of the Restoration drama. The form's pre-eminent practitioner was William Congreve, who enjoyed a brief yet large success with five shrewd comedies of manners. In *Love for Love* (1695) Congreve's character Valentine depicts the predictable life of the city:

> Prayers will be said in empty Churches, at the usual Hours. Yet you will see such Zealous Faces behind Counters, as if Religion were to be sold in every Shop. Oh things will go methodically in the City, the Clocks will strike Twelve at Noon, and the Horn'd Herd Buz in the Exchange at Two. Wives and Husbands will drive distinct Trades, and Care and Pleasure separately Occupy the Family. Coffee-Houses will be full of Smoak and Stratagems.

Congreve evokes a society in which politics, fashion and rhetoric collude, and the coffee house was the capital of modish intrigue – a place, moreover, tinged with foreignness.

The first English coffee house was opened some time in 1652 or 1653 by Daniel Edwards, a merchant who had spent several years in Anatolia. When he returned to London from Smyrna, he was accompanied by Pasqua Rosee, who would run his business in St Michael's Alley off Cornhill, and he brought back not only coffee, but also an armoury of coffee-making equipment. Many followed his example, and the coffee houses became important meeting places, open to people of all ranks and religions. It would be no exaggeration to say that the coffee houses were instrumental in shaping the very notion of 'public opinion'. The London Stock Exchange would have its beginnings in a coffee house, and so would its counterpart in New York.

From an early stage pamphlets attacking coffee were frequent, and they were nationalistic in flavour, for the beverage was associated with Turks and other Muslim 'infidels', and the democratic nature of the coffee house meant it was typically linked with the political opposition. In 1675 Charles II issued 'A Proclamation for the Suppression of Coffee-Houses' to counter their 'very evil and dangerous effects'; the meetings held in them helped spread 'False, Malitious and Scandalous Reports', and they had become 'the great resort of Idle and disaffected persons'.[25] The word *coffee* is recorded in Dr Johnson's *Dictionary*, which says it is 'originally Arabick, pronounced *caheu* by the Turks, and *cahuah* by the Arabs'. Actually, *qahwah* is more like it – the Turks pronounced it *kahveh* – and the bracing drink seems related etymologically to an Arabic verb meaning 'to lack appetite'. The term *café* caught on in the nineteenth century as coffee-drinking, having become a polite form of public sociality, needed to be detached from the imagery of subversion.

The diaries of Samuel Pepys are a wonderfully engaging source of information about the machinations and manners of the period. In January 1660, soon after he began keeping a diary, he joined a club that met at a coffee house called the Rota, and he would often sit for an hour or two over a cup, enjoying 'the diversity of company – and discourse'. He drank his first cup of *tea* on 25 September 1660. Six years later, during the Great Fire of London, he buried his wine and *parmesan* cheese in the garden to keep them safe. Fittingly, Pepys seems to have been the originator of the expression *to have a good time*: he may have found the formula in Montaigne.[26] His diary entries hint at his contemporaries' lively interest in the torrid zones of taboo: sex, human nature, the motions of the planets, the value or otherwise of the existing social order. He is quick to learn new words: he provides the earliest citations of *gherkin* and *gimp* (both from Dutch), and is an early adopter of that strange verb *to drub*, which derives from the Arabic *daraba*, the practice of flaying the soles of a man's feet as a punishment. He is also a vital source of detail about everyday life. For instance, on 18 July 1662 he mentions his decision to 'have my dining-room wainscoated, which will be very pretty'. This sort of panelling was fashionable, and its name opens up a subject that preyed often upon the minds of Pepys and his contemporaries.

Wainscot is a word that now has an archaic look about it. It may remind some readers of the passage in *As You Like It* where Jaques advises Touchstone to avoid having his marriage to Audrey conducted by Sir Oliver Martext – for 'This fellow will but join you / Together as they join wainscot; then one of you will / Prove a shrunk panel and, like green timber, warp, warp.' Or there is Walt Whitman, who itemizes the 'fluid utterances' of the 'solid forest': among them 'shingle, rail, prop, wainscot, jamb, lath, panel, gable'. To others it will simply be a term scented with the antique. First attested in 1352, it denoted, before it took on its present meaning, a special type of oak used to make fine panelling. Where does it come from? A clue: its language of origin is the same as that of *wiggle, rover, firkin, buckwheat, ogle, walrus, trigger, snack* and *dope*. No? How about if I mention *rijstafel*? The word *wainscot* is from Dutch – a corruption of *wagenschot* or *wagenskot* – and is one of a large group that we rarely recognize as stemming from that source. *Ogle* derives from the Dutch *oogheler*, 'a flatterer'; *dope* comes from a word simply meaning 'sauce'; *firkin* approximates to *vierdekijn*, which means 'a little quarter' and is thus a rather quaint term for the fourth part of a barrel. Dutch and Flemish are both, like English, the offspring of West Germanic, so it is not surprising that a good deal of those languages looks familiar. Dutch loanwords tend to be simple and concrete, with scarcely a whiff of scholarly sophistication about them.

Who have been the vectors of these words? Soldiers and sailors, for certain, and experts in the handicrafts such as weaving for which the Low Countries long enjoyed fame. Also fishermen, traders and religious refugees. When English wool was the best in Europe, Flemish weavers were its main buyers. The cloth industry in the Low Countries has given us *cambric, nap* (as in the nap of velvet), *selvage* and *stripe*. Admirers of Dutch and Flemish painters – Hals, Rubens, Brueghel and Rembrandt – are obvious candidates to have adopted *masterpiece*, a calque on *meesterstuk* which becomes common in the first part of the seventeenth century. *Etch, sketch* and *landscape* are also from the Dutch, and early mentions of the last of these preserved the Dutch spelling, *landschap*. *Easel* is another Dutch import; its literal meaning is 'donkey', and for an understanding of the connection we need only think of our words *clothes horse* and *sawhorse*. From the thirteenth century onward, large areas of land were reclaimed by the Dutch from the sea; whereas the English attitude to the sea was confident, the Dutch proved essentially defensive, and an English awareness of Dutch skill in keeping the sea at bay gave new life to the noun *dyke* and introduced *polder*. In a different sphere, Henry Lyte's *Herball* (1578) was a version of a work by Rembert Dodoens, and introduced many new terms from Dutch, as well as a handful from German. Among the former were *amelcorn, catkin, devil's milk, silverweed* and *whitewort*, and Lyte also provides the first sighting in an English book of *tulip*, that bell-shaped showy flower for which there was a craze in the Netherlands in the 1630s.

The sixteenth and seventeenth centuries were the richest period of contact. Trade between England and the Low Countries was largely controlled by the Dutch, and the thriving English fish markets depended on catches made by Dutch fishermen. In the last three decades of the sixteenth century, the move towards Dutch independence from Spanish rule propelled intellectual and economic freedom. Dutch and English seamen jostled for primacy in the East Indies. Nearer to home, the argot of the fishermen who worked the Thames contained a smattering of Dutch and titbits of Latin and French.[27] There was movement in both directions. Workmen from Middelburg helped improve English glassmaking; Dutch drainage experts worked the fens of Cambridgeshire and Essex, and Dutchmen laboured in the Cornish mines; English actors took touring shows to Amsterdam and Groningen; and a stream of Englishmen went to study at the university in Leiden. Dutch iron ice skates are mentioned by Pepys, as are Dutch chimney tiles and bricks, and both he and John Evelyn could not resist the temptation to go and see a 6 foot 10 inch Dutchwoman when she was paraded in London for public amusement.

An area of especially snug contact between the languages of Britain and the Low Countries has been Scotland. Beginning in the fifteenth century, and for a period of perhaps 300 years, incentives were offered to craftsmen from the Netherlands to settle there. These incomers worked in the Lanarkshire silver mines, set up presses at Aberdeen and Edinburgh, made pottery, and practised as weavers or sugar-refiners. At the same time, Scots traded freely with the Netherlands and Flanders, exporting fish, hides and cloth, while persecuted Presbyterians and Scottish Catholics took refuge there. One of the consequences was an influx of Dutch words into Scots; these were mainly associated with trade, farming and shipping, but included *mutchkin*, a word for three quarters of a pint, and, more remarkably, *golf* (from *kolven*, the Dutch name for a game played with clubs). More recently, contacts between Dutch fishermen and inhabitants of Shetland mean that there are

Dutch terms in Shetland speech, such as *dulhoit*, meaning 'lethargy', and *krook*, a word for a storage jar.[28]

Colloquially, the Dutchman was known as a 'butterbox' – at least as early as 1600 – because he tended to spread everywhere. In the seventeenth century he was to be found in the East Indies and Sri Lanka, in Guyana and Surinam, in Cape Town, off the coast of Nagasaki, and on the Hudson River. *Coleslaw* derives from the Dutch *kool-salade*, 'cabbage salad', and is first mentioned in a piece in the *Massachusetts Spy* in 1794. The borrowing of *boss*, *waffle* and *cookie* also resulted from contact with the Dutch in North America, and so did the derisive *Yankee*. (A now obsolete sense of *boss*, as a conduit for water, was introduced by Dutch engineers who travelled to England to lay important pipework in the sixteenth century.) The American connection also produced *cruller* (a twisted doughnut), the verb *snoop*, and *pit*, the name for a pip or stone in fruit. But the relationship goes back almost as far as the historian's eye can see. There were Flemish mercenaries in England in the twelfth and thirteenth centuries, and Henry I found it necessary to deport parties of Flemings from the area around the Tweed to Pembrokeshire. Families of traders and weavers from the Low Countries had settled in England for commercial gain before the Norman Conquest, while there were pre-Conquest clerical links with the busy intellectual centres of Utrecht and Liège.[29] Words borrowed from Dutch in the fifteenth century, such as *excise*, suggest the commercial link between the two countries. Older ones include *mangle*, *malmsey*, *mesh*, the verbs *to prate* and *to mingle*, and possibly also *to pamper* and *poke* (a bag).

It was in the final decades of the sixteenth century, while Englishmen were eyeing the Americas and bickering over inky polysyllables, that the Dutch became an imposing force in the Mediterranean. Dutch crews were known for their discipline; even aboard their pirate ships, prayers and psalm-singing were compulsory twice a day.[30] They had, in addition, an extensive jargon of seamanship, which impressed other sailors they met. People who spend their working lives at sea have, on the whole, a less acute sense of national identity than their counterparts on land, and the international companionship of sailors resulted in many of the Dutch terms of seamanship gaining wider currency. Examples include the nouns *skipper, boom, deck, sloop, reef* and *hull*, as well as the less commonly used terms *avast, bowsprit* and *orlop. Dock* was borrowed at the very start of the sixteenth century: it signified a bed where a ship could lie dry at low water, and was the word used of the dry wooden mooring yard constructed on the orders of Henry VII at Portsmouth in 1495.[31] *Landlubber* is Dutch, as are *schooner, decoy* and *keelhaul. On loof*, literally 'on rudder', was a Dutch phrase spoken by the captain of a vessel when he wanted to steer a course away from a hazard such as a reef. It became *aloof*, a word that extended this idea of avoidance and evasion. In the same sphere are *cruise, iceberg, halibut* and *to smuggle*, while *filibuster* is a corruption of *vrijbuiter. Yacht* rendered the Dutch *jaghte*, short for *jaghtschip*, which was literally a 'chase ship', a swift craft for flushing out enemy vessels. *Forlorn hope* was originally a technical naval term applied to a detachment of men chosen to commence an attack. It arose from the Dutch *verloren hoop*, which literally meant 'lost troop'. The term was commonly used of combatants who demonstrated frankly reckless levels of bravery, but only much later did it come to imply such things as a desperate venture, a faint possibility or a lost cause. Terms more generally connected with warfare that are derived from Dutch include – besides *onslaught* – *beleaguer* and *blunderbuss*. We should note the quite large number of verbs taken from Dutch: besides a few already mentioned, we have *shamble, snort, split, hanker* and *hustle.* Where we have borrowed verbs, we can be sure the relationship has been intense.

In the seventeenth century, this relationship was soured by a war that took on global proportions. It may be hard today to think of there being any animosity between the British and the Dutch, but disputes over lucrative sea routes sparked a series of conflicts. In the early part of the seventeenth century, Amsterdam was a commercial utopia. Writing around 1635, Descartes remarked that 'In this city there is nobody who does not trade in something.'[32] Traders from Poland, Hungary, Turkey and Spain gathered under the hawk-like gaze of Dutch merchant regents, and the city's Exchange Bank lubricated their deals. In the 1640s the Dutch became key players in the distribution of Spain's colonial plunder, and their maritime strength was embarrassingly obvious to the English, as Dutch craft brought great cargoes of fish, wine and textiles into England. Yet Dutch dominance of the world economy was not supported by great military power or a strong land base, and the republic was politically divided. Avarice and lethargy ate away at its foundations. The extrovert Dutch merchant elite, which had existed barely fifty years, was quite easily depressed. The Anglo-Dutch wars began in the fevered twinges of commercial jealousy.

The first of the wars ran from 1652 to 1654, the second from 1664 to 1667, and the third from 1672 to 1674. In June 1667 a Dutch fleet under Michiel de Ruyter even stole up the Medway as far as Upnor Castle, burning the defences and towing away the English flagship. There was a glut of anti-Dutch propaganda: pamphlets of the period pictured the Dutch as a nation of cheese-mongers and herring-picklers, muddy and greedy. The soldier Sir Roger Williams – no relation of the founder of Providence, Rhode Island – had set the tone in his *The Actions of the Lowe Countries* (posthumously published in 1618), characterizing the Dutch as 'unreasonable prowde with the least victorie . . . and deadly feare-full with the least overthrow'.[33] In 1653 Andrew Marvell issued a poem on 'The Character of Holland', which described the country as 'this indigested vomit of the sea', and in the same year an English pamphlet helpfully revealed the Dutchmen's pedigree – 'Showing how They Were First Bred and Descended from a Horse-Turd'.[34] We can trace to this period of antipathy a number of denigratory stereotypes that are still in use. A *Dutch widow* is a prostitute, and other expressions – *going Dutch*, a *Dutch uncle*, a *Dutch auction*, *Dutch courage* – will be familiar to all. The adjective *plump* was first used by Caxton, and the word was habitually applied to the Dutch, who were reckoned to be well fed, prosperous and dull. The stock Dutchman was short and squat – quite unlike today. It was with this in mind that the word *bumpkin* – deriving either from *bommekijn*, 'little barrel', or from *boomken*, 'little tree' – was used dismissively by Englishmen of their Dutch counterparts. The comparable *nitwit* comes from the Dutch *niet weet*, meaning 'I don't know.'

A very different perspective was offered by the progressive teacher Bathsua Makin, who wrote that 'One great Reason why our

Neighbours the *Dutch* have thriven to admiration, is the great care they take in the Education of their Women, from whence they are to be accounted . . . more useful than any Women in the World.'[35] As the historian Jonathan Israel points out, 'No aspect of Dutch freedom in the Golden Age struck contemporaries, especially foreigners, more than that enjoyed by women – of all classes and types.' It was noticeable that 'Dutch women, even young, unmarried women, were free to come and go, unaccompanied and unchaperoned, to work, conduct business, and engage in conversation almost like men.' Moreover, 'in Dutch society, wives were less subservient to their husbands than elsewhere.'[36]

But by the end of the seventeenth century, and as the following century wore on, the Dutch began to falter. Their overseas trade networks fell apart. Cattle virus wiped out many of their farms. Their urban economy shrivelled – a decline that speeded up from around 1720. Brewing, often an index of economic vitality, was hit hard; instead there was an appetite for the more swiftly intoxicating *brandewijn* ('burnt wine') and *genever* – from which we get the words *brandy* and *gin*. Gone, too, was the intellectual excellence of figures like Christiaan Huygens and Antony van Leeuwenhoek. As this happened, the Dutch influence on English began to dwindle. Yet its importance is clear. Certain words absorbed from Dutch suggest a state of mind – a Low Countries understanding and mastery of the sea, for instance – but there is also, plainly, a debt to Dutch technology, in the use of wind power and drainage techniques (exemplified by our borrowing of *pump*), in textile manufacture (*spool*), in ceramics (*delft*), as well as in the building and handling of ships.

Furthermore, in England the ultimate beneficiary of the seventeenth century's political tumult was a Dutchman. William of Orange was the Protestant nephew of Charles II and James II. As the Dutch *stadtholder*, he had long been threatened by the ambitions of Louis XIV. Replacing the autocratic James II offered the possibility of a grand alliance that could stand up to the French. He landed at Torbay in November 1688, and entered London in triumph on 18 December. Support for him was huge. William's *Declaration of Reasons for Appearing in Arms in England*, written by his political adviser

Caspar Fagel and translated into English by Gilbert Burnet, was an extraordinary piece of propaganda, designed to please people of all parties, and was distributed widely. His efficient presence promised to avert the threat of civil war. The following April, he and his wife, Mary, were crowned, and immediately he moved to limit French expansion.

William's rule kept French influence at bay, promoted religious tolerance, and repaired the relationship between Parliament and Crown, creating a constitutional monarchy and reversing the absolutism of the two previous monarchs. It also marked the beginning of a new chapter in the British experience overseas. Confrontations ceased between English and Dutch traders, much to the advantage of the English. While the Dutch busied themselves with other rivalries, the English strengthened their position. A new, commercially driven, East India Company was set up, and copied the Dutch policy of using as its trading bases a string of fortified military positions. Its merger with the old corporation, resulting in the creation of the United East India Company in 1709, produced an organization that combined naval power with sound banking resources and strategic expertise, as we shall soon see.

10. Connoisseur

A person well versed in one of the fine arts and competent to pass judgement on it; a judge in matters of taste

From the French, and ultimately from the Latin verb *cognoscere*, meaning 'to examine', 'to recognize', 'to know'

First, though, another story: about a period in which British pride, and incitements to such pride, grew impressively. And where better to begin than with that word *British*, which took on new significance at this time? The Act of Settlement, passed during William's reign, paved the way for the Act of Union under Queen Anne, and this second act, in 1707, created 'Great Britain'. *British* had once meant 'pertaining to the ancient Britons' or had referred to the Brittonic languages. In the works of Richard Carew it had denoted the people and culture of Brittany. Now it meant something else. While the word was in use as an adjective before 1707, the Act of Union gave it a status in law, and references to 'the British' increased from this time. Additionally, it began to be exploited in compounds like *British-built*, *British-born* and *British-owned*. Constitutional stability created confidence in the nation's identity, and this was boosted by what seemed the almost perpetual war with France: Protestant Britishness was defined through its antagonism to the Catholic enemy.[1]

The Act of Union was a watershed between the internal turmoil of the previous century and a new age of prosperity. As the century progressed, patriotic feeling grew, under Hanoverian rule, and it became one of the resources of government. The two seminal songs that embody it, 'Rule, Britannia' and 'God Save the King', date from the 1740s. (Britannia herself is a hangover from the days of Roman occupation, but it is in the eighteenth century that she acquires her familiar trident, enabling her to 'rule the waves'.) As this suggests, the period's patriotism was a kind of performance; the singing of 'Rule, Britannia', which had been written by the Scottish poet James Thomson, acted out loyalty and a myth of British resilience. This resilience was symbolized in the form of the 'native oak', whose roots apparently grew deeper in time of war. Indigenous art was essential to this myth. Figures such as William Hogarth – who was notably troubled by the popularity of the expression *je ne sais quoi* – stressed the need for a quick divorce from the cultural examples of Italy and France. But this divorce was never likely to be settled: the appetite for French fashion and culture ran deep, even against a backdrop of continual war and aggressive anti-Catholicism.

Writing in her journal in April 1793, the novelist Fanny Burney refers to a *soirée*. It is the first recorded use of the word in English, and we should not be surprised that it is Burney who employs it: she had a finely tuned ear for colloquialisms – especially for the speech of polite society and those who aspired to join it. She also enjoyed some exotic contacts: her brother James was friendly with Omai, the first Tahitian to visit Britain, and had a fine command of the Otaheite language, while her acquaintance with the well-connected Thrale family enabled her to meet the period's dominant literary figure, Dr Johnson. As it happens, Burney attracted scathing comments from some of her contemporaries, who felt she was a little too accepting of foreign phraseology like *vis à vis*, *manqué* and *zigzag*, and her marriage to a penniless French general – which resulted in her becoming Madame d'Arblay – was blamed for her talk of 'descending' to breakfast and a distinctly Gallic use of the verb *to accord*.[2]

Elsewhere in her diaries Fanny Burney is the first recorded user of the adjectives *passé* – of a woman's faded looks, rather than of an outdated fashion – and *puppyish*, while in her delicious novel *Evelina* (1778) she introduces such new words as *tea-party*, *grumpy* and *shopping* (these last two italicized in the first edition to suggest their novelty) and coins the unusual verb *to Londonize*. In *Evelina* she documents the Londonizing of a young lady from the provinces – the book's subtitle is 'The History of a Young Lady's Entrance into the World' – and portrays the social complexities of modish London living with a shrewdly satirical touch. Vogue words like *uppish* and *fuss* are in evidence, as are racy Gallic phrases such as *ma foi* and *mon dieu*. One character, told he might have benefited from spending some time abroad, sharply retorts, 'What, I suppose you'd have me to learn to cut capers? – and dress like a monkey? – and palaver in French gibberish?'

Concerns of this kind were common among Fanny Burney's contemporaries. There was a perpetual tension between those who seized on French buzzwords and those who had no stomach for them. But even sceptics privately acknowledged the excellence of the French in the arts, and it was easy to borrow their words, since, after all, this source had been repeatedly quarried in the past.

Fashionable folk were *bons vivants*, exhibiting *bon ton* and *goût*. A contributor to the *Gentleman's Magazine* in 1738 referred to 'the absurd and ridiculous' imitation of the French, which he claimed had 'now become the Epidemical Distemper of this Kingdom . . . [and] has even infected those whom one should have thought much above such Weaknesses'. 'We only ape their Imperfections,' he argued, 'and awkwardly copy those Parts which all reasonable *Frenchmen* themselves contemn.'[3] Yet for every commentator whose relationship with the French and their habits was sulphurous, there were a bevy of admirers who could point to the richness of French social and intellectual life. Voltaire, Rousseau and Montesquieu were widely, though by no means universally, admired, as were the polished, often lightweight, literary studies known as *belles-lettres*. There was an appreciation, too, of the sensual rewards of the *fête-champêtre* and the *jardin de plaisir*. French wine was a patrician necessity: to the eighteenth century we can trace the use in English of *château*, *bouquet*, *decanter* and *pétillant*, as well as knowledge of distinctive styles such as Sauternes, Barsac and Mâconnais. In Alexander Pope's four-book *Dunciad* of 1743 we find the earliest English reference to a *liqueur*, and the word seems already to have acquired a patina of absurdity that primes it for satire. From French the aspirational eighteenth-century citizen learnt to speak of a *connoisseur*, a *tête-à-tête*, a *jeu d'esprit* and a *billet-doux*. An *amateur*, rather than being a term of disparagement, signified someone who cultivated an art or a taste – philosophy, say, or sculpture or boxing. And the French reciprocated the interest: there was a clear current of Anglomania, reflected in a taste for British clothes and even British breeds of dog.[4]

The eighteenth century has been characterized as an age of politeness and commercialism.[5] Perhaps we should not be surprised, then, that it was during this period of dramatic financial expansion that *commerce* and *commercial* began to take on the pejorative sense that most of us would now recognize. The century witnessed an increased social mobility. The idea of 'travel' emerged from the shadow of its etymological forebear, *travail*. The art of conversation was cultivated – practised in the coffee house and the *salon* (1699) – and involved a range of skills such as *persiflage* (1757) and the epigrammatic neatness of *bons mots* (1735). Polite society, quick to police its boundaries, espoused new words of disapproval: *fatuous, prude, flippant*, and, as an at least half-damning word for an illicit relationship, *intrigue*.[6] Indeed, 'polite society' is a fabrication of this period. *Polite* had once meant the same as *polished*, and had been used of stones and metals. By the early sixteenth century it had come to suggest elegance and refinement, but was applied only to language or accomplishments; it took another hundred years for it to be used of people. The sense 'well mannered' arrives in the eighteenth century – as in Henry Mackenzie's *The Man of the World* (1773), where one character opines that 'The French are the politest enemies,' or William Pitt's definition of *politeness* as 'perpetual attention . . . to the little wants of those we are with'. This sense gained ground at the expense of the older *civil*.[7] *Politesse*, which originally meant something akin to 'smoothness', evolved more specific senses: 'intellectual culture', 'civilized behaviour', 'respect for the rules of propriety'. In Henry Fielding's *Joseph Andrews* (1742) the word has a sprightly freshness about it, and it does so still in Fanny Burney's diary more than thirty years later.

It is to the second half of this century that we can date the rise of a new fastidiousness about language – a new appetite for euphemisms and polite circumlocutions. (*Euphemism* is recognizably Greek – it's one of the Grecian oddities that Thomas Blount chose to explain in his *Glossographia*.) According to one study, when Jane Austen's Mr Darcy voices his approval of Elizabeth Bennet's 'dark eyes' he is really passing favourable comment on the size of her breasts.[8] In truth, the colour of her heroines' eyes is frequently of concern to Austen, but we may identify all the same with the experience of passing comment on a person's eyes when we mean to pay a more juicy compliment.

Another of Austen's heroines, Marianne Dashwood, is a study in exaggerated *sensibility* – a buzzword for a generation who saw hyper-sensitivity as a virtue. This quasi-religious cult of fine feelings involved a regard for the delicacy of mind and body, the cultivation of taste and sympathy, a kind of self-absorbed benevolence, and close attention to *physiognomy* (itself voguish – Swift deplored its shortening to *phiz*). Somewhat predictably, it was associated by many with the pernicious influence of Britain's neighbours across the Channel. In Maria Edgeworth's novel *Leonora* (1806), the scandalous and emotional Lady Olivia is uneasy with English companions, having 'known the charms of French ease, vivacity, and sentiment'. In this context *sentimental* became first a catchword, then a smear, and the fancy noun *presentiment*, also picked up from the French, was greeted with protest.[9] Particularly influential was Laurence Sterne's *A Sentimental Journey through France and Italy* (1768), based on a seven-month coach tour undertaken while Britain and France were at war. Sterne's short, unfinished book proved that conflict did not have to get in the way of tourism, and inspired a host of other 'sentimental' writings, which with varying degrees of success expounded a philosophy of pleasure.

One key figure in the evolving language of fine feeling was Lord Chesterfield, whom we earlier met as the first to refer to a picnic. In his prose Chesterfield is unmistakably keen on French words and phrases; he is almost certainly the first to write of *sang-froid* and *malaise*, of matters being *hors de combat* or *de trop*, and of a *début* (originally a term in billiards). Among the other words he imported were *gauche*, *soi-disant* and *faute de mieux*, and he helped naturalize *ennui*. He knew what he was doing. In a letter dating from 1768 he reports, 'I feel what the French call a general *mal-aise*,' adding that this is 'what we call in Ireland an *unwellness*'. He also uses *egotism* (although it was Joseph Addison who adopted this word from the French), and coined *etiquette*.

This last word, which eased aside *civility* in the second half of the century, embodied Chesterfield's ideas about proper conduct, and its widespread adoption was a symptom of a change in values. Manners, according to Chesterfield, are separate from morals; they are not absolute, but specific only to a social group. *Etiquette*, which may be glossed as 'a small ethics', consists not of doing good deeds that earn you admiration, but of being pleasantly conformist. (*Etiquette* could also signify a label or ticket, and codes of conduct were apt, at least in France, to be written down on cards.) Chesterfield argued that in social life it is small virtues rather than large ones that win us love and affection. For many, his concept of *etiquette* was alluring: it was better to be a chameleon than a paragon. While plenty of readers continued to cleave to the values set out in more puritanical conduct books, Chesterfield's model of behaviour inspired a new and rather malleable idea of correctness. *Etiquette* was essentially tactical. The art of social self-preservation involved 'vigilant self-control and perpetual observation of others'.[10]

In the opposite corner was Samuel Johnson, whose *A Dictionary of the English Language* had been briefly and ineffectually sponsored by Chesterfield. Yet, while plainly divided, the two men were united in their commitment to improving English. There were two responses to the linguistic licence so common in the previous two centuries. One was the idea of an English Academy, like the academy that existed in France: it would rationalize and standardize the language. The other consisted of individual attempts to send the language to school: grammars and dictionaries abounded, and none was more magisterial than Johnson's, commissioned by a group of powerful booksellers and published in April 1755. Both reflected a heightened concern with the means by which language advanced and the relationship between linguistic and social progress.

The diversity of English was considered a mixed blessing. It had been made all the more apparent by the Act of Union, which had integrated several ethnically disparate groups into one rather ambiguous unity. Johnson sensed the capacity of such diversity for causing disputes, and found the speech of his contemporaries 'copious without order': words had been picked up from many sources, and as a result 'wherever I turned my view, there was perplexity to be disentangled.' He believed that 'from the authors which rose in the time of Elizabeth, a speech might be formed adequate to all the purposes of use and elegance,' and he saw the language of the period before the Restoration as 'the wells of English undefiled'. He was dismissive of upper-class slang, much of which was sourced from French, and resisted 'barbarous jargon' – which tended to mean anything modish and foreign. Noting that 'our language, for almost a century, has . . . been gradually departing from its original *Teutonick* character, and deviating towards a *Gallick* structure and phraseology,' he urged that 'it ought to be our endeavour to recall it.' Unless the influx of Gallicisms was checked, his countrymen would be condemned to 'babble a dialect of French'. It is hardly startling, then, that in his *Dictionary* he omits words as widely used as *champagne, clique, façade, tableau, brochure* and *bouquet*, and most words of French origin were treated slightingly. Thus *ruse* is 'a French word neither elegant nor necessary' and *finesse* is 'an unnecessary word which is creeping into the language'. The obscure *souvenance* is 'a French word which with many more is now happily disused'. These terms, in his view, were the trappings of affectation; they were spouted by idiots seeking to impress even bigger idiots.

It is a nice irony, then, that the *OED*'s first citation in support of *civilization* ('a developed or advanced state of human society') is Dr Johnson's informing his biographer Boswell that he will not include this alien word in the revised fourth edition of his *Dictionary*. The great lexicographer would have associated this buzzword *du jour* with Voltaire and the whole dazzling business of Enlightenment. His own tastes ran more to Latin, as both his *Dictionary* and the essays he wrote while compiling it – with their hard words, like *equiponderant* and *terraqueous* – generously demonstrate. In Johnson's eyes the classical world was immutable, and its language was thus gratifyingly resistant to the vagaries of fashion. But others were not convinced: the historian and pamphleteer Owen Ruffhead thought that certain words Johnson used, among them *multifarious* and *indiscerpible*, were difficult to pronounce without breaking down in a fit of the giggles.[11]

One rather silly French word for which Johnson did find space in his *Dictionary* was *escargatoire*, which he defines as 'a nursery of snails'. His excuse would have been that it could be found in the works of a writer he esteemed, namely Addison. In Addison we see the gamut of the period's linguistic felicities and inconsistencies, as resonant in 1800 as in 1700. There is perhaps no better record of public taste in the early part of the century than Addison's magazine, *The Spectator*. It was influential in equating pure and proper use of language with moral excellence. Addison believed that English reflected the national character – 'modest, thoughtful and sincere'. His essays were at once urbane and didactic, and their style is strikingly sparing of metaphor and simile; comparison of his manuscripts and his published writings demonstrates that he took pains to repress imagery where he could.[12] He fretted about the use of foreign jargon (words like *bivouac* and *chamade*) in military reports sent from abroad, and even suggested that British troops have secretaries to help them convey their news in plain English. Certainly it was ironic that the Duke of Marlborough's troops could defeat the French, then ape their speech and style. Yet Addison seems to have been the first author to use such words as *hors d'œuvre* and *critique*, and some of his pet formulae – for instance, *fine taste* – are renderings of French expressions popularized by Jean de La Bruyère.

Others felt the same subtle literary influence. It was the influence of La Bruyère's *Les Caractères* (1688) that endowed *character* with connotations of good reputation and distinction. Voltaire boosted *tact*, and a later generation would mimic his phrase *capable de tout*. When, in his *Decline and Fall of the Roman Empire*, Edward Gibbon wrote of *public opinion*, he was recreating an expression he had found in Rousseau, while when Jeremy Bentham referred to *esprit de corps* he may well have found the phrase in the writings of Madame de Staël.

De Staël is now largely forgotten outside France, but she deserves a moment here as a shrewd commentator on France's national character. In her account of Germany she memorably noted, 'The great merit of the Germans is that of filling up their time well; the art of the French is to make it pass unnoticed.' She was struck that the Poles and Russians she met on her travels spoke only French. German, she felt, was 'a language . . . very copious in metaphysics, but very positive in conversation. The French language, on the contrary, is truly rich only in those terms of expression which designate the most complicated relations of society.'[13] The complex business of social relations has, as we know, endowed our own language with far more than has been drawn from the domain of metaphysics. Germans' 'positive' talk seemed to her, as to many others, too emphatic, too precise, too explicit; social skill consists in avoiding such dogmatism.

Nevertheless, there were vital sources of new lexis besides French. Here is the noted conversationalist and wit Richard Owen Cambridge, writing in the magazine *The World* in 1754: 'I must . . . beg leave . . . to doubt the propriety of joining to the fixed and permanent standard of our language, a vocabulary of words which perish and are forgot within the compass of the year.' He proposes instead 'a small portable vocabulary to be annually published'. Among the words that trouble him is the verb *to negotiate*, and he remarks that the late interest in China has led to much talk of *pagodas, junks* and *palanquins*.[14] These comments were a response to the previous week's issue of the magazine, in which Lord Chesterfield had extolled Johnson's imminent *Dictionary*. Chesterfield had remarked that 'Language is indisputably the more immediate province of the fair sex' and that 'The torrents of their eloquence . . . stun all opposition, and bear away in one promiscuous heap, nouns, pronouns, verbs, moods and tenses.' Women, he claimed, were 'forever enriching our language by words absolutely new'. It struck him that Johnson ought to add an appendix to his *Dictionary* – 'a genteel neological dictionary, containing those polite . . . words and phrases, commonly used, and sometimes understood, by the BEAU MONDE'.[15]

The need was clear. When do you think we find the first recorded use of the Norwegian word *kraken* or the Swedish *nickel*? What about *savoir vivre*, or indeed *reinsurance, water-closet* and *ungainliness*? And what about *baksheesh* and *baddish* – as in 'My command of the local dialect was baddish, but I knew I was being importuned for baksheesh'? As it happens, all these words are first found in 1755, the year Johnson published his great lexicon, and it is in a translation, dating from that year, of Erich Pontoppidan's *Natural History of Norway* that we first find the word *ski*. Contemporary critics thought these new words were depraved; Johnson was only one of many who worried about the 'degeneracy' of English.

Thomas Sheridan, father of the playwright Richard Brinsley, believed that the language's lack of inflexions made it vulnerable to barbarous incursions. Yet both accepted that, as knowledge increased, vocabulary had to increase too. Individual borrowings might be stigmatized, but, viewed more generally, borrowing was a mark of intellectual progress.

Inevitably, many of the freshly imported words were connected with fashion, popular delusions and the mania for collecting. Others conveyed more sinister images of abroad. Public knowledge of Pasquale Paoli's battle for Corsican independence, and his exile in Britain, raised awareness of the concept of the *vendetta*, which seemed to sum up the island's spirit of rugged violence. *Vampire* was a more fashionable yet disturbing import, perhaps from the Magyar language of Hungary or from Serbo-Croatian; in an essay in the *Gentleman's Magazine* for March 1732, readers were told how in that part of Europe 'certain dead Bodies called *Vampyres* had kill'd Several Persons by sucking out their Blood' and that 'those who have been tormented or killed by *Vampyres* become *Vampyres* when they are dead.'[16] It was not long before the word was being used of all manner of ruthless predators, of extortionate moneylenders, and even of bloodsucking bats.

Benedict Anderson has written that 'in Western Europe the eighteenth century marks not only the dawn of the age of nationalism but the dusk of religious modes of thought. The century of the Enlightenment, of rationalist secularism, brought with it its own modern darkness.'[17] An age in love with all things tangible, with discovering hard evidence and intriguing specimens, was inevitably sceptical, and, while there was a persistence of faith (as in the widespread conviction that language had been a gift from God), there was a new, almost profane, materialism.

The period witnessed an explosion of print culture. Its new phenomena included printed tickets, advertisements and receipts, as well as posters, political pamphlets, children's literature and street maps. Newspapers and magazines flourished. *Magazine* has its root in the Arabic *mahsan*, a storehouse; in 1755 Dr Johnson explains it as a 'repository of provisions', before adding that 'Of late this word has signified a miscellaneous pamphlet, from a periodical miscellany named the *Gentleman's Magazine*, by *Edward Cave*' – a nice puff for his sometime employer. A magazine is either a stock of explosives, a detachable container that feeds cartridges into the breech of a gun, a topical TV show, or, most often, a periodical such as *Time* or *Potato Grower*. Each embodies the idea of things being stored up for selective use and enjoyment. After 1774, when the old common-law 'perpetual' copyright was ended, another kind of storehouse was able to bloom: the *anthology*, literally 'a collection of flowers'. Inexpensive anthologies appealed to readers bent on self-improvement. They also created a sense of literary tradition, a canon of English literature.

As print culture burgeoned, and as its market grew, the man of letters became a figure of social importance. While at the start of the century more than a third of the adult population knew how to write, only one in twenty could do so fluently. But the number of readers was on the increase, and they were voracious in their appetite for printed material. The novel, concerned with realistically depicting individual characters and their experiences, reflected the middle-class appetite for coherent, believable fiction. A popular work like *Robinson Crusoe* (1719) was devoured by philosophers and kitchen maids alike, and its author, Daniel Defoe, strove for a supple, artless style that would make it accessible. The rise of the novel was one part of a pattern in which prose writing became more important. In 1695 Parliament had allowed the statute that permitted pre-publication censorship to lapse, mainly for commercial reasons; the result was a more vigorous public exchange of opinions in the press. A culture of patronage gradually gave way to one in which writers vied for success in the marketplace. At the same time, women writers began to prosper, new legislation improved the rights of authors, and public libraries were set up. As printed material became more common, language was increasingly systematized.

Since the middle of the seventeenth century, the most significant changes in English have been in vocabulary. In the eighteenth century, and especially in the second half of it, authors of grammar books established an ideal of English usage and busied themselves with disseminating it. They promised their readers the possibility of social advancement. According to their model, one's choice of words was crucial to one's public image. Propriety was their golden rule, and an aspect of 'proper' English was a freedom from foreign contaminants. The vision of Standard English that developed in the second half of the eighteenth century was an essentially prescriptive one, intolerant of regional usage and immune to the idea of the language's lush plurality. The period's grammarians, of whom there were a great number, spoke decisively, presenting their judgements as certainties. Readers looking at early editions of eighteenth-century novels can be surprised to find that most of the nouns begin with a capital letter – as in German today. This was a printing convention, yet it was the practice of many authors to stress nouns, as if marvelling at the sheer 'thingness' of the things about which they were writing. The grammarians, intent on putting an end to this, would here at least taste success.

What sorts of new word do we owe to the writers of the period? We have come across a few already, but there are many more worth comment. Thomas Sheridan, one of those most eager to send English to school, gave us the verb *to bother*; his son Richard gave us *dressing gown* and *amadavat* ('an Indian song-bird'). We owe *descriptive* to Johnson, *low-bred* to his friend the actor David Garrick, and *casino* to another of his friends, Hester Thrale. The novelist Samuel Richardson seems to have adopted the verb *to modernize* from the French. Edmund Burke's innovations included *colonial* and *electioneering*, and his responses to the political upheaval of the French Revolution include early sightings of the words *guillotine* and *sansculotte*. The radical philosopher Jeremy Bentham came up with the adjectives *secretarial* and *exhaustive*. The first author to use the word *adventuress* was Horace Walpole, who more famously coined *serendipity*, that once rare but now adored word for the faculty of making pleasant, unexpected discoveries, inspired by the old name of that teardrop of a tropical island, Sri Lanka.[18] John Gay, author of *The Beggar's Opera*, seems to have been the first letter-writer to sign off 'yours sincerely'.[19] *Optimism* we owe to Voltaire's satirical *Candide* (the full title of which was *Candide, ou l'Optimisme*), published in 1759; its first English user was the critic William Warburton, in a letter written that year. Appropriately, we owe *intolerance* to the grammarian Robert Lowth, whose *A Short Introduction to the English*

Language (1762) offered a narrowly prescriptive view of the subject – a first inspiration for all those letters to newspaper editors that fulminate against split infinitives and dangling prepositions.

One feature of the age was the growth of a highly subjective language of appreciation: *amusing, charming, exciting* and *fascinating,* as well as their antithesis, *boring*.[20] It is particularly fitting that *interesting,* although then a rather stronger adjective than it has since become, was first used in its usual modern sense by Sterne, in *A Sentimental Journey.* Sterne was a preacher and a lover of the salon; his works suggest the pleasures of eloquent company and its pitfalls – the importance to people of their particular hobby horses, the strange conflicts between words and body language, the comic possibilities of ambiguity. A literary magpie, he lifted ideas and phrases from Rabelais, Robert Burton and John Locke, and his language is a mix of lightly worn borrowings and zesty originality. 'To write a book is for all the world like humming a song,' he suggested, and his writing pulses with the music of conversation. He is the *OED's* first source for *bambino,* but also for a wealth of words connected with types of feeling and behaviour, such as *good-tempered, lackadaisical, muddle-headed, sixth sense, uncheery* and *whimsicality.* His was an era in which 'a culture which had been dominated by oral transactions came to be replaced by a culture predominantly based on the written text . . . [and] where printed communication took precedence.' During this transition, 'the ear is replaced by the eye in shifting perceptions of language . . . [and] the eye is ascribed the primordial role of deciphering words upon the printed page.' Accordingly, in this period 'language took precedence over images in aesthetic debates' and 'writing was often deemed . . . superior to speech.'[21]

Sterne plays joyously with the possibilities of the printed word. Nietzsche could pronounce him 'the most liberated spirit of all time', which is perhaps overdoing it, but Sterne's writing is fanciful and strewn with innuendo, a performance stimulated by the sense that low things are always sprouting through the gaps between lofty ones. 'I will tell you in three words what the book is,' says Tristram Shandy of the work that bears his name. 'It is a history.' Sterne repeatedly conveys a delight in disorder, a game embrace of chaos.

Tristram Shandy's huge audience was united in feeling it was a book that played fast and loose with conventional morality. Yet its humour did not prevent seriousness. The novel is deeply concerned with failures of communication – with 'the unsteady uses of words', the 'unhappy' and inconvenient associations of particular terms, and also the difficulties of making sense of gesture.

Uncertainty is at the heart of Sterne's work and its appeal. You can be sure of nothing, he seems to say, and his writing had lasting appeal for an audience intent on deliberately altering their perceptions. In Britain during the second half of the eighteenth century there emerged a fresh scientific, philosophical and cultural understanding of the business of looking and seeing. The smoked convex lens known as a *Claude glass*, which could be easily obtained from an optician, earned its name because it gave the landscapes reflected in it the shady, even gloomy, look of the paintings of Claude Lorraine. It was made fashionable by the cult of the *picturesque* – the French term popularized by Cumbrian clergyman William Gilpin – and other devices equally valuable as aids to perception were the *camera lucida* and the *camera obscura*. The *panorama* took its name from Greek; its innovator Robert Barker originally called it *La Nature à Coup d'Oeil*. (*Coup d'œil* was generally felt to be 'a needless Gallicism', but had credibility in military circles.)[22] Barker first exhibited in Scotland in 1788, and the following year he took his 'step-in' spectacle to London. Panoramas, which created impressively realistic effects, were soon all the rage; they paved the way for the development of the *stereoscope*. This was successfully created by Sir David Brewster, an enterprising Scot, who also invented the *kaleidoscope* in 1817. Later came the *zoetrope*, initially known as the *daedalum*. Its flickering impression of simulated movement fascinated nineteenth-century audiences.[23]

The quest for new vistas contributed to the contemporary passion for climbing – an erotic embrace of danger summed up in a new word, *mountaineering*. The *Critical Review* took pains to define *avalanche*, only to observe, we may think a little stupidly, that 'there can be no English word for a phenomenon of which there is no example in England.' The *Gentleman's Magazine* provided a detailed and incorrect explanation of *jokul*, an Icelandic synonym for the recently established *glacier*.[24] *Débâcle*, before it acquired the sense we usually now understand, was a term in geology for a violent deluge that breaks up ice or other barriers. Moreover, the striking new perspectives were not just available to climbers: you could also see different things from a *balloon* – the term borrowed from the French following the Montgolfier brothers' successful ascent in 1783, though it had been around for a couple of centuries as the name of a ball game imported from Italy. One of the results of these fresh ways of looking at the world was the rise, beginning in the eighteenth century, of a new type of observer for whom vision was active rather than passive.

The period's optical and visual developments exemplified the ways in which Isaac Newton's natural philosophy penetrated every area of the nation's life. Newton's insights into the physics of colour were revolutionary, and so were his laws of motion. Significantly, whereas his *Principia Mathematica* (1687) was published in Latin, his *Opticks*, seventeen years later, was in English; Newton's ideas were difficult, but while Latin allowed an immutable precision of argument, the use of English was an aid to wider public understanding. The popular grasp of the kind of knotty, important science Newton practised was enriched through lectures and demonstrations – often held in coffee houses which doubled as theatres. After all, people were eager to lap up theories which showed that time was without limit. 'The most important achievement in natural philosophy in the eighteenth century was a burgeoning public interest,' observes Larry Stewart. 'Nature . . . had entered the realm of public property,' and 'The production of knowledge, of scientific facts, increasingly depended upon the victory of a market model of public competition and consumption.'[25] The natural world existed to be used, and the advance of scientific knowledge was understood to run in parallel with the advance of trade. 'A palpable spaciousness animates late-seventeenth- and eighteenth-century natural philosophy,' writes George Steiner, 'a confidence that there are worlds enough and time for even the most forward-vaulting of sensibilities to draw a deep breath.' Instead of 'containment by the crystalline and concentric' and Pascal's 'terror of the void', the new thinkers are set free by 'the largesse of an unbounded future'.[26]

John Ray's *The Wisdom of God Manifested in the Works of the Creation* took frank pleasure in a world 'too great for any Man, or Generation of Men . . . to discover and find out all its Store and Furniture, all its Riches and Treasures'.[27] Ray's executor, William Derham, produced the popular *Physico-Theology* (1713), and pushed this idea further: it was a man's duty to make the most of God's Creation through experiment and exploration. As Newton's legacy was popularized, a financial relationship grew between the pioneers and the public. Important new books were published by subscription, which allowed many ambitiously conceived works to reach quite substantial audiences. Natural philosophy was equated with the 'public good', and an appropriate public language emerged. The very word *science* was beginning to bend to new purposes. In the second quarter of the eighteenth century it began to acquire a new sense, defined by the *OED* as 'a branch of study which is concerned either with a connected body of demonstrated truths or with observed facts systematically classified and more or less colligated by being brought under general laws, and which includes trustworthy methods for the discovery of new truths within its own domain'. Isaac Watts, now chiefly known for his hymns, is cited as the first to use the word in this more modern sense, in 1725.

Side by side with this was a shocking proliferation of pseudo-science and quackery. The practices of the quack are as old as history itself, but in eighteenth-century Britain they enjoyed special success. *Quack* is an abbreviation of *quacksalver*, which comes from the Dutch *Kwakzalver*, a person who quacks (that is, boasts) about the special properties of salves and ointments he offers for sale. *Mountebank* can be traced to the Italian *montar in banco*, 'to climb up on a bench'; it was used of practitioners whose work was heavily theatrical. The English quacks of the eighteenth century were aping the Italian *ciarlatani*, whose chicanery was mentioned by Ben Jonson in *Volpone*. Foreign quacks flocked to Britain, travelling from Italy, the Netherlands, Germany and Poland. Their wares were cordials, snuffs and lozenges. They promised dramatic results, and were apt to vanish when these results failed to materialize. To give a single example, an audacious woman called Joanna Stephens set herself up as an expert on how to relieve kidney stones; she was so persuasive that

Parliament paid her the magnificent sum of £5,000 for the secret of her remedy, which turned out to consist largely of dried snails, carrot and burdock seeds, soap and honey. Her success encouraged imitators, many of whom prescribed soap as a cure for gallstones. No less a figure than Sir Robert Walpole was so smitten with this form of treatment that at the time of his death he was reckoned to have consumed about 80 kilograms of it.

The quacks were enthusiastic manipulators of language. They made extensive use of obscure words, energetically appropriating the terms of natural philosophy. Anything that smacked of Latin learning was especially good, and so was any ingredient that could claim to have been sourced abroad – the balsam of Gilead, Japanese powders, Egyptian pills.[28] It is during this period of rampant quackery that *bona fide*, used adverbially since the sixteenth century, begins to be used as an adjective – a salesman's suspiciously vigorous assurance of sincerity. It is an example of a term that starts out as an element of legal jargon and in time becomes a commercial or academic buzzword before being fully absorbed into the mainstream; *caveat* is another such example, as are *ad hoc, in re, pro rata* and *verbatim*. Such terms were often to be found in newspapers, along with more recondite Latin snippets: *summum jus est summa injuria*, for instance, or *noli prosequi*.[29]

At the same time as Britain's consumer culture drew in foreign opportunists, it stimulated travel to their countries of origin. The period witnessed the second phase of heavy borrowing from Italian. Fashionable Britons spoke of venturing *alfresco*, or of harbouring private thoughts *in petto*. Hester Thrale could refer without explanation to *villeggiatura*, the habit of holidaying in the country. The old Puritan hostility to Italian culture was remedied by volumes such as William Huggins's new translation of Ariosto and by the popular *An Account of the Manners and Customs of Italy* (1768), written by Dr Johnson's friend Giuseppe Baretti. Addison's *Remarks on Several Parts of Italy* was another eloquent stimulus. Travel in Italy was considered a desirable part of a young man's education (the Grand Tour had first been mentioned in Richard Lascelles's *A Compleat Journey Through Italy* in 1670), and, as the masterworks of Italian art and literature were fetishized, so words such as *portfolio* were borrowed.

A less glamorous Italian word, *influenza*, cemented its position during an outbreak of the illness in 1743; in Italian, it had commonly been used of any epidemic, its name suggestive of the 'influence' of inexplicable occult forces.[30] *Malaria* first appears in 1740, in a letter of Horace Walpole's, complaining of the fevers suffered by summer visitors to Rome; early uses, including Walpole's, tended to be spelt *mal'aria*, which signals the word's origins in the Italian for 'bad air' – traceable at least as far back as a treatise published in 1560 by Francesco Sansovino.

There was also a cult of Italian musicians and singers, and the amounts earned in London by castrati such as Farinelli were the stuff of legend. Some of the castrati trafficked between the Protestant courts at Berlin, Braunschweig, Stuttgart and Bayreuth, periodically appearing at public operas, while others were active in Vienna, Munich, Hamburg and Mannheim. London was not among the most frequent ports of call, but it was a lucrative part of a complex international performance network.[31] The *mandolin* made its first appearance in 1707, when a Signior Conti performed in London 'upon his great Theorbo, and on the Mandoline, an instrument not known yet'.[32] The specifically musical sense of *maestro* was adopted in 1724; *concerto* in 1730; *impresario* in 1746; *bravura* in 1788. The approving cries *bravo* and *bravissimo* also achieved currency at this time. Meanwhile, a mass invasion of Italian violinists was inspired by the success of the Neapolitan Nicola Matteis; the phenomenon was noted by Fanny Burney's father, Charles, in his *A General History of Music* (1776–89), which introduced *melodrama, polyphonic* and *choreography*. London's musical culture was entrepreneurial, yet patronage also played a part, and the success of the *virtuoso* – whose very name, though etymologically indicative of virtue, became during this period something of a slur – was dependent on his ability to flatter affluent and well-connected socialites.[33] Hester Thrale appalled Dr Johnson by marrying her daughters' music master, Gabriel Piozzi: men such as Piozzi were supposed to sing and play the violin or spinet, not marry rich widows.

The success of impresarios and of the artists whose talents they paraded was a symptom of a booming consumer culture. The eighteenth century is commonly considered to have witnessed a 'shopping revolution', in which traditional markets and fairs were superseded by fixed commercial outlets. While the reality is more complex – with different retail circuits coexisting happily – it seems fair to say that increasing consumption and a burgeoning appetite for luxury goods are arresting features of the age, which has been dubbed the 'century of the shopkeeper'.[34] Dr Johnson could in 1755 trace *luxury*'s development, from 'addictedness to pleasure' via 'lewdness' and 'exuberance' to 'delicious fare'. His occasional antagonist the philosopher David Hume was one of the most impressive apologists for the appetite for what he called 'innocent luxury': for consumer goods like Hepplewhite cabinets and Axminster carpets, and for imported articles such as calico from Gujarat (which as Johnson explains is 'sometimes stained with gay and beautiful colours') and Japanese lacquerware. Chinese *porcelain* was popular, too. The word comes from the Italian for a cowrie shell; literally, *porcellana* was a 'little pig', and the connection seems grounded in the glossy shell's resemblance either to a pig's back or to a sow's glisteningly crinkled vagina.[35] Silks from Syria and Persia, Turkish mohair and West Indian coffee flowed into Britain's ports, and in the opposite direction there travelled woollens and furnishings. One area of real British excellence was metalwork: in the handsome new shops of London's Piccadilly and St James's, glittering buttons and buckles, ladles, spoons and candelabra competed for attention, and shoppers travelled across Europe to buy British toys and metalware.[36] Entrepreneurial craftsmen from Sheffield and Birmingham satisfied the desire for cheaper, more fashionable, designs. Novelty was vital to commercial success, and with it came slick jargon and a habit of grandiloquent puffery. Philosophically freighted words such as *enthusiasm* and *ideal* began to free themselves of their historical burdens and become part of the everyday language of sensory relish.

The increase in people travelling for pleasure created a market for books offering basic guidance about foreign languages. *The Traveller's Interpreter* (1728) was one such publication, containing 'A Vocabulary of select and necessary Words' in English, Dutch, French and Italian, and 'Rules for pronouncing each Language'. Intrepid Britons were usefully informed how to refer when abroad to a 'silly fellow' or a trollop, and how to name such everyday essentials as sundials, turpentine and muffs. Different reasons for needing to be competent in other tongues are implicit in James Willson's *The Soldier's Pocket Dictionary, Or Friend in Need* (1794), which provides guidance on words 'In General Use, and most likely to occur in Military Service' in English, German, Dutch, French, Italian and Spanish, including such phrases as 'Are there any marshes in the way?', 'My wound bleeds afresh' and – a wonderful solution when all else fails – 'Look into this little book.'

Travel literature shows the broadening horizons of English-speakers' authority. Soon after the accession of George III, John Duncombe could salute the new king with the mock-Horatian assurance that 'Britain's righteous laws' and 'Exulting commerce' encompassed giant tracts of land:

> The faithless Cherokee obeys,
> Rich Senegal her tribute pays,
> And Ganges' tyrant shakes with fear,
> For vengeance whispers, 'Clive is near.'[37]

One prolific source of new terms connected with abroad was Lady Mary Wortley Montagu. She was an accomplished networker, who brought to Britain the practice of inoculation against smallpox and started a magazine entitled the *Nonsense of Common-Sense*. Above all, she travelled: to Florence, Geneva, Avignon, Brescia and Venice, and through Hungary, Bohemia and Germany. She spent seventeen months in Turkey, with her husband, Edward, who was the British ambassador in Constantinople. A prodigious letter-writer, Lady Mary penned 'highly polished bulletins'. Yet what look to be 'the epistolary equivalent of *vers de société*, products of a decorative, brittle sensibility', are sustained by both 'the strong undertow of melancholy' and a gift for embellishment.[38] Her imports are wide-ranging: she can ask for a letter to be directed *chez* an aristocratic friend, or refer to a *fracas* breaking out in polite company, in addition to adopting words like *cicisbeo* (a married woman's approved bit on the side) and *feridgi* (a Turkish garment, not unlike a nightgown). She may well be the first British author to use *née* to introduce a married woman's maiden name, to refer to the pleasurable condition of *volupté*

(although *voluptee*, meaning 'lust', can be found in Wyclif's translation of the Bible), and to mention an *homme d'affaires* – explaining,
'Every pasha has his Jew, who is his *homme d'affaires*.'

Montagu's writings were an antidote to the often ill-informed
works of her contemporaries. For instance, John Campbell and
Charles Thompson both managed to produce accounts of the Levant
without ever going there. There was, moreover, a fashion for imaginative and sometimes moralistic forays into the Islamic world,
which can be dated to the Antoine Galland's 1704 translation of the
Arabian Nights. Their subject matter includes caravans, elephants and
camels, flowers and jewels, and a common trope is the impenetra-
bility of the East, its religions and mysteries.[39] Thus in Samuel Johnson's
play *Irene*, which was written in the 1730s, we hear of the nymph
known as a *houri*, in William Beckford's *Vathek* (1786) of a *ghoul* (from
the Arabic), in Thomas Moore's *Lalla Rookh* (1817) of a *kanoon* (a
type of harp), and in Felicia Hemans's unfinished poem 'Superstition
and Revelation' (*c*.1820) of 'the glistening serab' – that is, a mirage.

Although trade with the Near and Middle East shrivelled in the
eighteenth century, the distribution of traders was wider than ever.
Syria exported to London mohair yarn, raw silk and galls for use
in the production of dyes, while indigo and spices from British
India and woollens from England were sent to the markets at
Aleppo.[40] Robert Wood's *The Ruins of Palmyra* (1753) and *The Ruins
of Balbec* (1757) heightened interest in Islamic architecture, while
Richard Pococke's *Description of the East* (1743–5) provided for non-
specialists an account of Egypt, Syria, Palestine and Cyprus. Pococke
affords us a first sighting of the word *fellah*, a term for Egyptian
peasants – commonly encountered in the plural *fellahin*. In the next
century the challenge of understanding the Middle East would be
taken up by A. W. Kinglake and Sir Richard Burton, among others.

The literature of exploration contained a multitude of different
voices. Italy and France remained the most popular destinations for
tourists, but a few more serious travellers made for the Low Countries
and the Balkans. Mary Wollstonecraft's *Letters Written during a Short
Residence in Sweden, Norway, and Denmark* (1796) promoted the image
of a romantically moonlit Scandinavia, complete with castles, water-
falls and vast wildernesses. William Tooke's *View of the Russian Empire*

(1799), the fruit of more than twenty years as chaplain to the British trading station at St Petersburg, included such novelties as *kibitka*, a circular tent covered with felt, the sleeveless cloak called a *sarafan*, a fish known as *sudak*, and a type of leather called *yuft*. African travel offered a more dangerous romance: the quest for Timbuktu or a route through the Niger valley, and later David Livingstone's opening of 'God's Highway' along the Zambezi River. Livingstone would discover the *soko*, an ape that lived in the area around Lake Tanganyika, and would introduce *tampan*, a bloodsucking tick, and *lechwe*, the Sesuto name for a water antelope. Long before him his fellow Scot the explorer Mungo Park had noted in his bestselling *Travels in the Interior Districts of Africa* (1799) the *koonting*, a kind of guitar, and the *kora*, a stringed instrument much like a harp. These words presage outlandishness, not utility.

The North and South Poles were also keenly sought. It was on Constantine Phipps's mission to the North Pole in 1773 that a young Horatio Nelson narrowly evaded the clutches of a polar bear. That same year James Cook became the first man to cross the Antarctic Circle – though the continent itself would not be sighted until 1820. But it is for other pioneering journeys that Cook is known. Between 1768 and 1779 he led three expeditions to the Pacific. In October 1769 the crew of Cook's *Endeavour* made the first of several contacts with New Zealand Maoris. The following month his party's chief naturalist, Joseph Banks, could note in his journal that he had seen a Maori stockade and that it was known as a *pa*. Cook's crew were in an unfamiliar zone; there was a world of wonders in each new landfall.

In July 1770 Cook encountered aboriginal Australians speaking Guugu Yimidhirr, a language in which there is a whole special vocabulary for talking to one's brother-in-law.[41] One of these natives 'had a hole through the Bridge of his nose in which he stuck a piece of bone as thick as my finger'.[42] There were further surprises: flying foxes, hundreds of new species of plant, and the kangaroo – two were shot and eaten by members of Cook's party, who reported that they tasted just like venison. It has been charmingly alleged that the word *kangaroo* resulted from a misunderstanding – that the explorers asked what the animal was, received in the local language the answer 'I don't know,' and interpreted this as the creature's name – but in fact it was a corruption of the Guugu Yimidhirr *gangurru*, the word for a large black male roo. As it would turn out, the native languages were even more vulnerable than this creature. Within seventy-five years of contact with Europeans, the Aboriginal peoples of Tasmania were wiped out, and with them disappeared their speech.[43] When an authoritative history of the Australian language family was published in 1980, the author could report that of the approximately 200 languages spoken in Australia before Europeans set foot there, at least a quarter had become extinct. Another 100 were 'on the path towards extinction'.[44]

Cook devoted nine years to his voyages, acutely aware that he was charting previously unknown territories. In his journals he notes local words: the Tahitian girdle known as a *maro*, the woven cloak called a *kakahu*, the Tongan tomb known as a *fa'itoka*. These terms have hardly imprinted themselves on English, but in his papers we also find the first mentions of not just the *kangaroo*, but also *taboo*. The word was used among the so-called Friendly Islanders – as an adjective – of items set aside for the use of priests and potentates. Cook had no grasp of the subtleties of the Tongan language, and in importing the word he gave it a more general purpose, claiming it 'has a very comprehensive meaning; but, in general, signifies that a thing is forbidden'. He wrote as well of the practice of 'tattowing' – the first sighting of the word we know as *tattoo*. (The other kind of *tattoo*, the military display, comes from the Dutch *taptoe*, meaning 'Close off the tap,' a cry accompanied by a drum beat as tippling soldiers were summoned back to their garrison.) In 1774, when Fanny Burney met Omai, she noted that his hands were liberally covered with tattooed designs, and the *Gentleman's Magazine* displayed an image of a native New Zealander 'curiously Tataowed', which showed 'the manner in which . . . [they] both paint and ornament themselves . . . different from anything of the like kind hitherto discovered'.[45]

In the eyes of the British public, Cook was a hero. By increasing their knowledge of science and geography without doing obvious damage, he made Britons proud of their technology (he used new instruments to help him makes his charts) and allowed them to feel comfortable about their country's imperial role. Modern Australia began as a penal colony, to which around 160,000 convicts were deported, and until 1830 convicts outnumbered free settlers by at least four to one. Beginning in 1787, it was populated – in the words of Robert Hughes – 'to defend English property not from the frog-eating invader across the Channel but from the marauder within'. This colonial experiment transformed the unexplored continent into a giant jail: 'The space around it, the very air and sea, the whole transparent labyrinth of the South Pacific, would become a wall 14,000 miles thick.' The landscape pulsated with oddities – 'koalas clambered through the gum-tree branches or sprawled sedately in the comfortable forks munching their bunches of leaves', and then there were wombats, bandicoots, spiny anteaters.[46] Borrowings from the native languages consisted largely of words for the island's bizarre fauna, and included the *boomerang* (from *bumarin* in the Dharuk language of New South Wales) used in hunting them, but the often awkward relationship between the Aboriginal peoples and the incomers kept these verbal infusions to a minimum.

Writing to his aunt in 1793, the artist Thomas Watling, sentenced to fourteen years in Australia for forging a banknote, depicted the colony as a 'luxuriant museum', full of birds and plants 'that must baffle the happiest efforts of the pencil'. Yet of the natives he remarked, 'Irascibility, ferocity, cunning, treachery, revenge, filth, and immodesty, are strikingly their dark characteristics – their virtues are so far from conspicuous, that I have not, as yet, been able to discern them.'[47] Watling's attitude was representative. His peers took little interest in the language of the island's long-standing inhabitants. The Aborigines had been there for about forty millennia; the sudden surge of European-style civilization barely touched them. When the newcomers did pick up words used by the indigenous peoples, their motives were pragmatic. For this reason Aboriginal words have gained almost no hold beyond Australia. An English-speaker in Alice Springs may have some use for the words *pitchi* and *cooliman* (types of vessel used for carrying, respectively, food and water), but they are hardly a help to a Chicagoan or a Glaswegian. *Corroboree*, a term for a ceremonial dance, is typical of the type of

Aboriginal word that has made a small impression on Australian English, but has hardly become important beyond Australia. In the same class are *billabong*, *didgeridoo* and *quokka*. More familiar is *cooee*, which the OED defines as 'the call or cry used as a signal by the Australian aborigines, and adopted by the colonists in the bush'. Only a handful of other widely circulated English words have originated in Australia. Some will be familiar to anyone who has seen Barry Humphries's comic creations Barry McKenzie, Sir Les Patterson and Dame Edna Everage – and indeed to anyone who has spent much time socializing with Australians, who are on the whole both gregarious and addicted to foreign travel. Thus *larrikin*, *dinkum* and *plonk* (cheap wine). Despite concessions to multicultur- alism, the character of modern Australia is prosperous, coastal, urban and white. The country's deep history of linguistic diversity has barely been registered by the rest of the world, or indeed by the majority of Australians. Its proud independence notwithstanding, Australia is powerfully affected by the influence of America, and, culturally at least, little travels in the opposite direction.

Not long after Cook discovered New South Wales, the first British settlement in South Africa was established when an expeditionary force invaded. A larger, more secure, settlement was founded on the Eastern Cape in the 1820s. The Portuguese, Huguenots and Dutch had all preceded the British in colonizing the region, as had the Bushmen and Khoikhoi, and the positions inherited by English as it became the official language of the region were riddled with ethnic and linguistic tensions. English in South Africa has absorbed huge numbers of words from the black languages and also many from Afrikaans, the language seeded there by the Dutch settlers who began to arrive in the seventeenth century. Yet only a few South African words have become well known, and the matters with which they deal are plainly African: *trek*, *biltong*, *wildebeest*, *veldt* and *meerkat*. *Kraal*, derived from the Portuguese *curral*, meaning 'farmyard', has been confined to South and Central Africa, whereas its sister *corral* has travelled more widely.

In 1840, the year the transportation of convicts to eastern Australia was ended, the Treaty of Waitangi provided for New Zealand to become yet another British colony. *Kiwi*, *tutu* and *haka* are the Maori words most familiar to English-speakers, while foreign visitors to New Zealand cite *kumara*, a sweet potato, and *paua*, a kind of shell used for making jewellery, and English-speaking New Zealanders may consider as part of their own word-stock items such as *tui*, a parrot-like bird, and *totara*, an indigenous species of girthy tree. Samoan terms, however, have made a negligible impact outside New Zealand's own Samoan community.

In Australia, South Africa and New Zealand, then, the contributions of the indigenous languages to the English word-stock have been modest. But in another colony – older than any of these three, more deeply explored, and also more responsive – the story could not have been more different.

11. Teapot

A vessel in which tea is made and brought to the table

A compound of *tea* – a word probably learnt from Dutch
merchants, who had acquired it via Malay from the Amoy
dialect of Chinese – and *pot*, a word found occasionally in
Old English (its source unclear) and reinforced in Middle
English by the influence of French

The narrator of Salman Rushdie's novel *The Moor's Last Sigh* (1995)
sums up the Western enthusiasm for India. 'Pepper', he says, 'brought
Vasco da Gama's tall ships across the ocean, from Lisbon's Tower of
Belém to the Malabar Coast: first to Calicut and later, for its lagoony
harbour, to Cochin. English and French sailed in the wake of that
first-arrived Portugee.' Then, for extra frisson, he quotes an observation of his mother's: 'From the beginning, what the world wanted
from bloody mother India was daylight-clear. They came for the
hot stuff, just like any man calling on a tart.'[1]

As we have seen, the European appetite for spices was a significant driver of imperial expansionism, and in European lore India was
often presented as a sort of exotic pantry, stocked with condiments
and elixirs. The fate of imperial Rome served as a warning of how
costly the lust for such delicacies could be. Decadent Roman appetites
had necessitated a succession of wildly expensive forays into the Indian
market: pepper, cinnamon, saffron and cardamom were especially
valued, and of these cinnamon was the most sought after and the
most expensive. Spices were used not only in cooking, but also in
the manufacture of perfumes. The Romans had little to trade with
the Indians – except their silver and gold.[2] It seems appropriate that
Petronius's gaudy Trimalchio, whose dinner menu includes dormice
sprinkled with poppyseed and honey, considers sending to India just
for some mushroom seed. Such extravagance steadily depleted Roman
reserves of currency, and the large caches of Roman coins found in

modern Kerala (and as far afield as Vietnam) suggest where much of it ended up. A craving for 'the hot stuff' cost the Romans dear.

Da Gama's Portuguese were thus renewing an old connection. The risks were high – in the early voyages, they lost half their ships – but the rewards were believed to justify them. Trade was always a higher priority for them than conquest, and to facilitate it they set up *feitorias* – possibly the immediate source of the English word *factory* – on the coasts of Africa and Asia. In 1445 they positioned the first of these fortified bases at Arguin off the coast of modern Mauritania; their first in India was built at Cochin in 1503, followed a couple of years later by another at Cannanore. In 1518 a fort was established at Colombo. With their presence in Brazil to boot, Portugal's power spanned four continents. Their national poet Luis de Camões conceived his epic *The Lusiads* while soldiering in India. An apostle of empire, he boasted of his country's mission 'por mares nunca dantes navegados' – that is, 'for seas no one had sailed before'.

The Portuguese spread their language, which became a lingua franca of African and Asian commerce, and with it their Catholic faith. In India their stronghold was Goa, a position created when Afonso de Albuquerque grappled it from the Sultan of Bijapur in 1510, and formalized two decades later. Control of Goa, Ormuz and Malacca ensured their dominance of the key spice routes in the Indian Ocean. While they were about it, they muscled in on the trade in Arabian horses, but cloves and cinnamon were their real business.[3] The Portuguese presence in India gave English the words *monsoon*, *betel*, *mango* and *tamarind*, and it was in India that they first saw the *coconut*, which took its name from its base's supposed resemblance to a grinning face – in Portuguese, *coco* signifies a grin or a grimace. *Amah*, the Anglo-Indian name for a wet nurse, derives from this language too, and it appears that an encounter with Portuguese adventurers in Mauritius in 1628 alerted English-speakers to the existence of the *dodo*, so called after the Portuguese *doudo*, 'a simpleton', and once known to scientists by the sad name *Didus ineptus*.

British interest in India began, like that of the Portuguese, with a desire for strong flavours. An enduring feature of the British kitchen is a taste for foods that combine sweet and sour – for Worcester sauce, pickled relishes, and chutneys. But, for the British,

India's riches were not just gastronomic. Commerce drove the relationship. Fine muslins, colour-fast painted and printed chintzes, carpets, jewellery and household ornaments, opium and tea were sourced in India, and porcelain was sent home from further east. Ralph Fitch, who journeyed to India in the 1580s, enthused about 'very rich rice', 'great store of cloth' and people digging gold from the earth, and a generation later the diplomat Sir Thomas Roe could expatiate freely on the rubies, diamonds and 'massie gold' with which the nobles bedecked themselves.[4] In July 1661 Samuel Pepys recorded spending 34 shillings on an Indian gown, and in September 1663 he mentioned that he had had a stressful time of buying his wife 'a painted Indian callico' with which to line the walls of her study.

Half a century later, Charles Lockyer's account of trade in India sheds light on some of the goods most prized: rattan and sago, betel nuts, Nankeen fans, ivory, 'Cardamums from the *Malabar* Coast', 'Acheen from the *Syndi* Islands', 'Palampores, Pelongs, flower'd Damasks', turmeric, 'Sugar and Sugar Candy from *Bengall*', saltpetre, 'Hubble-bubble Canes', and from China 'Plates with blue Flowers, thin and well burnt' as well as silk flowers and brass locks.[5] Lockyer also mentions a snake he shot that had swallowed two hens and five chickens, the monkeys held in religious regard by the Hindus ('I cannot tell if we are allow'd to shoot them'), and jackals 'remarkable for Howling in the Night'.[6]

Lockyer's is a splendid display of early eighteenth-century taste, but words of Indian origin had been edging into English since the reign of Queen Elizabeth. Some are easily recognized: others are not. How many of us immediately see the Indian origins of, say, *cushy* or *swastika*? In the late nineteenth century, Henry Yule and Arthur Coke Burnell created a glossary of words from this source: *Hobson-Jobson*. 'Of words that seem to have been admitted to full franchise, we may give examples in *curry, toddy, veranda, cheroot, loot, nabob, teapot, sepoy, cowry*; and of others familiar enough to the ... English ear ... *chowry, baboo, mahout, aya.*' In addition there are items 'long since fully assimilated, which really originated in the adoption of an Indian word, or the modification of an Indian proper name': examples are *gingham, palanquin* and *chintz*. Yule and Burnell note a further class of 'words which are essentially Portuguese, among Anglo-Indian colloquialisms'; this includes *caste, mosquito, joss* and *cobra*.[7]

Hobson-Jobson takes its name from what they describe as 'an Anglo-Saxon version of the wailings of the Mahommedans as they beat their breasts in the procession of the *Moharram*'. What the British heard was '*Ya Hasan! Ya Husayn!*'; the two names were those of Muhammad's grandsons, killed fighting for their faith. Its anglicized form was 'typical . . . of the most highly assimilated class of Anglo-Indian *argot*'. When Yule and Burnell were writing, the phrase was in frequent use by British soldiers in the Punjab to refer to 'a native festal excitement': now it is remembered only as the title of this strange, discursive dictionary. But other words have held fast. Next time you see or refer to a *dinghy*, pause a moment to recall that it is Bengali, and, when you wash your hair, reflect perhaps on the origins of the word *shampoo*, which are in the imperative (*champo*) of the Hindi *champna*, a verb that conveys the idea of kneading and pressing the body to relieve fatigue and stimulate the circulation.

Similar examples abound. A *thug* was originally in Hindi a cheat or impostor, and the word was applied by the British to 'phansigars', who throttled travellers – supposedly for sacrificial purposes, but often for more immediate and obvious reward. *Bungalow* is Hindustani, and means literally 'belonging to Bengal'. From the same source we get *bandanna* and *gymkhana* and the *tom-tom* drum. From Hindi we get *bangle* – its original is *bangri*, which denoted a ring of coloured glass. From this language we also derive *toddy*, which we now use to refer to a hot, spiced drink; its root, *tarri*, is the name of fermented palm sap. The breakfast dish *kedgeree* takes its name from the Hindi *khichri*, and when we use the word *cot* of a light bedstead it is a corruption of the Hindi *khat*, a term which could also signify a hammock or couch.

Pyjamas is another import from India. In fact *pyjama* derived from the Persian words for 'foot' and 'garment', and in its Indian context it was used only of loose-fitting trousers, rather than of the entire ensemble of bedwear. *Catamaran*, spotted by William Dampier, can be traced to the Tamil *kattu-maram*, meaning literally 'tied wood', and the same language is the source of *mulligatawny*, *vetiver* and *pagoda* (the last picked up via Portuguese). Urdu provides words which strike us immediately as having an Indian context: the respectful title *sahib* and the soft cheese known as *paneer*. *Tank* is considered in *Hobson-Jobson* 'one of those perplexing words which seems to have a double origin, in this case one Indian, the other European'; in the Marathi language of western India *tanken* is the word for a reservoir or water butt, and the Portuguese used *tanque* ('pond') of Indian reservoirs and wells. *Polo* is traceable to a Tibetan word for a ball. *Cashmere* is named after the province in the western Himalayas where that soft wool, so beloved of moths, has traditionally been harvested.

Other terms have travelled a long way from their Indian origins. *Pundit* is one: originally it was the name for a learned Hindu versed in Sanskrit – that ancient, lexically rich and now ceremonial language that has given us the Upanishads, the Mahabharata and the Kama Sutra. The very name of Sanskrit means 'synthesized'; it denotes the formal language set out in textbooks, rather than the naturally occurring dialects, and it hints as well at the process of *sandhi* ('putting together') which allows the boundaries between individual words to blur into a fluid yarn of syllables. Pundits were required to unpack its ambiguities. Even after Muslim invaders had seized control of the subcontinent – a process that began in the tenth century as they thundered down on horseback from Afghanistan, and was completed in stages over the next half a millennium – Sanskrit remained. The incomers spoke Turkic, prayed in Arabic, and read Persian literature, and Persian became established as the language of administration. But, though Sanskrit lost its position as 'the representative language of culture' in the region, its status as the sacred language of Hinduism and Buddhism ensured that it did not fade into oblivion.[8] The pundit preserves its rhythms and instructions.

Sanskrit itself lies behind many English words, such as *mantra*, *avatar* and *yoga*, which literally mean 'instrument of thought', 'descent' and 'union'. *Jungle* derives from the Sanskrit *jangala*, which was used to denote a desert or wasteland. As the word filtered into other languages, it came to signify any section of land that could not be cultivated, and among Anglo-Indians it meant 'a forest; a thicket; a tangled wilderness'. For its part *juggernaut* can be traced to the

Sanskrit name of the god Krishna, although its English sense derives directly from Hindi. The annual festival of this deity involves its idol being dragged along on a giant carriage, and many devotees are crushed beneath its wheels. Hence the word's use of any heavy vehicle – and hence Mr Enfield's description, in *The Strange Case of Dr Jekyll and Mr Hyde*, of the deformed Hyde being 'like some damned Juggernaut'. Sanskrit also furnishes *nirvana* (literally 'blown out', like a candle, and thus suggestive of a state where one has gone beyond mere sentient existence). *Karma* is from the same source; the *OED*'s nice definition – 'in Buddhism, the sum of a person's actions in one of his successive states of existence, regarded as determining his fate in the next' – can hardly fail to make one think of how irreverently the term is now used. Another such irreverence: whether wittingly or not, the drug *Viagra* preserves the Sanskrit *vyaghra*, meaning 'tiger'.

The accumulation of these many borrowings was gradual, but it hints at the different British approaches to India: magisterial, curatorial, exoticist. Either the British were preoccupied with the exercise of power, or they minutely catalogued and exhibited Indian life and culture, or they dwelt on the country's wonders.[9] The imperial experience in India was different from that in America. India was 'a place of passage, not of settlement', and, as the Persian chronicler Ghulam Husain Khan remarked in the late eighteenth century, the English were accustomed to 'coming for a number of years, and then . . . going away to pay a visit to their native land, without any one of them showing an inclination to fix himself in this land'.[10] While there were individuals and families who entrenched themselves, there was little desire for the fixity of settlement; riches, not self-reinvention, were the goal.

Reaching back to examine the beginnings of this connection, we can see its special character. The East India Company was granted a royal charter by Queen Elizabeth on 31 December 1600, at a time when the American experiment seemed to be in jeopardy. The Company's 218 petitioners were to be permitted a monopoly on all English trade in Asia and the Pacific. Many were Levant merchants, eager to diversify as the price of pepper slumped. Their focus was, as the Company's name suggests, the East Indies.

It was a fabulous opportunity, a shimmering fantasy of drugs and silks and perfumes; but trade in the region was dominated by the Dutch. They had supplanted the Portuguese after King Sebastian's disastrous invasion of Morocco in 1578 had shattered Portugal's army and trading interests. The Dutch, united in their own company, had a huge slice of the global trade in pepper, sandalwood, camphor, mace and cloves, and their other exports from Indonesia included gold, gems, pearls, rare birds and tortoise shells. They posed a threat to English interests in the Levant, and it was vital to check Dutch progress in Asia.

The English joined the race for control of the East Indies in 1601. In 1603 they secured a toehold on Pulo Run, one of the tiny volcanic Banda Islands. Their main goal was to bring back nutmeg, a spice believed to have extraordinary properties. It was reputed to detoxify the spleen and the stomach, improve eyesight, and cure dysentery and head colds. It was also understood to act as a powerful aphrodisiac. Nutmeg sold in England for more than 500 times as much as it cost on Run. The island would in due course form part of a symbolic exchange: although Peter Stuyvesant had surrendered the Dutch colony of Manhattan to the English in September 1664, a neat exchange was effected under the Treaty of Breda three years later, when the English formally renounced their right to Run in exchange for this apparently unpromising American territory.

The East India Company's early voyages were profitable, and the level of profit rose with each expedition. But the focus began to shift. In 1607 the Company sent ships east via the Arabian Sea. One of the senior officers, William Hawkins, was commissioned to explore the potential of the territory we now know as Gujarat.[11] English traders arrived at Surat, the trading centre of the Mughal Empire, in late August 1608. John Jourdain was one of a second party who passed via Table Bay and Zanzibar to Aden, and from there on to Surat, where he bought 'some cloves and baftas' (the latter being a kind of cheap fabric), noted another Englishman's 'dieing with eateing opium', and remarked with some amusement the local overlord's 'delight . . . in strange toyes'.[12] Here in miniature is the story of the English in India: the acquisition of goods either rare or cheap, the reckless intoxication, and the Indians' appetite for English curios, in return for which they would bestow their favour.

In the sixteenth century a few Hindi words were learnt. *Rajah* is one of the first to be met, in 1555. There were far more in the century that followed: *juggernaut* and *kedgeree* I have mentioned, but we also get *guru, dhoti, ghee, dungaree* and *pukka. Dungaree* is a corruption of the name of a part of Bombay once noted for its rough calico. *Pukka* signified in Hindi a plethora of qualities: being strong, ripe, properly cooked, secure, or made of brick.

The factory the English built at Surat, stoutly fortified, was the launchpad for trade routes into Persia and what is today Indonesia. Indigo was one of the main materials to be ferried back to England; another was cotton, prized as a light and washable alternative to more traditional textiles. John Keay explains in his history of the Company that 'Indian cottons were about to invade English domestic life. Napkins and table-cloths, bed sheets and soft furnishings, not to mention underwear and dress fabrics, quite suddenly became indispensable to every respectable household . . . Having first invaded the larder, Eastern produce was about to take over the linen cupboard.'[13]

The Company's imports and exports were controversial: they appeared to be damaging English manufacture, and were of little use to the majority of the population. The entire business seemed to embody the height of decadence. And, while James I took a passionate interest in the Company's affairs, those who followed him were less enthusiastic. Charles I and Cromwell both received huge loans from the Company, which they had no intention of repaying. The Company's fortunes teetered. Investment in consolidating its position in India was all but impossible. Moreover, communication was a persistent problem. Missionaries found they had to have a command of Portuguese to make much progress with would-be converts. Yet in the end it was these patient men of faith who did the most to spread a knowledge of English.

The East India Company's key bases were at Madras (now called Chennai), Bombay (now usually Mumbai) and Calcutta (now Kolkata). The first of these was achieved in 1654; the others followed in 1668 and 1690. Madras has its origins in a grant made to the East India Company in 1639; a fort was founded on the narrow strip of sand by one of the Company's factors, Francis Day. Before the early nineteenth century, Bombay was an archipelago of seven islands; they were taken by the Portuguese in 1534, formed part of the dowry when Charles II married Catherine of Braganza in 1662, and were leased to the Company for the sum of £10 a year. Calcutta is generally believed to have been founded by Job Charnock, the Company's agent at Hugli; it would in due course serve as the British capital in India for almost 140 years. In each case, local rulers granted territory and trading rights to the settlers: the colonial presence was achieved through 'Indian permission, partnership and complicity in the business of making money'.[14]

Only in 1717, when it achieved exemption from paying customs duties in Bengal, did the Company's Indian fortunes truly begin to rise. What had started as an affiliation of Elizabethan men of business would become a behemoth of mercantile power, metamorphosing from a commercial venture into a vast political and military machine. A nineteenth-century commentator aptly described it as 'a Company which carries a sword in the one hand, and a ledger in the other – which maintains armies and retails tea'.[15] Yet the persistence of political squabbles with France and Spain inhibited trade; the expanding Company's expenses spiralled upward; and the tragedy of the Black Hole of Calcutta depressed public perception of the opportunities the colony had to offer.

Victory at the Battle of Plassey in 1757 was a pivotal moment in establishing the East India Company's political power, although it took time for this to be recognized. Robert Clive comprehensively defeated the Nawab of Bengal, Siraj ud-Daula, having already coaxed the Nawab's subjects into his thrall. Siraj's successor, Mir Jafar Ali Khan, awarded Clive a *jagit* – a handsome share of agricultural revenue worth almost £30,000 a year. The controversial Englishman was to prove an efficient and overbearing engineer of British supremacy in India. Thus a Muslim raj was supplanted by a British one, and, according to superstition, this was destined to last a hundred years before being supplanted in its turn by a Hindu raj. Plassey made an indelible imprint on native minds: the British, with their small-calibre cannon and howitzers, were seen as masters of technology. Once the French had been defeated at Wandiwash in 1760, and following the capture and trashing of their base in Pondicherry the following year, the British position was cemented. Thereafter, a programme of treaties and measured aggression was conducted, and its material rewards were huge. In the year of the success at Plassey, a contributor to the *Gentleman's Magazine* could write of Bengal, 'According to the report of travellers, [it] is one of most fruitful countries in the world, superior even to *Egypt* itself.' It abounded with 'rice, corn, and fruits of all kinds, which the inhabitants candy and preserve . . . [and] *European* ships supply themselves with biscuit, fowls, pork, and other provisions at very easy rates'. It also yielded 'opium, wax, civet, long pepper, and ginger'.[16]

It was clear, though, that the British in India had to face many hindrances and hazards: dust, disease (for instance, *beriberi*, which takes its name from a Sinhalese word meaning 'very weak'), snakes and scorpions, the occasional tiger, a riot of bowel complaints, the complexities of Indian society with its approximately 200 languages and countless protocols, and also boredom. To this list Emma Roberts, in her *Scenes and Characteristics of Hindostan* (1835), adds another unhappy detail: the 'incessant clamour' of the tom-tom, 'an instrument which is introduced into every mansion . . . for the ostensible purpose of charming the young folks', but which permits an 'almost constant drumming . . . from morning until night, a horrid discord, which, on a very hot day, aggravates every other torment'.[17]

A further risk was drug-induced folly. As early as the 1670s, a seaman by the name of Thomas Bowrey saw Bengalis drinking *bhang*. He and a few other sailors bought pints of this cannabis-based concoction in the bazaar; the result was a mixture of merriment and anguish. As Richard Davenport-Hines observes, a 'sailor who fancied himself an emperor, and his distracted colleague who hid his head inside . . . [a] jar, provided prototypes of Western behaviour that have endured over three centuries'. Puritan habits of thought 'had turned such experimental pleasures into an illicit pursuit': the result was that use had to be clandestine, and this increased its excitement.[18] Bowrey had stumbled on the principle that little can do more to advertise an illicit pursuit than an exotic name. Today, mixed with yoghurt, this explosively named substance makes the 'special lassis' beloved of thrill-seeking tourists. Bowrey was an early thrill-seeker, but suffered no ill effects. He would go on to compile the first Malay–English dictionary, a useful volume from which one could even learn the Malay for 'The Kingdom of this World is only a similitude of the Kingdom of the World to come, which is exceeding great, and there is no end to that Kingdom.'[19] He is the first Englishman to mention the *pelandok*, a yellow muntjac which is a staple of Malay folklore. (*Muntjac* itself is from Sundanese, a language spoken in the west of Java.) He also provides explanations of Malay words with which we are now quite familiar: *amok, bamboo, gong* and *sarong* – the last of these magnificently defined as 'a Sheath, a Scabbard, Case, Coope, Hive, Nest, Frame, as of a picture, Quiver for arrows, the Maw of any living creature, a Webb'.

What Thomas Bowrey witnessed in Bengal were the hazards inherent within India's bounty. Negotiating a path through the subcontinent's complex and often dangerous hinterland required the use of local expertise. Of necessity, business was done through bi-lingual go-betweens. A sound knowledge of Portuguese was even more valuable for men of business than it was for those trying to spread the word of God. In the provinces of Gujarat and Bengal the native who lubricated contact was known as a *banian* (the word was first recorded by Hakluyt, and now means a merchant or entre-preneur). Elsewhere he was often a *dubash* – the Hindi name for a person competent in two different languages.[20] When John Fryer, author of *A New Account of East India and Persia* (1698), fetched up in the fishing port of Masulipatnam on the Coromandel Coast, he was surprised to be offered the services of a local man who had this title. Fryer's book is worth pausing over; it was the fruit of nine years' travel, and includes such novelties as *to snickersnee*, a verb to convey the idea of fighting with a long knife, best known now for its appearance (as a noun) in Gilbert and Sullivan's *The Mikado*. Fryer, a Cambridge-educated doctor – soppy-stern if we credit the image that serves as his book's frontispiece – is the first Englishman to mention a *maharaja*. He is also the first to use *pukka*, and at various points in his account he can report that a fishing town is 'peculiarly notable for a Fish called the *Bumbelo*', that anyone who fails to pay customs duties is threatened with 'a *Chawbuck*, a great Whip' (compare the Afrikaans, *sjambok*), that the Indian ships are built with a timber he identifies as *teak*, and that the natives use *congee* for starching clothes.[21]

The dubash and the maharaja were at two ends of a spectrum of subtly graded status. Titles in India were minutely hierarchical, and roles rigidly defined. A grandee could be a *nawab* or a *rajah* or a *pasha* or many other things besides. A *rajput* was a member of the Hindu warrior caste; a *talukdar* was the holder of a hereditary estate. In Bengal, land could be held by *zamindars* or *ryots*. A *jama* was a revenue demand payable by zamindars; a *patwari* was a zamindar officer who kept a village's accounts; a *kist* was an instalment of the payment made by tenants to the zamindars or by the zamindars to the government.[22] David Gilmour's study of life in the Victorian Raj, entitled *The Ruling Caste*, begins of necessity with a two-page glossary of Indian and Anglo-Indian terms, featuring a mixture of the fairly well known (*purdah*, *ayah*, the snack known as *tiffin*) and the distinctly bizarre – such as *poodle-faker*, a word for a master of seduction, and *chota hazri*, a term for a light early breakfast. Here too we find *badmash*, a rogue; *kheddah*, the capture of wild elephants; *mali*, a gardener; *tonga*, a two-wheeled vehicle usually drawn by ponies; and *zenana*, 'the area in a household where the women are kept secluded'.[23] There were no English equivalents for such terms. To understand the structure of Indian society (or really structures, for a religious hierarchy existed side by side with a secular one), the colonists had to get to grips with the local terminology. Europeans tended to feel that India was in a state of perpetual chaos, and the plurality of languages exacerbated this impression. At first, using the right titles was essential, and so were efforts to adopt the right idiom: trade could be conducted only after establishing a suitable climate of deference. Later, as British might grew, obsequious niceties could be abandoned. English alone could never fully convey the subtleties of Indian society, nor indeed of Indian thought and feeling. But philology and dictionaries helped shape British India – to produce an image of a unified territory, even though this unity was one that few native inhabitants would readily recognize.

Go-betweens were key players both in enlarging what the British knew of Indian languages and in adopting English words into their own tongues. Learning an 'intruder' language will always open up career opportunities. As an Indian, if you wanted to get anywhere under the British, you needed to have a grasp of English. Acquiring it was considered a means of self-improvement; even if the language didn't ennoble the soul, it certainly meliorated business, made it possible to climb the ladder of administration, and allowed access to the scientific advances achieved within the English-speaking world. In education, the better the institution and the more advanced the course it offered, the more central English was in its curriculum. All the while, the assimilation of Indian vocabulary into English was part of the imperial programme of ownership: to claim and modify Indian words was to anglicize not just the words themselves, but the things for which they stood. *Lascar*, a term for an East Indian sailor and later for a man employed to pitch tents, was a crass misunderstanding of an Urdu word for an encampment, and another word borrowed from Urdu, *sepoy*, was used not in its original sense of 'horseman', but to denote a private soldier in the infantry.

A further example in this vein is *pariah*, which survives as a fairly well-known word for a person to be shunned or avoided. Its particular origin is intriguing. At Indian festivals drums are played – but only those who stand to lose nothing from touching the drums' taut leather skins feel able to do so. Traditionally, the expert drummers are Dravidians and are known by the Tamil name *Paraiyar*. These drummers, hailing mainly from Kerala and Tamil Nadu, often used to work for Europeans as servants, and they were thus frequently involved in practices formally regarded as unclean. For this reason they were deemed by most Hindus to be of low caste, or even to be outcasts. But *Paraiyar* was simply the name of a group united by their occupation, not a catch-all term of abuse or infamy. The English colonists did not pick up on this: they understood only that the servant-drummers were called *Paraiyar* and were held in low regard by Hindus, and *pariah* became an English word for an outcast and then, by extension, a term of contempt.

Words such as *pariah*, *lascar* and *sepoy* became staples of English colonial usage – casually callous misprisions of Indian culture, typical of the 'magisterial' approach. The native peoples were organized by the British, who apparently believed that India would disintegrate if left to its own devices. British society was narrow and exclusive. On the one hand Samuel Foote's play *The Nabob* (1773), which significantly increased the currency of that word, mocked the upstarts who had made their fortunes in India. On the other, Thomas Williamson's *The East India Vade-Mecum* (1810), the fruit of two decades in Bengal, set the agenda for those seeking such fortunes. Williamson was concerned to 'facilitate the progress of . . . young gentlemen', and explained, for instance, that the bearers of a palan-quin, known as *cahars*, should 'carry the *chowry*, (or whisk,) and swing a kind of *punkah*, (or fan,) made either from a large palm leaf, or with split bamboo, and printed cotton', adding that the best protection from the sun would be afforded by 'a *chattah*, (or umbrella)'.[24] The 1,000 pages of Williamson's two volumes are littered with words his readers are expected to pick up – words such as *sircar, choolah, babachy, maylah, ghaut*. His readers must often have been baffled by the information he set before them: 'Carpenters . . . tremble for their tools, whenever the *cowah* is to become subject to their labors'; 'About thirty-two years ago, the common raw sugar, known by the name of *g'hoor*, was to be had at three rupees per maund of 96lb.'; 'The *bickty*, (or cockup,) . . . grows to an enormous size.'[25]

Williamson's *Vade-Mecum* marks the beginning of the great period of borrowing from Indian languages. When Queen Victoria came to the throne, in 1837, British India consisted of slightly less than half the Indian subcontinent; within twenty years its portion had increased to two-thirds. The acquisition of Sindh was completed in 1843; the Punjab was annexed in 1849. In the year of Victoria's accession the Scottish missionary Alexander Duff could hail a 'new era' in the English language's role in India – its use in education to allow the country's youth access to 'the pure fount of European literature and science' and to 'all the really useful knowledge which the world contains', as well as its help in the 'demolition of the superstitions and idolatries of India'.[26] In Duff's imagination, English was a lever capable of moving India into the modern age. This did not happen as Duff envisaged, yet when Lord Curzon arrived in

India as its new viceroy, in 1899, he felt able to proclaim the British achievement there 'the miracle of the world'. But, as David Gilmour shows, at a time when vast numbers of Britons were emigrating to Australia, Canada and America, the British population of India was peculiarly small – a total of 154,961, in the year of Victoria's death, of whom almost half were soldiers.[27]

Language was the key. Although English was the language of administration, the administrative process necessarily involved a grasp of local terminology. Rather as Spanish had usurped the positions of the native languages in South America, English in the nineteenth century advanced parasitically, exploiting power structures that had been created by Persian.[28] As Richard Bailey has pointed out, 'without the aid of a glossary, the letters sent from one English officer to another from the beginning of the Raj until its end are now virtually unintelligible'. The administrative language of the East India Company was 'crammed with loanwords for the various economic practices that were involved in the extraction of riches from the subcontinent'.[29] George Whitworth's *An Anglo-Indian Dictionary* (1885) was the sort of resource Bailey has in mind. It glosses the familiar words (*bungalow* and the like), but also explains terms at once peculiar and useful: *bela*, an area of forest kept as a game reserve; *jalakara*, 'one who searches in goldsmiths' sweepings for gold'; *khubber*, meaning news or information; *sala*, 'a wife's brother' and also a 'very common form of abuse'.

Writers like Whitworth were collectors of useful titbits. They had little use for a more scientific approach to language. Yet it was precisely by examining Indian words that Sir William Jones initiated a more technical appreciation of language as a whole. In 1783 Jones was appointed to the Supreme Court of Judicature at Fort William in Bengal. Already a distinguished orientalist, having learnt Arabic while a schoolboy at Harrow, he would make vital connections between Sanskrit, Latin, Greek and the majority of modern European languages, in addition to unlocking some of the mysteries of the Hindu and Islamic civilizations. His insight that related languages spring from a common source laid the foundation for the study of the Indo-European family and its ancestry. It is no exaggeration to say that Jones was the central figure in stimulating

European intellectual interest in India, correcting the long-standing view of Indian culture and ritual as absurd and deviant, and disentangling the truth from the sort of lurid fictions that could be traced back as far as *The Travels of Sir John Mandeville*.

Jones's writings, on judicial subjects as well as on language, deploy borrowed terms out of respect for the complexity of Indian civilization. He catalogued Indian plants, collected inscriptions, wrote essays on the scaly, sticky-tongued pangolin and the slow loris, explained Indian knowledge of music and the zodiac, recorded details of local medicines, and above all immersed himself in Sanskrit, a language he considered far more refined than either Latin or Greek. He was the first to write of an *avatar*, the sweet song of the *bulbul*, the Indian lute called a *veena*, and *dharma* (a fusion of custom, truth and law, popularized in the title of Jack Kerouac's 1958 novel *The Dharma Bums*). Although he remained loyal to the Church of England, India was his Arcadia, and from his retreat at Krishnagar he quietly revolutionized the understanding of languages, raising the possibility of a proto-Indo-European language that could have sired such different tongues as English, Russian and Persian. The scientific study of Eastern languages opened up a range of related subjects, and the comparative grammar pioneered by Jones established the tenor of nineteenth-century language studies and opened a new channel into the very archaeology of human experience.

Jones's grasp of the qualities of the region's culture was scholarly and inquisitive. The East, he understood, could enlighten the West. But nineteenth-century Britons' image of India was more emphatically shaped by a very different figure. This was James Mill, who began his *The History of British India* in 1806, and completed it twelve years later without having visited the country about which he was writing. Mill savaged Jones's positive portrait of Indian civilization, sniping at what he saw as its dangerous inadequacies. He claimed that his own ignorance of the native languages worked to his advantage, allowing him to view India objectively. His was a 'philosophical' brand of history.

William Jones the empirical philologist and James Mill the cold utilitarian: it is telling that Mill was the more popular of the two, for, despite Jones's important intellectual legacy, the India known to outsiders has been Mill's. The subtleties of India have held less interest for the rest of the world than a broad impression of those subtleties. The archetypal vision in this respect is that of Lord Macaulay, who wrote in his 'Minute on Indian Education' (1835), 'I have no knowledge of either Sanscrit or Arabic. But I have done what I could to form a correct estimate of their value.' It probably goes without saying that Macaulay's 'correct estimate' was not a high one.

This stupendous chauvinism is typical of imperial rapaciousness: the art of taking what you want and pronouncing everything else worthless. And there is more: India was energetically used as a springboard for accessing other cultures. The loss of Britain's colonies in America – of which more very shortly – diverted attention eastward. India was a base for pushing further east, and the Pacific was to become by 1800 'a British lake'.[30] The acquisition of Penang in 1786 was crucial, but Penang's importance was eclipsed in 1819 with Sir Thomas Stamford Raffles's foundation of Singapore. Burma opened up in the 1820s, and was occupied in stages. Between 1815 and 1880 the majority of British interests abroad were menaced by no foreigner save the indigenous peoples, and this absence of external pressure allowed Britain's empire to grow at a rate of about 100,000 square miles a year during the half-century after the defeat of Napoleon. Some of the acquisitions were strategic, others commercial, and still others the result of white settlers' arrogant self-assertion.[31]

The greatest opportunities lay in China. The Portuguese had begun to trade with the Chinese around 1540, and had established themselves in Macau by 1560. It seems that the first English travellers to visit Macau did so in the final years of the sixteenth century, but the first useful records of contact between British and Chinese traders date from 1637. The diaries of Peter Mundy, the son of a Cornish pilchard merchant, record his experiences as a trader in the East, describing the Chinese in some detail and documenting the abundance of commodities like porcelain, pepper, ginger and silks. Mundy's writings contain novel words such as *chopsticks* and *kimono*, and he offers what would appear to be the first diagnosis of the difficulties faced by Chinese-speakers in their attempts to pronounce English – evident in their calling him *Pe-tang Mun-ty*.[32]

For a long time after Peter Mundy, China remained a land of mystery, disengaged from the rest of the world. Abstaining from seaborne imperialism, it consolidated its power westward, over land. For Sir Thomas Browne, a man never averse to verbal embroidery, the Chinese were quite simply the people 'who live at the bounds of the earth'. The Chinese, meanwhile, 'dealt with foreigners as uncouth barbarians'; before the nineteenth century the only foreign influence to make a broad impact on China was Buddhism, which had begun in northern India. Their language and culture developed in a vacuum.[33] Some of the rewards of their civilization filtered westward, but always through intermediaries, and slowly: for instance, in China gunpowder was developed during the ninth century AD, and formulae for its composition were published at least as early as 1044, but there was no European science of its manufacture until the thirteenth century. The Chinese people's ideogrammic written language and subtly tonal speech prevented outsiders from readily getting to grips with their accomplishments. Chinese innovations such as paper, the compass and mechanical clockwork were impressive to those few who saw them, yet, while their practical value was quickly apparent, the precise means of their use and manufacture could not easily be conveyed. The writings of the trailblazing Mundy point up the kind of words that English-speakers have been best able to extract from Chinese. Attitudes to China have tended to be either scathing or apprehensive: the prospect of China's political and economic rise, which is bruited every generation or so, causes fear. The one area of comparative safety is food.

The utensils we call *chopsticks* are known to the Chinese as *kwai-tsze*, which literally means 'nimble boys'. *Chopsticks* is a crude equivalent, partly inspired by the pidgin word *chop*, 'quick'. (The pidgin English exclamation *chop chop* replicates the Chinese *kwai kwai*.) William Dampier explains, 'At their ordinary eating they use two small round sticks about the length and bigness of a Tobacco-pipe. They hold them both in the right hand, one between the fore-finger and thumb; the other between the middle-finger and fore-finger,' and adds that 'they are called by the English seamen Chopsticks.' It is easy enough to think of a dozen or so other Chinese words connected with food and eating that have been absorbed into commonplace

English. Dampier refers enthusiastically to the *kumquat*, which is the Cantonese dialect term for the little golden orange more widely known in China as *kin ku*. The *lychee*, native to southern China, is first mentioned by Hakluyt's friend Robert Parke in his translation of Gonzalez de Mendoza's history of that land, and turns up in Dampier. (The *mandarin*, which we might expect to have something to do with Chinese, gets its name from Swedish.) *Dim sum* comes from Cantonese, while the Amoy dialect of what is today southern Fujian is the source of *ketchup* – originally a brine in which fish were kept, and described in a dictionary of cant in 1690 as a 'high East-India Sauce'. Then of course there are the widely known *chow mein*, *chop suey* and *tofu*. *Ginseng* derives from *jen shen*, which has usually been interpreted as 'man root' – a reference to the forked fleshy root of the plant, which resembles a pair of legs; John Ray mentions it in his *The Wisdom of God Manifested in the Works of the Creation* (1691), where he gives it the name *nisi*. The toast *chin chin* (1795) is a version of the Mandarin salutation *ts'ing ts'ing*. And the Cantonese *wok* started to appear in English-language books about Chinese cookery in the 1950s and '60s.

The advent of Chinese words in English began in earnest as a result of the East India Company's trading in opium and tea. Opium had long been traded privately by the Company's employees, who shipped chests of the drug from Calcutta to Canton and Macau. It had been introduced to China as early as the first century BC, but mass export into the region was initiated by the Dutch in the 1660s. Prohibited by imperial edict in 1729, it was nonetheless in high demand, and Indian opium was of a quality far superior to the Chinese opium grown mainly in Yunnan. In 1773 the Company took monopoly control of the production of opium, and between 1767 and 1790 the volume of exports to China quadrupled.[34] Emperor Qian Long could write to George III that his celestial empire contained 'all things in prolific abundance and lacks no product within its own borders', but this was manifestly not the case.[35] The Indian opium paid for Chinese tea; by 1833 about 35 million pounds of tea were being imported annually by the Company.[36]

The noun *tea* seemed novel to Samuel Pepys in 1661 (he explains that it is 'a Chinese drink'), but in Pope's *The Rape of the Lock* (1712–14) it needed no gloss. Where once the practice of drinking tea had been made popular by the spread of Buddhism, now it grew first through the influence of Charles II's Portuguese wife and then through a very English affection for any pastime that involves a ludicrous mass of paraphernalia (summed up in the twee eighteenth-century coinage *tea-things*). More words were adopted thanks to the eighteenth-century spate of fascination, right across Europe, with all things Chinese. This *chinoiserie* was evident in Thomas Chippendale's festive bedroom furniture, the architectural designs of Sir William Chambers and William Halfpenny, George Bickham's wallpapers, and also Thomas Percy's *Miscellaneous Pieces Relating to the Chinese* (1762). While knowledge of China certainly improved at this time, its manifestations in art and literature rarely rose above a stylized, largely imaginary representation of the country and its culture.

Subsequent borrowing from Chinese had much to do with the region's infiltration by British and American missionaries, and in the nineteenth century with business dealings. In Hong Kong, doing business was easy; Britain's occupation of this free port was confirmed by the Treaty of Nanking in 1842, and companies such as Jardine Matheson and Butterfield & Swire profited. A vocabulary dating from as early as 1824, 'intended as an Aid to Correspondence and Conversation', suggests the nature of relations between British and Chinese, full as it is with glosses of words and expressions like *dissolve partnership, fair price, monopoly* and *undersell*.[37]

Clearly, when Chinese words are borrowed into English they are spelt out in the English alphabet, and this can have implications for their pronunciation. For instance, the Chinese root of the word *kaolin* consists of two characters and two syllables, but the form adopted into English is pronounced with three syllables. Another pertinent example is the verb *kowtow*, which literally means 'to knock the head' – as one does in prostrating oneself before a superior. *Kowtow* was adopted in the early nineteenth century as a noun; the first author to use it as a verb – and to use it figuratively – was Benjamin Disraeli, in 1826. In English it is treated as a single unit: we say, 'He kowtowed repeatedly,' not the more picturesque 'He kowed his tow repeatedly.' Moreover, the particularity of a word's connotations can be lost. We tend to use *taipan* to signify the head of a large company, but it was formerly used of a dance-hall manager or the man in charge of a public convenience.[38]

A few more examples of borrowings from Chinese will suggest the flavour of this debt. Thus there is the game *mahjong*, the first English account of which was written by the ethnographer Stewart Culin. Its name literally means 'sparrows': the clattering of the tiles with which the game is played has been likened to the sound of sparrows squabbling over crumbs. *Cheongsam* (literally 'long garment') is probably the best-known style of clothing to have been adopted, while a few Chinese breeds of dog have achieved popularity, such as the *shih-tzu* (literally 'lion dog'). *Feng shui* is a direct import from Mandarin, where the two words signify 'wind' and 'water'. We may be surprised by how long the expression has had a place in English: the *OED*'s first citation dates from 1797, and the term was quite casually used by Rudyard Kipling more than seventy years ago. *Gung ho* was adopted by Evans Carlson, a colonel in the US Marine Corps during the Second World War. It derives from *kung*, 'work', and *ho*, 'together', and Carlson's marines, striving to present a united front, took *gung ho* as their motto. *Kung fu* made its first known appearance in *Punch* in September 1966. The skills it denoted were of great antiquity, but the term *kung fu* was quite a modern development; it burst into international view only with the rise of martial-arts films and the emergence of Bruce Lee as a bankable star in the late 1960s. *Typhoon* may well have been picked up from Chinese sailors, but it entered Chinese from Arabic, and the Arabic word *tufan* can in turn be traced to Greek, where it was used by Aristotle among others.[39] The verb *to shanghai* is attributable to the once very brutal means by which sailors were recruited for voyages to the Far East.

The source of these words will easily be identified by most speakers of English. We may also, I think, say that a large part of the history of the relationship between English and Chinese has been painted over. Tom McArthur writes, 'English and Chinese constitute two of the most powerful language complexes on earth and it seems highly likely that their influence on one another in future will transcend anything that has so far transpired between them.'[40] This sounds plausible. But when we reflect on English's debt to Chinese, it is hard not to perceive a certain awkwardness, a lack of trust on both sides; and this persists.

In his essay 'Shooting an Elephant', George Orwell recalls an episode from his time as an imperial policeman in Burma:

> It was at this moment, as I stood there with the rifle in my hands, that I first grasped the hollowness, the futility of the white man's dominion in the East. Here was I, the white man with his gun, standing in front of the unarmed native crowd – seemingly the leading actor of the piece; but in reality I was only an absurd puppet pushed to and fro by the will of those yellow faces behind. I perceived in this moment that when the white man turns tyrant it is his own freedom that he destroys. He becomes a sort of hollow, posing dummy, the conventionalized figure of a sahib. For it is the condition of his rule that he shall spend his life trying to impress the 'natives', and so in every crisis he has got to do what the 'natives' expect of him. He wears a mask, and his face grows to fit it.

Orwell reimagines his experience of this puppetry in the novel *Burmese Days*. There he trowels on the local colour, with abundant use of words like *pukka*, *pani-wallah*, *chokra* (a young male servant), *burra sahib*, *sampan*, *thugyi* and *mamoty* (a tool that looks a bit like a hoe). The effect is cloying, and deliberately so. Orwell perfectly evokes the way the English grasp of the language of the 'East' seems not to bring it closer, but to keep it at arm's length.

12. Blizzard

A sharp blow or knock; a blast of blinding snow

The word is 'more or less onomatopoeic' (*OED*), and was apparently popularized by the American press during the hard winter of 1880–81, although it had been used perhaps as much as half a century earlier

The colonists have put some distance between themselves and 'alien' usage, and so have the colonized. In my opening chapter I pictured Samuel Sewall breakfasting in 1690s Boston on venison and chocolate. Reading his diaries, which cover a period of more than half a century, we see him worrying about his children, eight of whom died before reaching adulthood, and fishing for cod beyond Massachusetts Bay, complaining about the wearing of wigs, and propagating the Gospel among the natives. Amid its frank records of social and spiritual life, Sewall's diary is full of pleasing detail; on one occasion he calls for a chamber pot, the bottom of which falls out when he uses it, prompting the reflection, 'How unexpectedly a man may be expos'd! There's no security but in God.'¹ Yet, even as Sewall emerges from the diary's pages as a man loyal to his English roots, others' murmurs of discontent are audible. In less moderate circles they were loud. The distance was growing between the British idea of America and the American experience of America, and language registered this. Many words that were once seen as symptoms of the political and cultural gulf have been appropriated by users of English who have never set foot on American soil, but the Americanization of Standard English – abhorred by Samuel Johnson, almost unthinkable in the age of Samuel Sewall – has its origins in American resistance to British sovereignty.

The organization of the land was one early area of tension. By 1700 there were as many as 140 towns in New England, and along the eastern seaboard there lay not just Boston, but a string of other well-planned communities: Philadelphia, Charles Town, Newport and New York. Even though British America was still predominantly rural, its landscape was regular, parcelled into convenient lots.[2] And while for a large part of the eighteenth century most of the white inhabitants of the American colonies thought of themselves as free subjects of the British monarch, there gradually rose a resistance to this convenient parcelling-up of land, and there rose as well an appetite for self-reliance.

In 1705 Robert Beverley, writing anonymously in his *The History and Present State of Virginia*, pronounces himself an Indian. It seems a strange gesture for a man who had been educated in Yorkshire and was living at the time in London, but in doing this he is explicitly distancing himself from English habits and English rule. He did not call himself an American: that word was still somewhat ambiguous – a term habitually used of the indigenous peoples, and just beginning to be used by some colonists of themselves, although not with the pride that it would later connote. Beverley was unimpressed by English achievements in Virginia, yet he was smitten with Virginia itself. He was not alone in sensing an impending divorce. Aphra Behn's play *The Widdow Ranter, or, The History of Bacon in Virginia* (first performed in 1689) identifies Virginia not as an extension of England, but rather as a fascinatingly distinct place, alive with new possibilities and possessed of its own potently bizarre language.[3] While many settlers felt the need to advertise their English credentials, others identified with the land where they lived, not with the land of their ancestors. The drudgery of settlement had dampened individualism, but in the early eighteenth century British America began to develop its own culture. In 1721 Hugh Jones, a professor at William and Mary College in Williamsburg, Virginia, put together the first American guide to English grammar, and bolder statements of the distinctiveness of British America were to follow.

Francis Moore, who travelled to Georgia in 1735, may well have been the first Englishman to snipe at 'American English', complaining that the barbarous Americans called the bank of a river a *bluff*, and around the same time Richard Owen Cambridge became the first to argue the need for a glossary of Americanisms. Many who ventured from Britain to America were taken aback by the good usage prevalent among Americans; one, an adventurous farmer's son from Derbyshire called Nicholas Cresswell, recorded in his journal in July 1777 that American English was better than the standard version spoken in Britain.[4] Yet most British writers and thinkers of the period were simply uninterested in American speech and American literature. When this began to change, around 1830, American English was routinely trashed by commentators such as Frances Trollope and Frederick Marryat. The reason? Probably it was a renewed flow of Americanisms into British English – at first through the works of writers such as Thomas Jefferson and James Fenimore Cooper, and then, more vividly, as slang. Marryat scorned the American habit of punctuating speech with *uh* and *um*, but picked it up all the same.

As eighteenth-century Americans resisted British rule, so a distinctively American form of English became a badge of anti-British sentiment. At institutions such as Harvard and Yale, students aspired to the genteel manners of the British elite, as did many cosmopolitan capitalists in New York and Philadelphia, but, more commonly, Americans' use of English telegraphed their distance from Britain and from Britons. The American Revolution brought a tidal wave of 'visible and auditory terrorism' – a tumult of slogans, bonfires, processions and topsy-turvydom.[5] One word for it was *hubbub*, a Gaelic term formerly associated with the shrill wail of the bagpipes. By the 1770s the gulf between American and British Englishes was widening quickly, and it became more pronounced after the Declaration of Independence in 1776. This founding document promoted 'liberty' and 'the pursuit of happiness', and Americans' political independence galvanized a sense of linguistic independence. An American Philological Society was formed in 1788 – a response to the arguments put forward by, among others, John Adams, who had suggested an American Academy to the president of Congress in two letters dated September 1780.

Adams played a key role in defining the political values of America, so it seems fitting that he was the first to employ the word *caucus*, in his diary in February 1763, although as the stertorous *caw-cauwwassoughe* this word for a private meeting of political leaders had appeared in John Smith's *Generall Historie of Virginia*.[6] More than thirty years later, a group of federalists in Congress would be publicly excoriated for meeting in caucus to sponsor Adams's candidacy to be the country's second president. As for Adams's goal of a national academy, that would be realized through the American Academy of Language and Belles Lettres, founded in 1820 with his son John Quincy Adams as its president. But by then the Americanness of American English had been trumpeted across the nation by a single reformist member of the Philological Society. This was the Connecticut schoolmaster Noah Webster, an energetic Calvinist and Federalist, whose strong ideas and shameless self-promotion made him the most influential architect of the divergence between British and American usage.

Already when Webster began his work, America was more diverse − ethnically and linguistically − than any country in western Europe. Besides the remaining speakers of French, Spanish and Dutch, there were Germans in Pennsylvania and Maryland, Welsh in New England, Swedes in Delaware, and Sephardic Jews in Manhattan. The range of American experience was also stunning. As one commentator observed, 'How tame will his language sound, who would describe Niagara in language fitted for the falls at London bridge, or attempt the majesty of the Mississippi in that which was made for the Thames?'[7]

Webster's dictionaries would reflect this sense of newness: new ideas and new ways of being and seeing, a novel and independent national character and destiny. His productions flaunted their distance from Britishness with patriotic titles − *The American Spelling Book*, *An American Dictionary of the English Language* − and a niggling disparagement of the quintessentially English authority of Dr Johnson. He also took note of American coinages such as *lengthy* and *skunk*. Webster was in favour of making spellings more straightforward − writing *color* instead of *colour*, for instance, *music* rather than *musick*, and *check* rather than *cheque*. There were etymological reasons for such preferences, as well as practical ones, although some of the other spellings he initially favoured − *groop* and *tung*, for instance − failed to impress even his keenest supporters. In any case, Webster's persistent and patriotic lexicography was never hindered by anxieties about whether he was genuinely right. His approach was in many respects unsuccessful, but one aspect endures: tellingly, when American language mavens complain about what they perceive to be incorrectness, they proffer logical explanations and emphasize the need for simplicity and clarity, while their British counterparts tend to display a mixture of masochistic Victorianism and unreasoning bluster.

Linguistically, the next 150 years in America were lush, as the works of Emerson, Melville and Whitman were to prove. In the short term, and simultaneous with the emergence of a distinctive and determinedly American form of English, there was a vast improvement in Americans' knowledge of their land. Works including James Adair's *The History of the American Indians* (1775) and Washington Irving's *Astoria* (1836), as well as the westward expedition of Lewis and Clark, whose reports were published in 1814, marked the Americans' conquest of their own country. These men's stories fertilized dreams of a country united from sea to shining sea. Penetrating the extremities of their continent, driven forth by the power of industry and technology, and buoyed by improved schooling, the American people attained their 'manifest destiny'. Their country was an experiment in hopefulness and self-assurance.

Today, the most immediately obvious difference between American and British Englishes is their distinct 'tunes', but divergence of pronunciation, while easily mimicked and ridiculed, has rarely been as aggressively targeted as disparities in vocabulary. The word *Americanism* was first used in 1781 by John Witherspoon, later the president of Princeton University, who wrote a number of articles for the *Pennsylvania Journal* about 'ways of speaking peculiar to this country'. *Briticism* and *Britishism* were coined in the following century. Many words once stigmatized as Americanisms have since been universally adopted: a few examples are the already mentioned *lengthy* (a favourite of Thomas Jefferson's) and *blizzard*, the adjective *brash*, the Germanic verb *dunk* (be it of a basketball or a doughnut), *hindsight*, *roustabout*, and the word *bindery* for a bookbinder's workshop. In his *American Notes* (1842), Dickens proposed that the quintessential Americanism was *fix*, a word with a host of applications.

American usage added new resonance to *emancipation* and

abolitionist, and could popularize a usage as apparently ephemeral as *sideburn* – an inversion of the name of a notably whiskery Civil War commander, Ambrose Everett Burnside.[8] John Farmer's dictionary of Americanisms, published in 1889, includes a host of altogether more obscure items, such as *burgaloo*, the name of a type of paper (and a corruption of the French *virgalieu*); *sapsago*, a kind of cheese known to the Germans as *Schabzieger*, and *blauser*, a corruption of the Dutch name for the deaf adder. Farmer is an alarmingly insensitive guide ('It would have been strange indeed', he remarks, 'had the Red Man failed to leave the most distinct impress upon the life and surroundings of the American nation'), and his celebration of 'perverted and obsolete English words' and the 'rare ingenuity and versatility of the American mind' bulges with oddities.[9]

It should be emphasized that, while there is a long history of resistance outside America to American words and forms, plenty of commentators, including Virginia Woolf and Robert Bridges, have defended them. Much of what was once derided or feared as Americanism is now not even recognized as such: *stampede, advisory, bandwagon, squatter, split-level, gobbledygook, isolationism, badlands, law-abiding, curvaceous, It girl, haywire, elevator, mileage, slapstick, unshakable, stunt* and, in the colloquial sense, *spring chicken*. If we think about some of these words, even briefly, their American roots resurface, or we can imagine where they lie: *stampede*, for instance, comes from the Mexican Spanish *estampida*, and was first used of the thunderous flight of panicked cattle, and *badlands* is a calque of *mauvaises terres*, which is what the first French settlers called the rugged terrain of the upper Missouri valley. But common use has put distance between these words and their origins.

As American society has developed along different lines from that of Britain, accommodating different proportions of immigrants and enjoying different cultural contacts, its language has inevitably assimilated its own loans and has been hospitable towards them. Many of these have been brought about by contact with Spanish-speaking peoples both within and beyond American borders. Some, like *hobo* and *vigilante*, have become very widely known. Familiar borrowings from other tongues include *bogus*, which was at first the name for a counterfeit coin and originated in the Hausa language of West

Africa, and the name *goober* for a peanut, which is from Kongo. Contact with French-speakers in North America has yielded *pumpkin, crevasse, to sashay, rotisserie* and *praline*, along with *shanty, prairie* and *chowder*, while German has introduced *noodle, nix* and *hoodlum*. As I have mentioned, words such as *boss* and *cookie* were absorbed through contact with the Dutch in North America, as were *bedspread, stoop* (the raised entrance to a house), *caboose* and *sleigh*, and it's worth pausing to remark some of the place names that have the same source, notably in New York: Brooklyn, Harlem, the Bowery and the Bronx, and Gramercy Park (a corruption of the Dutch for 'crooked knife', *krom mesje*, the name of a stream that ran down what is today 21st Street). The Latin *alumnus* and *alumni* first achieved currency in American universities. More recently, words adopted in the US that have found global usage among English-speakers have included the Italian *barista* and the seemingly Germanic *feisty*.

H. L. Mencken justly observed that 'In the treatment of loan words, English spelling is much more conservative than American,' noting the 'rapid naturalization' in America of words from French and Spanish. The original words' accents were quickly discarded, and plurals were formed without affectation: Mencken observed that while fastidious British users would refer to *libretti* or *sanatoria*, Americans were straight away comfortable talking about *virtuosos* and *dilettantes*.[10] He convicted his countrymen of a 'spacious disregard for linguistic nicety': in reality, American English tends to be more condensed than its British counterpart.

Nonetheless, American English has in certain respects proved conservative and archaic. Some of the usages that seem distinctively American to British speakers of English are in fact British in origin. The habit of saying *gotten* instead of *got* reflects the standard British usage of a couple of hundred years ago. The preference for *fall* rather than *autumn* now seems distinctively American, but *fall* was used in this sense by Sir Walter Scott, Thomas Carlyle and John Evelyn, to name but three. Equally, saying *I guess* isn't a Valley Girl tic, but a locution as old as Chaucer.[11] Geoffrey Hughes cites other examples: *dumb* as a casually unpleasant synonym for *stupid, trash* as a word for household waste, *mad* meaning 'angry', and *skillet* for *frying pan.*[12] The word *spry* is almost an archaism in British English, but not in American English. Yet, just to give one counter-example, American English has lost *fortnight.*

Since the early nineteenth century, native speakers of English have been in a minority among America's new immigrants. The country has absorbed significant numbers of people who speak as their first language Spanish, Italian, Russian, German, Polish, Greek, Arabic, Persian, Vietnamese, Tagalog, Korean or Chinese, as well as a variety of other tongues including African, Indic and Scandinavian languages. But by 1800 the position of English was entrenched – America would be an English-speaking country, in perpetuity – and by the end of the nineteenth century English was the common language of a territory thirty times the size of Britain. 'Within a single century,' notes Nicholas Ostler, 'a linguistic monoculture had grown to overwhelm a sparsely scattered cornucopia of over two hundred different languages.'[13] Those other voices are, for today's English-speaking majority, 'noises off', most of them very faintly heard.

Benjamin Franklin, who testified to the American love of English manners and customs, was one of the architects of this, proposing that his countrymen curb the use of all languages other than English. But there have always been communities where English has barely risen above the status of 'necessary second language', and the bilingualism of many Americans has impregnated American English with the exotic.

Many of its borrowings are exclusive to a single region. Literary tributes to local styles of speech have been paid by writers such as Mark Twain, Damon Runyon and Sarah Orne Jewett, yet the evidence confronts us most straightforwardly when we hear it for ourselves.

In Louisiana, which takes it name from Louis XIV and was purchased from the French by Thomas Jefferson for $15 million in 1803, you will hear the French influence in *levee, Mardi gras* and *lagniappe* – the last of these, meaning a gratuity or something to make up good measure, a French corruption of a Spanish word learnt from Quechua – as well as in the archaic dialect Cajun. The first word of Louisiana French to find common acceptance was *bayou,* which comes from the Choctaw *bayuk*; its Choctaw abbreviation *bok* became in French *boque*, which survives, as *bogue*, in place names like Bogue Sound in North Carolina.[14] The dialects of the West, the Inland South and the Midland are coloured by their different clusterings of immigrants. In Minnesota, which in the nineteenth century attracted many struggling farmers from Sweden and Norway, you'll hear Nordic words like *lutefisk* and idioms that are essentially calques of Scandinavian idioms – as in talk of 'cooking coffee'. In Maine, where as much as a quarter of the population has French ancestry, you may hear a stray hair called a *couette*, and in parts of Ohio *please* is used in the same way as the German *bitte*, to invite a person to repeat something just said – apparently a remnant of the bilingual schooling once available in Cincinnati.[15]

As for Spanish influence, it is one of the true distinguishing features of American English. Florida, discovered by Juan Ponce de Leon in 1513 (and named after Pascua Florida, the 'flowery festival' of Easter), was sold to the Americans for $5 million in 1819.[16] Oregon, Texas and the Mexican territories in the south-west followed in the 1840s. Hispanisms were picked up in all these areas. The Mexican War of 1846–8 increased borrowings. English-speaking trappers, traders and woodsmen had been venturing south into New Mexico for almost half a century. The war and the campaigns and treaties that followed, together with the many new schools run by missionaries, diffused English through the region. As this happened, Spanish words, much more than Indian ones, were acquired by osmosis.

Discussing Spanish in North America, Harold Bentley writes just a little fancifully of words 'hauled into the English language by British seamen' or 'picked up on the Santa Fe trail, lassoed . . . by the vaqueros on the broad mesas, cultivated by the colonists of Texas, bartered by merchants, or come upon by intrepid explorers'.[17] Yet the essential thrust of his account is correct. Where Spanish is concerned, farming, cowboys and horsemanship, architecture and construction have all figured prominently.[18] Thus many terms to do with ranching are Hispanic in origin; for instance, the legendary *ten-gallon* hat takes it name from *galon*, the Spanish word for a band used to decorate one's headgear. The nineteenth-century goldrushers were not the first people to penetrate California, and the Spanish legacy is evident in *bronco, caporal, corrida* and *corral*. There too English-speakers came across the *abalone*, with its bleeding-mushroom flavour; the word was a Spanish reworking of a term long used by the Costanoan fishermen of Monterey Bay. A farm's squat *adobe* dwellings, *patio* and whitewashed *casa grande* are plainly Hispanic, while *bonanza* 'originally signified good weather on the ocean . . . [but] has come to mean a vein of rich ore in a mine' – and, figuratively, any big payday or burst of good fortune.[19] *Hacienda*, an estate where workers busy themselves with farming and mining, stems from the Latin *facienda*, 'things to be done'. *Rodeo* is another word that stands out. Literally a round-up of cattle, it was employed in this sense by Darwin in *The Voyage of the Beagle* (1839), but has chiefly been used of cowboy stunts since around 1900. According to Bentley, 'One of the first instances of word writing in the sky by airplane was on the occasion of advertising a *rodeo* in Madison Square Garden in New York'.[20]

This Spanish influence has continued to the present day; at least 15 per cent of Americans are of Hispanic origin. Its charisma is strongly evident in the south-west, especially in California, Texas and New Mexico, but in Florida and the north-east too, and derives not just from Mexicans, but also from people whose origins are in Puerto Rico, El Salvador, Honduras, Cuba, Colombia and the Dominican Republic. More recent borrowings have often involved politics (*Contra, Sandinista, Zapatista*), food and drink (*taco, fajita, nacho, picante, tequila*), and questions of occupation and status (for instance, *numero uno, gonzo*, and the kind of US-owned sweatshop known as a *maquiladora*).[21] A particularly fertile area of transfer is street slang. The narcotics trade in the US has deep roots in Latin America. Early on, settlers in the south-west discovered *mescal* and *peyote*, both of which are Spanish renderings of Nahuatl terms. Then the connection ramified. Today one can readily hear the word *caballo* used for heroin (compare the English slang *horse*), *rojas* ('reds') for barbiturates such as Seconal, *cura* for a fix, and also *carne* for heroin.[22] Furthermore, a product of tensions between Hispanics and white Americans is the large number of derogatory or dismissive terms in common use for Hispanics – words like *chico, hombre, pedro* –

while *gringo* and *gringa* have since the eighteenth century been used slightingly by Hispanics of non-Hispanics, and *gringo* was fully assimilated into English in the twentieth.

Stereotypes of Hispanic Americans may be odious, but they have contributed repeatedly to the common American word-stock, insinuating themselves into power relationships, and reinforcing anxieties and oppositions. *Cojones* makes its first appearance in Hemingway's *Death in the Afternoon* – 'It takes more cojones to be a sportsman where death is a closer party to the game' – and has become an emblem of ostentatious masculinity. This concept is summed up, of course, in the Spanish *macho* and *machismo*; significantly, in Mexican Spanish *machismo* equates simply to 'manliness', but, borrowed by English, it has morphed into a distinctly pejorative term. *Vamos* and its derivative *vamoose* connote a kind of butch criminality. *Hasta la vista*, long a popular phrase of leave-taking, gained global popularity when uttered by Arnold Schwarzenegger's murderous cyborg in the *Terminator* films. Other American Hispanisms evoke a culture of slow-paced leisure. Thus for instance *siesta* and *mañana*. The latter, a catch-all for the supposedly Hispanic trait of procrastination, gained popularity in the nineteenth century; D. H. Lawrence and George Orwell both felt able to use it without explanation. And borrowings of a different stripe continue. A recent one is *descanso*, a Spanish term for a place of rest for a dead person, now gaining popularity as a term for a memorial erected at the site of a fatal road crash. Another is *huarache* – the name, in the language of the Purepecha people of northern Mexico, of a kind of sandal, adopted by Nike in the early 1990s to denote a strappy sports shoe with a shock-absorbing heel insert.

What finds its way into the mainstream of American English will usually find its way into British English.[23] A giant study – potentially fascinating, potentially stultifying – could be made of this transatlantic drift. It is a cliché of Anglo-American entente that where one of us speaks of the *sidewalk* and insists on 'getting in line', the other speaks of the *pavement* and 'joining the queue'; that one of us says *realtor, pants* and *basin* where the other says *estate agent, trousers* and *mixing bowl*. American English and British English are adjacent parts of the big continuum of intelligibility known simply as 'English', and accounts that emphasize the differences are likely to originate in some sort of Pooterish xenophobia, or in the feigned incomprehension of social and cultural myopia. I am concerned here not with the capacity of American forms to win out over British ones (or with marvelling at the fact of one country's preference for *billfold* over *wallet*), but rather with what American English has borrowed and with the radiation of these borrowings through the whole breadth of global English.

American's one-time colonial presence in the Philippines has resulted in a handful of borrowings from the most commonly spoken local language, Tagalog. The best example is *boondocks*. Originally in Tagalog it signified a mountain, but, when poor natives explained that they came from mountainous areas, outsiders imagined the word was a general term for any slummy or primitive place. Other examples, less intimately bound up with American involvement, are *yo-yo*, *sampaguita* (a Spanish–Tagalog hybrid term for Arabian jasmine), the card game *panguingue*, and the custard-fragranced flower *ylang-ylang*.

A much bigger source has been Yiddish. About 2.5 million Jews emigrated from Europe to the United States between 1877 and 1917. They set up Jewish schools and shops, charities and synagogues, and the language of these institutions was Yiddish. More than 150 Yiddish newspapers and periodicals were started in New York between 1885 and 1914, and the language was central to the flourishing Jewish theatre scenes in New York, Chicago, Philadelphia and beyond. Some of the words that entered American English were straightforwardly Yiddish, like *schlep* and *kvell*; others, such as *schvartzer*, arose 'in response to the social context of Jewish life in the US'.[24] Inevitably, Yiddish was Americanized, and many immigrants gave up speaking Yiddish in order to avoid anti-Semitic prejudice and violence. Yet, since the Second World War, pride in Jewish ethnicity has been resurgent, and whereas Jews long regarded Yiddish as a sort of lower-class jargon, in the last half-century or so many have come to look on it as a vital element of their culture.[25]

Certain elements of Yiddish are widely known across the English-speaking world. Examples are *bagel*, *bar mitzvah* and *drek*. *Kabbalah*, which is really just the Hebrew word for 'tradition', has come to signify a particular dogma favoured by celebrities tripping on mysticism. The well-known *kosher* has come to mean 'legitimate' or 'good quality', although it of course retains the fastidious sense 'acceptable according to the rules of Jewish dietary law as executed under rabbinical supervision'.[26] The almost as familiar *chutzpah* has been drolly defined as 'the quality shown by the man who murders his mother and father, then asks the judge to forgive a poor orphan'.[27] Most vividly, there are the expressive adjectives – an unusually high percentage of borrowings from Yiddish are adjectives – like *meshuge* or *zaftig*. The latter, meaning 'juicy', tends to be used of voluptuous women, and thus increasingly of any woman who doesn't resemble a matchstick.

Yiddish abounds with pungent denominations for people. For instance, a *nebbish* is a timid, luckless simpleton. The word is related to the Czech *neboky*, meaning 'unfortunate'. The classic nebbish is the sort of character played by Woody Allen in most of his own films. A nagging or disastrously boring person will be a *nudnik*; the word comes from the Yiddish verb *nudyen*, meaning 'to pester'. A nineteenth-century example can be found in *Bleak House*, where Jo the crossing sweeper is described as an obstinate 'gonoph' – a version of the Yiddish *gonef*, a word for a thief. *Schmuck* can mean 'penis', 'fool' or 'hypocrite'. Its German root is a word meaning 'jewel': it's not hard to see how this became a slang term for a man's favourite pendant, and any word for the penis sooner or later becomes a term of abuse. The dismissive *sch* sound can also be heard in *schtick*, *schlock* and *shlep*. Strictly, spelling these words with *sch* rather than *sh* makes them look German; Yiddishists prefer to drop the *c*. But it's hard to avoid the Germanic twang. For instance, *schmaltz*, which is in Yiddish a term for anything dripping with corny sentiment, is the German word for 'lard'.

A personal favourite among borrowings from Yiddish is the suggestively onomatopoeic verb *khrop*, meaning 'to snore'. Another favourite is *kibitzer*, a person who looks over the shoulder of someone playing cards or chess – and then, typically, needles and distracts him with comments on the quality of his hand. *Katzenjammer*, literally 'cat's wailing', feels much more heady than *hangover*. What's more, several popular expressions are translations of popular Yiddishisms: when we refer to *the bottom line* we are expressing, for the most part unwittingly, the Yiddish idiom *di untershte shure*, heard in the common phrase 'Vos iz di untershte shure?'[28]

The Yiddish voice has been promoted by many American writers – Philip Roth, Saul Bellow and Cynthia Ozick are just a few examples – and by a vast number of American comedians, including Woody Allen, Lenny Bruce and Larry David. Millions of English-speakers with no Jewish connections are familiar with *lox*, *shtick* and the exclamation *oy vay*, as well as with distinctively Yiddish expressions such as 'I need it like a hole in the head'. The role of Yiddish in Jewish folk culture has enriched its poetic colour. I've heard it said that comics are to literature as Yiddish is to English – an analogy likely to meet with objections, yet pertinent in its emphasis on the capacity of Yiddish for graphic storytelling, and also intriguing when we think of how many of the great American comic book artists and cartoonists have been Jewish: Stan Lee and Jack Kirby, Joe Shuster and Jerome Siegel, Will Eisner and Art Spiegelman.

The contributions of the languages just mentioned and of others are tangible in Merriam–Webster's *12,000 Words* (1986), which furnishes details of words and meanings that have become established in American English since *Webster's Third New International Dictionary of the English Language* was published in 1961. About a tenth of these are borrowed – all but a few of them nouns. We find *après-ski*, *linguine* and the Brazilian Portuguese *favela* (for a contemporary context, think of Fernando Meirelles's seethingly brilliant film *City of God*). Here too are the Yoruba *dashiki*, the Hindi *tabla*, the Vietnamese outfit called an *ao dai*, and *ikebana*, the Japanese word for flower-arranging.

Unsurprisingly, however, in *12,000 Words* the Spanish element is to the fore, and, in the more than two decades since, the number of borrowings from Spanish has escalated. It is now possible to imagine that at some point in the not too remote future the growing Spanish-speaking population of the US will demand that their language be accorded official status at a national level, though of course the Constitution at present grants no such status even to English.

For comparison, we may look at Canada. Canadian English has been touched by the influence of many immigrants, including those from Germany, Ukraine and China, and this influence has been cemented through political support for the teaching of 'Heritage Languages'. But the main linguistic tension has been between English and French. In the closing decades of the seventeenth century, English adventurers began to penetrate the lucrative Canadian fur industry, which had up till then been dominated by the French, and the English language began to assert itself. In due course the French would surrender their claim to Newfoundland, and settlers moved north from New England to Nova Scotia. English-speaking loyalists fled to Canada in the aftermath of the War of Independence, and were followed by British and Irish immigrants in the nineteenth century. For a brief moment in the 1780s the Nova Scotian coastal town of Shelburne was the largest city in British North America.[29] But French held on, in Quebec and also in communities dotted through Labrador, Newfoundland and northern Ontario. The confederation of Canada's provinces in 1867 forged a political unity which was essentially anglophone but made some provision for bilingualism. Thereafter, as the use of French was curtailed, the relative statuses of the two languages became a blazing political issue. The Official Languages Act of 1969 formally recognized both English and French, and its revised version in 1988 consolidated bilingual policy.

There are numerous French words in Canadian English. Anglophones in Quebec, most of whom reside in Montreal, may refer unselfconsciously to a *dépanneur* (corner store) or a *caisse populaire* (credit union), to the widely spoken *joual* patois (its name a rural pronunciation of *cheval*), and to the knitted cap known as a *tuque* or the meat pie called a *tourtière*. Yet at present less than quarter of Canadians are francophone, and there is less seepage into English from French in Canada than there is from Spanish in the most Hispanic parts of the US.

Today there are more Hispanics in the US than in Spain, and their median age is well below thirty. They promise to write important chapters in the histories of not just one language, but two.

13. Ethos

The characteristic spirit of a people or community; the 'genius' of an institution or system

From Greek *ēthos*, meaning 'character' or 'disposition'. Initially it was used in English with particular reference to Aristotle's definition of the term in his *Rhetoric*, where it denoted the moral and intellectual qualities that enabled a speaker to appeal to his audience.

Ethnic and regional tensions are a motif of American history. In 1860, when Abraham Lincoln became the first Republican president, he did so without the support of a single Southern state. Lincoln's election prompted disgruntled Southerners to secede from the Union, laying the ground for the Civil War. That same year New Zealand Maoris revolted against British control of their land, and the Second Opium War, which had pitted the British against China's Qing Dynasty, ended with the Convention of Peking, under which the opium trade was legalized and the British established a permanent diplomatic presence in the Chinese capital. At this time, too, Italy was in the process of unification, Japan was emerging from the shadows of feudalism, and the Russian Empire was being overhauled (serfdom was abolished in 1861), while, in the wake of the Indian Mutiny of 1857 and the dissolution of the East India Company, the British role in India was also in the throes of reform. Nevertheless, against this background of upheaval, the real stories of the nineteenth century played on, uninterrupted: a great swell of invention and technology, together with urbanization, the reign of coal and steam power, the growth of religious doubt, the proliferation of ideologies, and the contest between progressives and reactionaries, as well as new ideas about social responsibility, the class system, education and manners.

In a letter dating from October 1860, Queen Victoria writes to her eldest daughter requesting 'a photo'. We may be tickled by her doing so, but we shouldn't be surprised. The word, which was of course an abbreviation of *photograph*, was becoming common. *Photograph* was itself a new coinage, built from Greek components, but *photo* signalled the wide acceptance of this little bit of mechanical magic – invented by William Fox Talbot, and independently accomplished (with greater fanfare) by Louis Daguerre, a one-time taxman whose name is preserved in the noun *daguerreotype*. Talbot preferred to speak of *photogenic drawing*; it was Sir John Herschel who pressed for the adoption of *photography*, and the greater pliability of that word meant that it caught on, along with *photograph* and *photographic*. The popularity of the practice and of the word would rocket during the First World War, when photos helped construct the shared experience of being caught up in conflict.

The abbreviated form *photo* chimes with the immediate appeal of amateur photography and also with the medium's brisk documentary usefulness, first experienced in Britain through Samuel Bourne's pictures of 1860s India and Roger Fenton's of the landscapes of the Crimean War. The photo's quick (and by the end of the century affordable) combination of the artistic and the mechanical symbolized the way technology could redraw the boundaries of aesthetics. Yet photography met with hostility – as indeed did the word itself. John Ruskin, writing in 1872, could argue that photos, though 'worth anything' in the fields of geology and geography, 'for art purposes' had a value 'a good deal less than zero'.[1]

A related word is *cliché*. At the start of the nineteenth century it was a term among printers for a plate or cast used in type foundries. Charles Babbage could employ it with a sense of wonder in 1832; a generation later it was used quite casually by Darwin. But by the end of the century it had acquired a new figurative sense – one with which we are all now familiar. An expression repeated too often bears the shallow mechanical imprint of the printing plate: you can hear in the word the wet click of a machine and then a metallic emptiness. The semantically related word *stereotype* derives from an eighteenth-century printing technique; around the middle of the nineteenth century it began to signify something endlessly and tediously repeated, and its application to simplistic, preconceived ideas (of people, places, situations) grew out of this.

These two words, *cliché* and *photo*, can be seen as tokens of the age. One signifies both the trend for specific, professional vocabulary to be slipped into everyday talk and the way polite or popular usage tends to become mechanical: the other suggests the passionate striving after new ideas, embodied in language, and its mixed reception hints at the resistance that can greet it. *Photograph* is a symptom of the period's appetite for the technical majesty of Greek. *Photo* typifies the way the technical gets stripped down, softened and even bastardized – a perennial concern among nineteenth-century commentators. *Cliché* is, for its part, another fine example of a French word that, with time, has drifted further and further from its birthplace; for, while both common pronunciations of the word preserve its Gallic bouquet, the term is used without a trace of the self-consciousness with which we might utter *santé* or *touché* – and its Frenchness may strike those who hear it less forcibly even than that of *café*.

Right at the end of the eighteenth century, and in the early part of the nineteenth, French imports asserted themselves, and so did numerous words directly connected with French affairs. Many of these have long since become detached from their original context: the French Revolution, which convulsed Paris in the summer of 1789, taming the monarchy and ushering in a programme of 'rational reform'. The events of that summer bequeathed to English *emigré*, *civism*, *terrorist* and *democrat* – the last two of which, especially, have been freed from their historical moorings. Edmund Burke could write in 1795 of 'those Hell-hounds called Terrorists', enjoying the newness of the term; by then, Thomas Jefferson and James Madison had established their status as *democrats* opposed to the Federalist politics of Alexander Hamilton. It was a Frenchman intimate with the United States, Alexis de Tocqueville, who proved instrumental in popularizing *ancien régime*, a formula not current before 1789.

The republican spirit of the Revolution was rapturously embraced. Percy Bysshe Shelley could write in *Prometheus Unbound* (1820) that 'The loathesome mask has fallen' and that man was now 'Exempt from awe, worship, degree'. Seizing on the implications of a society free from hereditary distinctions, he claimed in *A Defence of Poetry* that poets were 'the unacknowledged legislators of the world'. The classic image of the Romantic poet is of a figure at once solitary and political, contemplative and energetic. Shelley was all these things and more: a visionary moralist, he crusaded against his fellow men's instinctive desire to impose their will on others, even embracing a vegetarian diet as a sign of idealism. Yet, with his famously sweet tooth, he was also an enthusiastic consumer of the unctuous rewards of empire, even as he reviled the means by which they were harvested. Strikingly, his oriental poems are full of decorative fauna and flora, the 'shimmering' materials of a 'fabricated East'. It is a paradox of his poetry that its progressive understanding of gender and national identity was grounded in classics of colonialism like Edward Moor's *Hindu Pantheon* (1810) and Sydney Owenson's *The Missionary* (1811).[2]

The poets we group together as Romantics rebelled against the orderliness of their predecessors. Their writing celebrated spontaneity, and illuminated the natural world. To see the world was to create it anew, to sharpen what Shelley called our 'blunted' senses. Romantic poetry reclaimed the basic act of feeling, and its lyricism was ecstatically personal – exclamation marks are frequent; sincerity is more important than craft. The individual was glorified, and there was beauty in his or her melancholy. Yet, to look forward, the Romantics felt they had to look back. 'We are all Greeks,' Shelley could write in the preface to his *Hellas*, and 'our laws, our literature, our religion, our arts have their root in Greece.' His creative contemporaries shared this sense of the past as a hive of honeyed detail, into which they could reach for inspiration. They were passionate in reviving time-worn diction, especially where it seemed to connect them with a lost naturalness. They had grown up at a time when traditional ballads were being recuperated – and when the atmospheric medievalism of the *Gothic* (a word on the whole used as a slight) was in vogue. The literature they created was much closer to the norms of speech than the elaborate 'correctness' of the previous century. To be Romantic was to claim back imagination, emotion and freedom.

Quarrying the past could be profitable in more ways than one. The 'plainer and emphatic language' acclaimed by Wordsworth was a national treasure, a 'simple and unelaborated' expression of an intrinsic Britishness, but others cast about for a more commercial kind of treasure. A huge inspiration was Thomas Percy's *Reliques of Ancient English Poetry* (1765), which presented in detail the illustrious history of English folklore. Scottish anthologists also profited from the fresh interest in folklore, and so did Scottish poets. When Robert Burns reclaimed Scottish dialect in his poems and songs, the ensuing success enabled him to shelve his desperate plan of emigrating to Jamaica. In Bristol, the teenage poet Thomas Chatterton plundered an early-eighteenth-century dictionary by John Kersey for the antique lexis he needed to stamp authenticity on his medieval forgeries. The very titles and openings of his poems signal his archaic inclinations: 'Ynn auntient Dayes, when Kenewalchyn Kynge', 'Knightes Templaries Chyrche', 'Ethelgar. A Saxon Poem'. Here there was an appetite for a rather morbid, ancient Englishness. In much the same vein John Keats, who was capable of imagining himself bellowing in the trenches alongside Achilles or wafting along the banks of the river Styx, slaked his craving for beauty and 'fine excess' with quaint Spenserian coinages like *upfurled*, *bosomer* and *tittlebat*.

Romantic art was, according to Thomas Carlyle, a replacement for the decayed functions of the Church, and was indeed a new and 'proper' Church. Its liturgy was bold. In the itinerant and peasant folk of Dorset, whom he initially dismissed as an assortment of cheats and thieves, Wordsworth came to see what he would later call 'the depth of human souls' – souls, he added, 'that appear to have no depth at all / To vulgar eyes'. His sympathy for rural living led him to employ what he considered to be true rustic speech. He revived the Norse *ghyll* as a word for a wooded ravine, albeit deeming it necessary to supply an explanatory note – Sir Walter Scott felt able to use it without any such explanation. And both Wordsworth and Coleridge fetched up the Norse *tarn* to signify a small mountain lake. They could have found it in John Ray's *A Collection of English Words Not Generally Used* (1674), but not among their contemporaries.

Wordsworth and Coleridge are often paired. They met in 1795, became firm friends two years later, and in 1798 jointly produced *Lyrical Ballads*, a venture that was at first published anonymously but later, when their authorship was disclosed, ensured that their names would for ever be entwined. Yet Wordsworth's style was always distinct from that of Coleridge, and after their friendship collapsed in 1810 they moved in markedly different directions – reflected in Coleridge's criticism of Wordsworth in *Biographia Literaria* (1817). At the risk of generalization, one might suggest that Coleridge's language is more exotic and highly coloured than Wordsworth's, especially in his choice of adjectives, and that Wordsworth's metaphors are more deeply embedded in his poetry.[3] Wordsworth borrows less because his language is more organic: Coleridge reaches for the magical properties of others' achievements in science and literature, hoping to transcend what seems to him a rather dank sort of English empiricism.

Like many of his contemporaries, Coleridge was emboldened by reading Captain Cook's accounts of his voyages. What another poet, William Cowper, called 'the honey of . . . deep research' was a delicious source of nourishment. Coleridge's exoticism is perfectly illustrated in the well-known 'Kubla Khan'. He combines vocabulary typical of the Gothic – *cavern, chasm, tumult* – with lusciously foreign touches like *honeydew*, the brilliantly made-up *pleasuredome*, and the *dulcimer* belonging to an Abyssinian maid. His Xanadu brings to mind the imagery of paradise that had invigorated Mediterranean adventurers half a millennium before. Yet its details cannot be mapped: Coleridge suggests that the British appetite for the Orient originates in fantasy, and that its destiny is also fantasy, a projection of the traveller's own psyche and desires. In 'The Rime of the Ancient Mariner' his archaism authenticates his supernatural subject matter. In its imagery there is a connection with the deep past of English verse – audible in lines such as 'And now the Storm-blast came, and he / Was tyrannous and strong' or 'And every tongue, through utter drought, / Was withered at the root.' There is, moreover, a strong Anglo-Saxon element, including the marvellously mildewed adverb *eftsoons*.

There were other influences saturating Coleridge's mind. In *Biographia Literaria* he can employ the seemingly archaic *aglow* and *homelike*, yet also the German term *pasquillant* (a composer of lampoons) and the fiendishly technical *incorrespondency*. His challenging register prompted Byron to write, in the dedication to *Don Juan* (1819–24):

And Coleridge, too, has lately taken wing,
But like a hawk encumber'd with his hood –
Explaining metaphysics to the nation –
I wish he would explain his Explanation.

Byron was understandably confused, for Coleridge's language was strikingly stylized. His reading in German – and above all of Immanuel Kant – endowed him with a vocabulary of abstract thought, of hypothesis and metaphysics and the imagination. He adopts the word *clerisy* as a collective term for men of learning, and writes of the *esemplastic* power of the imagination, to suggest its unifying force, taking his lead from the German *Ineinsbildung*. He borrows the adjective *derb*, meaning 'solid' or 'rough', and also, on the model of the German, speaks of *humanism*. He is an early user of the adjective *aesthetic* – adopted into German by Alexander Baumgarten, popularized by Kant, and seen by Coleridge as a highly esoteric term, although to us it looks quite normal. Baumgarten and those who followed stressed the importance of the senses: Coleridge wished he could find an easier word to do the job, especially as others found this one so pedantic.[4] But for Coleridge it was necessary to have the right words with which to mark what he considered important conceptual distinctions, and he coined and imported terms to satisfy this need.

The ten months Coleridge spent in Germany in 1798–9 were a revelation. They ensured his esteem not just for that country's wines, brass doorbells and variety of soups, but also for German prowess in natural history, theology and philosophy – and for the whole broad sweep of European intellectual life. His subsequent borrowings from German were inspired by the studies in which he engrossed himself while at Göttingen. A few examples are *Messianic*, *misology* (a word for hatred of discussion, from Immanuel Kant's *Misologie*) and *Naturphilosophie*. Although not many such terms caught on, Coleridge can be recognized as an early disciple of a Teutonic intellectualism that would have longer-lived consequences.

Coleridge was excited by the white heat of the intellectual present. By contrast, the prolific and internationally successful Walter Scott, though he shared with Coleridge the distinction of being much admired in Russia, was inspired by the past. Scott's desire to 'contribute somewhat to the history of my native country' led him to collect old songs and ballads, and he was influential in bolstering the position of Scottish words in English: *blackmail*, for instance, which Nicol Jarvie in *Rob Roy* (1817) finds it necessary to explain to the Englishman Frank Osbaldistone, and *cosy*, which derives from the Gaelic *cosagach*; the ghostly *eldritch* and the daunting *awesome* and *gruesome*; the softer *winsome* and crackling *guffaw*; *faraway*, *uncanny* and *wizened*, which in dialogue became 'wuzzent'; the expression *kith and kin*; and many more.[5] One scholar has gone so far as to suggest that 'He gave to the English language possibly more English words than any author since Shakespeare.'[6] He popularized *glamour*, a word which at that time conveyed the idea of magical enchantment; only in the last hundred years has it calcified and come to suggest a hard-edged and rather less mysterious kind of attractiveness. These words now seem far removed from their Scots Gaelic origins, but in using them Scott was either introducing something new into English vocabulary or reviving a word that had long since fallen into disuse. Scottish words we now take for granted have baffled previous generations. *Kipper*, when encountered by Daniel Defoe during his tour of Great Britain in the 1720s, seemed odd enough to warrant explanation. *Glen* was adopted as early as the sixteenth century by Spenser, but when Samuel Johnson used it in a letter in 1773 he still felt he had to provide a gloss.

Scott also popularized a few words of 'Eastern' hue, including *dervish*, but the main influence in this area was Byron, who spent almost a third of his life abroad, as if to compensate for missing out on the Grand Tour. His 'Oriental' poetry was coloured by both wide reading and his experiences in Greece, Albania and Turkey. 'With those countries, and events connected with them, all my really poetical feelings begin and end,' he could write to his friend Thomas Moore in 1816.[7] Fidelity to the true local colour is deemed essential, although Byron, like contemporaries such as Goethe, seems more provoked by the idea of the East than absorbed in actually understanding it. He subscribes to a collective fantasy of Eastern promise. In *The Giaour* (1813) we hear 'the browsing camels' bells . . .

tinkling'; altogether more exotic are the sharp *ataghan* sheathed in silver and the euphoric cries of *Bismillah*. In *The Bride of Abydos*, published in the same year, we are presented with a *comboloio* (a Muslim rosary made up of ninety-nine beads), while in the following year's *The Corsair* the strongest reek of the exotic is the 'dissolving cloud' that rises from the Turkish pipe called a *chibouque*. He employs words such as *bulbul, camise, alma* and *tambourgi*, and is comfortable enough with *kiosk, gazelle* and *minaret* to use them as rhyme words.[8] His use of *Stamboul* rather than *Istanbul* was also much copied.

Byron was forever snuffing up the flavours of the places he visited, all so different from the 'Babylon' of London, and acquiring exotic language was an activity to be savoured. In Athens, for instance, he learnt Italian from a polyglot teenage boy, Nicolo Giraud, and took particular pleasure in conjugating both the ancient and modern Greek equivalents of the verb *to embrace*.[9] Later, he found the 'bastard Latin' of the Venetians 'sweet', and one of his projects during his time in their city was to learn Armenian – an Indo-European language with its own 38-letter alphabet – from a group of exiled Mechitarist monks. Byron's *Marino Faliero* (1820), about an ambitious fourteenth-century doge, was a flawed attempt at Italianate drama, as was his friend Shelley's tragedy *The Cenci* (1819). Shelley's writing is coloured by his taste for Italian opera, and by imagery absorbed from Hindustani lyrics and airs.[10] Yet such pleasures could be wearing, and it barely seems a coincidence that Byron is the first to write of someone being *blasé* – Don Juan, to be precise.

While the French Revolution had inspired both artistic and political reform on a grand scale, as the rise of the middle classes fostered new styles of liberal democracy, a second upheaval, very different and less abrupt, brought more tangible changes. The *Industrial Revolution* – the coinage is Arnold Toynbee's – created wealth, a new working class and a whole new culture of work, a new urban landscape, and a modern economy, yet it also exacerbated social schisms and imperilled the environment. (It is doing so still, especially outside Europe.) The rural workers idealized by Wordsworth were migrating to the crowded cities. By the time of the 1851 census, half the UK's populations lived in cities or in towns. 'First came steam and steel,' wrote H. G. Wells in his brisk, novelistic *A Short History of World*, 'the railway, the great liner, vast bridges and buildings, machinery of almost limitless power, the possibility of a bountiful satisfaction of every material human need, and then . . . the hidden treasures of electrical science were opened.'[11] Philosophically, the transition was from man using tools to man being a tool: new technologies revised the very idea of 'work', and laid fresh emphasis on labour as power.

Britain was the world's richest country. In the middle of the century it accounted for about a fifth of the world's manufacturing. It was, as historians have since repeatedly intoned, 'the workshop of the world'. And while its population was growing at a rate of more than 1 per cent a year, its annual gross national product was rising at more than 2 per cent.[12] In *The Coal Question* (1865) the economist William Stanley Jevons, who pioneered the theory of *marginal utility*, could write triumphally:

> The plains of North America and Russia are our corn fields; Chicago and Odessa our granaries; Canada and the Baltic our timber-forests; Australasia contains our sheepfarms, and in Argentina and on the western prairies of North America are our herds of oxen; Peru sends her silver, and the gold of South Africa and Australia flows to London; the Hindus and the Chinese grow tea for us, and our coffee, sugar and spice plantations are in all the Indies.[13]

Jevons spoke for an age that demanded 'progress', expected it to continue indefinitely, and saw empire as the key instrument for achieving this. Part of Britain's success, as he saw it, was the export of ideas. He was the first British author to refer to the Japanese *yen* and the Swedish *krona*, and did so in a discussion of the international development of a gold standard – established in Britain in 1844, and adopted by many of the world's major powers in the 1870s. The Victorian embrace of corporate activity – energized by new legislation in the 1840s and '50s – was signalled by the borrowing of *entrepreneur* and *laissez-faire*, as well as by the emergence of *capitalist* and *stakeholder*.

Even learning was mechanized and commodified. Visiting Britain in 1848, Ralph Waldo Emerson informed American readers that 'The logical English train a scholar as they train an engineer. Oxford is a Greek factory, as Wilton mills weave carpet, and Sheffield grinds steel.' 'The atmosphere is loaded with Greek learning,' he went on, and 'The English nature takes culture kindly.'[14] The nineteenth century proved generous in its rehabilitation of Greek words as terms of English-language science and scholarship. It is to this period that we owe such Grecian coinages as *colostomy* and *brachycephalous*, the more palatable *ethos* and *neuron*, and markers of technological development like *gramophone* and *telegram*. In 1878 the world's first telephone network, in the Connecticut town of New Haven, had 21 subscribers; seven years later, 150,000 Americans owned a phone.[15] The pioneering electrical work of Thomas Edison and those who followed him gave rise to what was humorously dubbed 'Schenectady Greek'.[16] Besides inventing the light bulb, Edison seems to have initiated the habit of answering the phone with the exclamation *hello* – once a ferryman's call, yet touched with just a hint of Grecian colour.

Greek prefixes were also lavishly productive: *meta-*, *epi-* and *hypo-* are notable examples. Their temper is academic and assertively technical. The period's classic discussion of human achievement and excellence, Samuel Smiles's *Self-Help* (1859), is a paean to technical genius. Smiles, whose work was translated into more than fifty languages, was not the first to write of *self-help*, but the concept as we now understand it was a new one. In a memorable episode, he describes the mathematician Edmund Stone being asked how, despite his humble origins as the son of a gardener, he had got to grips with Newton's *Principia Mathematica*. Stone had replied, 'One needs only to know the twenty-four letters of the alphabet in order to learn everything that one wishes' – a distinctly mechanical view of what it means to read.

Mention of Smiles and South African gold, and of Darwin and Ruskin, will conjure for many of us a single potently emotive word: *Victorian*. We tend to feel we know what the Victorians were like. Perhaps this is because, in Britain, the spirit of Victorianism seems never quite to have faded. In a recent history of the British middle class, Lawrence James writes that 'We are the inheritors of Victorian civic and private benevolence. It has provided us with parks, libraries, museums, town halls, hospitals, universities, schools, churches, swimming baths, public lavatories, horse troughs and those now derelict drinking fountains with brass scoops. These conveniences perfectly reflected that Victorian blend of compassion and practicality.'[17]

We may think also of the Victorian music halls, which were home to volcanic displays of patriotic zeal, or of humanitarians as disparate as the Bradford mill-owner Sir Titus Salt and Dickens's terrifyingly feckless Mrs Jellyby. We may think of an age in which the waning of religion was answered by a faith in culture. More than anything, we think of orderliness and propriety – and sometimes, too, of prudery, even as we are aware that the once-popular image of Victorian primness has been made more ambiguous and complex by modern scholarship.

In science and technology, the Victorian period produced a succession of visionaries. Increasingly specialized, science was also increasingly apt to excite the public, and Victorian achievements in the field were interleaved with controversies. Charles Lyell's *Principles of Geology* (1830–33) advanced the contentious idea that the Earth had been shaped by forces that operated slowly and over long periods of time. This was dubbed *uniformitarianism*. The view which it supplanted, more consistent with the Bible's teachings, was that over a comparatively short period the planet had been shaken by a succession of sudden, brief and extreme events. In a review of the *Principles'* second volume, William Whewell coined the word *catastrophist* to denote the traditional belief against which Lyell was arguing. Lyell's influence was profound. Darwin devoured the *Principles of Geology* while aboard the *Beagle*, and his own radical theories began as an expansion of Lyell's. Moreover, the dissension surrounding the *Principles* sparked huge public interest in earth sciences.

Mineralogy, like philosophy and the social sciences, was an area in which German expertise was fabled. (Incidentally, the use of *expert* as a noun is a nineteenth-century development, though the adjective had been around for half a millennium.) As long ago as the 1570s the German assayer Jonas Schutz had been brought in to supervise the smelting works on the royal manor at Dartford, while

Somerset miners in the seventeenth century used a kind of German dowsing rod known as a *Wunschelrute*. It is from contact with German expertise that we get *cobalt*, *quartz*, *shale*, *gneiss* and *zinc*. From the same source we derive a great many specialist terms in the field, like *bergschrund*, *thalweg* and *geest*. In German folklore, cobalt's reputation for enfeebling the miners who brought it up from the ground was linked to the presence in the mines of a malign spirit known as a *Kobold*. The association between digging underground and coming across wicked sprites was popular: the English *nickel* comes from Swedish, but can be traced back to the German *Kupfernickel* – the half of this word that the English preserves is another German term for a mischievous, mine-dwelling imp.

Geology sabotaged the credibility of the Bible's account of time, and the fashion for the subject – evident in Harriet Martineau's claim that in the 1830s the middle classes were buying five times more geology books than novels – created an imposingly difficult vocabulary.[18] By contrast, the linguistic effects of Darwinism were subtle. Words were repositioned. Thus *development* became associated, almost impalpably, with *evolution* and *natural selection*.

As for the wider scientific language, a large portion of its novelties were classical and decidedly obscure. Among those to have found currency are *palaeontology*, *bacteria*, *altimeter* and *jurassic*. *Dinosaur* was coined by Richard Owen in 1842. The word meant 'terrible lizard'; Owen had scrupulously examined the fossils discovered by collectors such as William Buckland, and the noun testifies to the astonishing taxonomic moment inspired by the realization that such fearsome reptiles once roamed the planet. Other coinages were more insidious. Darwin's polymathic cousin Francis Galton came up with *eugenic* in 1883; the politics of Social Darwinism were made respectable by means of a handsome Greek name. In the same vein there was the neo-Greek *moron*, coined in 1910 by H. H. Goddard, the pioneer of the IQ test and director of New Jersey's Vineland Training School for Feeble-minded Girls and Boys. (The word had previously existed, but only to denote a particular kind of dark-skinned salamander – something Goddard probably didn't know.) It rapidly became a term of abuse or disdain, and its usefulness as a technical term for people with mental retardation diminished as it did so. But it was minted in a spirit of eugenic elitism. At the same time there emerged a new vocabulary of terms to denigrate religion. *Pietistic* is one. *Pious*, which had been acquiring connotations of self-righteousness since the seventeenth century, became more obviously pejorative. Meanwhile, *agnostic* was coined by 'Darwin's bulldog', T. H. Huxley, who was the period's leading commentator not just on science, but on the implications of science for humanity.

The increasing sense of the world and indeed the universe as essentially mechanical places found expression in a distaste for 'spiritual' explanations of existence. This was an age of -*isms*, self-conscious intellectual and moral positions, typically outside the purview of religion. Owen Barfield sums it up shrewdly: 'We are hardly conscious at all of being *human*, more so of being *humane*, more still of being *humanitarian*, and very conscious . . . of *humanitarianism*.'[19] A more self-inspecting attitude tends to call for, or give rise to, a vocabulary more clearly touched by science – or by the illusion of scientific nicety.

In the nineteenth century -*isms* not only came increasingly to be identified by that name, but also began to be stigmatized. Classicism was cherished, then impugned, then cherished afresh – a return to the altercations of the Inkhorn controversy. At this time the rather scientific prefix *non-* became vastly popular, and we find authors using words like *non-native*, *non-paying*, *non-white* and *non-sectarian*, as well as George Washington's coinage *non-discrimination*. A more scientific spin was even imparted to the approximate, with the increased use of the pretentiously classical *circa*. The habit of dignifying the ordinary with Latin tags was long established. Victorians who labelled their books *ex libris* or adopted such novel terms as *in absentia*, *genius loci* or *status quo* were simply adding to a tradition of advertising their education (or their aspirations) by means of highly polished insignia. They did so in the face of a process, begun in the previous century, which involved converting Latin tags and Latin borrowings into more congenial English forms.

An eloquent few craved a return to the supposed purity of Anglo-Saxon diction. Dickens and Thomas Hardy pushed for it, and so did Gerard Manley Hopkins, who had a particular taste for odd coinages such as *spendsavour* and *lovescape*, akin to Willam Barnes's *wheelsaddle* and *nipperlings*. Thomas Carlyle dreamt up *anywhen* on the model of *anywhere*, coined adjectives such as *hawkish* and *wrongish*, had a taste for forming his own peculiar negatives (*ungorgeous*, *unlucid*, *unphilosopher*), and favoured words ending -*dom*, following the model of a whole range of German words that ended in -*tum*. Tellingly, when he wrote of *bureaucracy* he fastened it between inverted commas and deemed it a 'Continental nuisance'. The second half of the nineteenth century witnessed a surge of enthusiasm for Norse litera-ture. William Morris took refuge from modernity (and, naturally, from Frenchness) in an imaginary medieval past, and his Nordic enthusiasms were palpable in a string of almost Viking coinages: *manfolk*, *unangry*, *unwrongful*, *eastering*, *wind-drift*, *hillward* and, his special verb for a heron's guttural croak, *to squark*. One of his inheritors was J. R. R. Tolkien, who shared his philological appetites and devel-oped for his imaginary Middle Earth a raft of Elvish languages. In grasping for the Germanic roots of English, Tolkien created fantasy out of what was in fact a lost reality. The affection for what were seen as Anglo-Saxon or Teutonic qualities was encouraged, in the 1850s and '60s, by a wave of revulsion for the French. According to this view, the Norman Conquest had been an aberration, and it was vital to assert the role of the Anglo-Saxons as England's founding fathers. Thomas Nicholas, in *The Pedigree of the English People* (1868), drew up a table which demonstrated – to him, at least – that the English were a compound only of Celtic and Teutonic influences.[20]

Nonetheless, *medieval* at this time became a slur, and it was the mechanical impulse that predominated in an age where even human behaviour was codified as if to be manufactured. Chesterfield's notions of etiquette were now formalized. The emphasis was on practicality, on systems of regulated decorum. In Henry John Todd's revision of Johnson's *Dictionary*, published in 1818, etiquette was explicitly calibrated against 'rank, and place'. Conduct could be quantified; manners were not the equivalent of morals, but were instead a question of knowledge, of rules and conventions. The best-selling *Enquire Within Upon Everything*, a guide boasting expertise in matters from burying a relative to making a wax model of a flower, advises, 'Be discreet and sparing of your words', 'A gentleman walking, should always wear gloves' and 'Never be without a handkerchief.' 'Moderation, decorum, and neatness distinguish the gentleman,' readers are counselled. 'The correctness of his mind induces him to bend to etiquette, but not to stoop to adulation.'[21] Significantly, books of this kind were written for financial gain, rather than out of any great sense of moral urgency.[22]

The Great Exhibition of 1851 highlighted the quasi-religious ardour with which Victorian Britain cultivated domestic virtues. Its 2,000-page catalogue boasted of being 'a book of reference to the philosopher, merchant, and manufacturer'. Dickens complained that the exhibition contained too much – that the atmosphere of this temple to material abundance was thoroughly oppressive. But for its apologists, such as Charles Babbage, it was a chance to give the intricacies of technology an aura of religious magnificence. Six million visitors paid homage. One of the exhibitors was Adolf Sax, a Belgian, who proudly displayed a set of instruments to be played by military bands, including his recent invention the *saxophone*. Other exhibits propelled new words into the limelight: *lorry, lithograph, hydromechanics*, and some long since forgotten articles, like *dhoop*, a piney resin from Bhutan, the commercially worthless *hyawaballi* wood of Guyana, a Philippine fabric called *jusi*, and *serpentcleide*, a wooden bass bugle.

Technology promised to extend the domain of the human mind, and British pre-eminence in the field was considered a given. Less secure, though, was the status of the language needed to maintain this. One recurrent theme among technophiles was that mechanical sophistication mattered more than elegance; as far as language was concerned, it was better to avoid felicitous foreign novelties and instead concentrate on 'correctness'.

Techniques of correctness were strenuously moralized. *The Habits of Good Society*, a volume on etiquette dating from 1859, suggests that 'Perhaps the most useful accomplishment . . . is a knowledge of languages . . . [for] you are liable in really good society . . . to meet with foreigners having a very slight acquaintance with English. From them you may derive a vast amount of information . . . [and] you will rarely meet with a Frenchman, Italian, or German, from whom you may not gather much curious information which will serve you elsewhere.'[23] However, 'the worst vulgarity is an assumption of refinement in the choice of language': the author explains that 'the best speakers will never use a Latin word where an Anglo-Saxon one will do as well.'[24] Another publication, more directly concerned with languages, was *A Dictionary of Daily Blunders* (1880), whose author, Thomas Preston, assailed such vices as Americanisms and inept metaphors, while reserving special distaste for those who 'introduce foreign words and phrases into ordinary writing at every opportunity, when there are English words to express the same meaning equally well'.[25] 'A slip of the tongue is bad enough, but how much worse is a slip of the pen!' Preston exclaims, adding that, while 'blunders are occasionally frivolous,' for any reader who 'discovers he has been innocently blundering, the book will be well worth its cost'.[26] Resistance to this kind of attitude was common. In *Middlemarch* it is summed up by Fred Vincy, who denounces 'correct' usage as 'the slang of prigs'.

Anxieties about the state of the language were nothing new, but there was a fresh sense that urgent efforts were needed in order to keep barbarisms at bay. In part this was cultural xenophobia, in part moral anxiety. To the most extreme purists, each new word that entered the language seemed to mark a cultural trauma. In some cases we can precisely determine the moment this happened. There may be no better example than *radioactive*, first used by Pierre and Marie Curie in a report to the French Academy of Sciences on 18 July 1898; ten days later the word appeared in the British magazine *Nature*. *Sociology* was coined by the philosopher Auguste Comte in 1830, was first used in an English text in 1843, and was eagerly taken up by Herbert Spencer, who was responsible for the phrase often wrongly attributed to Darwin, 'the survival of the fittest'. The Crimean War gave rise to *cardigan* and *balaclava*, and popularized *ambulance*, which derived from *hôpital ambulant*, a 'walking hospital'. At the risk of merely listing instances, I'll briefly note a few more. The *omnibus*, which drew its name from the Latin meaning 'for all', was launched in Nantes in the 1820s and introduced to Britain by George Shillibeer in 1829 – his service ran from Paddington into the City of London. *Mascot* was made known by Edmond Audran's comic opera *La Mascotte*, which premiered in December 1880; the word derives from a Provençal term for a magic charm. We should be aware, however, that *La Mascotte's* first performance would not have been called a *premiere*, for that word was not used in its theatrical sense until 1889. It was short for *première représentation*, a mouthful that certainly wasn't going to catch on. Early in the next century we find *superman*, which is George Bernard Shaw's calque of the German *Übermensch*, a motif of Nietzsche's philosophy. Shaw also introduced *Wunderkind*, and was a great one for turning people's names into adjectives, coining for instance *Tiepolesque* and *Rodinesque*, *Strindbergian*, *Mendelssohnic* and the clumsy *Beethovenian*. (Is the dreadful *Shavian* his payback for doing so?) More usefully, he brought in *realpolitik* and, long before D. H. Lawrence employed the phrase in *Lady Chatterley's Lover*, the muckily erotic *nostalgie de la boue*.

For its part, the word *neologism* first appeared in 1799, and in 1841 Isaac D'Israeli, so savage in his criticism of the verbose Hamon L'Estrange, could write of the way 'neologisms have fertilised the barrenness of our Saxon, and the finest geniuses in Europe have abandoned the language of Cicero, to transfuse its grace into an idiom whose penury was deemed too rude for the pen of the scholar.'[27] Irony abounds here, and others took up the cudgels in unambiguously moral terms. Henry Alford, a pious cleric who had at the age of ten produced a pamphlet with the wonderfully earnest title *Looking unto Jesus: The Believer's Support under Trials and Afflictions*, published *A Plea for the Queen's English* in 1864 – by which time he was fifty-four and dean of Canterbury. Alford was much concerned with misspelling in newspapers, the overuse of commas, and the abundance of silly nicknames. He worried about 'American debasements' – 'their reckless exaggeration' and 'blunted sense of moral obligation' – and counselled readers to 'avoid . . . all *slang* words,' as this kind of talk was fit only 'for raw schoolboys, and one-term freshmen, to astonish their sisters with'.[28] He would doubt-less have been shocked to read a letter Queen Victoria wrote in December 1863, in which she described the sky as *lilacky*. And still more painful to him would have been those American imports of the period we have already seen: *blizzard, graveyard, loafer* and *lengthy*.

The number of words borrowed from French decreased in the early part of the nineteenth century, after the heyday of post-

Revolutionary loans, but it was still the living foreign language that English-speakers were most likely to learn, and by 1840 imports were on the rise again. Peter Mark Roget's celebrated *Thesaurus* (1852) contains a noticeably large volume of French terms and phrases, as we might expect given his francophone background. New words and phrases from French included *rapprochement* and *camaraderie, clairvoyance* and *allure, noblesse oblige* and *amour propre. Abattoir*, a word current in French after Napoleon's reforms of 1810, began to displace the less hygienic-sounding *slaughterhouse*. French was usually associated with *politesse* and fashionable living, although it was often criticized, as for instance by Thomas De Quincey, who claimed that its 'very power . . . as a language for social intercourse, is built on its impotence for purposes of passion, grandeur, and native simplicity'.[29] It was also associated with louche living, epitomized in new borrowings of the period like *agent provocateur* and indeed *louche* itself, which derived from the French word for 'squinting'. In *Vanity Fair* (1847–8), the brilliantly scheming Becky Sharp is welcomed into Parisian society and is courted by 'English men of fashion', but is dismissed by their wives, who label her a *parvenue*.

In her account of nineteenth-century English, Lynda Mugglestone notes the popularity of *engougement* – a word meaning 'unreasoning fondness' – and observes as well Benjamin Disraeli's liking for *betise* and the widening adoption of words like *luxe* and *débâcle*. Robert Peel was known for his foreign turn of phrase – or rather *tournure de phrase*.[30] Modish Gallicisms included *cachet, milieu, enfant terrible, aide-mémoire* (often with its acute accent), *pastiche, risqué, savoir faire*, and that insipid word for a decent thing, *bonhomie. Slice of life* was a calque of the French *tranche de vie. Croquet* migrated via Ireland into England in 1851, achieving considerable popularity in the 1860s. Another vogue was for using the French *femme* in combinations such as *femme du monde, femme de ménage* and *femme incomprise*. In a volume from 1879 entitled *Society Small Talk* the anonymous author, a self-styled 'member of the aristocracy', is determined to stamp out 'vulgarisms' yet displays a grating enthusiasm for snippets of French: *rencontre, tapis, gaucherie, mauvaise langue*.

Nevertheless, the use of foreign words and phrases – especially those from French – was commonly ridiculed. Jane Austen was one author who had fun at the expense of characters who went in for pretentious Gallicisms. Another, in the Victorian heartland, was Elizabeth Gaskell; in *Wives and Daughters* (1866) Mrs Gibson takes a particularly risible pleasure in referring to her household ornaments as *objets d'art*. The less well-known John Moore, in *Mordaunt: Sketches of Life, Characters and Manners, in Various Countries* (1800), has one character refer slightingly to a Lady Mincing, who often prefers French words to English ones and uses *embonpoint* instead of *plumpness*.

Others were defensive when they introduced snippets of French. In *Shirley* (1849), Charlotte Brontë refers to a character's *bonté* and explains, 'I use this French word, because it expresses just what I mean; neither goodness nor good nature, but something between the two.' Later in the novel she uses the noun *reflets* and in a note avows, 'Find me an English word as good, reader, and I will gladly dispense with the French word.' In Disraeli's novel *Vivian Grey* (1826) a character uses the French verb *résumer*; the author comments in a footnote that 'I have ventured on using this word, in spite of the plaintive remonstrances contained in a pretty little article in the last number of the *Quarterly Review*', and adds, 'I deprecate equally with the reviewer "the *hodge-podge* of languages" now so much in vogue . . . although I am not quite prepared to say that I consider this practice "as nauseous as wearing perfumes".' As for the reviewer's taste for 'the tritest Latin quotations', he feels only regret: the enthusiasm is 'worthy of a very young schoolboy, or a very ancient schoolmaster'.

If French had to be used, it was advisable to mangle it. R. S. Surtees's Mr Jorrocks refers to *blanquettes de veau* as 'blankets of woe', while *poissons* fatally loses an *s*. Foreign learners of English were encouraged to dispense where possible with French turns of phrase. A guide to English and Portuguese conversation presented by Pedro Carolino in 1869 emphasized that the phrases it contained were 'clean of Gallicisms, and despoiled phrases'. Paradoxically, in a section entitled 'For to speak French', Carolino offered readers such alarming locutions as 'It must to study for to learn it. How long there is it what you learn it?' and 'I know him it is long; he has teached a many of my friends. Don't he tell you that it must to speak french?'

Another significant phrase was 'You do well the french language becomes us all days too much necessary.'[31]

The Victorians were the first to have a vision of English as a true world language. Right across Europe, national languages were blossoming, but English was, as the German philologist Jacob Grimm recognized, 'a language of the world' and 'destined to reign . . . over all parts of the globe'. Lord Macaulay hailed 'our own language' as 'pre-eminent even among the languages of the West'. Matthew Arnold, a more restrained writer, was no less fervent an apostle of English and its culture, intuiting their capacity for achieving 'moral effects'. Britain's imperial reach could be secured and even extended by means of a standard language. Literacy rose sharply at this time, and publishing flourished. Moreover, free trade was embraced – a process begun in the eighteenth century, but shaped by Robert Peel in the 1840s and completed by Gladstone in the next decade. During this period, for the first time, English began to export more words than it imported.[32]

Simultaneously, there was a new interest in the language's history and diversity. The study of its history, invigorated by Sir William Jones, now led to the creation of *The Oxford English Dictionary* under the stewardship of James Murray. Concerted work on the *OED* was begun in 1860. The principle of accepting the testimony only of written texts meant that many colloquialisms went unrecorded. So did dialect forms, although Joseph Wright's *English Dialect Dictionary* (1898–1905) would compensate for this. But for the makers of the *OED* there were other pressing concerns. Their work was a celebration of what they considered a unique cultural tradition. It was also an attempt to catch up with the philological progress of German scholars and improve on Dr Johnson's delightful yet outdated volumes. Predictably, they worried about including French words such as *cahier*, and some even dubbed them 'vermin'.[33] It says something, surely, about Victorian morality that the word *condom* was deliberately omitted from the first edition. Yet *fiancé* managed to displace *betrothed*, and *menu* to supplant *bill of fare*.

William Hodgson, in his *Errors in the Use of English* (1881), is fidgety about 'spurious words'. He quotes the amusingly conservative Kington Oliphant – 'Our hard-working fathers had no need of the word *ennui*; our wealth, ever waxing, has brought the state of mind; so France has given us the name for it.' Then he cites John Camden Hotten's recent dictionary of slang: 'an unmeaning gibberish of Gallicisms runs through English fashionable conversation', and 'servants . . . appropriate the scraps of French conversation which fall from their master's guests at the dinner table, and forthwith in the world of flunkeydom the word "know" is disused, and the lady's-maid, in doubt on a particular point, asks John whether or no he "saveys" it.' To Hodgson, the plural forms of adopted nouns were a significant irritant: 'None but the grossly uneducated commit gross errors in the use of English nominal inflections, these being as familiar as they are few and simple; but foreign nouns, borrowed by English, yet retaining their original inflections, have often provided pitfalls to unwary writers.' Problem nouns included *miasma, cherub, bandit* and *magus.* 'Of pseudo-Latin plurals one need not speak at length,' he adds. 'It is enough to remark that men have been heard to talk of "the throngs of *omnibi* that ply the London streets" . . . [and] that Thackeray is said to have known an eminent female grammarian who spoke of witness "taking their *affiesdavit*".'[34]

In volumes like Hodgson's and Henry Alford's we see the strong Victorian sense of nationhood, grounded in the idea that the few should lead the rest. The same belief resonated in Sir John Seeley's *The Expansion of England*, published in 1883, which emphasized the unity of the nation and the Empire. Seeley argued that 'the English Empire . . . broadly may be said to be English throughout,' and declared that 'England has left Europe altogether behind it and become a world-state.'[35] For Seeley, the nation's future was not at home, but abroad. Its unity was achieved through language, literature and religion. His book stayed in print until 1956, the year of the Suez Crisis. Seeley characterized his country as 'pre-eminently . . . maritime, colonising and industrial', dating this 'vocation' to the age of Elizabeth. But he saw also that 'bigness' was not the same as 'greatness', and that Britain should not dilute its moral character simply in order to expand its possessions. The contemporary image of empire was steeped in contradiction: on the one hand it was the creation of military triumph, and existed to be exploited, yet on the other it was an instrument of benevolence. Questions about the nature of empire were a feature of the period's public discourse. What did empire 'mean'? What obligations did it entail?

This interrogative spirit was a mark of a time when social and technological change were not just brisk, but also highly visible. The structure of the known world was being rearranged. Yet, as social changes unfolded, language preserved distinctions that were highly suggestive of users' class, education and position. Certain words, for instance, were not used by anyone who could lay serious claim to the qualities of which they were tokens: genteel folk did not speak of being *genteel*, and to refer to someone as a *lady* or a *gentleman* suggested a certain plebeian unctuousness. In Thomas Hardy's *A Pair of Blue Eyes* (1873), Elfride Swancourt is chastised by her stepmother for referring to 'gentlemen': 'We have handed over "gentlemen" to the lower classes, where the word is still to be heard at tradesmen's balls and provincial tea-parties.'[36]

Elfride Swancourt is one of several characters in Hardy's novels whose lives unfold in the shadow of the railway. Empire had created fresh opportunities for travel, and so now did the steamship and the locomotive. Besides diplomats, natural historians, missionaries and soldiers, there were many travellers who simply craved adventure and the status that came with it. Some of the most audacious were women, like Constance Gordon Cumming, who wandered through Sri Lanka (then called Ceylon), Fiji, China and Japan, or Isabella Bird, who clambered up Mauna Loa and rode into the Rocky Mountains wearing a pair of baggy Hawaiian trousers.[37] Nineteenth-century Americans flocked to Europe, armed with Roswell Park's *A Hand-Book for American Travellers* (1853) or, later, Grant Allen's *The European Tour: A Handbook for Americans and Colonists* (1899), to soak up what Henry James would call its 'denser, richer, warmer . . . spectacle'. Park is quick with words like *portmanteau*, *embarcadère*, *loggia* and *vettura*, and informs readers that 'an American may travel on the . . . mainland of Europe, without knowing aught beforehand of any language save his own.'[38] Allen commends Europe's opportunities for 'free use of lungs and limbs' and, while dropping in a few foreign words, strikes a less serious tone, insisting for example that 'to see Rome before you have seen Florence is *a fatal blunder*.'[39]

British travellers could be a pretty dismal bunch, fretting about the real possibility of fatality and the inevitability of blundering. Reeking waterways, pipe smoke, garlic and mosquitoes were common causes of complaint. The caustic Frances Trollope fusses about 'the want of drains and sewers . . . [in] all the cities in France' and the 'seared and blunted conscience' of Americans.[40] John Henry Newman bemoans the horrors of the Sicilian flea. Matthew Arnold draws from Holland a 'general impression . . . of mortal *ennui*'.[41] Shelley agitates about the 'stupid and shrivelled slaves' he sees walking the streets of Milan, and Algernon Swinburne, bordering on incoherence, characterizes Italy as a 'leprous, blotched, mangy, grimy, parboiled, country *without* trees, water, grass, fields − *with* blank, beastly, senseless olives and orange-trees like a mad cabbage gone indigestible'.[42] Diet is a frequent worry. 'Not uncommonly in southern climes an egg with the shell on is the only procurable animal food without garlic in it,' writes Thomas King Chambers in 1875.[43] A 'polyglot dialogue book' aimed at English travellers in the Levant hints at the bilious experiences of those who journeyed there, offering Greek and Turkish equivalents for phrases such as 'My head aches terribly,' 'Your tongue is foul' and 'Don't let me forget to buy some handkerchiefs.'[44] The experience of being put in quarantine to prevent the spread of cholera familiarized travellers with the Italian *lazaretto*, where they might even be fumigated. More agreeably, they grew accustomed to previously unknown conveyances − the *britzska*, the *carriole*, the *vetturino*, the *trekschuit*.

Books for travellers, explaining where to go and what to take, were in high demand. Long before E. M. Forster satirized Lucy Honeychurch's craven reliance on Baedeker's *Handbook to Northern Italy*, British tourists were subjecting themselves to a compressed and compartmentalized version of the Grand Tour. Travel was regimented − work more than play. The *Practical Guide* series provided information to tourists about wintering places on the Mediterranean, the Italian lakes, Paris and the Rhine, Switzerland and so on. Travellers were advised 'not to attempt sentences; but pronounce boldly and baldly the one or two words which mainly imply the meaning'.[45] No change there, then. One was, however, allowed to drop into speech such resonantly Continental words as *chalet, edelweiss, strudel* and *contessa*, or indeed *kursaal* and *permis de séjour*. From more remote climes came *troika*, *tundra* and *laager*. *Tundra*, for instance, was first attested in 1841; it hails from the language spoken by the Sami people of the Kola Peninsula bordering the Barents Sea.

Writings on art provided a more majestic view of Continental culture. *Artistic* was a Victorian buzzword, and with it came talk of the *artistic temperament* as well as the distinction between an *artist* and that less exalted performer, the *artiste*.[46] Most of the Victorian writing about art happened in periodicals such as *Art-Journal* and the *Illustrated London News*. The dominant figure in an age of frequently incompetent and insensitive reviewery (a good Victorian word, coined by Robert Louis Stevenson) was John Ruskin, an exceptional polemicist, who created nothing less than a new way of looking at paintings and buildings.

The aestheticism of Ruskin and Walter Pater had its own analytical language that translated everything the eye could see into a whirl of words. In his *Studies in the History of the Renaissance* (1873), which is barely a history at all, Pater writes a fluid prose that exists to stimulate with its richness. Yet his borrowings are few – *ben trovato* is the only one of note. By contrast, Ruskin's writings, which are of a more educational bent, abound with new technical terms, and his tastes are unmistakably classical, as he adopts or confects a great many terms – *aesthesis* ('mere sensual perception of the outward qualities and necessary effects of bodies'), *vaporescence, interfenestral* (as in the 'interfenestral piers' of an apse in *The Stones of Venice*), *chromolithotint*, the Italian *scuola* and the pseudo-French *blottesque*. To be educated was to be 'learned in the peerage of words', grasping the ramifications of their ancestry and their distant relationships. Art history has embraced this principle. One of the difficulties of writing about art is that, while historians want to enlarge their critical lexicon by finding or making new words, such items are 'cultural orphans', dissociated from any proper semantic framework. A description of a painting by Rembrandt will violate our experience of actually looking at the painting.[47] In the field of art criticism, sensitivity to the nuances and historical resonances of language has made borrowing at once seductive and troublesome.

New words connected with art included *macramé*, which was related to an Arabic word for a bedcover, *vitrine*, *trompe l'œil* and *œuvre*. The *Encyclopædia Britannica* could gamely adopt Sebastiano del Piombo's notion of Michelangelo's *terribilità* – 'the tempest and hurricane of the spirit which accompanied his unequalled technical mastery and knowledge'. The arts were the field in which Italian was most valued; loans of this period include *prima donna*, *magenta*, *studio*, *scenario*. Another is *graffiti*, in 1851; oddly, it was first used in English not of a curse inscribed at Pompeii or the Coliseum, but of a Stone Age runic inscription found in Orkney. At the same time *fiasco* was adopted; it derived from a word for a bottle, perhaps because glassblowers who made a mess of a delicate piece of work would end up having to turn their creation not into art, but into a mere receptacle. *Impressionist* art is mentioned by Henry James in 1876, two years after Louis Leroy's article in *Le Charivari* which coined the term to insinuate the triviality of Monet, Renoir and Degas. It's worth adding that individual works of art (and cultural artefacts more generally) have made particular words and phrases well known, and that these can be detached from their original contexts: just as we may know what *pietà* is without necessarily thinking of Michelangelo, so we can use without recalling their origins such phrases as *jeux sans frontières* and *j'accuse*.

The word *decadence*, which once signified little more than decay, is now at once highly suggestive and vague, suggesting a woolly melodrama of transgression, and this too can be historically located. Until the late nineteenth century the word was not attached to people: things and conditions and the temper of public life might be convicted of decadence, but individuals could not be. The century's final generation changed this. In 1886 a minor French poet by the name of Anatole Baju founded a magazine called *Le Décadent*, and in the first issue he trumpeted the emergence of a new type of person – 'a man of progress'. Surprisingly to us, Baju's image of decadence was essentially rational – his imagined 'precursor' of a brightly decadent future was 'economical, hard-working and straight in all his habits' – but others were promoting an image that we will much more easily recognize. While the Marquis de Sade a hundred years before had hinted at a cult of unreason as he commended the extremes of depravity, claiming that true happiness was the fruit of widespread moral corruption, the 1880s and '90s witnessed a flowering of decadent aesthetics. The paintings of Gustave Moreau and the violently expressive prose of Joris-Karl Huysmans made a mixture of lasciviousness and artifice seem the height of glamour. The principal character of Huysmans's *À Rebours* (1884), which has been dubbed the 'bible of Decadence', possesses a 'nervous system altogether modern in its morbid sensitiviness'.[48]

In the 'yellow' 1890s, which seem to have been the first decade identified as having its own peculiar hue, the art of luxurious decay was practised by androgynous young men. Oscar Wilde's Dorian Gray does likewise: here is a pair of lemon-coloured gloves, here a cigarette laced with opium, here a lamp bedizened with turquoises. Fashionable words associated with this *demi-monde* (itself a fashionable word, coined by Alexandre Dumas *fils*) included *mystique*, *ambiance* and *folie*. The phrase *fin de siècle* became voguish in the century's final decade. Applied as an adjective, it connoted from the start a welter of unreason and purple excess. Critics used it ominously: participants, excitably. *Entourage* meanwhile became increasingly a term associated with artists and intellectuals, as was the less recently adopted *coterie*, and the dashingly expressive *panache* first made an appearance in the English translation of *Cyrano de Bergerac* in 1898.

A less radical arm of the arts was dance, yet this proved an area of sustained eastern-European influence. The *minuet* was French and graceful, the *gavotte* French and lively, the *waltz* German and smooth, the *forlana* Italian, stately and brisk; all were recreational. By contrast, Polish forms, such as the *gorlitza*, the *krakowiak* and the *redowa*, began as folk dances and had as a result a spirit and authority that they retained when transplanted to the ballroom and the theatre. The country dance known as a *mazurka* was Polish in origin, and became widely known in western Europe thanks to either German or Russian influence. Another dance, the *polka*, which originated during the Polish uprising of 1830–31, gained popularity in Bohemia; its name is actually Czech. The *csardas* was a further style of dance new to Victorian audiences. Hungarian in origin, it provided themes for works by Brahms and Tchaikovsky, and was a courtship dance, though apparently related to the *verbunkos*, which was used during army recruitment ceremonies. As industrialization squeezed the communities where these folk dances had grown up, admirers began deliberately to conserve them, and conservation systematized the different styles' gestures and rituals.

Hungarian, Czech and Polish were, to nineteenth-century English-speakers, objects of only mild curiosity, if even that. By contrast, German eminence in the sciences meant that the German language seemed a threat to English, in academic circles at least. As Coleridge's borrowings have suggested, many important Englightenment ideas were first expressed in German. While ultimately the language of the Germans made a negligible impact beyond their country's borders, it resonated with intellectuals, who relished its agglutinative nouns, which crisply expressed complex ideas. German compounds are said to be 'self-explaining', as Old English was and Modern English frequently isn't.

The term *Zeitgeist* was adopted by Matthew Arnold, who first used it in a letter in 1848 and gave it a public airing in *Literature and Dogma* in 1873. The word was made well known among those of a philosophical bent by Georg Hegel early in the nineteenth century, yet it was still being used only tentatively by English writers in the 1930s. Today, though, it has been freed from its philosophical and poetic moorings: in an episode of *Sex and the City*, Carrie Bradshaw is asked to speak to university students taking a course in 'Cultural Zeitgeist', and the word is used by Google as an umbrella term for prevailing Internet search trends. It is, quite simply, one of those words that endows an everyday idea with both seriousness and glamour; comparable examples with German backgrounds include *ersatz*, *wanderlust*, *doppelganger* and *Kaffeeklatsch*. German nouns, as we have already seen, begin with a capital letter: here I have kept the initial capital only for those that still seem resolutely German.

In Britain, German loanwords are often connected with scholarship, outdoor recreation and politics. In the first of these domains a few choice examples are *festschrift*, the scientist's *ansatz* (an assumption made to facilitate the solving of an equation) and the drama student's *Verfremdungseffekt* (the Brechtian technique of alienation), the calque *animal magnetism* from Franz Anton Mesmer's *thierischer*

Magnetismus, Leibniz's coinage *infinitesimal* and the literary-critical *Bildungsroman*, as well as the much less obvious calque *academic freedom*. A related example is the Greek *ecology*, which became known only through an awareness of the work of Ernst Haeckel. In the second category we might readily think of *rucksack* or *to yodel*, a number of words to do with climbing and winter sports (*abseil*, *alpenstock*, the calque *outrun*), and several familiar breeds of dog – the *rottweiler*, for instance, and the *dachshund*, which was originally favoured for hunting badgers (*dachs* being the German for 'badger'). The third, in which I include the language of war, is represented by *hinterland*, *diktat* and Marx's concept of the *Lumpenproletariat*. Other examples are *zeppelin*, *blitz* and *flak*, alongside the more surprising *spanner*, which was originally a device to wind up the spring in a firearm. This category also incorporates some lasting calques: *power politics* is modelled on the German *Machtpolitik*, while *Gastarbeiter* is rendered as the only superficially respectful *guest worker*.

Another area of conspicuous influence is psychology. Some of the terms in this field are quite plainly German: Christian von Ehrenfels's concept of *Gestalt*, for instance. Others have classical roots, but were popularized by German-speakers. Thus *imago* and *libido*, and thus too the specialized psychological sense of *complex*, which was coined by Albert Neisser in 1906 and given publicity by Freud, and the Greek-sounding *empathy*, an English rendering of Theodor Lipps's notion of *Einfühlung*. *Psychoanalysis* itself is a word clearly Greek in origin, but it was Freud who originated this method of treatment and used *Psychoanalyse* as a more succinct form of *Psychische Analyse*.[49] He also used the word *Todeswunsch*, which has been rendered in English as *deathwish*. Yet another borrowing in this field that has found wide use is *angst*, while *Hackliste*, originally a term restricted to studies of animal behaviour, is the source of the expressive *pecking order*.

Not all areas of Germanic achievement made an impression. In the age of Bach (d. 1750), Mozart (d. 1791) and Beethoven (d. 1827), no musical term of note was borrowed from German.[50] But then Italian had provided such a wealth of musical terminology that little more was needed. And plenty of other domains were represented. For example, *kindergarten* was quickly adopted after its coinage by

Friedrich Froebel as a name for the activity centre he had set up in 1837. Then there were words to do with religion: *papist*, which was coined by Luther; *selfhood*, which is a calque of Jacob Boehme's *Selbheit*; and some of the terms introduced in sixteenth-century translations of the Bible, such as *mercy seat*, which is William Tyndale's rendering of Luther's *Gnadenstuhl*. The negative associations of the noun *culture* – felt mainly by those who think the word smacks of elitism or chauvinism – stem from a growing sense in the nineteenth and early twentieth centuries of the German notion of *Kultur*; the English word does not come from German, but *Kultur* was at once well known and tainted by associations with a nationalist view of German civilization with which few English-speakers felt at ease.

Food and drink also figure – we might think straight away of *pretzel, muesli, lager, spritzer* and *schnapps*. Another obvious loan in this area is *hamburger*, first attested in 1889, although this is really an Americanism on a German model. *Frankfurter* is an abbreviation of *Frankfurter Wurst*; along with *delicatessen* – now usually just *deli* – it makes an early appearance in *Kettner's Book of the Table* (1877), a volume collecting the culinary wisdom of Auguste Kettner, whose Soho restaurant was a favourite haunt of Oscar Wilde. The evidence of *delicatessen* notwithstanding, we can infer something about the British perception of the German diet – and indeed about the true essence of the German diet – by comparing these rather indelicate borrowings with those words borrowed in this field from Italian or French.

For a perspective on Victorian eating habits, we could do a lot worse than turn to Isabella Beeton's famous *Book of Household Management*. Published in 1861, it drew on received wisdom from Britain, Ireland, France, Italy and Germany. Especially handy was its list explaining French terms – words at once necessary and somewhat unfamiliar – such as *bouillon, purée, remoulade* and *café noir*. Mrs Beeton was not the only successful English food writer of her day. *Spaghetti*, which she defines as 'a smaller kind of macaroni', is 'Naples vermicelli' in Eliza Acton's *Modern Cookery for Private Families* (1845).[51] At the start of Acton's bulky volume there is a helpful 'vocabulary', explaining what is meant by *casserole, meringue, purée* and the like, and there is a brief section on 'Foreign and Jewish Cookery', which includes recipes for Indian lobster cutlets, kedgeree, various pilaffs (Syrian, Turkish, Arabian, Indian), Milanese risotto, a Swiss mayonnaise, Viennese soufflé, and a German drink made from white wine, orange and woodruff.[52] As one history of the period's language explains, 'More than any other linguistic community then or earlier, Anglophones in the nineteenth century explored the remotest parts of the globe and encountered new things described in languages new to them'.[53]

We have touched already several times on food – on the appetites of English-speakers – and on language's omnivorous capacity. The subject is worth a digression. As we have seen, food has played a significant part in shaping history: our appetites have drawn us into conflict and inspired grand projects of piracy and conquest. In English, the language of food signals both our imperial contacts and our cosmopolitan aspirations, while also testifying to deeper continuities. In recent years travel and culinary evangelism have enlarged our tastes and our knowledge. Even if they are not to your liking, you may well be familiar with *harissa* from North Africa, Mexican *fajitas*, *pad thai*, *gyoza*, Cypriot *halloumi*, Cajun *jambalaya*, *raclette* from Switzerland, Russian *shashlik* and *zakuski*, Japanese *edamame*, and *tabbouleh* from the Middle East. Our taste in drinks may be a little less wide-ranging, but we can recognize the different sources from which we get *grappa*, *sake*, *Eiswein*, *cognac*, *tequila*, *slivovitz* and *port*, and adventurous types may also manage *raki*, *kumis* and *aguardiente*.

The core of our diet is much older, and this is evident lexically. The words *bread*, *meat*, *fish* and *cheese* can be traced back to Old English, as can *wine* and *beer*. Later additions to the language are less generic, but they still strike us as having a venerable quality – we can imagine Chaucer tucking into what they denote. In Middle English we find *bacon*, *mushroom* and *jelly*, along with *claret*; Chaucer's Summoner loves to consume 'garleek, onions, and eek lekes, / And for to drynken strong wyn', while in 'The Merchant's Tale' the ageing January drinks several kinds of sweet wine in an attempt to boost his sexual potency. The sixteenth and seventeenth centuries see an influx of new items. Gervase Markham's *The English Housewife* (1615) mentions 'paste of Genoa', which is made using soft quinces, and the recent introduction of hops, which resulted in a new distinction between *ale* and *beer*. The period's other novelties include *banana* and *anchovy*, as well as *tea*, *coffee* and *lemonade*. *Anchovy* comes from Spanish, and is first sighted in English when Shakespeare's Falstaff is found to have spent 2*s*. 6*d*. on an after-supper binge of wine and pickled fish. Bananas are mentioned by Purchas and Dampier, but a clue to their general unfamiliarity is Jules Verne's explanation in *Around the World in Eighty Days* (published in French in 1872) that 'the fruit . . . [is] as healthy as bread and as succulent as cream.' Both word and object possess a faint air of the ridiculous, which may explain the large number of colloquialisms involving them, from *banana republic* and *banana oil* (meaning nonsense) to talk of *going bananas* or *being driven bananas*. Five years after Verne's novel, the first refrigerated ship was launched, and fresh foods of an ever greater diversity began to cross the seas.

In the eighteenth century we find *meringue* and *ice cream*; in the nineteenth, *grapefruit*, the Arabic *kebab* (an updated spelling of the older *cabob*) and *Coca-Cola*. The last of these is described, in an advertisement dating from 1887, as a 'brain tonic and intellectual soda fountain beverage'. At five cents a glass, it was alleged to alleviate headaches and impotence. More recent accessions include Italian *pizza* and Arabic *falafel*; a slightly older one is *goulash*, the invention of Hungarian herdsmen − its name combining *gulyas*, 'herdsman', and *hus*, 'meat'. The critical ingredient in goulash is *paprika*, which was introduced to Hungary by the Turks in the sixteenth century. It was initially known as *Török-bors* (Turkish pepper), but its Hungarian name was influenced by a Croatian word, and was the form that caught on across Europe.

A puzzling adoption, dating from the 1920s, is *bistro*. The Russian *bystra* means 'hurry', and it is sometimes suggested that the Russians who occupied Paris during the Napoleonic Wars would call this out when service was sluggish. Alternative explanations identify it as a word in the dialect spoken around Poitiers, meaning 'junior servant', or as a corruption of *bistrouille*, a term for low-grade *eau de vie*. The very mention of *eau de vie* is enough to set word-lovers' tongues wagging, in any case. The reason for this excitement is that its name is a symptom of a strange and long-standing connection. The Scandinavians have their *akvavit*. The word *whisky* derives from *usquebaugh,* a Gaelic calque of the Latin *aqua vitae. Vodka* is borrowed from Russian, and is a diminutive form of *voda,* meaning water. This association of water and intoxicating spirits testifies at once to the habit of identifying hard liquor as one of life's essentials and to the tendency to pass it off as something innocent. The notion that alcohol offers health benefits is attractive; we can trace it back at least as far as the Greek physician Asclepiades in the first century BC. The semantic linkage between water and alcohol attests the latter's symbolic and ritual use – its mythic, magical and metaphorical power.

Love of food has fostered a figurative debt to the kitchen. John Ray could record the saying 'What's sauce for the goose is sauce for the gander' in 1670, while Robespierre is alleged to have been responsible for the observation that 'You can't make an omelette without breaking eggs.'[54] A few words have entered the English lexicon as kitchen terms and have later become more generalized. For instance, *liaison* comes from the Latin *ligari* 'to bind', and was originally imported via French into the kitchen, where eggs were used to achieve the 'liaison' ('thickening') of sauces. It was first used to suggest intimate social links in the nineteenth century, and the *OED* cites Lord Byron as the first to use it of illicit relations – a sense adopted by his friend Shelley, who wrote of Byron's 'permanent sort of liaison' with the Contessa Guiccioli.

As we can hardly fail to see, it is the French contributions to the menu that have been most profound. *Menu* itself was adopted from French in the nineteenth century, along with *restaurant, à la carte* and *gourmet* – the last a word that had originally meant a wine-taster. From the time of the Norman Conquest at least, the techniques of French cooking have been influential. And the language of the kitchen is peppered with inimitable French words, such as *aïoli, ratatouille* and Provençal *bouillabaisse.* The last of these advertises in its name the two processes involved in making it – first boiling, then reducing (*abaissement*) – yet the word itself is dreamy. So is *daube,* a stew cooked from cold, which is named after the narrow-necked, big-bellied pot in which it is cooked, the *daubière.* In *To the Lighthouse,* Virginia Woolf revels in describing the *boeuf en daube* prepared for the Ramsays by their cook: its 'soft mass' gives off 'an exquisite scent of olives and oil and juice', and Mrs Ramsay admires the pot 'with its shiny walls and its confusion of savoury brown and yellow meats and its bay leaves and its wine'. The recipe is her grand-mother's – 'Of course it was French. What passes for cooking in England is an abomination . . . It is putting cabbages in water. It is roasting meat till it is like leather. It is cutting off the delicious skins of vegetables.'

Resistance to French culinary methods has always been vocifer-ous. Only in the eighteenth century did the sturdy sort of medievalism embodied in volumes like Robert May's *The Accomplisht Cook* (1660) give way to a more progressive style, learnt from works such as François Massialot's *Le Cuisinier roial et bourgeois* (1691).[55] The French have written about food with a verve and sophistica-tion unparalleled in English, and the very names of the great French food-writers are a succulent cavalcade: Jean Anthelme Brillat-Savarin, Edouard de Pomaine, Prosper Montagné, Alexandre Grimod de La Reynière, Antonin Carême. (Brillat-Savarin, however, was convinced that his own language's resources were limited, and made a point of taking what he could from elsewhere.) English writers on the subject have tended to be more prosaic.

One of the enduring myths of the English kitchen is that Henry I died of a 'surfeit of lampreys' – eel-like fish that take their name indi-rectly from the Latin *lambere*, 'to lick', and *petra*, 'stone'. It hardly conjures up a favourable picture of the national diet or eating habits. The first English cookbook, known as *The Forme of Cury*, was compiled around 1390 and gives such unappetising advice as 'Cranes and Herons shul be armed with lard of Swyne and eten with gyng.'[56] It also includes details of how to make a 'salat' out of parsley, sage and garlic, dressed with vinegar. Later volumes contained more tasty counsel. One example is Elizabeth Moxon's successful *English Housewifery* (1741), which gives advice on how to pickle nasturtium buds or make a pie out of a calf's feet. Yet practicality has always been paramount. It was a sophisticated foreigner, Brillat-Savarin, who furnished the nineteenth-century formula for a perfect dinner party, but the details were left to Mrs Beeton and *The Habits of Good Society*.

French food has always been served more seductively – as *cuisine* or, better still, *haute cuisine*, which translates cooking into a form of high art. The word *chef* is another nineteenth-century borrowing, suggestive of a presidential role far greater than the Old English *cook*. The Victorians soaked up French sauces – *mayonnaise, béchamel, hollandaise* – and acquired as well *brioche, gâteau, éclair* and *crouton. Mayonnaise* takes its name from Port Mahon in Minorca, captured by the French under the duc de Richelieu in 1756. *Brie* and *Camembert* are recorded in the fifth edition of the *Encyclopædia Britannica*, which was published in 1876. *Crème brûlée*, first recorded in France in the seventeenth century, became popular in Victorian Britain. *Charcuterie* also appears at this time, while *patisserie*, first attested in the late sixteenth century, becomes a common term.

Moving closer to the present, we can see the expansion of British gastronomic horizons. What links *bruschetta* and *taleggio* to *crudités* and *salade niçoise*? The answer is that the *OED* suggests that all are first attested in the writings of Elizabeth David, who pioneered the idea of the kitchenware shop and almost single-handedly persuaded a whole generation of Britons that food was among life's chief pleasures. More recently, the proliferation of Indian and Chinese restaurants, together with growing numbers purveying the cuisines of Lebanon, Greece, Turkey and Japan, to name a few, have accustomed our palates to new sensations.

In the cuisine of Greece and southern India, for instance, a staple item is the soft, fleshy, smoky *eggplant*. This unattractive word can be traced back about 250 years. It seems originally to have referred to the white-fruited variety of the plant, although it has since been used of the dark-fruited kind. *Eggplant* remains the preferred term in the US, but in Britain the plant is usually known as the *aubergine*, and has been since the early nineteenth century. This word comes, via French, from the Catalan *alberginia*; the Catalan derives from the Arabic *al-badinjan*, which can itself be traced back to the Middle Indo-Aryan *vatingana*. Minus its prefix, the Arabic word also accounts for the Castilian *berenjena* and for the Anglo-Indian *brinjal*, which can still be heard in South Africa. In the Caribbean, *brinjal* has been corrupted into the rather more appealing *brown jolly*. Aubergine is much used in Italian cooking, and the Italian word for it is *melanzana* ('mad apple'), which looks less remote if you replace the initial *m* with a *b*. The association between aubergines and madness is of long standing, dating back to old Arabic lore about the vegetable's capacity to bring on melancholy.

The South Asian influence has become so entrenched that a good deal of it is hardly recognized as such. Many of us will have come across someone saying 'What could be more English than a good curry?' Famously, Britain's most popular curried dish, chicken tikka masala, is unknown to Indians. In 2001 the Labour politician Robin Cook, who was Foreign Secretary at the time, gave a speech to London's Social Market Foundation in which he celebrated Britishness. Cook cited chicken tikka masala as 'a perfect illustration of the way Britain absorbs and adapts external influences'. Explaining that chicken tikka was originally an Indian dish, he observed that the sauce was added 'to satisfy the desire of British people to have their meat served in gravy'.[57]

Many twentieth-century borrowings from Indian languages have happened outside India and have shown this concern with food. 'Concern' may not quite capture the mood, though: as the example above shows, Indian cuisine been enthusiastically bastardized. A large part of its international vocabulary is Urdu. The national language of Pakistan, Urdu is also the official language of Kashmir, is spoken in urban parts of Afghanistan, and can be heard in many Indian cities, such as Hyderabad and Bangalore. It will be familiar to many from the menus in so-called Indian restaurants, which are often run by immigrants from Pakistan and Bangladesh. Your lamb pasanda or karahi, your mutton korma, murgh masala, naan, paneer and creamy rogan josh are all Urdu by name and by nature. So are such familiar words as the previously mentioned *nabob* – first found in an English text 400 years ago – and *pashmina*, fashionable only since the 1990s, but in use since the Victorian era.

It is hardly a revelation that what we know of other cultures we often know through food and drink. But typically it reaches no deeper than familiarity with a few words. The nineteenth century bequeathed to the twentieth the conviction that knowing words was intrinsically a good thing – that the breadth of a person's vocabulary signified the breadth of his or her intelligence. Knowledge of foreign words was believed to indicate sophistication, learning, cosmopolitanism. Yet it could often be little more than a smokescreen, a miasma of delusion. So it still can be. Furthermore, it has the potential to tell, obliquely yet agonizingly, of lost worlds, effaced cultures and obliterated identities.

14. Voodoo

A form of religious witchcraft, prevalent in the southern United States, ultimately of African origin

The noun probably comes from the word *vodun* ('spirit') in the Fon language, which is spoken in modern-day Benin.

In the closing years of the nineteenth century, the British Empire's boundaries increased. The Empire came to comprise India, Canada, Australia and New Zealand, a substantial part of the Far East, and also a much greater portion of Africa, control having been gained over Kenya, Uganda, Sudan, Nigeria, Transvaal and the Orange Free State. By 1900 it comprehended 12 million square miles and around a quarter of the people on the planet. But its pre-eminence in industry and business was on the wane. All the while, the economy of the United States was growing; American productivity had soared in the second half of the century – the production of coal, for instance, climbing by 800 per cent between the end of the Civil War in 1865 and the outbreak of the war with Spain in 1898. By 1914 the national per-capita income of the US was $377 a year, compared with $244 in Britain, $184 in Germany and $41 in Russia.[1]

Britain's energies had been sapped by the so-called Scramble for Africa. The term, reportedly dating from 1884, summed up the madly internecine competition between Britain, France, Belgium, Germany, Italy, Spain and Portugal. What had begun for the British as a mission to safeguard Indian Ocean sea routes had turned into a lust for the gold and gems buried in Africa's interior. The continent's promised riches could restore the nation's balance of trade. Yet, while Britain assumed control of about a third of Africa's population in the three decades leading up to the First World War, colonial Africa proved disappointing – a theatre for moral postures, but not the abundant mine of resources that its advocates had claimed.

The climate and natural obstacles (deserts, deficient ports, apparently malevolent rivers) made settlement difficult and unattractive. The Treasury was reluctant to fund expansion, and public enthusiasm for an African strategy was meagre. The most significant products were not gold and gems, but rubber and ivory. Imports of the latter peaked in 1890, at more than 700 tons a year.[2] It was used to fashion a range of consumer goods including chess sets, knife handles, billiard balls and piano keys. Such indulgent uses were symbolic of the destructive greed practised in colonial Africa. And when, in the twentieth century, the process of decolonization was played out, it too seemed to serve the gluttonous interests of Europe more effectively than it did the interests of Africans.

The lexical legacy of these scrambles into and out of Africa looks modest. It is broadly true that borrowed words of African origin have specialized uses, beyond which they have not been stretched. So, for instance, there are words like *shifta*, adopted from Somali to describe a group of armed nomadic freedom-fighters found in northern Kenya, and *shea butter*, a sort of gloop used in primitive soap-making and supposed to be a cure of rheumatism, which takes its name from the Bambara word for the tree whose kernels are its source. From Igbo comes the plant *okra*, the fruit of which is excellent for thickening a stew; from one of the languages of coastal Ghana, the wasting disease *kwashiorkor*; from Luganda, *matoke*, a dish of mashed green bananas. Much better known is *safari*, the most commonly used loanword from Swahili (it can be traced back to the Arabic *safar*, 'a journey'), and from the same language we have adopted *uhuru* as a word to signify an African nation's independence, *piri-piri* as the name for the hot red pepper sauce that tastes so good on barbecued chicken, the infectious fever *dengue*, the verb *yam* as a synonym for *eat*, and *panga*, a word for a serious-looking knife that is used for cutting undergrowth.

Knives, fevers, peculiar food: early visitors to Africa flinched from these things and spoke of the continent's 'strangeness' and 'dreadfulness'. Typical of its darker aspect was *mumbo-jumbo*, seemingly a corruption of the Mandingo name for a secret society. It appears in Francis Moore's *Travels into the Inland Parts of Africa* (1738), and in Mungo Park's *Travels* it signifies 'a strange bugbear . . . much employed by the Pagan natives in keeping their women in subjection'. *Jumbo* was understood to signify something large and unwieldy; in due course, P. T. Barnum and Thomas Edison would coax the word in a more positive direction.[3] Later contacts have given us *tsetse*, *baobab* and *zebra*, which come from Bantu languages, and Anglo-Zulu conflict in the nineteenth century created an awareness of other Bantu terms that have since fallen out of use. Another South African language, Xhosa, has contributed quite a number of items. Besides *dagga*, a word for a kind of mortar made out of mud and dung, and *mbongo*, a word for a political 'yes-man', there is *tokoloshe*, a delightful yet necessarily obscure term for a libidinous hairy dwarf believed to have a single buttock and a giant penis. Xhosa has also indirectly contributed the more familiar *gnu* and – a calque of *umkhaya* – *homeboy*.

One final word worth mentioning in this category is *palaver*, which first appears in journals kept by eighteenth-century seafarers. Traders and sailors picked it up in West Africa, where it was used in the local pidgins. It had been adapted by the inhabitants from *palavra*, the Portuguese for 'talk'. Conversation with Portuguese traders had traditionally been quarrelsome, disputatious and uncomfortable; accordingly, *palaver* became a word for an argument, for complicated business, for all-round hassle. In fact *palaver* was the pre-colonial name for an assembly at which grievances were aired and consensus attempted – the institution has even been enshrined as part of the modern political framework of Mali – but to outsiders looking in it resembled raucous chaos, something to be dismissed rather than understood.

Misprision has urged on the European desire to 'civilize' many who are already civilized. Languages, in particular, have on the flimsiest of grounds been dismissed as barbaric. The Kenyan author Ngugi wa Thiong'o has written that 'Language . . . has a dual character: it is both a means of communication and a carrier of culture.' In describing his upbringing, as part of a family of 'about twenty-eight children', he draws attention to the gap between his home life and the formal education he received. English was the language of the latter, and 'one of the most humiliating experiences was to be caught speaking Gikuyu in the vicinity of the school. The culprit was given corporal punishment . . . or was made to carry a metal plate around the neck with inscriptions such as I AM STUPID or I AM A DONKEY.'⁴ It is implicit that the author suffered this indignity himself, and his experience highlights the institutional suppression of African languages. This was practised by colonialists throughout Africa, and also by the owners of Africans transported as slaves across the Atlantic. Its effect, of course, was to drive these languages underground. Over time, fragments of their vocabularies have teased their way into the languages of the very people responsible for their suppression.

Examples are not hugely numerous, but they are forceful, even if we must hedge them round with qualifiers. Many have first come to light in America, where the legacy of slavery has been hauntingly profound. America's slave population originated in a range of countries that included Ghana, Senegal, Angola and Nigeria. The slaves' speech kept elements of their ancestral cultures alive. Eventually, as humanitarian reformists tackled slavery, and as segregation and discrimination were challenged, African traditions, cultural and linguistic alike, became more visible and audible to the rest of the population, in music, dance, literature, folklore, diet, clothing and the everyday use of language. For example, aspects of African culture have been nurtured in America by the Traditional Black Church, an independent institution that has felt no pressure to become Eurocentric.⁵ Oral tradition has been critical to the creation of African American culture. So has a capacity for combining the old with the new. The words that have emerged from this background seem steeped in the contrasting colours of freedom and suffering.

What are these words? *Voodoo* we have already seen. The Kongo language spoken today in Angola has provided *zombie* as well as its less common relative, *jumby*. Hausa, now mainly spoken in Niger, provides *juju*, 'a fetish', which is seemingly related to the French *joujou*, while *honkie*, a familiar term of disparagement for white people, derives from *honq*, the word for 'pink' in Wolof, which is spoken in Senegal, Mauritania and Gambia. *Hip* is thought to come from the Wolof *hipi* ('to open one's eyes' – the hipster is open to experience in all its many hues), and the verbs in expressions such as 'I'm *digging* this music' and 'You're *bugging* me' may also have Wolof origins. It is possible, too, that *OK* has its origins in the Wolof *waw kay*. That said, the expression has also been claimed as Greek, Finnish, Gaelic, Choctaw and French; as an abbreviation of the faintly humorous misspelling *Orl Korrect* or of Obediah Kelly, the name of a freight agent who initialled documents he'd checked; and as an inversion of the boxing term *KO* (*knock-out*), used because a boxer who hadn't been knocked out was considered to be . . . well, OK. Less problematically, the linguist David Dalby suggests that the use of *bad* and *wicked* to convey positive rather than negative feelings originates in African languages such as Bambara, where there are 'frequent uses of negative terms . . . to describe positive extremes'. Dalby traces the habit of saying *uh-huh* to the same source.[6]

Another channel is the Gullah creole spoken in the Sea Islands and the nearby coastal areas of Georgia and South Carolina. A creole is a language that develops when people from different backgrounds are thrown together and have to arrive at a means of communicating. The vocabulary of Gullah contains words recognizably derived from West and Central African languages, among them Wolof, Hausa, Bambara, Ewe and Igbo. The creole's foundations seem to have been laid on the Rice Coast, a traditionally agricultural region stretching from Senegal to Liberia. Slaves from this region were sought after by plantation owners who needed workers with experience of tending rice. The Gullah people are descended from these slaves, and today their tongue has as many as 250,000 speakers, although only a handful of them speak no other language.

Gullah has been identified as the precursor of modern African American Language, and has provided *mojo*, as in Jim Morrison's nickname Mr Mojo Risin', as well as *ninny*, a slang term for a woman's breast. Furthermore, there is a Gullah term *juke* or *joog* which means 'disorderly' or 'wicked', which probably comes from the Wolof *dzug*, 'to live wickedly'. The Gullah word turns up in the Black American *juke-joint* and *juke-house*, both old names for roadside amusement parlours – establishments where the amusement was part musical and part sexual. These tended to have their own resident bands, but a machine enabling music to be played at the drop of a coin was always likely to prove at once more lucrative and more reliable: the 1890s saw the development of the coin-slot phonograph, and in the 1930s this was superseded by the Gothic triumph of tubes and chrome we know as the *jukebox*.

A related and more contentious subject is the etymology of *jazz*. The word seems first to have been used around 1913. Its early spellings were various (including both *jas* and *jascz*), and it was certainly in spoken currency before anyone troubled to write about it. One popular explanation traces it to the French Creole spoken in Louisiana. According to this school of thought, its antecedent is either the verb *jaser*, 'to chatter like a magpie', or *chasser*, meaning 'to hunt' – with its implications of spontaneity and wild movement. The trouble is, the use of this word to denote the style of music we know as jazz began in California, and only from there did it spread to Chicago and on to New Orleans. An alternative explanation is that *jazz* is linked to the Mandingo *jasi*, which means something along the lines of 'to become abnormal' or 'to become exaggerated'.

The soul of jazz is African American. Its correlative is African American Vernacular English, that direct, performative and rapidly evolving object of controversy. Today, the interplay of black talk and Standard English is fertile – the differences between them less extreme than tends to be claimed – and African Americanisms wield a small yet significant influence over the use and lexicon of Standard English. While there remains wide resistance to black language – which is perceived in certain quarters as lazy, solecistic, illogical, a mark of poor education and low academic ability, and inimical to its speakers' learning standard forms – the fact remains that it is commonly co-opted by advertisers, and nowhere is its presence more keenly felt than in music, a medium which quickly and memorably disseminates words and phrases among people (mainly young people) of very diverse backgrounds. As one recent account notes, 'African Americans are on the cutting edge of the sociolinguistic situation in the USA' and 'Hip Hop Nation Language' is 'the cutting edge of the cutting edge'.[7] Moving beyond the US, the impact of African American vernaculars is evident in 'a sense of the figurative possibilities behind the sentence; a sense of the flow and flavour of rhyme, meter, assonance, and alliteration'.[8] Plainly, yet also subtly, across a large part of the English-speaking world the cadences, vocabulary, tone and tenor of Black Englishes are asserting themselves. Each assertion is a reassertion.

So are Standard English and the locutions of African American and Black British English converging, or are they moving further apart? Observation suggests there is convergence. The widespread adoption of Black English usage by people of other heritages is a form of 'inward borrowing', a process whereby a word moves from a particular department of the language into more general use. This is a vital theme of Modern English.

15. Angst

Anxiety, anguish, neurotic fear, dread, guilt

The word is German, related to the Latin *angustus*, meaning 'narrow' or 'restricted'. It has been popularized through the works of Sigmund Freud, Carl Gustav Jung and Martin Heidegger.

In the twentieth century the English lexicon grew by some 90,000 words. Of these, around 5,000 were imported from other languages – a large enough number, but the smallest volume of borrowings in any century since the Norman Conquest. The variety of languages from which English borrowed was greater than ever. An increasing number of cultures were impinging on English, which in turn was impinging on an increasing number of others. Continuities were evident, but so were newly brittle patterns of usage.

John Evelyn could refer to a *chassis* in 1664, Tobias Smollett to a *cabriolet* in 1766, and Thackeray to a *hangar* in 1852, but the phenomena with which we now associate these words – as well as a host of others that share with them the distinction of originating in French, such as *limousine, chauffeur* and *fuselage* – are twentieth-century creations. Although the first internal-combustion engine was designed in the early years of the nineteenth century, large-scale manufacturing of cars did not begin until Ransom Olds launched his first assembly line in Detroit in 1901. Two years later, Orville and Wilbur Wright made the first controlled flight at Kitty Hawk, North Carolina. The implications of these events were huge. Both ultimately accelerated human relations. The car, especially, has liberated and mobilized us, affording us opportunities to see people and places we could never otherwise have seen, yet it has become a kind of shield, 'quasi-heraldic', a tool that is more than just a tool.[1]

The twentieth century witnessed many such doubled-edged achievements, both liberating and estranging. Man walked on the moon. The atom was split. Widespread electrification allowed us to tap into the world's energy resources. Other notable innovations included personal computers and television – and, on a smaller scale, nylon, oral contraceptives and the credit card. We might also flag up mechanized agriculture, dramatic improvements in water supply, the development of lasers and fibre optics, or the rise of household appliances like the electric oven and the vacuum cleaner. Concurrently, the age of empires folded. Western control in the East declined, and Japan and China became major world powers.

Yet this was above all a century of science, of technical and theoretical advances that to many observers seemed nothing short of sorcery, and a century of wars, of slaughter on a giant scale – 'the bloodiest century in modern history' according to one recent study, and 'far more violent in relative as well as absolute terms than any previous era'.[2] The two domains, war and science, were closely related. As the century unfurled, scientific endeavour's 'centre of gravity' moved from Europe to America, with obvious political and lexical consequences.[3] The wars, meanwhile, were of a kind not previously experienced – industrial, technologized.

War disrupts language even as it depends on it. Familiar assumptions are destabilized, as are everyday moral categories.[4] People used to speak of 'a boast of soldiers' – as they still do of 'a flock of sheep' or 'a futility of husbands' – and military vocabulary has a necessarily triumphalist ring. Moreover, soldiering lies behind many common idioms. If you choose explicitly to stick to your guns, dig yourself in, mark time, fall into line, steal a march or take somewhere by storm, you are exploiting this tradition. This is the talk of troops on the front line – to be supplemented by something more transient, the virile jargon that builds unity in the trenches and the barracks. Yet, as technology has become ever more central to military dominance, so the lexis has become more opaque: the language of modern warfare, as of modern policing, is robotic.

Whenever war is raging, we assimilate new words. The atrocities of modern combat are neutralized with talk of *friendly fire* and *collateral damage*, terms eloquent only of the bureaucratic nature of the modern military. Euphemisms rub epauletted shoulders with detachments of management speak and pseudo-science – plus the odd blackly humorous item like *gremlin*. In this context the verb *degrade* means *kill*, while *explosive device* and *physics package* take the place of *bomb* and *warhead*. The noun *incident* is used of almost any unsavoury occurrence. Today's army officers sound like business consultants, trading in impressive gibberish or fancy obfuscations. Violence is routinely disguised. Talk of *engagements*, *operations* or that old CIA favourite *clandestine activities* is, according to your perspective, quaint, diplomatic or appallingly evasive. In a truly dreadful moment of lexical perversion, the US military's deployment of troops on the island of Grenada in October 1983 was presented as a 'pre-dawn vertical insertion'. And, in a surprising return to the spirit of the spice wars, President Ronald Reagan whimsically excused the intervention on the grounds that Grenada was the world's richest source of nutmeg, explaining that 'You can't make eggnog without nutmeg.'[5]

Conflict also causes us to absorb words from our enemies' languages. As a result of the Napoleonic Wars, we have French terms like *battalion, bayonet, fusillade* and *grenade*. *Commando*, a word originally Portuguese, became highly visible at the time of the Boer War, as did *laager*, and the political tensions of Victorian South Africa lent currency to terms like *trek* and *kraal*. The First World War was remarkable for its violence and for the technical innovations it unleashed. From German we learnt a wave of new items – *ersatz*, *achtung*, the calque expression 'sunk without trace' – and from French *camouflage* and the suddenly popular *espionage*. In the wake of the war came the distress signal *mayday* (from French: *m'aidez*). The Spanish Civil War brought in the *fifth column* – one of its earliest adopters was Ernest Hemingway. The rise of fascism and the Second World War popularized *Weltpolitik* and *Herrenvolk*, and then *blitzkrieg* and *quisling*. *Scorched earth* was calqued on a Chinese expression, common under Chiang Kai-shek; Japanese involvement in the war gave an international profile to the code of honour known as *Bushido*. One of the features of the Second World War was a vocabulary of military 'philosophy', which James Dawes has called a 'rationalized organization of violence'. The six-year conflict 'saw language shattered in the centralizing bureaucracies of the military-industrial [powers] . . . and reinvented in the rise of international human rights law'.[6]

Our vocabulary of warfare comprises many other obviously foreign words: *torpedo, guerrilla, salvo, bazooka*. Of these, *guerrilla* is especially interesting, as it gained currency during the Peninsular War of 1808–14, when the British encouraged the efforts of Spanish partisans against Napoleon's army; the *OED* gives as the first recorded instance a dispatch written in 1809 by the Duke of Wellington. Literally meaning 'little war', it at first denoted wars against France and the French revolutionary cause. Only in 1959, with the Cuban Revolution, was the word appropriated by Marxists.[7] We associate it immediately with the handsome visage of Che Guevara, plastered on countless student bedroom walls. Yet we also know that the term has broadened its scope to include all manner of irregular and independent practices, not many of which are really belligerent. So, for instance, a trawl through a well-stocked bookshop will reveal titles such as *Guerrilla Marketing: Secrets for Making Big Profits from Your Small Business, Guerrilla Home Recording* and *The Guerrilla Guide to Credit Repair.* What we see here is common enough: small business and personal finance, as well as film-making and music production, are presented as exercises in military stealth.

The imagery of war, at first shocking and alien, rapidly gets attached to the trivial and everyday. Thus the term *kamikaze* is now most often used metaphorically and hyperbolically: of a rodeo rider, an aggressive driver or someone hooked on speed-dating. Yet *kamikaze* has the literal meaning 'divine wind' – something beautiful, ethereal, enormous – and was originally used in Japanese of a wind that destroyed a fleet of invading Mongols in 1281. It was adopted into English by the half-Greek, half-Irish travel writer Lafcadio Hearn at the end of the nineteenth century, and acquired greater currency after the suicidal attacks by Japanese pilots on Allied ships in the Pacific in the autumn of 1944. The *OED* cites the poet Sylvia Plath as the first to use the word figuratively to suggest any kind of reckless and self-destructive behaviour. In the context of Plath's pathos-laden writing, the word is potent, but its painful specificity has since been deadened by casual use. Many Japanese terms were transformed amid the carnage of the Second World War. The best example is *banzai*; once a cheer used in greeting the emperor, it became a vicious war cry, unavoidably associated with Japan's fanatical soldiers. Now it is probably best known as the name of a spoof gameshow and a hapless hyena in *The Lion King*, or, when shouted, as an expression of forced jollity. The post-war occupation popularized other Japanese words, such as *honcho*, which circulated among American servicemen in Korea and was later given an unwelcome boost during the Watergate hearings.[8]

A more extreme example of semantic blunting is *bikini*. This was the name of an atoll in the Marshall Islands where an atomic bomb was tested in July 1946, and it was adopted as a word for a signifi-cant explosion. The style of bathing suit we now know as the bikini existed before then, but got its name only when the designer Louis Réard chose to use it to draw attention to a collection he was showing a few days after the bomb test. *Bikini*, we might argue, should have become a word to sum up the devastation that a nuclear weapon can cause; instead it became a word for a skimpy piece of beach attire.

One word not transformed in this way is *holocaust*, which from the 1950s was – with an initial capital – the standard name for the Nazis' campaign of destruction against European Jews. It derives from the Greek rendering of a Hebrew word meaning 'completely burnt', and can be found in Tyndale's Bible in the early sixteenth century. The Hebrew term was connected with sacrifice – religious offerings had to be burnt in their entirety – but it clearly now has nothing to do with sacrifice in this sense. However, its force seems too specifically Jewish to allow wider use. Ideological purists prefer the half-Greek, half-Latin *genocide* to denote the mass destruction of an ethnic or religious group.

The changing theatres and practices of war continue to thrust new words into the limelight. A recent example is *jihad*, which I mentioned briefly in my opening chapter. The word has been used in English since the second half of the nineteenth century, but is now inextricably associated with the new breeds of militant Islamist who have emerged over the last decade. Whereas in Arabic, fighting and hostility are only parts of *jihad* – which can be understood as a larger struggle towards the realization of a perfect faith – the word is used in English of a form of violence without ethical limit, carried out in the name of religion but with obvious political intent.

Moreover, it has spawned *jihadist*, a word that manages to be at once ersatz and downright sinister.

In time of war, while new terms are swiftly acquired, some existing loanwords are demonized. Our pets and the food we consume are especially vulnerable to this. The dachshund, so strongly associated with Germany, became a 'liberty pup' during the First World War, and after it the increasingly popular German Shepherds were renamed Alsatians in light of persisting anti-German feeling. During the same period frankfurters and sauerkraut were relabelled as 'hot dogs' and 'liberty cabbage'. In the Second World War the Japanese showed a similar concern with eradicating traces of the enemy from their language, and dropped certain American terms customarily used in baseball – for instance, first base became *ichi ryu*.

Given the turbulent history of Russia in the twentieth century, together with its large presence in world events, it is hardly a surprise that the bulk of Russian borrowings into English occurred during that period. On the whole, those Russian words that are known to English-speakers are reserved for purely Russian phenomena: examples are *dacha*, *babushka* and *shashlik*. But there are exceptions. *Czar* and *tsar*, which came in during the sixteenth century, when trade with Russia was in its infancy, have slackened to suggest not just an emperor, but any dictatorial figure of authority, and other borrowings before the last century – *steppe*, *samovar*, *mammoth*, *pogrom* – have assumed wider significance. In the nineteenth century Russian literature was a conduit of influence on English, and in the twentieth science played the same role. But above all in the last century there was a large category of vivid, specialized borrowings needed to convey the workings of the region's politics. Now, as memories of the Cold War and Communism recede, the currency of these words diminishes. They were used to play up the difference between 'us' and 'them'; today the political motives for dramatizing that difference are less urgent.

Soviet and *Bolshevik* are used far less widely than they were a generation ago. The *cosmonaut* and *sputnik*, beacons of Soviet technical achievement, also seem superannuated. We no longer hear the once-common *kulak* or *ukase*. *Perestroika* and *glasnost* – both of which were indices of political and social changes in the Soviet Union in the mid-1980s, and were later used more generally – have declined in popularity, as have the values they denote. Those terms that live on are redolent of a half-interred past: examples are *agitprop*, *apparatchik* and *samizdat*. The last of these, which denotes the clandestine copying of state-suppressed texts, was coined by the poet Nikolai Glazkov, who was active in the 1930s and '40s. In an age where the Internet allows individuals to circulate messages with a minimum of state scrutiny, it looks doomed, though we should note the Chinese authorities' use of 'deep packet inspection' to identify subversive online communication. *Intelligentsia*, whose early adopters included H. G. Wells and Aldous Huxley, also seems to be a concept in decline, although readers of this book may demur. A few Russian-sourced calques have lasted: *fellow traveller*, *the party line*, and (possibly) *bogeyman*. But, overall, the Russian element in English is increasingly tinged with nostalgia. Since the break-up of the Soviet Union, the prospects for the Russian language have not looked auspicious, and significant loans from this source are from now on likely to be more scarce, despite the international wanderings of Russian-speaking plutocrats.

In the years after the First World War and the Russian Revolution there gathered the insurgent energies of Modernism. The movement's defining mission was a rethinking of fundamentals, in the service of the spiritually and practically enriching possibilities of new art, architecture and design, often to be facilitated by machines. 'We all make vows to ourselves on New Year's Eve,' writes Peter Conrad, and 'The twentieth century began with the bravest, most ambitious, perhaps the most foolhardy of such self-improving resolutions: a promise to make the world modern, which meant to create it all over again.'[9] For the innovators who sought to live up to this promise, the forces of progress needed a new analytical language.

Reviewing humankind's achievements in the twentieth century, it is impossible not to see the long shadows cast by Marx, Freud and Einstein, the architects of socialism, psychoanalysis and the atomic age. They renovated thought, and their achievements are legible in language we use every day. I shall say more about Freud soon, but for now it is worth pausing to reflect on the peculiarly post-

Einsteinian resonance of *photon, space-time, quantum* and *curvature,* as well as *relativity,* and of the Marxist tang of *alienation, bourgeoisie, hegemony, proletariat* and *praxis.* We should note as well that Marxist language now tends to convey an air of contempt that Marx would not have recognized.

The fixation of bourgeois citizens with drawing up an inventory of all things they possessed was guyed by the surrealists, whose work celebrated desire, the unconscious and the magic of madness. The noun *surréalisme* was coined by the poet Guillaume Apollinaire in 1917, and was adopted by André Breton as the name for a movement of convulsive artistic liberation. Cyril Connolly would use it with its French spelling in 1927; the English version became current a decade later. The word's tentative emergence may suggest a certain reticence about embracing this attention-seeking assault on order and conformism. At a time when political relationships within Europe were being nervously recalibrated, it seemed tactlessly self-indulgent.

The Marxist theorist Fredric Jameson has argued that an important trait of modernity is a move 'away from positive content, and from the various dogmatisms of the signifier'.[10] The key idea here is that the mechanisms we use to create meaning (words or signs) are not the same thing as the meaning itself; it appears to follow that one can create meaning without using those established mechanisms. Surreal and modernist art explored new ways of doing this. Hints of the period's artistic temper were contained in new borrowings from French: *collage, cubism, montage, élan vital* (coined by Henri Bergson), and, less seriously, *ooh-la-la.* The magazine *transition* was founded in 1927 by an American exiled in Europe, Eugene Jolas, and became a furnace of avant-garde creativity. Jolas craved what he called 'an enrichment of language', comprising 'new words, millions of words'. He sought to break down the barriers between different languages, celebrated the modern lexicon's 'scintillating assemblage of phonetic novelties', and made sure that the verbiage of high culture was spread as far as possible, in the hope of driving out the ideology of what he saw as 'a rotting civilization'. Borrowing from other languages created a 'fantasia of many-tongued words'; it promised to erase borders and inequalities.[11]

For Tristan Tzara, the founder of Dadaism, sound mattered more than sense. Some observers thought that *Dada* took its name from the French word for a hobby horse, but the Dadaists cultivated confusion about its etymology. Devotion to reason seemed destined to lead only to conflict; the Dadaists renounced bourgeois rationality and aesthetics, choosing instead anarchy – a preference for instinct rather than meaning. In an appealing irony, while the exiled Dadaists fermented raucous discontent at Zurich's Cabaret Voltaire, another exile, Lenin, drew up his plans for political revolution in an apartment nearby. (*Cabaret* had only lately come to signify a nightclub offering a floor show; originally it had meant a wooden shed or booth.) For a generation of radicals, even if actions spoke much louder than words, there had to be a new vocabulary of dissent and self-realization. This vocabulary is with us still. To the period between the wars we can trace the rise of *atonal, pressure group, escapism* and *technocrat; sociopath, autism* and *sex drive*; and, re-energized and repositioned, *nucleus, partisan, workshop, serious* and *stream of consciousness.*

Many of these words were offshoots of older ones or were clawed back from oblivion. To seminal writers such as James Joyce and T. S. Eliot, other people's leftovers were the ingredients of their urban masterpieces. In *Finnegans Wake* (1939) Joyce audaciously reversed the experience of Babel, making a universal language out of the cacophony of different tongues. The book, famously difficult, at once celebrated the possibility that we could all make sense of each other and invited a bleak sort of amusement at the expense of our mutual incomprehension.[12] It may also have inspired the adoption of the German word *quark*, literally a curd (and, less literally, an item of no consequence), to denote a tiny fundamental particle that is one of the building blocks of the atom. For his part Eliot redeemed words used in Sir Thomas Elyot's *The Boke Named the Governour*, while for Virginia Woolf's character Katharine Hilbery, in *Night and Day* (1919), there was to be a new language that could enable 'a riveting together of the shattered fragments of the world'. In 1922 – the year of Joyce's *Ulysses* and Eliot's *The Waste Land*, as well as of the Ottoman Empire's abolition and the founding of the BBC – newly used words included *anschluss* and *provocateur;* in the previous few years one could have spotted not only *fascist* and *putsch*, but also *yippee* and *blah*. Political nervousness precluded neither excitement nor world-weariness.

In radically different ways, ranging from vandalism to the most abstruse kind of scholarship, modernism's pioneers tried to replenish meaning by dismantling received ideas. As Peter Conrad observes, a central requirement of modernism was 'to insist on knowing how things work', and after Einstein's theoretical advances 'physics treated the universe itself as a kit of parts.'[13] The mechanics of experience could be picked to pieces: the possibilities of science and technology seemed boundless. In his play *R.U.R.* (1920) Karel Čapek used *robota*, a Czech noun related to the German noun *Arbeit* and meaning 'forced labour', to signify a new type of 'artificial' being, assembled like a car and programmed to be of service to humans.[14] This choice of word was inspired by a conversation with his brother Josef, a painter of the cubist school. It would become an emblem of the future's potential.

The first English reference to a *robot* is dated by the *OED* to 1923. That same year, in his *Vers une architecture*, the Swiss architect Le Corbusier presented a seasonable blueprint: the house as a *machine à habiter*. Le Corbusier's model dwelling had to be elegantly proportional, but also geared towards hygiene and warmth. The new purity he sought to introduce into the world of objects was embodied in his celebrated Villa Savoye, built at Poissy near Paris. The reinforced concrete stilts that supported the house's upper structure were called *pilotis*. The word seemed unfamiliar to English-speaking admirers, yet had been used in an English text as early as the seventeenth century – and by no less an eighteenth-century writer than Defoe. For Le Corbusier, the *piloti* was supposed to give the sense of a building floating in the air yet still connected to the ground. In acknowledging this paradox – the simultaneous desires for connection and disconnection – and in developing an architectural style that was geometric, machinist, anonymous and utopian, he grasped the architect's social responsibilities while also tapping into the rising spirit of consumerism, in which pleasure was presented as highly individual yet was assiduously mass-produced.

In person and in his philosophy, Le Corbusier insisted on a manicured anonymity. His real name was Charles-Edouard Jeanneret; he adopted his pseudonym as part of an attempt to prove that people, objects and communities could be refashioned. Yet his functional artefacts appealed to the adherents of *conspicuous consumption*. That phrase's originator, Thorstein Veblen, explained it as 'a means of reputability to the gentleman of leisure. As wealth accumulates on his hands, his own unaided effort will not avail to sufficiently put his opulence in evidence by this method. The aid of friends and competitors is therefore brought in by resorting to the giving of valuable presents and expensive feasts and entertainments.'[15] Veblen reported the tendency to buy goods for show – to satisfy psychological needs, not practical ones. This was not a new phenomenon, but it had become more perceptible in the 1880s with the development of the department store, and it ballooned in the early years of the century that followed. (For me, at least, 'conspicuous consumption' calls to mind Jay Gatsby's tear-jerking panoply of shirts and the Xanadu of *Citizen Kane*.) Among the most striking features of the twentieth century as a whole was the growth of the leisure industry, which became a bigger and bigger part of the world's industrialized economies. Work came to be seen as a necessary obstacle to enjoyment. Leisure meanwhile became narcissistic, and the language of leisure became self-involved.

One symptom of this has been the changing use of the word *addict*. Many of us think of *addiction* as properly referring to drug addiction, so it may come as a surprise to find Gladstone referring in 1858 to an 'addiction to agricultural pursuits' or Edward Phillips in 1675 mentioning Shakespeare's 'addiction to books'. The noun *addict* is a twentieth-century coinage, initially used exclusively of habitual drug-users. But it has come to encapsulate the pathological tendencies of modern living. We continually hear about addicts of sex, shopping, chocolate, slot machines, chatrooms, gossip, fashion and television. More than anything, these are addicts of the New. Addicts think of themselves as addicts, and this affects not just their self-image, but also their relationships.

Consumerism has generally altered the way we classify people. We judge those around us by what they own and how they spend their money. The emergence of the *teenager* – of a self-conscious youth culture – was a phenomenon of the 1940s and '50s. It amounted to a youth-led revolution. The actual concept of a teenager was much older (and *adolescence* had been adopted by John Lydgate in the fifteenth century), but to the 1940s we can date a new, decisive, use of it as a means of classifying a large and diverse group through a single characteristic. In the same period there emerged *hipster, youth club* and *baby boom*, and in 1942 the Harvard sociologist Talcott Parsons explicitly identified what he called *youth culture*.

This appealed to the advertising industry. As we know, advertising propagates desire. In an essay that appeared more than 250 years ago, Samuel Johnson diagnosed that 'Promise, large promise, is the soul of an advertisement,' and explained that 'Advertisements are now so numerous that they are very neglectfully perused, and it is therefore become necessary to gain attention by magnificence of promises, and by eloquence sometimes sublime and sometimes pathetic.'[16] Advertising puts pressure on us to identify ourselves through what we consume. It would hardly be an exaggeration to say that it exists to make us feel bad about ourselves and salve our bad feelings by spending money. Companies commissioning advertisements certainly recognize the need to prey on insecurities. The General Motors executive Charles Kettering, who invented the electric ignition system for cars, aptly spoke of 'the organized creation of dissatisfaction'. What we are being sold is Hope.

Advertising has been around for several millennia – since at least 5,000 years ago, when Babylonian cobblers hung from their doors the shoes they had expertly mended – but it was in the first three decades of the twentieth century that it became a coherent, systematic business, grounded in market research. One of the architects of this change was King Gillette. Gillette's *The Human Drift* (1894) was a disturbing manifesto which envisioned a society where mass marketing would eliminate the very essence of human character and individuality.[17] Whereas Thorstein Veblen had had his pet terms, like the pejorative and pseudo-French *nouveaux arrivés* (along with *emulative* and *ostensible*), Gillette had no gift for neologism or indeed for prose. Mass distribution of disposable goods was his forte – he sold 168 razor blades in 1903, 12 million the following year – and his aggressive and shrewdly positioned advertising played a key role in shaping consumer culture. After Gillette, and then especially in the 1960s, the philosophy of advertising became scientific. As goods became less truly magical to those who acquired them, the methods of their promotion had to evolve. It seems relevant that the word *hype* – a debased scrag of Greek – acquired its present meaning in that decade; one early appearance noted by the *OED* is in an article in the *Sunday Times*, in August 1968, where the author explained, 'Hype is an American word for the gentle art of getting a tune into the pop charts without actually selling any records. Its methods are various: from the crudest bribery to devious techniques for upsetting the . . . calculations of chart-compilers.' We know this well, though it hardly now seems a 'gentle' art.

The business of advertising has its own cant, in which products effect miracles and realize fantasies. Vagueness is invaluable: empty claims are clothed in the illusory skeins of exactitude. An especially tired formula is the use of *luxury* as an attributive. Once, an advertiser had only to attach this word to a cruise, a flat or a brand of toilet paper and the item acquired cachet. Now, however, we tend to be suspicious of it. What was formerly 'luxurious' has been democratized. True luxury may have kept its sparkle, but in this realm the word *luxury* is avoided, as it is associated with vulgarity and striving aspiration. Most of us know, from our own painful experience, that any food described as *mouth-watering* and any hotel that boasts of its *old world charm* will leave us somewhere short of total satisfaction.

Among other conventions, such as never referring to consumers as 'old', advertising borrows exotic words to make ordinary products sound resplendent. More than half of the world's leading advertising agencies are American; in countries where English is not a major language, English words are dropped into advertisements to connote glamour or the benefits of pedigree, and in countries where English predominates a quick dash of a foreign language can pep up even the most humdrum offering. Audi's *Vorsprung durch Technik* may be the best-known German phrase in the English-speaking world; the foreign words lend an extra air of technical exactness to what is in fact a completely banal promise.

The rise of commercial advertising was central to an era hungry for pleasure and blessed with real purchasing power. Its products included hula hoops, Brylcreem, drive-in movies, moralistic TV shows like *Leave It to Beaver*, and jukeboxes playing Buddy Holly and Elvis Presley, but also, as traditional moral values appeared to slip, a rash of *juvenile delinquency* (a buzzword of the later 1950s, though of sufficiently old standing to have been used by Dickens in *Oliver Twist*). At the same time – and some observers made a connection here – many English-speaking countries were becoming much more ethnically diverse. Pockets of Britain, for instance, had been multiracial in the 1920s, and before the war there were sizeable communities of Arabs and Jews. But the arrival in Tilbury on 22 June 1948 of the SS *Empire Windrush*, with its 492 Jamaican passengers, appeared to open a new chapter in Britain's multi-racialism. The numbers increased: there were 3,000 immigrants from the Caribbean in 1953, twenty times as many in 1961. Indians and Pakistanis also began to arrive in significant numbers during the 1960s, and there were visibly busy communities of Chinese, Poles, Cypriots and Maltese.

We can draw from the dictionary an impression of changing pleasures and passions. Among the newly borrowed words of 1950 are *passegiatta* and *Vespa*, *chipotle* and *filo*, *ayatollah* and *maven*, *Mau Mau* and *dianetics*, *mano a mano* and *appellation contrôlée*. Move on a decade and the list includes *bricolage*, *arugula*, *crudités*, *Hezbollah*, *meritocrat*, *shura*, *yé-yé* and *New Wave* – the last of these calqued on *nouvelle vague*. The latest styles of music and dance often had foreign inspirations: hence *bossa nova* (Brazilian Portuguese), *ska* (Jamaican patois) and *mambo* (Cuban Spanish). Increasingly, borrowings dealt less with fundamental concepts and more with the edges of day-to-day existence: with things to eat and fads to follow, and with the forces that put them under threat or merely grazed the margin of most people's consciousness.

Submerged beneath all of this is a story of desire. It is by no means trivial: the politics of the world's most economically developed countries have in the last few generations been increasingly bent towards satisfying appetites rather than putting into effect real principles. The use of the Latin word *status* has grown and grown over this period – and the thing itself, a modern religion, has often been confused with love. To paraphrase the historian Daniel Boorstin, image has taken the place of ideals.

When was the first time you drank a *cappuccino*? In Italy it is consumed with a spoon, standing up, before eleven o'clock in the morning: ordering a cappuccino after one's evening meal is a gastronomic crime and may sometimes be treated as if it were a moral one to boot. But in Britain and America cappuccino is everywhere. To anyone under the age of twenty, the years 'B. C.' (Before Cappuccino) may sound like the time of myth. And for many younger consumers the drink is inextricably associated with Starbucks. The giant coffee chain was founded in 1971, but originally it sold coffee beans and equipment for making coffee, and it was only in the late 1980s, steered by Howard Schultz, that the firm began to expand. Its first branch outside North America opened in Tokyo, as recently as 1996. The drink and its purveyors haven't been around all that long.

The now-common word *cappuccino* derives from the name of the Capuchin order of monks. In Robert O'Brien's *This is San Francisco* (1948), the link is made explicit. O'Brien takes us inside 'a world of Neapolitans and Tuscans, Romans and Venetians and assorted *paisani* from the toe to the knee of the Italian boot': there 'you leave behind the kingdom of *chow mein* and *jow won ton* and jasmine tea, and enter the realm of *ravioli*.' Immersing yourself in this little Italy, where Caruso records play endlessly, 'you drink a *cappuccino*, gray, like the robe of a capuchin monk . . . and heated by steam forced through coffee.'[18]

The cappuccino is a typically modern appropriation: it's been taken from somewhere else, reinvented, glamorized, cheapened (yet made more expensive), and sent out, repackaged, into the rest of the world. It is a convenient emblem for a large part of modern living: indulgent, ephemeral, frothy. The takeaway cup of coffee is a fashion accessory, a romantic object of connoisseurship, and our addiction to its contents is as much social as somatic. Ever since Achille Gaggia patented his first espresso machine in the late 1930s, the paraphernalia of coffee-making and coffee-drinking has possessed an air of considered urbanity.

It is easy to forget how recently some of our pleasures and necessities were born. In his fine history of Britain in the 1960s, Dominic Sandbrook points out that 'At the beginning of the sixties, lager accounted for a mere 3 per cent of the British beer market, and some brewers' predictions that it would one day eclipse bitter seemed very far-fetched.'Yet within just a few years it exerted an iron grip on the market, and, as Sandbrook points out, 'While the sale of wine and lager seemed to mark a convergence of British and European tastes, there was an even more pronounced transform-ation in what people ate . . . Avocadoes, aubergines and courgettes were becoming increasingly familiar . . . More and more people drove German cars, took their holidays on the Spanish coast, drank French wine and copied the latest Italian fashions.'[19] Since then, the popularization of foreign commodities has widened its reach: the cars may well be Korean, the holidays in Turkey or Thailand (complete with the obligatory *dervish* show or hit from a *bong*), the wine Chilean, the fashions Japanese or Scandinavian. Xenophobia persists, but even the most impassioned nationalists will eat foreign food and vacation in foreign resorts.

Against this background, the equation of linguistic nicety with moral or social rectitude has managed to hold on. Talk of 'U' and 'non-U' may now be infrequent, but the spirit of the distinction between upper-class usage and usage that is not upper class abides. It brings to mind Nancy Mitford, though the terms were coined in the 1950s by Alan Ross, a scholar of Old English who had worked as a government code-breaker at Bletchley Park during the Second World War. The idea was not new: in the sixteenth century, Pietro Aretino had somewhat flippantly made the same kind of distinction, suggesting for instance that a window was not to be called a *finestra*, but should properly be known as a *balcone*. Ross, whose paper on the subject was published in the intimidat-ingly titled Finnish journal *Neuphilologische Mitteilungen*, began from the position that the British aristocracy was separated by its use of language from the middle and lower classes. Pronunciation was part of this, and we may well still make inferences about a person's background from his or her pronunciation of particular words; borrowings – *conduit, turquoise, loggia* – being prominent among these. But also 'proper' language substantiated seemingly import-ant principles: a respect for public property, purity of mind, moder-ation, a distrust of redundancy and fanciness. In Nancy Mitford's view, the last of these was paramount, and it is noticeable that she abhors *cruet*, *pardon*, *serviette*, *dentures* and *perfume*, all of which are from French.

We are back again with the purists, who believe all change is for the worse and pretend that the English word-stock can be set in aspic. Recent loanwords are, understandably, the ones that look and feel most alien, and now as then they elicit the loudest protests. Yet their alien status is quickly lost, and indeed, as we have seen, it can be part of their appeal – a badge of status, of being informed, educated, modish. We think of such terms as buzzwords, tokens of the hum of commerce and vogue. *Buzzword* itself can be dated back to the 1940s; the *OED* cites a 1946 article in the journal *American Speech*, which explains that 'Students at the Graduate School of Business Administration at Harvard University use a specialized vocabulary known as "buzz words" to describe the key to any particular course or situation.' It can hardly come as a surprise that the word was popularized among MBA students at Harvard, for there are certain areas where new words, be they borrowed or confected, prove especially abundant, and in the world of business they multiply feverishly, often without any logic or grammar.

The modern world of finance is encrusted with these verbal trinkets, many of them repugnant. This, after all, is an environment in which the word *aggressive* marks approval. The term *dead cat bounce* has been around since the mid-1980s; it signifies a temporary and illusory improvement in the price of a stock – little imagination is needed to feel the force of the image. A declining stock is a *falling knife*; someone will eventually get skewered. When investors dump stocks that appear to be underperforming, they *shoot the wounded*. A corporate meltdown results in *blood on the floor* or, worse, *blood on the walls*. A broker who encourages clients to buy into a stock he holds, then offloads his holding at the newly inflated price, is said to have *pumped and dumped*.

Furthermore, capitalism and free enterprise have 'liberated' words from their less euphoric past. *Purchase*, *pay* and *fee* were long ago relieved of their dominant connotations of, respectively, hunting, appeasement and the requirement to settle a debt.[20] It is not hard to see that *finance* contains some idea of finality (think of the French word *fin* or the Latin *finis*, meaning 'end' or 'limit'), and at first the word denoted specifically the idea of 'ending' or 'settlement'. We still come up against this when we're hit with a *fine*. It is only in the seventeenth century that we come across *financiers*, and that *finance* begins to mean 'money management'. In business, the official terminology tends to be Latinate, but there is an undercurrent of irreverent slang, much of it self-consciously brash and crude. There is also a persistent element of facetiousness. A City of London trader will gamely refer to money as *moolah* – the word is probably Romani – or to £5 as a *ching*, perhaps after the Italian *cinque*. The once popular but at the moment unfashionable *dosh* comes from a word in an African language (no one seems clear which) for a bribe or backhander.

Businesspeople are forever finding new ways of vilifying the very culture within which they operate: new ways of referring to the levels of boredom they feel during meetings and presentations, new ways of trashing not just underachievers, but also colleagues who are pedantic, gung ho, overzealous. Meanwhile, the jargon of sport is often transplanted into business talk for the purpose of asserting a sort of manly excellence. Referring to a colleague or a rival as a *heavy-hitter* or claiming that your team has *bench* betrays the machismo that prevails in the modern workplace, yet this imagery is used playfully, as if to say 'It's all a game.'

In the accelerated world of commerce, new words are legion, coming at us daily and from every angle. Seen as a whole, the twentieth century was a period of ebullient growth in English vocabulary, and this continues apace in the twenty-first. Borrowings are no longer dominant among the novelties: most new words are formed creatively from the language's existing resources. Thus, while loans remain plentiful in popular culture, politics, sport and science, as well as among drug-users and backpackers, today the alien languages from which we borrow most freely are outposts of our own language: office jargon, the savvy talk of music fans, the language of chatrooms, newsgroups and blogs. Online communities, which are nothing if not eclectic, prove an especially rich breeding ground for new words. At its extremes – and the online world tends to look as though it consists in large measure of extremes, many of them in fact densely populated – the language is deliriously ludic. As technology grows ever more interactive and personalized, the reign of subjectivity will manifest itself in an array of communications at once massively numerous and determinedly localized.

Interactivity is nicely embodied in the concept of a *Wiki*, a type of website which can be modified by anyone. Its name was coined by a computer programmer, Ward Cunningham, who was told by a worker at Honolulu International Airport to take a 'Wiki Wiki' shuttle bus between the airport's terminals. The name played on the Hawaiian *wiki-wiki*, meaning 'quick', and it stuck in Cunningham's mind. He went on to develop software that enabled online collaboration – the most famous result of which is Wikipedia, the free web-based encyclopedia created by Larry Sanger and Jimmy Wales.

The Internet constantly begets new words of this kind: David Crystal describes it as a 'lexical goldmine'. It is a medium where everything is logged, complete with date and time; coinages can be traced back to their origins – and to their originators. Moreover, Internet terms are rapidly adapted to purposes far removed from computing. The use of *spam* in an IT context is fifteen years old; now its original meaning, dating from the 1930s, feels secondary, despite its celebration by Monty Python. But this is not all: today *spam* denotes not just the unwanted communications clogging your email inbox, but also other kinds of 'unwanted utterance' or evasion – an unwelcome break for advertisements on TV, or the patter of a pushy shop assistant.[21]

This is the inward borrowing I described a few pages ago. The process remains the same as before, even if the sources have changed. The words are transplanted from the margin to the heart of our public and private language – or shift there, perhaps sweetly, perhaps insidiously – because they are needed to denote new or newly important experiences, or for reasons of chic, or simply to inject fresh life into our discourse. Fundamentally, the model is this: you know something I don't, or you appear to, and I want to know it too and possess it and use it to enhance by the very slightest fraction my perceived worth (the perception may be others', or it may be my own). The pattern is exemplified by the case of *epicentre*, a specialized term in seismology which has come to be used as an alternative to *centre*. *Epicentre* is considered better because it sounds more technical, more in-the-know. The term, when first adopted, seemed less debased by ordinary usage than poor *centre*: now we may be nostalgic for the older, simpler word.

Professionalism thrives on stripping the meaning out of words, or at least on impoverishing them and dulling their subtleties. Every profession has its characteristic verbal tics and postures. Rudyard Kipling could describe the language of trade as 'a toothsome amalgam of Americanisms and epigrams'; Frank Zappa characterized rock reporters as 'people who can't write interviewing people who can't talk for people who can't read'; John Galsworthy noted, with careful irony, that the heyday of journalese coincided with the setting up of Britain's Ministry of Health. As I observed some time ago, we often hear the cliché that 'language is power,' but the power does not necessarily lie with those who utter it. Language betrays frailties, anxieties and the precariousness of self-image. We can see past the bogus superlatives of advertising or what George Steiner has called the 'vehement obscurity' of sociology. We know, too, what lies behind the opaque utterances of academics and management gurus with their talk of *discourse* or *hermeneutics*, of *adding value* or *operationalizing* a brand. There seems to be a language of science (complex, metaphorical), of religion (poetic, oracular), and of sport (hyperbolic, platitudinous). Then, too, we have the 'over-manicured' and 'turgid' style of lawyers.[22] These occupational dialects build affiliations, and can betray them.

As Tony Thorne observes in his amusing look at contemporary jargon, *Shoot the Puppy* (2006), 'One reason why fewer foreign terms make it into English in the twenty-first century may be that these days a different sort of person is coining new language. A hundred years ago it was poets, ambassadors and international sophisticates . . . Today it's IT specialists, management consultants and financiers.' Yet now and then these people do reach for foreign terms. Thorne cites the example of *chasse gardée*, a recently adopted way of designating private property or a no-go area, which might be used in a sentence like 'Central America has traditionally been the USA's chasse gardée.' He mentions a handful of other imported words and phrases used in business: *gaijin*, the Japanese term for a foreigner, the Spanish *mano a mano*, beloved of corporate tough guys, and the more obscure *Fingerspitzengefühl*, a charming if offputtingly long word for a 'feeling in the tips of one's fingers', which is to say an instinctive grasp – presumably for one of the more complex areas of business. With more than a touch of irony, Thorne points out that 'it's a *sine qua non* that English, or rather American, is the *lingua franca – par excellence* – of world business.'[23]

One of the less appealing forms this takes is the widespread adoption of 'management-speak', which starts as bureaucratic flummery and mutates into a kind of mandatory tag of professional know-how. Management speak is an essentially male institution – a means of institutionalizing self-importance. Dickens sends it up in *Little Dorrit*, where the Circumlocution Office is deemed to be the most important government department; its chief talents are for addling business and churning out hopelessly ungrammatical correspondence. Readers will have their own experience of this wearisome argot, which makes people sound like machines. It is probably fair to say that the young and the old treat such language with suspicion; its originators and protectors are those in between, caught between the urge to seem professional and the urge to be modish. Writing in 1978, Kenneth Hudson stated that 'the most notorious jargon-producers' were 'politicians and political propagandists, East and West; those engaged in the social sciences, particularly in psychology; spokesmen for the armed forces; people writing about or publicising hotels, restaurants and the entertainment industry; economists and management consultants; writers on education; bureaucrats; and critics of literature and the arts'. The reasons for their succumbing to this infectious lingo were diagnosed as insecurity about the value of their services, feelings of shame about their work (resulting in the need 'to find suitable language with which to gild their activities'), the desire for 'an extra ration of size' and an awareness that they 'have nothing really to sell'.[24] As we read this, we may be reminded of the Inkhorn disputants of the sixteenth century and the notion that polysyllabic excesses 'make all things darke and harde'.

Most of us will cringe on hearing certain words used in a political or official context: terms such as *efficiency* and *initiative* seem invariably to be deployed only in situations where neither is in evidence. Very little of this type of language is borrowed from abroad. Instead, it thrives on clumsy compounding – sometimes imagined to be pithy or humorous, yet often just grotesque. But some foreign words do play a role: formerly dignified, they now become laughable. The Hindi *guru*, deriving ultimately from a Sanskrit word meaning 'weighty' or 'dignified', has come to signify in many cases an opportunistic celebrant of capitalism. The psychologist Adrian Furnham comments, 'It has been said that journalists first used the term "guru" to describe management theorists because they could not spell the word "charlatan".'[25] The word's freight of sacred significance has been lost amid the antagonism of puffery and irony.

Gurus are the bad poets of our connected world, vying for the laurel with those who satirize them. The growth of the Internet and of businesses that trade online has incubated a wealth of new terms. Some, such as *dot.com* and *e-commerce*, are ubiquitous and widely understood. Others are more obscure. Much of this new terminology has been coined by disaffected observers, who dismiss the *get-rich-click* schemes of blithe young technophiles and belittle the technophiles themselves as *dot snots* or *entreprenerds* or *sneaker millionaires*. Among the practitioners rather than the observers, the general tone is snappy, witty and a little smug; after all, 'the future just happened.' The hallmark of this language is a brisk way of dealing with complex ideas. *First-mover advantage* is a concept that can hardly be conveyed more succinctly. All the same, the economy of the expression suggests a rather testy cast of mind. Email and instant messaging have accelerated the urge towards brevity: everything must happen faster and more compactly.

As long ago as the 1960s the Canadian theorist Marshall McLuhan announced that changing modes of communication had created a Global Village: all of us were plumbed into a single giant nervous system, a cognitively stifling electronic brain. 'For most people in the industrialized countries,' wrote Richard Maltby two decades later, 'the consumption of media has come to occupy more time than any other activity except sleeping and working.'[26] A sceptical reader might wonder if the last four words are still needed. In particular, the obsession with celebrities – with reading about their exploits, peeking inside their homes, learning how to imitate their looks, hearing their opinions about global warming or diet crazes or other celebrities – has become frantic. Federico Fellini's film *La Dolce Vita* (1960) highlighted the intrusions of press photographers; one character, Paparazzo, is a hovering, buzzing snapper who finds he can earn princely sums for pictures of celebrities behaving badly. Fellini believed the character's name called to mind a darting insect: others have pointed out that in the Abruzzi dialect *paparazzo* is a name for a clam, the opening and closing of which may suggest a camera lens. Whatever the real inspiration, it was *La Dolce Vita* that immortalized *paparazzo*. It is now more commonly found as the plural *paparazzi* – after all, snappers tend to hunt in packs. The modern media, driven by faster technologies and the energies of global business, ape the paparazzo's lust for the latest image, the 'exclusive' and the most extreme.

Amid the resulting flurries of communication, insecurity is rife. Our relationship with technology is neurotic. For instance, mobile phones have become like pets: we take them for walks, fit them with little outfits, use them as displays of our status, and expect them to provide emotional solace. Devices created as aids to communication often lead to superfluous exchanges, but can also be isolating. Like the characters in E. M. Forster's prescient story 'The Machine Stops', we shun face-to-face talk, preferring to exchange our deodorized thoughts remotely. Forster's narrator remarks that in the Age of the Machine, 'Men seldom moved their bodies; all unrest was concentrated in the soul.' I have alluded already to the solipsistic self-pities of our atomized society, and social fragmentation results in linguistic separatism. It also results in language that evokes our dividedness – from each other, and from ourselves. We possess today a prolific language of self-inspection and self-description. Much of this can be traced back to the writings of Sigmund Freud, which gave new significance to the word *repression* and, as I have already mentioned, boosted *libido* and *angst*. These words are now common outside the realm of professional psychology, and among the other terms in this field that have been gained by everyday speech are *inhibition*, *psychotic* and *wishful thinking*. Freud's one-time colleague Carl Gustav Jung promoted *persona* and *psyche*, along with *extrovert* and *introvert*. Even Henry Havelock Ellis's *coitus interruptus* has found popularity, often in a non-literal sense. *Paranoia*, originally a precise medical term, has become a flailingly general one; appropriately, the first quotation given in the *OED* as evidence of this development is from Nabokov's *Pnin* (1957) – 'There is nothing more banal and more bourgeois than paranoia.'

One of the consequences is a relentless quest for new wellsprings of meaning. As concerns rise about poverty and overpopulation, climate change and the depletion of natural resources, terrorism and a fresh wave of nuclear proliferation – all of which are subjects that are negotiated in terms either evasive or polemical – we are also witnessing a rabid pursuit of new paths to enlightenment. *Kabbalah* I have briefly mentioned, but other new sites of spiritual excitement and superstition are vastly numerous, typically centred on charismatic preachers and teachers. The rise of Western enthusiasm for Buddhism and yoga has enlarged familiarity with once-obscure terms such as *mandala, chakra, mantra* and *sutra*. Faiths and cults lacking Buddhism's integrity have fostered other new shibboleths, such as the now widely known and widely satirized language of Scientology, with its *thetans, auditing* and *isness* (defined by founder L. Ron Hubbard as 'an apparency of existence'). The unifying feature of all words in this field is that they are hugely impressive to initiates yet in the eyes of everyone else appear laughable.

In 1997 Collins, the publishers of a popular dictionary, produced a list of words – each new in its day – that could be said to have defined the twentieth century. It ranged from *radioactivity* (1896) to *Blairite* (1997), and included *allergy* (1907), *television* (1926), *psychedelic* (1957), *workaholic* (1971), *AIDS* (1983) and *road rage* (1995). If we divide the century into decades we can identify areas of particular lexical growth. Thus the 1930s brought in many new words to do with transport, while with the 1950s, '60s and '70s we can associate significant rises in language to do with, respectively, youth culture, drugs and computing.

The language of politics has been a steady force throughout. Political language has long been stereotyped as revolving around the avoidance of truth. Its manners are anaesthetic; politicians evade simple, unpleasant statements of reality. We still know what they mean, but somehow their euphemisms indemnify them against resentment. We avoid talking about death, grave sickness, excretion, sex, menstruation and people's age: they avoid talking about anything that threatens to be 'divisive'. Euphemisms are essentially dishonest, but their evasiveness insulates the user from the charge of insensitivity. Social creatures need to be diplomats, and diplomacy is, as humorists like to say, the art of telling someone to go to hell in such a way that he looks forward to the trip.

This kind of talk extends into other domains. *Life insurance* is really *death insurance*, after all. Attempts to proscribe biased or insensitive language are often classified as political correctness, and involve replacing terms that are perceived as denigratory with artificial alternatives. The thinking here is clear enough: the ways in which we refer to ethnicity, sexual orientation, gender and disability can convey deep hostility or bias, and a more sensitive approach can eradicate not only disparaging language but also the very attitudes and prejudices that underpin such disparagement. Yet, to quote the British journalist Melanie Phillips, the purpose of such acts of verbal hygiene is 'less to protect the ostensible targets of prejudice . . . than to demonstrate the moral purity of the expurgators'.[27] This cultural sensitivity, which tends to be most visible in academia and social work, can mutate into patronizing tokenism, a licence for political ineptitude or inertia, and a grotesque repression of personal freedoms. At its most extreme, political correctness is capable of destroying family life and rewriting history.

We all know that words are ideologically charged. Disputes over language can be bloody: witness the reaction to Franco's exclusion of Catalan from Spain's public life, or, more recently, to repression of Romanian in the Trans-Dniester region of Moldova. The word *politician* was initially depreciative, used of schemers and masters of intrigue. When in the first part of Shakespeare's *Henry IV* Hotspur refers to 'this vile politician, Bolingbroke' his insult is two-pronged. He goes on to characterize Bolingbroke as 'this king of smiles' – a description that will pique anyone tired of the white-toothed blandishments of contemporary politicos. (*Politico*, although it may feel like a recent coinage, can be dated back at least as far as 1630.) Contemporary political language, so assiduously manipulated, often has religious overtones. For powerful examples one need only think of George W. Bush's rhetoric about the 'axis of evil' and a 'just war'. The former was coined by speechwriter David Frum; it is worth noting that he originally and less emotively called it the 'axis of hatred'.

In politics, religiosity goes hand in hand with pomposity – an inflation of language, a bombastic puffing-up of terms. George Orwell observed in his essay 'Politics and the English Language' that 'Bad writers, and especially scientific, political and sociological writers, are nearly always haunted by the notion that Latin or Greek words are grander than Saxon ones.' Good writing, he felt, had to be purged of gratuitous classicism. Orwell's purism may be a form of nostalgia, but his diagnosis is sound. We've all baulked at the inadequacy of politicians' favoured euphemisms: *explosive device, industrial action, incident*. The classical tendency in political language reflects a wider perception, which I have touched on several times, that foreignness is sophisticated, abstract and often usefully fuzzy. A couple of borrowings that seem irretrievably associated with political evasiveness are *scenario* and *personnel*, which tend to be used, respectively, of sinister military plans and of people regarded as being not much better than mere office furniture. If we open out beyond the political sphere, we can quickly assemble a quaint cabinet of borrowings whose chief purpose is evasion: *erotica, lingerie, poppycock, pudenda, facetiae, derrière*. It is quite widely known that *poppycock* comes from the Dutch for 'doll's shit', and as recently as the 1980s was ruled 'unparliamentary' by the Speaker of the House of Commons, but for most people it probably calls to mind the delicately textured scarlet poppy.

I have recently come across *than*, a euphemism for 'bed' that is used by speakers of Vlax Romani and seems to have crept into the English of immigrants from parts of south-eastern Europe. It is certainly not an established borrowing, but it's a striking one. After all, Romani, the language of the group commonly though controversially known as Gypsies, whom we associate with Transylvania and the Balkans, is usually thought of as being concerned not with delicacy, but with secrecy.

There is a submerged history of English borrowings – persistent, even if modest – from Romani. Speakers of English and Romani are reckoned to have been in contact for more than 500 years, and it is estimated that there were 10,000 Gypsies in England in the reign of Elizabeth I.[28] Over time, Gypsy communities in Britain have largely taken to speaking English, but with a distinctive smattering of Romani elements – comprising a vocabulary of up to about 1,000 items. Romani words in common use include *minge*, *kushti* (often spelt *cushty*), *wonga* and *lolly* (both meaning 'money'), *gaff* as slang for the place where one lives, and the briefly ubiquitous *chav*. Another word of Romani origin, *nark*, can be used of a police informer or a policeman, as well as of anyone or anything that proves a source of irritation. *Moniker*, meanwhile, may come from Shelta, the language of the Irish Travellers. In an essay on the subject, Anthony Grant cites also *drum*, a slang word for any place of residence, and *pal*, together with the words *rum* as a synonym for *strange* and *conk* meaning the nose.[29] Peripatetic workers have spread this language, and it has enjoyed periods of popularity as a form of secret code among beggars, journeymen and petty criminals. Lately, some of these words – notably *drum* – have become common terms in the speech of Britain's urban youth. For them Romani has the scope to serve as a cryptolect, an arcane jargon which can usefully baffle their families, the authorities and their less street-smart peers.

Frequently, as a group or community appears to grow, so does a vocabulary used of that community by those outside it. This vocabulary may well be appropriated from the language of the community itself. Thus in Britain apprehensiveness and snobbery about Travellers has made *chav* one of the defining English words of the past decade, and from there the word's use has been liberalized to the point where it seems it can be attached to anyone who lacks education or some blurry notion of 'class'. Similarly, the changing use of the word *mafia* suggests a tendency to see certain types of community as threats – be those threats to moral standards or, perhaps, aesthetic ones. *Mafia* is still used of the secret society that originated in Sicily (where the word has connotations of bragging or chicanery, and is probably formed on the model of an Arabic term for an outcast), but its use has become much broader, to include pretty much any group felt to be at once secret and toxic. Thus we can have a mafia of opera singers, publishers, bloggers or art collectors, whose interactions are felt to be in some way deplorable.

In passing judgement on these groups, we say more about our own affiliations. Some of these are deeply ingrained in our language. Common English expressions quietly voice the norms of our culture and world view. For example, compared with other languages, English has an unusually large number of 'downtoners' – words used for purposes of understatement, such as *relatively, somewhat, hardly* and *almost*. There is, moreover, a subtle tendency for colloquial English to express 'the values and standards of scientific discourse' – manifest in our saying 'to be precise' or 'Exactly!' – and for facts to be assiduously distinguished from opinions in a way apparently striking and bizarre to a speaker of, say, Arabic, Swedish or Polish. 'I think', 'to the best of my knowledge', 'as far as I can tell': such formulae are apt to bemuse speakers of these and many other languages. The notion of 'hard facts' is peculiar to English, and so, it seems, are many of our elaborate linguistic mechanisms for avoiding telling people what to do – our modes of inviting and offering and suggesting, which so strenuously avoid impinging on the autonomy of those we are addressing, and which can seem archaic or just plain weird to foreigners.[30] Many everyday metaphors subtly convey ideology: the imagery of flow and liquidity, when we talk about finance, equates money with blood; systems are represented as machines; ethnic classifications suggest links between race and morality (just think of the typical associations of the words *white* and *black*); and the language we use of sex expresses male sexuality in terms of violence.[31] Some of these metaphors may have biological origins, and are thus universal, but others are rooted in our history. This is all 'cultural baggage' – a collection of concepts by which we live, and which on the whole we do not notice: secrets woven into the fabric of our words. It is this contexture that borrowed language reputedly threatens to rend.

16. Shabash

An exclamation conveying the sense 'Well done!'; a modern counterpart to 'Bravo!'

Of Hindi or Urdu origin, the word was known among soldiers serving in India by the middle of the nineteenth century. It has become increasingly familiar in the last couple of decades, especially to devotees of cricket.

'*Shabash! Shabash!* Oh, well done, little one! . . . Now, slowly, let us hear what befell afterwards – step by step' – Rudyard Kipling, *Kim* (1901)

'The tongue of Eden was like a flawless glass,' George Steiner has written. 'A light of total understanding streamed through it.'[1] But for as long as history has been recorded we have lacked this total understanding, because we have spoken different tongues.

One consequence of English's wealth of borrowings is that we can be presented with a sentence in a foreign language and manage to work out what it means. This is obviously not going to work with Korean or Yoruba, but other European languages, with which English has more in common, can be at least partly deciphered. Take the following: 'Giv os i Dag vort daglige Brød.' Or another version of the same request: 'Geef ons heden ons dagelijksch brood.' Once we have spotted what this means – without consciously knowing a word of the languages in which they written, namely Danish and Dutch – we are likely to be struck by the very different look of the Spanish, which is 'Danos hoy nuestro pan cotidiano,' yet we shall probably also feel that this would have made sense to us even outside the context just provided. In these three versions of a sentence that will be familiar to most English-speaking readers, we achieve a very quick impression of what English shares with three other languages, as well as of where it differs from them.

Sometimes we are arrested by basic similarities, and sometimes we are startled by divergence: an arm is called an *arm* in English, German, Dutch, Swedish and Danish, but a pencil is a *Bleistift* in German, a *potlood* in Dutch, a *blyertspenna* in Swedish, and in Danish a *Blyant*.[2]

Pleasant connections notwithstanding, incomprehension is the norm. Today there are around 6,900 different, mutually unintelligible natural languages. A mere eleven of these account for the speech of more than half the world's population. These are Mandarin Chinese, Spanish, Hindi, Arabic, French, Bengali, Portuguese, Russian, German, Japanese and English; the origins of all bar Arabic are in Europe or the southern and eastern parts of Asia. Realistically, fifty years from now the world's 'big' languages may be just six: Chinese, Spanish, Hindi, Bengali, Arabic and English.[3] The last two of these, and the final one especially, are distinguished by having significant numbers of non-native speakers.

The future of English needs to be understood in the context of a dramatic change in the whole global system of languages, for at the opposite end of the scale are the languages teetering on the brink of extinction. Some countries are home to a truly remark-able variety of tongues: notably, around a sixth of the world's living languages are spoken on the lush Oceanian island of New Guinea. Its eastern section forms the main part of Papua New Guinea, a country which, although it has a population not much above 5 million, harbours more than 820 indigenous languages. Many, such as Aruop and Matepi, are spoken by a tiny number of people; and some, such as Gorovu and Susuami, are close to dying out. In fact, by the time you read these words, they may already be gone. Other sites of exceptional linguistic diversity include Australia, India, Cameroon and Mexico. In Sudan there are currently more than 130 languages in use; in Indonesia the figure was reckoned, the last time I checked, to be 737. According to Nicholas Ostler, 'over half the languages in the world . . . have fewer than five thousand speakers, and over a thousand languages have under a dozen.'[4] Ninety-six per cent of the world's languages are spoken by 4 per cent of its inhabitants, and four-fifths in only one country, with the result that their fortunes are closely tied to the politics of their governments. Languages are continually disappearing. A recent study has estimated that a language becomes extinct about once a fort-night.[5]

There seems little chance of English becoming extinct or even fragile. It is the world's most widespread language, and its global position has for some time appeared to be strengthening. Indeed, some languages survive only in so far as elements of their vocabulary have been assimilated into English. For members of smaller speech communities, the need to study foreign languages is strong, and English tops the list, as it occupies a dominant position in so many fields. Among these are diplomacy, trade, shipping, the entertainment industry and youth culture. English is the lingua franca of computing and technology, of science and medicine.[6] Its position is prominent, if not dominant, in education, international business and journalism. It is the working language of the United Nations. It holds sway, too, in academia – in scholarly research and publications. English language teaching, commonly known as ELT, is less a branch of pedagogy than a fully developed industry. And there are other, less glamorous, areas of dominance: when you are on a plane, the safety instructions will always be relayed in English, and English is used right across the globe as the language of air traffic control.

There are several ways for a language to increase its number of speakers. One is reproduction – we could look, for instance, at China, whose population has increased from around 550 million in 1950 to nearly 1.4 billion today. Other means, as we have seen, include conquest and imperialism, trade, migration and the proselytizing zeal of religion. The last of these may sound improbable in the twenty-first century, but the present rise of Islam has spread knowledge of Arabic, as the Prophet's teachings can properly be conveyed only in their original language. The continuing diffusion of English is, we can see, a consequence of capitalism and globalization, conflict and the Americanization of popular culture. English-speakers won two world wars, and in the Cold War, which spanned five decades, English was presented by the West – and widely regarded in the Communist 'East' – as the 'language of freedom'.[7] Once upon a time you might have learnt English so that you could read its literature, digest the heady ideas contained in its scientific volumes, or follow the Bible and the Book of Common Prayer. Today, however, learners of English are more concerned with commerce, fashion and the entertainment industry. It is a language of material, not spiritual, aspiration.

One field that brings together the material and spiritual impulses is popular music, and here the global appeal of English is flamboyant. In the 1960s, British and American music became associated with radicalism and protest. Since then, the foreign policies of Britain and America have failed to tarnish the image of their music: its range of styles and idioms has increased, and so have its fluidity and its allure. You will very likely have had a few curious experiences of this. I have found myself feebly trying to explain The Smiths to a melancholic student in Hiroshima, and have been waylaid by children on the streets of Lisbon whose entire knowledge of English appeared to have been picked up from the lyrics of Snoop Dogg. While an unfamiliar musical style may be quite readily appreciated, lyrics in an unfamiliar tongue can make a song baffling – yet those lyrics are picked up even if they are not understood. Some French musicians go in for what is known as *chanter en yaourt* ('singing in yoghurt'), which involves composing a sort of gibberish of vaguely English-sounding lyrics at the time of writing a song: the lyrics fit the rhythms and melodies of their music, and the actual content can be improved later. In an essay on Indonesian underground rock music, the American ethnographer Jeremy Wallach explains that many young Indonesians, influenced in part by English-language music, employ English words for the purposes of romance and use English expletives, because doing so is either safer or sexier than using indigenous languages – it frees them from some of the inhibitions they would otherwise feel.[8] In South Korea, young musicians use English to construct an image of menace or sexual daring, and to emphasize the contentious, uninhibited nature of their art.[9]

The intrusiveness of English is undeniably bound up with globalized entertainment. It is the language, for instance, of countless advertising jingles and catchphrases ('Coke. It's the real thing' or McDonald's 'I'm lovin' it') which insinuate themselves into people's minds. Native English-speakers are frequently embarrassed to realize which bits of their language leave the clearest imprint on other cultures. Plenty of people will smile knowingly at the words of Sir Richard Turnbull, the penultimate governor of Aden, who claimed that 'when the British Empire finally sank beneath the waves of history, it . . . [left behind] only two monuments: one was the game of Association Football, the other was the expression "Fuck off".'[10] A less deliberately provocative view would be that, while liberal capitalism is the most powerful legacy of empire, the English language is the most conspicuous.

Its cultural consequences can be devastating. Benedict Anderson, reflecting on the success of his book *Imagined Communities*, comments, 'Had . . . [it] originally appeared in Tirana, in Albanian, or in Ho Chi Minh City, in Vietnamese, . . . it is unlikely to have travelled very far.' The book's success, in his view, owed much to 'its original publication in London, in the English language, which now serves as a kind of global-hegemonic, post-clerical Latin'.[11] We can extrapolate beyond Anderson's argument: things that don't happen in English are likely to be marginalized in favour of very possibly less worthy things that do happen in English.

The dominance of English is not guaranteed. Great linguistic empires have fallen before. Cultural earthquakes occur. As Ovid pointed out, there are fields of wheat where Troy once stood. Moreover, the circumstances that enable a language's spread are not the same as those that maintain it. For political reasons, English is in some parts of the world seen in a negative light. In Iraq or the Philippines or Sri Lanka or Puerto Rico, it is perceived very differently from the way in which readers of this book will tend to view it. English is associated with shallow consumerism, big business or the so-called War on Terror. Gandhi once protested that the English language had enslaved the minds of Indians, and a Nazi critique denounced the British Council for its role in bringing Western civilization to its knees.[12] Today the advance of English symbolizes for many people the erosion of their own identities and interests. It equalizes values and desires, without doing the same for opportunities. English-speakers may think the spread of their language facilitates global connections, but to many who hear the language spoken it is indicative of America, and for others it may call to mind the Christian faith or some dark colonial agenda. It is no exaggeration to argue that the status of English is now intimately dependent on the status of globalization and on international attitudes towards this phenomenon.

That said, anyone actually experiencing the supposedly homogenous 'world culture' on the ground is likely to be less sure that we are in the throes of linguistic apocalypse. To return to music: in countries as different as Poland and Tanzania, the rhythms, politics and iconography of American hip-hop have been copied, and so have its idioms. But these do not stamp out the distinctive identities of local forms. What happens, instead, is a subtle refashioning in which the global language of the genre meshes with the authentic local sound. Performers find this invigorating; to them, even if not to those who pass judgement on their art, it marks no tragic loss of identity. In any case, the flow of influence is two-directional: the global increase in multiculturalism means that in the very communities where the identity of English seems most rooted, its character is being energetically contested and altered. As readers of this book will probably be aware, urban Britain and America are abundantly multilingual. A study in 2000 showed that children in London's schools spoke a total of more than 300 languages.[13]

So what is English in the twenty-first century? The idea of 'World English' was first paraded in the 1920s. Now it is a reality. Today there are more people using English as a second language than there are native speakers. English is spoken, with at least some degree of fluency, by more than a billion people. In truth the figure may be closer to double that, especially if we are prepared to accept competence in lieu of expertise. The number of people actively learning English may soon reach 2 billion. This still means that there are more people who speak no English than there are people who have some command of it. But for now its life force continues to grow. And, as it does so in the future, the language will change in ways that many native English-speakers are likely to find disconcerting.

English is not monolithic. Rather, there is a family of many different Englishes, and some of this family's members would strike most readers of this book as alien. There are more fluent speakers of English in India, where it persists as a 'subsidiary official language', than in Britain. In affluent Singapore, there are four official languages – English, Mandarin, Tamil and Malay – and English bosses the other three, but there is also a homegrown, slangy hybrid known as Singlish. At the extreme, there is Spanglish, spoken mainly by Hispanic Americans, who also call it *español pocho*, 'stunted Spanish'. We can get a sense of what it is like from utterances such as 'No me gusta hablar con Melissa because she is too gossipy' or 'We would have salido si supiéramos la verdad.'[14] Is this a form of English, or a form of Spanish, or both, or neither? We may think of it as a language in its own right, which permits Hispanic Americans to maintain dual identities – or which suggests the cultural limbo in which they can find themselves.

While we may disagree about what count as 'new' Englishes, as well as about their psychological climates, the facts of their existence and proliferation are beyond doubt, and they suggest the way the 'Englishness' of English is being diluted. Amid all this, native English-speakers may be at a disadvantage. Many of our elaborations and much of our cultural baggage prove confusing. Nonnative speakers of English often find it easier to speak to each other than to native speakers. It seems entirely possible that in the not too distant future there will be deep rifts between forms of English that at present appear intimate.

English is creeping into vernacular Mandarin, where the Internet, which is changing the very ways in which English is taught and learnt, is known as the *Interwang*, and words such as *cool* and *DVD* are in common use. English has also become the language of cultivated, business-minded Europeans. As the historian Tony Judt points out, before the Second World War German was 'in active daily use from Strasbourg to Riga', yet this situation has since changed dramatically, and the authority of French has also declined sharply.[15] A generation ago there were perhaps 60 million Continental Europeans who knew enough English to hold a conversation. Now the figure is about twice as great, and it is rising quickly. When polled, more than four-fifths of people in the Netherlands and Sweden claim to be able to speak English. The figure is around 50 per cent in Germany, Slovenia and Finland, and closer to 30 in Italy, France and the Czech Republic.[16] An interesting study has recently shown that among students in the United Arab Emirates 'Arabic is associated with tradition, home, religion, culture, school, arts and social sciences,' while English is 'symbolic of modernity, work, higher education, commerce, economics and science and technology'.[17]

Inevitably, all such facts have implications for the future of English. Its centre of gravity has moved. Its future may well be defined in India and China, not in Britain or America – above all, by the new economies of Bangalore, Beijing and Shanghai. Outside its heartlands it is more and more a language of urban middle classes. Additionally, as technology has broken down borders, it is no longer sensible to think, as we used to, of a clearly defined association between particular languages and particular territories.

If you hear a woman speaking Italian, you can be confident that she *is* Italian. Sitting on the London Underground, I am able to recognize that the group of young men opposite are Poles: I hear words and phrases that are familiar to me from my travels in Poland, and I am pretty confident that only Poles speak Polish. But when we hear someone speaking English we can draw no such conclusions. It is a language nobody owns. Instead of being a badge of nationality, the ability to speak English has become a sign of aspiration – of the desire to be educated, to succeed in business or as a public official, to study science or imbibe the intoxicating creations of Hollywood. People who learn English don't even necessarily do so in order to converse with its native users. The one medium contains many voices. Indeed, there is a long and distinguished history of people using English for anti-English ends – of writers and orators asserting in English their distance from Englishness or Britishness or Americanness. For many creative artists, imbuing English with weird flavours has been a way of reclaiming their heritage while working in a medium that has allowed them to reach a wide audience. Making English 'different' has proved a means of resisting norms and all that they imply.

English remains omnivorous. Today the areas in which the language is most quickly assimilating new terms are reckoned by one observer to be 'food, martial arts, health remedies and therapies, science and plants'.[18] An older perspective – succinct and accurate – is afforded by William Safire, for many years the *New York Times*'s arbiter of all things linguistic: 'The new foundations of argot are the media, kids' talk, diplomacy, and sports.'[19] For all the eminence of British and American performers, music is another rich domain, as listeners seek out new sounds: do you know the difference between *baile funk*, which is Brazilian Portuguese, the Punjabi *bhangra*, and *bashment*, the name of which derives from Jamaican patois? Perhaps you do not think these are 'proper' English words, but to many they are just that – fully assimilated, fully functioning, and urgently relevant.

The new words being absorbed into the language testify, as they always have, to new experiences and priorities. Thus recent acts of terrorism in America and Europe have fomented a vocabulary *about* terrorism. Whereas the twentieth century was steered by achievements in physics, it seems likely that the twenty-first will be ruled by biology, and biological lexis is set to become more popular as this science proves both essential and incendiary. We can expect, over the next generation, a wave of adoptions from Arabic as the Islamic world continues to occupy a central position in global events – and as the rest of the world tries harder to get to grips with it. In the US, as I have suggested, the volume of Spanish loans stands to increase. In Britain, we can expect more gains from Hindi, Urdu and Punjabi. We are seeing them already: the plaudit *shabash*, the revival of *badmash*, which seems increasingly to mean not so much a hooligan as a mischief-maker, *achcha* ('all right'), and *nang*, another term of approval, which probably originated in Bengali, along with borrowings from South Asian English, like the verb *to prepone* (modelled on *postpone*). Acquisitions from the various Caribbean Englishes show no sign of slowing; among recent ones are *creps* and *bare*, meaning 'trainers' and 'lots of' respectively.

Language is always changing. No living language can stand still; rather, each moves in a current of its own making. It is this vitality that ensures language is so sustaining a subject. As long as there are groups on the move, languages will change. Such groups at present include migrant labourers, students, troops and aid workers, refugees, tourists and businesspeople. Think, for a moment, of their influence: the ideas they propagate, the pleasures they share, the dramas they witness, the opportunities they create, exploit or implore.

A few visionaries have predicted a linguistic utopia in which men and women communicate by some more direct means. In the 1850s Alexander Melville Bell developed a 94-letter alphabet as part of what he hoped would be an international Visible Speech; out of his endeavours grew the more potent vision of his son Alexander Graham Bell, who imagined that his telephone might restore unity to what he saw as an increasingly divided America. In *Men Like Gods* (1923) H. G. Wells imagined a future where individuals could exchange thoughts by 'direct transmission': 'People began to *get* the idea before it was clothed in words and uttered in sounds. They began to hear in their minds, as soon as the speaker had arranged his ideas and before he put them into word symbols even in his own mind. They knew what he was going to say before he said it.' The principle is one we can just about credit, but it is part of a future most of us picture nervously, if at all. Much might be gained by direct transmission, but much, we sense, would be lost. A similar vision is presented in *The Hitch-Hiker's Guide to the Galaxy* (1979), where Douglas Adams imagines the Babel fish, a creature like a leech which feeds on people's brainwaves and excretes them into the minds of others, thus enabling speakers of different languages to communicate freely.

For now, as the number of languages in the world declines, their diversity is something to cherish, just as we should cherish the diversity of human interests, energies and traditions. The differing creative potential of different languages, their particular understandings of the world, the ways in which they embody the cultures and histories of those who use them, the ways moreover in which they empower their native speakers: these are the very limbs of civilization. Languages blossom in ways that the speakers of a single language, however worldly, cannot fully grasp. Cultures are subtly interrelated. The empires of language may rupture, but they can also intertwine.

Acknowledgements

Anyone writing about the English language is profoundly indebted to those who have gone before. Where I have been sure of my obligations to others, I have made them clear either in the text or in my notes, but inevitably there are some I have failed to recognize or remember. In order to keep end matter to a reasonable minimum, some quotations have been included in the text without a full reference. Where a quotation is from a well-known source, such as the Bible or Shakespeare, or where it can readily be found in a dictionary or an online resource, a detailed reference has not been provided. For quotations from works that are less readily available I have given details of the source.

My continual recourse to *The Oxford English Dictionary* has enriched my sense of quite how extraordinary a feat of scholarly collaboration it is. We consult dictionaries rather as the Bible was once consulted – for definitive truth. Faith in dictionaries is often blind. As Dr Johnson pointed out, 'dictionaries are like watches,' since 'the worst is better than none, and the best cannot be expected to go quite true.' But the *OED* has served me magnificently, again and again. So have other dictionaries and works of reference, notably *The Oxford Dictionary of National Biography*. In the interests of concision and readability, I have not always explicitly marked these debts in my text.

In the course of my work I have received kindnesses from David Crystal, Joanna Gray, Helen Hawksfield, Kwasi Kwarteng, Guy Ladenburg, Douglas Matthews, Dan O'Hara, Rowan Routh, Benedict Shaw, James Spackman and Christopher Tyerman, as well as from the patient staff of the British Library, London. For greater acts of generosity I wish to thank Richard Arundel, Joshua Burch,

Alex Burghart, Christopher Burlinson, Jonty Claypole, Bob Davenport, Sam Gilpin, John Mullan and especially Robert Macfarlane.

My agent, Peter Straus, immediately understood what sort of book I wanted to write, and his support has been invaluable. At John Murray, Anya Serota embraced the idea, and Eleanor Birne skilfully and trustingly saw it through to fruition.

My greatest debts are to my parents, generous as ever in many ways, and to Angela, whose support has been at once tactful, affectionate and unstinting.

Notes

Chapter 1: Ensemble

1. *The Diary of Samuel Sewall*, ed. M. Halsey Thomas, 2 vols. (New York: Farrar, Straus and Giroux, 1973), I, 380. Regarding the choice of Torrey as president of Harvard, see Josiah Quincy, *The History of Harvard University*, 2 vols. (Cambridge, Mass.: John Owen, 1840), I, 38.

2. James Harris, *Hermes: Or, A Philosophical Inquiry Concerning Language and Universal Grammar* (London: Nourse and Vaillant, 1751), 408–9.

3. My examples of animal communication are borrowed from Jean-Louis Dessalles, *Why We Talk: The Evolutionary Origins of Language*, trans. James Grieve (Oxford: Oxford University Press, 2007), 3–29.

4. Nicholas Ostler, *Empires of the Word: A Language History of the World* (London: HarperCollins, 2005), 557.

5. George Steiner, *After Babel: Aspects of Language and Translation*, 3rd edn (Oxford: Oxford University Press, 1998), 24.

6. Vladimir Nabokov, *Bend Sinister* (London: Weidenfeld & Nicolson, 1960), 125, 140.

7. The case is made engagingly, though incompletely, in M. J. Harper, *The History of Britain Revealed* (London: Nathan Carmody, 2002).

8. The question of how the Indo-European languages spread is still moot. The hypothesis mentioned here was first advanced by Colin Renfrew in the 1980s.

9. John McWhorter, *The Power of Babel: A Natural History of Language* (London: William Heinemann, 2002), 95.

10. Dieter Katsovksy, 'Vocabulary', in Richard Hogg and David Denison (eds.), *A History of the English Language* (Cambridge: Cambridge University Press, 2006), 199.

11. I borrow this useful phrase from T. E. Hope, 'Loanwords as Cultural and Lexical Symbols', *Archivum Linguisticum* 14 (1962), 120.

12. Linda and Roger Flavell, *The Chronology of Words and Phrases* (London: Kyle Cathie, 1999), 165.

13. Horace, *On the Art of Poetry*, in *Classical Literary Criticism*, trans. T. S. Dorsch (Harmondsworth: Penguin, 1986), 80–81.

14. David Crystal, *How Language Works* (London: Penguin, 2005), 225.

15. Stanley M. Tsuzaki and Samuel H. Elbert, 'Hawaiian Loanwords in English', *General Linguistics* 9 (1969), 22–40.

16. Christopher Ball, 'Lexis: The Vocabulary of English', in W. F. Bolton and David Crystal (eds.), *The English Language* (London: Penguin, 1993), 182–3.

17. John Lanchester, *The Debt to Pleasure* (London: Picador, 1996), 43.

18. Don Paterson, *The Book of Shadows* (London: Faber, 2005), 154.

19. Louis Deroy, *L'Emprunt linguistique* (Paris: Société d'Edition 'Les Belles Lettres', 1956), 215.

20. Examples from Jean Aitchison, *Language Change: Progress or Decay?* 3rd edn (Cambridge: Cambridge University Press, 2001), 142, and Pius N. Tamanji, 'Indirect Borrowing: A Source of Lexical Expansion', in George Echu and Samuel Gyasi Obeng (eds.), *Africa Meets Europe: Language Contact in West Africa* (New York: Nova Science, 2004), 78.

Chapter 2: Invade

1. Ralph Waldo Emerson, *English Traits*, ed. Douglas Emory Wilson (Cambridge, Mass.: Harvard University Press, 1994), 27–28, 132.

2. The designation 'Celts' was not used in British history until the sixteenth century, and in the eyes of specialists it is a rather lazy catch-all for the peoples who lived in Britain and Gaul before the rise of the Roman Empire. I use the term here because it is convenient and commonly understood.

3. Barry Cunliffe, *The Ancient Celts* (Oxford: Oxford University Press, 1997), 5–6.

4. Celtic also, at least on the Continent, made some impact on Latin. The subject is discussed in J. N. Adams, *Bilingualism and the Latin Language* (Cambridge: Cambridge University Press, 2003). Adams notes that 'Latin took a considerable number of terms to do with transport and horsemanship from Celtic, a reflection of Gaulish expertise in such matters and of trading contacts between Gauls and Latin speakers' (p. 184).

5. It seems significant that the Latin *schola* explicitly denoted a place of study, whereas the older Greek word *scholē* denoted leisure – which among Greeks was expected, though not guaranteed, to be given over to study.

6. This information comes from Helena Drysdale, *Mother Tongues: Travels through Tribal Europe* (London: Picador, 2002), 129.
7. Clearly, under Roman rule, some people had permanently transplanted themselves to Britain from the Mediterranean, but they were in the minority.
8. Markku Filppula, Juhani Klemola and Heli Pitkanen (eds.), *The Celtic Roots of English* (Joensuu: University of Joensuu, Faculty of Humanities, 2002), 6.
9. In his book *Catastrophe: An Investigation into the Origins of the Modern World* (London: Century, 1999), David Keys has argued for another factor in the changing fabric of Britain: a huge natural disaster around AD 535, possibly a volcanic eruption or asteroid collision, that resulted in famine, migration and political change. He explains, for instance, that 'Tree-ring evidence from the British Isles shows that tree growth slowed down significantly in 535–6 and did not fully recover until 555' (p. 110), and identifies this period as one of 'climactic chaos' (p. 112) characterized by freak storms and exceptionally bitter winters.
10. Albert C. Baugh and Thomas Cable, *A History of the English Language*, 5th edn (Upper Saddle River, NJ: Prentice Hall, 2002), 82.
11. The original title of his work was *Historia Ecclesiastica Gentis Anglorum*.
12. The subject is given far more detailed treatment than is possible here in Hans Sauer, 'Old English Words for People in the *Épinal-Erfurt glossary*', in Hans Sauer and Renate Bauer (eds.), *Beowulf and Beyond* (Frankfurt am Main: Peter Lang, 2007), 119–81.
13. *The Anglo-Saxon Chronicles*, trans. and ed. Michael Swanton (London: Phoenix, 2000), 55–7.
14. John Geipel, *The Viking Legacy* (Newton Abbot: David & Charles, 1971), 31.
15. Else Roesdahl, *The Vikings*, trans. Susan M. Margeson and Kirsten Williams, 2nd edn (London: Penguin, 1998), 193–8.
16. Peter Sawyer, *Scandinavians and the English in the Viking Age* (Cambridge: Department of Anglo-Saxon, Norse, and Celtic, 1995), 7.
17. David Miles, *The Tribes of Britain* (London: Phoenix, 2006), 218.
18. Roger Lass, *The Shape of English: Structure and History* (London: J. M. Dent, 1987), 53.
19. Bruce R. Smith, *The Acoustic World of Early Modern England* (Chicago: University of Chicago Press, 1999), 289.
20. Emerson, *English Traits*, 28, 75.
21. Matthew Townend, 'Contacts and Conflicts: Latin, Norse, and French',

in Lynda Mugglestone (ed.), *The Oxford History of English* (Oxford: Oxford University Press, 2006), 82–3.

22. The subject is treated in depth in Sara M. Pons-Sanz, *Norse-Derived Vocabulary in Late Old English Texts* (Odense: University Press of Southern Denmark, 2007).

23. More recent loans from Scandinavian languages include *silt*, *troll*, *lemming*, *cosy*, *queasy*, *saga* and *ombudsman*. The *dahlia* takes its name from a Swedish botanist, Anders Dahl, although somewhat confusingly the Swedes call this flower a *georgine*.

24. Simon Winchester, *The Meaning of Everything: The Story of the Oxford English Dictionary* (Oxford: Oxford University Press, 2003), 9.

25. Drysdale, *Mother Tongues*, 50.

26. The Isle of Man and the Hebrides were the last two outposts of Norse influence. The last speakers of Norn, a Norse dialect known in Shetland, Orkney and Caithness, seem to have died in the eighteenth century.

27. Ernest Barker, 'An Attempt at Perspective', in Ernest Barker (ed.), *The Character of England* (Oxford: Clarendon Press, 1947), 556. In the whole of the British Isles, the furthest point from the sea is reckoned to be 1 mile south-east of Coton in the Elms, South Derbyshire.

28. Details from Terttu Nevalainen and Ingrid Tieken-Boon van Ostade, 'Standardisation', in Hogg and Denison (eds.), *A History of the English Language*, 301.

29. Baugh and Cable, *A History of the English Language*, 91.

30. *The Anglo-Saxon Chronicles*, ed. Swanton, 199.

31. M. T. Clanchy, *From Memory to Written Record: England 1066–1307*, 2nd edn (Oxford: Blackwell, 1993), 6. It is now accepted that the final years of the Anglo-Saxon state were also quite heavily documented. However, these records have mostly been lost, having become redundant after the Conquest.

32. David Crystal, *The Stories of English* (London: Allen Lane, 2004), 135.

33. Nevalainen and van Ostade, 'Standardisation', in Hogg and Denison (eds.), *A History of the English Language*, 273.

34. Frederick Bodmer, *The Loom of Language*, ed. Lancelot Hogben (London: Allen & Unwin, 1943), 223.

35. Seth Lerer, *Inventing English: A Portable History of the Language* (New York: Columbia University Press, 2007), 49.

36. Richard W. Bailey, 'English Among the Languages', in Mugglestone (ed.), *The Oxford History of English*, 336.

37. Mario Pei, *The Story of the English Language* (London: Allen & Unwin, 1968), 41.

38. 'Given' names quickly lose their air of novelty, and we seem after very little time to lose sight of their origins. How often do we *really* think of Karen as a name borrowed from Danish, or of the name Natasha being Russian?

39. Stephanie Barker, Stefankai Spoerlein, Tobias Vetter and Wolfgang Viereck, *An Atlas of English Surnames* (Frankfurt am Main: Peter Lang, 2007), 9.

40. Charles Hughes (ed.), *Shakespeare's Europe: Unpublished Chapters of Fynes Moryson's Itinerary* (London: Sherratt & Hughes, 1903), 213.

41. Geoffrey Hughes, *Words in Time* (Oxford: Blackwell, 1988), 45.

42. W. Rothwell, 'Adding Insult to Injury: The English Who Curse in Borrowed French', in Hans F. Nielsen and Lene Schosler (eds.), *The Origins and Development of Emigrant Languages* (Odense: Odense University Press, 1996), 41–54.

43. See Crystal, *The Stories of English*, 145, 154.

44. W. Rothwell, 'Arrivals and Departures: The Adoption of French Terminology into Middle English', *English Studies* 79 (1998), 151.

45. Quoted in Douglas A. Kibbee, 'The Case of Anglo-French', in Hans F. Nielsen and Lene Schosler (eds.), *The Origins and Development of Emigrant Languages* (Odense: Odense University Press, 1996), 5.

46. W. Rothwell, 'The Missing Link in English Etymology: Anglo-French', *Medium Aevum* 60 (1991), 183–4.

47. Geoffrey Hughes, *A History of English Words* (Oxford: Blackwell, 1999), 113.

48. Richard FitzNigel, *Dialogus de Scaccario*, trans. and ed. Charles Johnson, with corrections by F. E. L. Carter and D. E. Greenway (Oxford: Clarendon Press, 1983), 52–3.

49. A detailed account of the tenacity of Law French can be found in David Mellinkoff, *The Language of the Law* (Boston: Little, Brown, 1963).

50. See Suzanne Romaine, 'The English Language in Scotland', in Richard W. Bailey and Manfred Görlach (eds.), *English as a World Language* (Cambridge: Cambridge University Press, 1984), 56–8.

51. Robert Burchfield, *The English Language* (Oxford: Oxford University Press, 1985), 18.

52. Melvyn Bragg, *The Adventure of English* (London: Hodder & Stoughton, 2003), 51.

53. C. S. Lewis, *Studies in Words*, 2nd edn (Cambridge: Cambridge University Press, 1967), 18.

54. Quoted in David Graddol, Dick Leith and Joan Swann (eds.), *English: History, Diversity and Change* (London: Routledge, 1996), 7.

Chapter 3: Saffron

1. *Kohl* sounds German, but derives from *kahala*, an Arabic verb meaning 'to stain'.
2. Andrew Breeze, 'Old English *Ealfara*, "Pack-Horse": A Spanish-Arabic Loanword', *Notes and Queries* 38 (1991), 15–17.
3. Fernand Braudel, *A History of Civilizations*, trans. Richard Mayne (London: Penguin, 1995), 304.
4. In Spanish the *al-* prefix has been retained – even if not always completely, owing to conventions in Arabic surrounding the pronunciation of the *l* in the prefix *al-* before certain letters. *Algodon* is the Spanish word for cotton, *azucar* for sugar.
5. See Rosamond E. Mack, *Bazaar to Piazza: Islamic Trade and Italian Art, 1300–1600* (Berkeley: University of California Press, 2002), 15.
6. Olivia Remie Constable, *Trade and Traders in Muslim Spain* (Cambridge: Cambridge University Press, 1994), 215–16.
7. David Abulafia, 'The Impact of the Orient: Economic Interactions between East and West in the Medieval Mediterranean', in Dionisius A. Agius and Ian Richard Netton (eds.), *Across the Mediterranean Frontiers: Trade, Politics and Religion, 650–1450* (Turnhout: Brepols, 1997), 10.
8. Ostler, *Empires of the Word*, 94–6.
9. R. W. Southern, *Western Views of Islam in the Middle Ages* (Cambridge, Mass.: Harvard University Press, 1962), 13.
10. Richard Fletcher, *The Cross and the Crescent: The Dramatic Story of the Earliest Encounters between Christians and Muslims* (London: Penguin, 2004), 78.
11. Christopher Tyerman, *God's War: A New History of the Crusades* (London: Allen Lane, 2006), 913.
12. See Bernard Hamilton, 'The Impact of the Crusades on Western Geographical Knowledge', in Rosamund Allen (ed.), *Eastward Bound: Travel and Travellers, 1050-1550* (Manchester: Manchester University Press, 2004), 15-34.
13. See Suzanne Conklin Akbari, 'The Diversity of Mankind in *The Book of John Mandeville*', in Allen (ed.), *Eastward Bound*, 156-76.
14. See Katharine Scarfe Beckett, *Anglo-Saxon Perceptions of the Islamic World* (Cambridge: Cambridge University Press, 2003).
15. Lorraine Daston and Katharine Park, *Wonders and the Order of Nature 1150–1750* (New York: Zone Books, 1998), 26.
16. The Arabic word is linked to an ancient Assyrian term, *meturgeman*.

This passed into Aramaic and was used of the men who translated the Hebrew scriptures.

17. Bernard Lewis, *From Babel to Dragomans: Interpreting the Middle East* (London: Phoenix, 2005), 33-4.

18. Ostler, *Empires of the Word*, 407.

19. I use the word *trader* as a shorthand form, for, besides those who actually performed the transactions, there were also sailors, bankers, carters, various kinds of agent, and an assortment of other menial workers as well as men with technical expertise in, for example, the practicalities of moneylending.

20. Robert S. Lopez and Irving W. Raymond (eds.), *Medieval Trade in the Mediterranean World: Illustrative Documents* (New York: Columbia University Press, 2001), 423.

21. See Jack Turner, *Spice: The History of a Temptation* (London: HarperCollins, 2004), 114-15.

22. *Sakk* is related to the verb *sakka*, meaning 'to mint money'.

23. S. D. Goitein (ed.), *Letters of Medieval Jewish Traders* (Princeton: Princeton University Press, 1973), 16-17.

24. Ibid., 78, 189.

25. W. Montgomery Watt, *A History of Islamic Spain* (Edinburgh: Edinburgh University Press, 1965), 51.

26. Kees Versteegh, *The Arabic Language* (Edinburgh: Edinburgh University Press, 2001), 228.

27. L. P. Harvey, *Islamic Spain, 1250 to 1500* (Chicago: University of Chicago Press, 1990), 325.

28. The first (poor) translation into English, by Alexander Ross, was published in 1649.

29. Peter's polemic did not circulate widely, but the very fact of its existence is further evidence of the desire to engage with Islam intellectually rather than militarily. However, as Richard Fletcher has pointed out, Peter was at the same time writing to Louis VII of France 'expressing the hope that he would smash the Saracens as Moses and Joshua had destroyed the Amonites and Canaanites of old'. See Richard Fletcher, *Moorish Spain* (London: Weidenfeld & Nicolson, 1992), 154.

30. Pococke's career is covered in detail in G. J. Toomer, *Eastern Wisedome and Learning: The Study of Arabic in Seventeenth-Century England* (Oxford: Clarendon Press, 1996).

31. References to *Mecca* not in Islamic contexts, but simply to denote a place of special interest, date from the middle of the nineteenth century.

32. Ostler, *Empires of the Word*, 108.

33. Louis Heller, Alexander Humez and Malcah Dror, *The Private Lives of English Words* (London: Routledge, 1984), 110.

Chapter 4: Volume

1. See Jean Gimpel, *The Medieval Machine: The Industrial Revolution of the Middle Ages*, 2nd edn (Aldershot: Wildwood House, 1988).
2. Piers D. Mitchell, 'The Infirmaries of the Order of the Temple in the Medieval Kingdom of Jerusalem', in Barbara S. Bowers (ed.), *The Medieval Hospital and Medical Practice* (Aldershot: Ashgate, 2007), 225.
3. Quoted in Lerer, *Inventing English*, 88
4. For a detailed account of the life of John Trevisa, see David C. Fowler, *The Life and Times of John Trevisa, Medieval Scholar* (Seattle: University of Washington Press, 1995).
5. Thorlac Turville-Petre, *England the Nation: Language, Literature, and National Identity, 1290–1340* (Oxford: Clarendon Press, 1996), 181.
6. S. Thrupp, 'The Grocers of London', in Eileen Power and M. M. Postan (eds.), *Studies in English Trade in the Fifteenth Century* (London: Routledge, 1933), 248.
7. Ibid., 284–5.
8. Regarding the Italian influence on Chaucer, see Piero Boitani (ed.), *Chaucer and the Italian Trecento* (Cambridge: Cambridge University Press, 1983).
9. Christopher Cannon explains, 'The subtle movements of Chaucer's words encouraged the view that his English was new, but Chaucer also had a direct hand in this encouragement – although his touch was exceedingly light. Daring statements were hemmed in by qualification and great ambition was couched in significant reserve. The careful reader may search but will search in vain for lines in which Chaucer *says* that he "invented" English literary language, but that same reader will be equally likely to come away from Chaucer's texts with the impression that he has claimed precisely this.' See *The Making of Chaucer's English: A Study of Words* (Cambridge: Cambridge University Press, 1998), 136.
10. This example is hardly original, having been used in several books about Chaucer. For instance, it appears in John H. Fisher's *The Importance of Chaucer* (Carbondale: Southern Illinois University Press, 1992), and Fisher comments, 'The substantive vocabulary is almost wholly French ("March" and "palmers" preserve the Anglo-Norman forms instead of the Parisian French; until Chaucer, French "Averil" was the most

common spelling in England, and . . . "Zephirus" is directly from Latin)' (p. 31). Fisher also states that in *The Canterbury Tales* the amount of French-derived vocabulary varies 'from a low of 26.7 percent for the Miller's Tale to a high of 51.3 percent for the Parson's Tale, with the average about 40 percent' (p. 29).

11. Peggy A. Knapp, *Time-Bound Words: Semantic and Social Economies from Chaucer's England to Shakespeare's* (Basingstoke: Macmillan, 2000), 15.

12. Lerer, *Inventing English*, 78.

13. I have borrowed some of these examples from Simon Horobin, *Chaucer's Language* (Basingstoke: Palgrave Macmillan, 2007), 83–4.

14. The idea of English as an 'upstart language' comes from N. F. Blake, *A History of the English Language* (Basingstoke: Macmillan, 1996), 184.

15. Translated from the Latin and quoted in Richard Foster Jones, *The Triumph of the English Language* (London: Oxford University Press, 1953), 261.

16. Lerer, *Inventing English*, 84.

17. David Burnley, *The History of the English Language: A Source Book*, 2nd edn (Harlow: Pearson Education, 2000), 171–2.

18. Lisa Jardine, *Worldly Goods* (London: Macmillan, 1996), 171.

19. Julia Boffey, 'From Manuscript to Modern Text', in Peter Brown (ed.), *A Companion to Medieval English Literature and Culture* (Oxford: Blackwell, 2007), 114–15.

20. Elizabeth L. Eisenstein, *The Printing Revolution in Early Modern Europe*, 2nd edn (Cambridge: Cambridge University Press, 2005), 92.

21. These details are taken from Bailey, 'English Among the Languages', in Mugglestone (ed.), *The Oxford History of English*, 339.

22. Baugh and Cable, *A History of the English Language*, 215, n.

Chapter 5: Bravado

1. As Nicholas Ostler points out, the colony at Roanoke in Virginia had been set up several years before, but 'no one in England then knew if it was still in existence' (*Empires of the Word*, 477).

2. Mack, *Bazaar to Piazza*, 25.

3. On this last subject, see Neva Ruth Deardorff, *English Trade in the Baltic during the Reign of Elizabeth* (PhD thesis, University of Pennsylvania, 1911).

4. Fernand Braudel, *The Mediterranean and the Mediterranean World in the Age of Philip II*, trans. Siân Reynolds, abridged by Richard Ollard (London: HarperCollins, 1992), 444–5.

5. For a detailed account, see Nabil Matar, *Turks, Moors, and Englishmen in the Age of Discovery* (New York: Columbia University Press, 1999).

6. Roy Strong, *Gloriana:The Portraits of Queen Elizabeth I* (London:Thames and Hudson, 1987), 91.

7. See Fraser Mackenzie, *Les Relations de l'Angleterre et de la France d'après le vocabulaire*, 2 vols. (Paris: E. Droz, 1939), II, 130.

8. Turner, *Spice: The History of a Temptation*, 40.

9. David B. Abernethy, *The Dynamics of Global Dominance: European Overseas Empires, 1415–1980* (New Haven:Yale University Press, 2000), 5.

10. See Matthew Restall, *Seven Myths of the Spanish Conquest* (Oxford: Oxford University Press, 2003), 143.

11. Tim Ecott, *Vanilla: Travels in Search of a Luscious Substance* (London: Penguin, 2005), 24.

12. The diverse means of glorifying Elizabeth are explored in detail by Helen Hackett in *Virgin Mother, Maiden Queen: Elizabeth I and the Cult of the Virgin Mary* (Basingstoke: Macmillan, 1995).

13. Robert Claiborne, *The Life and Times of the English Language* (London: Bloomsbury, 1990), 148.

14. Ostler, *Empires of the Word*, 382.

15. Felipe Fernández-Armesto, *Pathfinders: A Global History of Exploration* (Oxford: Oxford University Press, 2006), 136.

16. A pidgin is a system of communication that develops among people who have no language in common.

17. J. H. Elliott, *Empires of the Atlantic World: Britain and Spain in America 1492–1830* (New Haven:Yale University Press, 2006), 224.

18. Lawrence James, *The Rise and Fall of the British Empire* (London: Little, Brown, 1994), 17, 31.

19. Hugh Thomas, *The Slave Trade: The History of the Atlantic Slave Trade: 1440–1870* (London: Picador, 1997), 136.

20. Figures from David W. Galenson, *Traders, Planters, and Slaves: Market Behaviour in Early English America* (Cambridge: Cambridge University Press, 1986), 5.

21. Elliott, *Empires of the Atlantic World*, 220.

22. William Dampier, *A New Voyage Round the World* (London: James Knapton, 1697), 222, 464.

23. Linda Colley, *Captives: Britain, Empire and the World, 1600–1850* (London: Jonathan Cape, 2002), 375.

24. Niall Ferguson, *Empire: How Britain Made the Modern World* (London: Allen Lane, 2003), xxii.

Chapter 6: Genius

1. See James Shapiro, *1599: A Year in the Life of William Shakespeare* (London: Faber, 2005), 209.

2. Richard Verstegan, *A Restitution of Decayed Intelligence* (Antwerp: Robert Bruney, 1605), 204–5.

3. Isaac D'Israeli, *Amenities of Literature* (London: Frederick Warne, 1867), 361.

4. Ralph Lever, *The Arte of Reason* (London: H. Bynneman, 1573), 'The Forespeache'.

5. F.W. Bateson, *English Poetry and the English Language* (Oxford: Clarendon Press, 1934), 31, n. 1.

6. Lerer, *Inventing English*, 141.

7. I draw my statistics and much else in this paragraph from Thomas N. Corns, *A History of Seventeenth-Century English Literature* (Oxford: Blackwell, 2007), 1–22.

8. Richard Helgerson, *Forms of Nationhood: The Elizabethan Writing of England* (Chicago: University of Chicago Press, 1992), 133.

9. It is in John Florio's 1603 translation of Montaigne that we first find the word *dogmatism*.

10. G. Hughes, *A History of English Words*, 163.

11. Richard Mulcaster, *The First Part of the Elementarie* (London: Thomas Vautroullier, 1582), 81–2.

12. Owen Barfield, *History in English Words* (London: Faber, 1954), 148.

13. John Stow, *A Survey of London Written in the Year 1598* (Stroud: Sutton, 2005), 327.

14. Greene was also the author of *A Notable Discovery of Coosnage. Now daily practised by sundry lewd persons, called Connie-catchers and Crosse-biters . . . with a delightfull discourse on the coosnage of colliers* (1591), a book which memorably displays the copiousness of Elizabethan slang.

15. These details are from Elspeth M. Veale, *The English Fur Trade in the Later Middle Ages*, 2nd edn (London: London Record Society, 2003), 136–46.

16. Edmund Coote's *The English Schoole-maister* (1596) laid the groundwork for Cawdrey's volume and could legitimately claim to be the first such dictionary, although it has tended to be dimissed as no more than a 'spelling list'.

17. I have borrowed this expression from N. F. Blake, *The Language of Shakespeare* (Basingstoke: Macmillan, 1989), 55.

18. Many common expressions have their roots in sport. For instance, bowls is the source of the now widely used *bias*. When I *let fly*, the image comes from archery; if I *turn the tables*, backgammon provides the idiom; *keeping one's end up*, *knuckling down* and *acing* something (such as an exam) are from cricket, marbles and tennis respectively.

19. Hilda M. Hulme, *Explorations in Shakespeare's Language* (London: Longman, 1962), 315–40.

20. Stephen Greenblatt, *Will in the World: How Shakespeare Became Shakespeare* (London: Jonathan Cape, 2004), 72.

21. Donald Sassoon, *The Culture of the Europeans from 1800 to the Present* (London: HarperCollins, 2006), 22.

22. For a detailed examination, see Gustav Ungerer, *Anglo-Spanish Relations in Tudor Literature* (Madrid: Clavileño, 1956), 81–174.

23. This subject is discussed in detail in Heather C. Easterling, *Parsing the City: Jonson, Middleton, Dekker, and the City Comedy's London as Language* (New York: Routledge, 2007).

24. John Green, *A Refutation of the Apology for Actors* (London: W. White, 1615), 41–2.

25. See James T. Henke, *Gutter Life and Language in the Early 'Street' Literature of England* (West Cornwall, Conn.: Locust Hill Press, 1988).

26. A detailed treatment of the experiences of English travellers in the first two-thirds of the seventeenth century is John Stoye's *English Travellers Abroad 1604–1667*, rev. edn (New Haven: Yale University Press, 1989).

27. Peter Burke, 'The Language of Gesture in Early Modern Italy', in Jan Bremmer and Herman Roodenburg (eds.), *A Cultural History of Gesture* (Cambridge: Polity, 1993), 80.

28. Laura Pinnavaia, *The Italian Borrowings in the Oxford English Dictionary* (Rome: Bulzoni, 2001), 146–51, 153.

29. Its first use in the context of chess appears to have been not in Italian, but in Spanish around 1560.

30. Knapp, *Time-Bound Words*, 179–80.

31. Thomas's *The Historie of Italie* was also composed at this time.

32. For a full discussion of this, see Jeannette Fellheimer, 'The Section on Italy in the Elizabethan Translations of Giovanni Botero's *Relationi Universali*', *English Miscellany* 8 (1957), 289–306.

33. Thomas Coryat, *Coryat's Crudities*, 2 vols. (Glasgow: James MacLehose, 1905), I, 228, 274, 303; II, 17, 48.

34. Ibid., I, 229.

35. Ibid., I, 413, 370.

36. Markus Klinge, 'Milton's Balcony in *Areopagitica*, II, 524', *Notes and Queries* 52 (2005), 298–304.

37. G. Gregory Smith (ed.), *Elizabethan Critical Essays*, 2 vols. (Oxford: Clarendon Press, 1904), II, 289–90, 293.

38. I am indebted for this curious piece of information to Luigi Luca Cavalli-Sforza, *Genes, Peoples, and Languages*, trans. Mark Seielstad (London: Allen Lane, 2000), 183.

Chapter 7: Powwow

1. The word *colonist* does not appear to have been used until the early eighteenth century.

2. *A Counterblaste to Tobacco* (London: Robert Barker, 1604). This volume is not paginated.

3. The Spanish influence is especially clear today. You have only to think of all the American communities bearing names like Buena Vista or El Dorado. In California, the maps show – among many others – Cresta Blanca, Escondido, La Jolla, Monte Vista, Palo Alto, Tiburon and Yerba Linda, in addition to the very well-known San Francisco, San Diego, Sacramento and Los Angeles.

4. Kirkpatrick Sale, *The Conquest of Paradise: Christopher Columbus and the Columbian Legacy* (London: Hodder & Stoughton, 1991), 4.

5. Samuel Purchas, *Purchas His Pilgrimage*, 2nd edn (London: Henry Fetherstone, 1614), 451.

6. Susan Brigden, *New Worlds, Lost Worlds: The Rule of the Tudors 1485–1603* (London: Allen Lane, 2000), 279.

7. Peter C. Mancall, *Hakluyt's Promise: An Elizabethan's Obsession for an English America* (New Haven: Yale University Press, 2007), 94, 144.

8. Quoted in Charles Nicholl, *The Creature in the Map* (New York: Morrow, 1995), 24.

9. David Beers Quinn (ed.), *The Roanoke Voyages 1584–1590*, 2 vols. (London: Hakluyt Society, 1955), I, 95–106.

10. Ibid., I, 403–64.

11. Ibid., I, 204–5.

12. Jerry Brotton, *Trading Territories: Mapping the Early Modern World* (London: Reaktion Books, 1997), 21–5.

13. James Rosier, *A True Relation of the most prosperous voyage made this present yeere 1605, by Captaine George Waymouth, in the Discovery of the land of Virginia* (London: George Bishop, 1605). This volume is not paginated.

14. Samuel Purchas, *Purchas His Pilgrimes. In Five Books* (London: Henry Fetherstone, 1625), 1667.

15. This theme is developed in an original and detailed fashion by Peter Charles Hoffer in his *Sensory Worlds in Early America* (Baltimore: Johns Hopkins University Press, 2003).

16. In *After Columbus: Essays in the Ethnohistory of Colonial North America* (New York: Oxford University Press, 1988), James Axtell imagines the process of social and linguistic change, poetically writing of the latter, 'Native gutturals were to give way to the smooth sibilants and languid labials of . . . English' (p. 110).

17. Richard White, *The Middle Ground: Indians, Empires, and Republics in the Great Lakes Region, 1650–1815* (Cambridge: Cambridge University Press, 1991), ix–x. It is worth pointing out that the French exported young women – *filles à marier* – in an effort to keep their settlers from consorting with and marrying local females. Children born of such unions would, after all, have been unlikely to learn much French, and the French administration understandably wanted French America to be unequivocally francophone.

18. Two years later, William Strachey, whose colonial exploits were one of the inspirations for Shakespeare's *The Tempest*, describes 'a beast they call *arocoune*, much like a badger'.

19. Dorothy and Thomas Hoobler, *Captain John Smith: Jamestown and the Birth of the American Dream* (Hoboken, NJ: Wiley, 2006), 249.

20. Purchas, *Purchas His Pilgrimes*, 1772.

21. Philip L. Barbour (ed.), *The Jamestown Voyages under the First Charter 1606–1609*, 2 vols. (Cambridge: Cambridge University Press, 1969), II, 348.

22. George Sandys, *Ovids Metamorphosis Englished* (Oxford: John Lichfield, 1632), 497.

23. Mark Monmonier, *From Squaw Tit to Whorehouse Meadow: How Maps Name, Claim, and Inflame* (Chicago: University of Chicago Press, 2006), 52–4.

24. Purchas, *Purchas His Pilgrimes*, 1861, 1868.

25. Elliott, *Empires of the Atlantic World*, 80.

26. Facts and figures are taken here from David Hackett Fischer, *Albion's Seed: Four British Folkways in America* (Oxford: Oxford University Press, 1989).

27. Elliott, *Empires of the Atlantic World*, 147.

28. One might imagine this excellent berry was the cranberry, but it seems to have been the fruit of a type of viburnum.

29. Roger Williams, *A Key into the Language of America* (London: Gregory Dexter, 1643), 98, 197.

30. This information is taken from Ives Goddard, 'Pidgin Delaware', in Sarah G. Thomason (ed.), *Contact Languages: A Wider Perspective* (Amsterdam: John Benjamins, 1997), 43–98.

31. Edward Finegan, 'English in North America', in Hogg and Denison (eds.), *A History of the English Language*, 388–9.

32. *An Interesting Account of Those Extraordinary People the Esquimaux Indians, From Baffin's Bay, North Pole; to which is affixed, A Vocabulary of Esquimaux Words, translated into English by George Niagungitok* (Sheffield: George Ridge, 1825), 4.

33. Dale Blake (ed.), *Inuit Life Writings and Oral Traditions: Inuit Myths*, (St John's, Newfoundland: Educational Resource Development Co-operative, 2001), 32–4.

34. Francis Jennings, *The Invasion of America: Indians, Colonialism and the Cant of Conquest* (Chapel Hill, NC: University of North Carolina Press, 1975), 172.

Chapter 8: Bonsai

1. Richard Eden, *The History of Travayle in the West and East Indies, and other countreys lying eyther way, towardes the fruitfull and ryche Moluccaes . . . with a discourse of the Northwest passage*, ed. Richard Willes (London: Richard Jugge, 1577), 255.

2. BL Add. MS 31301, fol. 159.

3. Shoko Tsuchihashi, 'History of Japanese Loanwords in English', in *The Twenty-Third LACUS Forum 1996*, ed. Alan K. Melby (Chapel Hill, NC: The Linguistic Association of Canada and the United States, 1997), 685.

4. See Tom McArthur, *Oxford Guide to World English* (Oxford University Press, 2003), 368–70.

Chapter 9: Onslaught

1. Roland Barthes, *Empire of Signs*, trans. Richard Howard (London: Jonathan Cape, 1983), 9.

2. Barfield, *History in English Words*, 146, 154, 164–6.

3. This subject is explored in detail in Anna Wierzbicka, *English: Meaning and Culture* (Oxford: Oxford University Press, 2006).

4. Jonathan Scott, *England's Troubles: Seventeenth-Century English Political Instability in European Context* (Cambridge: Cambridge University Press, 2000), 231.

5. C. L. Barber, *The Idea of Honour in the English Drama 1591–1700* (Göteborg: Acta Universitatis Gothoburgensis, 1957), 332.

6. G. Hughes, *Words in Time*, 2.

7. Hamon L'Estrange, *The Observator Observed: Or, Animadversions upon the Observations on the History of King Charles* (London: Edward Dod, 1656), 2.

8. D'Israeli, *Amenities of Literature*, 136–7.

9. William Walker, *Phraseologia Anglo-Latina or, Phrases of the English and Latin Tongue* (London: Richard Royston, 1672), preface.

10. Ibid., 157, 289.

11. Adam Nicolson, *Power and Glory: Jacobean England and the Making of the King James Bible* (London: HarperCollins, 2003), 230.

12. *The Declaration of John Robins and Other Writings*, ed. Andrew Hopton (London: Aporia Press, 1992), 22.

13. See Lilo Moessner, 'The Vocabulary of Early Modern English Scientific Texts', in Ute Smit, Stefan Dollinger, Julia Hüttner, Gunther Kaltenböck and Ursula Lutzky (eds.), *Tracing English through Time* (Vienna: Braumüller, 2007), 235–52.

14. Ostler, *Empires of the Word*, 228.

15. Johannes Veslingus, *The Anatomy of the Body of Man*, trans. Nicholas Culpeper (London: George Sawbridge, 1677), 23–4.

16. Keith Thomas, *Religion and the Decline of Magic* (London: Weidenfeld & Nicolson, 1971), 9.

17. This is the subject of George Steiner's essay 'The Retreat from the Word', in *Language and Silence* (London: Faber, 1985).

18. *Memoirs of John Evelyn*, ed. William Bray (London: Frederick Warne, 1900), 628–9.

19. Susie I. Tucker, *Protean Shape: A Study in Eighteenth-Century Vocabulary and Usage* (London: Athlone, 1967), 108.

20. Logan Pearsall Smith, *The English Language*, 3rd edn (Oxford: Oxford University Press, 1966), 108.

21. The poem appears in the annotated third edition of Edward Fairfax's *Godfrey of Bulloigne*, a translation of Torquato Tasso's *Gerusalemme Liberata*.

22. Quoted in Manfred Görlach, *Eighteenth-Century English* (Heidelberg: Winter, 2001), 161.

23. Dryden may actually have made up *double-entendre*, rather than taking it from a French source.

24. Samuel Johnson, *Lives of the English Poets*, ed. George Birkbeck Hill, 3 vols. (Oxford: Clarendon Press, 1905), I, 463–4.

25. Quoted in Markman Ellis, *The Coffee-House: A Cultural History* (London: Phoenix, 2005), 86.

26. Mackenzie, *Les Relations de l'Angleterre et de la France d'après le vocabulaire*, II, 144.

27. Peter Ackroyd, *London: The Biography* (London: Chatto & Windus, 2000), 160–61.

28. See David Murison, 'The Dutch Element in the Vocabulary of Scots', in A. J. Aitken, Angus McIntosh and Hermann Palsson (eds.), *Edinburgh Studies in English and Scots* (London: Longman, 1971), 159–76.

29. A number of these details are from J. F. Bense, *Anglo-Dutch Relations from the Earliest Times to the Death of William the Third* (The Hague: Martinus Nijhoff, 1925).

30. Jonathan I. Israel, *The Dutch Republic: Its Rise, Greatness, and Fall, 1477–1806* (Oxford: Clarendon Press, 1998), 679.

31. Linda and Roger Flavell, *The Chronology of Words and Phrases*, 111.

32. Quoted in Geert Mak, *Amsterdam: A Brief Life of the City*, trans. Philipp Blom (London: Harvill, 1999), 100.

33. *The Works of Sir Roger Williams*, ed. John X. Evans (Oxford: Clarendon Press, 1972), 64.

34. See Simon Schama, *The Embarrassment of Riches: An Interpretation of Dutch Culture in the Golden Age* (London: Collins, 1987), 262–3.

35. Bathsua Makin, *An Essay to Revive the Antient Education of Gentlewomen* (London: J. D., 1673), 28.

36. Israel, *The Dutch Republic*, 677.

Chapter 10: Connoisseur

1. For an extensive treatment of the emergence of this national identity, see Linda Colley, *Britons: Forging the Nation 1707–1837* (New Haven: Yale University Press, 1992).

2. Tucker, *Protean Shape*, 35.

3. *Gentleman's Magazine* 8 (1738), 586.

4. Jeremy Black, *Natural and Necessary Enemies: Anglo-French Relations in the Eighteenth Century* (London: Duckworth, 1986), 175.

5. See for instance the title of Paul Langford's important history of the period, *A Polite and Commercial People: England 1727–1783* (Oxford: Oxford University Press, 1992).

6. Barfield, *History in English Words*, 158.

7. See Terttu Nevalainen and Heli Tissari, 'Of Politeness and People', in Graham D. Caie, Carole Hough and Irené Wotherspoon (eds.), *The Power of Words: Essays in Lexicography, Lexicology and Semantics in Honour of Christian J. Kay* (Amsterdam: Rodopi, 2006).

8. Judith S. Neaman and Carole G. Silver, quoted in Patricia Beer, 'Elizabeth Bennet's Fine Eyes', in D. J. Enright (ed.), *Fair of Speech: The Uses of Euphemism* (Oxford: Oxford University Press, 1985), 120–21. In Victorian Britain, *trousers* became *indescribables*, *prostitutes* were *fallen women*, and a collector of dog excrement was a *pure-finder*. See Joss Marsh, *Blasphemy, Culture, and Literature in Nineteenth-Century England* (Chicago: University of Chicago Press, 1998), 215–30.

9. Tucker, *Protean Shape*, 107.

10. Norbert Elias, *The Civilizing Process*, trans. Edmund Jephcott, rev. edn (Oxford: Blackwell, 2000), 400. For a detailed discussion, see also Jorge Arditi, *A Genealogy of Manners: Transformation of Social Relations in France and England from the Fourteenth Century to the Eighteenth Century* (Chicago: University of Chicago Press, 1998), 182–220.

11. *Monthly Review* 20 (1759), 428.

12. For a full discussion, see Jan Lannering, *Studies in the Prose Style of Joseph Addison* (Uppsala: Appelbergs Boktryckeri, 1951).

13. Madame de Staël, *Germany*, with notes and appendices by O. W. Wright, 2 vols. (New York: Hurd and Houghton, 1871), I, 91.

14. *The World* 102 (12 December 1754), 611–15.

15. Ibid. 101 (5 December 1754), 606–10.

16. *Gentleman's Magazine* 2 (1732), 681.

17. Benedict Anderson, *Imagined Communities: Reflections on the Origin and Spread of Nationalism*, rev. edn (London: Verso, 2006), 11.

18. Walpole also shares Chesterfield's special taste for Gallicisms, as does the diarist and philanthropist Hannah More.

19. These examples come from Ingrid Tieken-Boon van Ostade's essay 'English at the Onset of the Normative Tradition', in Mugglestone (ed.), *The Oxford History of English*.

20. Barfield, *History in English Words*, 170.

21. Alexis Tadié, *Sterne's Whimsical Theatres of Language* (Aldershot: Ashgate, 2003), 12–14.

22. Tucker, *Protean Shape*, 18.

23. Martin Kemp, *The Science of Art* (New Haven: Yale University Press, 1990), 213–17.

24. Quoted in Tucker, *Protean Shape*, 12.

25. Larry Stewart, *The Rise of Public Science: Rhetoric, Technology, and Natural*

Philosophy in Newtonian Britain, 1660–1750 (Cambridge: Cambridge University Press, 1992), xxiv–xxv.

26. Steiner, *After Babel*, 160.
27. John Ray, *The Wisdom of God Manifested in the Works of the Creation*, 7th edn (London: William Innys, 1717), 370.
28. For a full and fascinating treatment of the subject, including details of many individual quacks and their bizarre medicines, see C. J. S. Thompson, *The Quacks of Old London* (London: Brentano, 1928).
29. See Udo Fries, 'Foreign Words in Early English Newspapers', in Smit et al. (eds.), *Tracing English through Time*, 115–32.
30. Tucker, *Protean Shape*, 20.
31. See Reinhard Strohm, 'Italian Operisti North of the Alps, c.1700 – c.1750', in Reinhard Strohm (ed.), *The Eighteenth-Century Diaspora of Italian Music and Musicians* (Turnhout: Brepols, 2001), 1–59.
32. John Ashton, *Social Life in the Reign of Queen Anne*, 2 vols. (London: Chatto & Windus, 1882), II, 38.
33. See Simon McVeigh, 'Italian Violinists in Eighteenth-Century London', in Strohm (ed.), *The Eighteenth-Century Diaspora of Italian Music and Musicians*, 139–76.
34. For a full discussion of shopping behaviour and the circuits of commerce, see Bruno Blondé, Peter Stabel, Jon Stobart and Ilja Van Damme (eds.), *Buyers and Sellers: Retail Circuits and Practices in Medieval and Early Modern Europe* (Turnhout: Brepols, 2006).
35. For anyone wishing to uncover the seedier side of eighteenth-century English, the place to begin is the *Dictionary of the Vulgar Tongue* published in 1785 by Francis Grose, the son of a Swiss jeweller.
36. Maxine Berg, *Luxury and Pleasure in Eighteenth-Century Britain* (Oxford: Oxford University Press, 2005), 157–8.
37. Quoted in James, *The Rise and Fall of the British Empire*, 73.
38. Bruce Redford, *The Converse of the Pen: Acts of Intimacy in the Eighteenth-Century Familiar Letter* (Chicago: University of Chicago Press, 1986), 31.
39. This is explored in detail in Edna Osborne, *Oriental Diction and Theme in English Verse, 1740–1840* (Lawrence: University of Kansas, 1916).
40. Abdul-Karim Mahmud Gharaybeh, *English Traders in Syria 1744–1791* (PhD thesis, London University, 1950), 12.
41. My source here is Anatole V. Lyovin, *An Introduction to the Languages of the World* (New York: Oxford University Press, 1997), 257. The Latin word *aborigines* had originally been used in the sixteenth century of the first occupiers of Italy and Greece; only at the end of the eighteenth century

did it come to be used of those natives who had possessed a land before the arrival of European settlers.

42. *The Journals of Captain Cook*, ed. Philip Edwards (London: Penguin, 1999), 152.
43. Suzanne Romaine, *Bilingualism*, 2nd edn (Oxford: Blackwell, 1995), 39.
44. R. M. W. Dixon, *The Languages of Australia* (Cambridge: Cambridge University Press, 1980), 18.
45. *Gentleman's Magazine* 44 (1774), 70.
46. Robert Hughes, *The Fatal Shore* (London: Collins Harvill, 1987), 1, 5.
47. Quoted in Elizabeth Webby (ed.), *Colonial Voices: Letters, Diaries, Journalism and Other Accounts of Nineteenth-Century Australia* (St Lucia: University of Queensland Press, 1989), 13–14.

Chapter 11: Teapot

1. Salman Rushdie, *The Moor's Last Sigh* (London: Jonathan Cape, 1995), 4–5.
2. Turner, *Spice: The History of a Temptation*, 88.
3. See C. R. Boxer, *The Portuguese Seaborne Empire 1415–1825* (Manchester: Carcanet, 1991), 39–64.
4. Quoted in Ram Chandra Prasad, *Early English Travellers in India* (Delhi: Motilal Banarsidass, 1980), 52, 146.
5. Charles Lockyer, *An Account of the Trade in India* (London: Samuel Crouch, 1711), 71–2, 124, 131, 248–50, 265.
6. Ibid., 85, 282.
7. Henry Yule and A. C. Burnell, *Hobson-Jobson: Being A Glossary of Anglo-Indian Colloquial Words and Phrases, and of Kindred Terms* (London: John Murray, 1886), xiv, xvii.
8. Ostler, *Empires of the Word*, 212–13.
9. This idea is put forward by Amartya Sen in his essay 'Indian Traditions and the Western Imagination' in *The Argumentative Indian: Writings on Indian Culture, History and Identity* (London: Allen Lane, 2005).
10. Anthony Pagden, *Peoples and Empires* (London: Weidenfeld & Nicolson, 2001), 100–101.
11. This William Hawkins was the grandson of the William Hawkins who reached West Africa in the 1530s, and was the nephew of John Hawkins.
12. *The Journal of John Jourdain, 1608–1617*, ed. William Foster (Cambridge: Hakluyt Society, 1905), 136–40.
13. John Keay, *The Honourable Company: A History of the English East India Company* (London: HarperCollins, 1991), 98–9.

14. Anthony Farrington, *Trading Places: The East India Company and Asia 1600–1834* (London: British Library, 2002), 64.

15. J. R. McCulloch, 'Revenue and Commerce of India', *Edinburgh Review* 45 (1827), 365.

16. *Gentleman's Magazine* 27 (1757), 309.

17. Tim Fulford and Peter J. Kitson (gen. eds.), *Travels, Explorations and Empires: Writings from the Era of Imperial Expansion 1770–1835*, 6 vols. (London: Pickering & Chatto, 2001), VI, 250.

18. Richard Davenport-Hines, *The Pursuit of Oblivion: A Social History of Drugs* (London: Weidenfeld & Nicolson, 2001), 2.

19. Thomas Bowrey, *A Dictionary of English and Malay* (London: printed by Samuel Bridge for the author, 1701).

20. A related term is *topaz* or *topass*, a low-caste attendant or interpreter.

21. John Fryer, *A New Account of East India and Persia* (London: Richard Chiswell, 1698), 67, 98, 142, 200–201.

22. Sirajul Islam, *The Permanent Settlement in Bengal: A Study of Its Operation 1790–1819* (Dacca: Bangla Academy, 1979), 257–9.

23. David Gilmour, *The Ruling Caste: Imperial Lives in the Victorian Raj* (London: John Murray, 2005), xxii–xxiii.

24. Thomas Williamson, *The East India Vade-Mecum*, 2 vols. (London: Black, Parry, and Kingsbury, 1810), I, 314.

25. Ibid., II, 76, 134, 155.

26. Alexander Duff, *New Era of the English Language and English Literature in India* (Edinburgh: John Johnstone, 1837), 18, 37–8.

27. Gilmour, *The Ruling Caste*, 10–11.

28. Ostler, *Empires of the Word*, 12.

29. Richard W. Bailey, *Images of English: A Cultural History of the Language* (Cambridge: Cambridge University Press, 1991), 140–41.

30. James, *The Rise and Fall of the British Empire*, 146.

31. Paul Kennedy, *The Rise and Fall of the Great Powers* (London: Fontana, 1989), 198–9.

32. See Kingsley Bolton, *Chinese Englishes: A Sociolinguistic History* (Cambridge: Cambridge University Press, 2003), 145.

33. Raymond Chang and Margaret Scrogin Chang, *Speaking of Chinese* (New York: W. W. Norton, 2001), 11.

34. Martin Booth, *Opium: A History* (London: Pocket Books, 1997), 110.

35. Emperor Qian Long's letter is quoted in Nayan Chanda, *Bound Together: How Traders, Preachers, Adventurers, and Warriors Shaped Globalization* (New Haven: Yale University Press, 2007), 35.

36. Ronald Hyam, *Britain's Imperial Century, 1815–1914*, 3rd edn (Basingstoke: Palgrave Macmillan, 2002), 123.

37. *A Vocabulary, Containing Chinese Words and Phrases Peculiar to Canton and Macao, and to the Trade of those Places* (Macao: The Honourable Company's Press, 1824).

38. See Mimi Chan and Helen Kwok, *A Study of Lexical Borrowing from Chinese into English with Special Reference to Hong Kong* (Hong Kong: Centre of Asian Studies, University of Hong Kong, 1985), 83, 88, 91.

39. Anatoly Lieberman, *Word Origins . . . and How We Know Them* (Oxford: Oxford University Press, 2005), 140.

40. McArthur, *Oxford Guide to World English*, 358.

Chapter 12: Blizzard

1. *The Diary of Samuel Sewall*, I, 543.

2. Elliott, *Empires of the Atlantic World*, 43.

3. See Peter C. Herman, '"We All Smoke Here": Behn's *The Widdow Ranter* and the Invention of American Identity', in Robert Appelbaum and John Wood Sweet (eds.), *Envisioning an English Empire: Jamestown and the Making of the North Atlantic World* (Philadelphia: University of Pennsylvania Press, 2005), 254–74.

4. See H. L. Mencken, *The American Language*, 4th edn (New York: Knopf, 1963), 5.

5. Hoffer, *Sensory Worlds in Early America*, 217–18.

6. David K. Barnhart and Allan A. Metcalf, *America in So Many Words: Words That Have Shaped America* (Boston: Houghton Mifflin, 1997), 70.

7. Quoted in Jill Lepore, *A is for American: Letters and Other Characters in the Newly United States* (New York: Knopf, 2002), 5.

8. Linda and Roger Flavell, *The Chronology of Words and Phrases*, 213.

9. John S. Farmer (ed.), *Americanisms – Old and New* (London: Thomas Poulter, 1889), x, xiii.

10. Mencken, *The American Language*, 498–501.

11. See Baugh and Cable, *A History of the English Language*, 360.

12. G. Hughes, *A History of English Words*, 284–5.

13. Ostler, *Empires of the Word*, 490.

14. Stuart Berg Flexner, *I Hear America Talking: An Illustrated Treasury of American Words and Phrases* (New York: Van Nostrand Reinhold, 1976), 20.

15. For this last example, see Beverly Olson Flanigan, 'Different Ways of Talking in the Buckeye State (Ohio)', in Walt Wolfram and Ben Ward

(eds.), *American Voices: How Dialects Differ from Coast to Coast* (Oxford: Blackwell, 2006), 122.

16. It is worth noting here that many other states have names that now seem prosaic but must once have been poetic: Alabama takes its name from a Choctaw expression meaning 'I open the thicket,' while Minnesota's comes from a Dakota Sioux word for 'sky-tinted water', and Kansas is, in Sioux, the 'land of the south wind people'.

17. Harold W. Bentley, *A Dictionary of Spanish Terms in English: With Special Reference to the American Southwest* (New York: Columbia University Press, 1932), 56.

18. John Algeo, 'Spanish Loanwords in English by 1900', in Felix Rodriguez Gonzalez (ed.), *Spanish Loanwords in the English Language* (Berlin: Mouton de Gruyter, 1996), 13–40.

19. Bentley, *A Dictionary of Spanish Terms in English*, 101.

20. Ibid., 197.

21. Garland Cannon, 'Recent Borrowings from Spanish', in Gonzalez (ed.), *Spanish Loanwords in the English Language*, 45.

22. Thomas E. Murray, 'Spanish Loanwords in Contemporary American English Slang', in Gonzalez (ed.), *Spanish Loanwords in the English Language*, 105–37.

23. Terms specific to particular regions are much less likely to make the journey. A non-American speaker of English will in all likelihood be flummoxed by the Southern *pulley bone* (*wishbone*), the Midland *spouts* (*gutters*) or the Northern *spider* (*frying pan*). Yet much American regional usage can be traced back to the colonial period.

24. Christian Mair, *Twentieth-Century English: History, Variation, and Standardization* (Cambridge: Cambridge University Press, 2006), 60.

25. My information here is taken mainly from Sol Steinmetz, *Yiddish and English: The Story of Yiddish in America*, 2nd edn (Tuscaloosa: University of Alabama Press, 2001).

26. This definition is provided by Gene Bluestein in *Anglish-Yinglish: Yiddish in American Life and Literature* (Athens, Ga.: University of Georgia Press, 1989), 57.

27. Quoted in Leo Rosten, *Hooray for Yiddish!* (London: Elm Tree Books, 1983), 85.

28. This example is from Steinmetz, *Yiddish and English*, 74.

29. Richard W. Bailey, 'The English Language in Canada', in Bailey and Görlach (eds), *English as a World Language*, 141.

Chapter 13: Ethos

1. Quoted in Doug Nickel, 'The Camera and Other Drawing Machines', in Mike Weaver (ed.), *British Photography in the Nineteenth Century: The Fine Art Tradition* (Cambridge: Cambridge University Press, 1989), 1.

2. Meena Alexander, 'Shelley's India: Territory and Text, Some Problems of Decolonization', in Betty T. Bennett and Stuart Curran (eds.), *Shelley: Poet and Legislator of the World* (Baltimore: Johns Hopkins University Press, 1996), 171–2.

3. See Frances Austin, *The Language of Wordsworth and Coleridge* (Basingstoke: Macmillan, 1989).

4. Raymond Williams, *Keywords: A Vocabulary of Culture and Society* (London: Fontana, 1988), 31–2.

5. This subject is covered in depth in Graham Tulloch, *The Language of Walter Scott* (London: André Deutsch, 1980), 182–266.

6. Manfred Görlach, *English in Nineteenth-Century England: An Introduction* (Cambridge: Cambridge University Press, 1999), 103.

7. *Byron's Letters and Journals*, ed. Leslie A. Marchand, 12 vols. (Cambridge, Mass.: Harvard University Press, 1973–82), V, 45.

8. Garland Cannon, 'Turkish and Persian Loans in English Literature', *Neophilologus* 84 (2000), 291–2.

9. Fiona MacCarthy, *Byron: Life and Legend* (London: Faber, 2003), 128.

10. In relation to the latter, see Tilar J. Mazzeo, 'The Strains of Empire: Shelley and the Music of India', in Michael J. Franklin (ed.), *Romantic Representations of British India* (Abingdon: Routledge, 2006), 180–96.

11. H. G. Wells, *A Short History of the World* (London: Collins, 1934), 274–5.

12. Kennedy, *The Rise and Fall of the Great Powers*, 187.

13. Quoted in Ostler, *Empires of the Word*, 511.

14. Emerson, *English Traits*, 115–16.

15. Sassoon, *The Culture of the Europeans from 1800 to the Present*, 596.

16. Pei, *The Story of the English Language*, 102.

17. Lawrence James, *The Middle Class: A History* (London: Little, Brown, 2006), 232.

18. See Michael Shortland, 'Geology', in Sally Mitchell (ed.), *Victorian Britain: An Encyclopedia* (New York: Garland, 1988), 327–8.

19. Barfield, *History in English Words*, 193.

20. Peter Mandler, *The English National Character: The History of an Idea from Edmund Burke to Tony Blair* (New Haven: Yale University Press, 2006), 86–7, 100.

21. *Enquire Within Upon Everything*, 69th edn (London: Houlston, 1884), 270–71, 280.

22. Michael Curtin, *Propriety and Position: A Study of Victorian Manners* (New York: Garland, 1987), 46–7.

23. *The Habits of Good Society: A Handbook of Etiquette for Ladies and Gentlemen* (London: James Hogg, 1859), 219.

24. Ibid., 49.

25. Thomas Preston, *A Dictionary of Daily Blunders* (London: Whittaker & Co., 1880), 56.

26. Ibid., 5, 7.

27. D'Israeli, *Amenities of Literature*, 361.

28. Henry Alford, *A Plea for the Queen's English* (London: Strahan, 1864), 6, 280.

29. Görlach, *English in Nineteenth-Century England*, 108.

30. Lynda Mugglestone, 'English in the Nineteenth Century', in Mugglestone (ed.), *The Oxford History of English*, 299.

31. Pedro Carolino, *The New Guide of the Conversation in Portuguese and English* (Peking: privately published, 1869), 109, 134.

32. Görlach, *English in Nineteenth-Century England*, 107.

33. For a full account, see Lynda Mugglestone, *Lost for Words: The Hidden History of the Oxford English Dictionary* (New Haven: Yale University Press, 2005), 102–9.

34. William B. Hodgson, *Errors in the Use of English* (Edinburgh: David Douglas, 1881), 65–6, 70.

35. J. R. Seeley, *The Expansion of England* (Leipzig: Bernhard Tauchnitz, 1884), 57, 304.

36. K. C. Phillips, *Language and Class in Victorian England* (Oxford: Blackwell, 1984), 1–23.

37. These details are taken from Dea Birkett, *Spinsters Abroad: Victorian Lady Explorers* (London: Gollancz, 1991).

38. Roswell Park, *A Hand-Book for American Travellers in Europe* (New York: Putnam, 1853), 48.

39. Grant Allen, *The European Tour: A Handbook for Americans and Colonists* (London: Grant Richards, 1899), 2, 190.

40. Hugh and Pauline Massingham, *The Englishman Abroad* (Gloucester: Alan Sutton, 1984), 60, 144.

41. Ibid., 107, 117.

42. Ibid., 47, 50.

43. Ibid., 17.

44. Anton Tien, *The Levant Interpreter; A Polyglot Dialogue Book for English*

Travellers in the Levant (London: Williams and Norgate, 1879), 102, 114.

45. *Practical Guide for the Wintering Places of the South* (London: Simpkin, Marshall & Co., 1872), xlix.

46. Williams, *Keywords*, 41.

47. See Michael Baxandall, 'The Language of Art Criticism', in Salim Kemal and Ivan Gaskell (eds.), *The Language of Art History* (Cambridge: Cambridge University Press, 1991).

48. See Richard Gilman, *Decadence: The Strange Life of an Epithet* (London: Secker & Warburg, 1979), 73–109.

49. Some of these examples are borrowed from Charles T. Carr, *The German Influence on the English Vocabulary* (Oxford: Clarendon Press, 1934).

50. Barbara M. H. Strang, *A History of English* (London: Routledge, 1989), 124. *Glockenspiel*, known from the 1820s, hardly counts, and *leitmotiv*, another word which might be considered an exception, comes much later.

51. Pasta comes in many forms. Most of us would recognize *macaroni* and *tagliatelle* as words absorbed into common use, but what of *mostaccioli* or *tonnarelli*?

52. Eliza Acton, *Modern Cookery, for Private Families*, rev. edn (London: Longman, 1865), 605–22.

53. Richard W. Bailey, *Nineteenth-Century English* (Ann Arbor: University of Michigan Press, 1996), 162.

54. Christine Ammer, *Fruitcakes and Couch Potatoes and Other Delicious Expressions* (New York: Plume, 1995), 100–101.

55. Massialot's book, arranged alphabetically, is described by Roy Strong as 'the great cookery classic of the eighteenth century'. Roy Strong, *Feast: A History of Grand Eating* (London: Jonathan Cape, 2002), 229.

56. *The Forme of Cury, A Roll of Ancient English Cookery* (London: J. Nichols, 1780), 67. *Cury* was a general term for cookery, deriving from the French *queurie*.

57. *Guardian*, 19 April 2001.

Chapter 14: Voodoo

1. Kennedy, *The Rise and Fall of the Great Powers*, 312–14.
2. Hyam, *Britain's Imperial Century*, 217–18.
3. Allan Metcalf, *The World in So Many Words* (Boston: Houghton Mifflin, 1999), 67–8.

4. Ngugi wa Thiong'o, *Decolonising the Mind: The Politics of Language in African Literature* (London: James Currey, 1986), 10–13.

5. Geneva Smitherman, 'Word from the Hood: The Lexicon of African-American Vernacular English', in Salikoko S. Mufwene, John R. Rickford, Guy Bailey and John Baugh (eds.), *African-American English: Structure, History, and Use* (London: Routledge, 1998), 209–10.

6. David Dalby, 'The African Element in American English', in Thomas Kochman (ed.), *Rappin' and Stylin' Out: Communication in Urban Black America* (Urbana: University of Illinois Press, 1972), 177, 185.

7. H. Samy Alim, 'Hip Hop Nation', in Edward Finegan and John R. Rickford (eds.), *Language in the USA: Themes for the Twenty-first Century* (Cambridge: Cambridge University Press, 2004), 396.

8. Lerer, *Inventing English*, 233.

Chapter 15: Angst

1. I take my lead here from L. J. K. Setright, *Drive On! A Social History of the Motor Car* (London: Granta, 2003), 178.

2. Niall Ferguson, *The War of the World: History's Age of Hatred* (London: Allen Lane, 2006), xxxiv.

3. I have borrowed this image from Eric Hobsbawm, *Age of Extremes: The Short Twentieth Century 1914–1991* (London: Michael Joseph, 1994), 523.

4. For a sustained discussion of the way war and its strategic violence influence language, see James Dawes, *The Language of War: Literature and Culture in the U.S. from the Civil War through World War II* (Cambridge, Mass.: Harvard University Press, 2002).

5. For the text of President Reagan's speech, see http://www.reagan.utexas.edu/archives/speeches/1984/12684h.htm

6. Dawes, *The Language of War*, 23.

7. Hobsbawm, *Age of Extremes*, 78–9.

8. Garland Cannon, *The Japanese Contributions to the English Language* (Wiesbaden: Harrassowitz Verlag, 1996), 63.

9. Peter Conrad, *Modern Times, Modern Places: Life and Art in the 20th Century* (London: Thames and Hudson, 1998), 13.

10. Fredric Jameson, *The Prison-House of Language* (Princeton: Princeton University Press, 1972), 195.

11. See Marjorie Perloff, *Differentials: Poetry, Poetics, Pedagogy* (Tuscaloosa: University of Alabama Press, 2004), 82–101.

12. I adapt this idea from Derek Attridge, 'The *Wake's* Confounded

Language', in Morris Beja and Shari Benstock (eds.), *Coping with Joyce: Essays from the Copenhagen Symposium* (Columbus: Ohio State University Press, 1989).

13. Conrad, *Modern Times, Modern Places*, 125.

14. A reference to *robota* can be found in an English translation dating from 1797 of a work by the conspiracy theorist Augustin Barruel. See Christopher Goulding, '*Robot*: Antedating the Entry in the Oxford English Dictionary', *Notes and Queries* 52 (2005), 380–81.

15. Thorstein Veblen, *The Theory of the Leisure Class* (New York: Macmillan, 1899), 75.

16. Samuel Johnson, *The Idler and the Adventurer*, ed. W. J. Bate, John M. Bullitt and L. F. Powell (New Haven: Yale University Press, 1963), 125.

17. John Hood, *Selling the Dream: Why Advertising is Good Business* (Westport, Conn.: Praeger, 2005), 32, 40.

18. Robert O'Brien, *This is San Francisco* (New York: Whittlesey House, 1948), 83–4.

19. Dominic Sandbrook, *White Heat: A History of Britain in the Swinging Sixties* (London: Little, Brown, 2006), 186–7.

20. For a fuller treatment of the subject, see G. Hughes, *Words in Time*, 67–91.

21. David Crystal, *By Hook or by Crook: A Journey in Search of English* (London: HarperPress, 2007), 271–2.

22. David S. Levine, '"My Client Has Discussed Your Proposal to Fill the Drainage Ditch with His Partners": Legal Language', in Leonard Michaels and Christopher Ricks (eds.), *The State of the Language* (Berkeley: University of California Press, 1980), 406.

23. Tony Thorne, *Shoot the Puppy: A Survival Guide to the Curious Jargon of Modern Life* (London: Penguin, 2006), 28–9.

24. Kenneth Hudson, *The Jargon of the Professions* (London: Macmillan, 1978), 14–15.

25. Adrian Furnham, *The Psychology of Managerial Incompetence: A Sceptic's Dictionary of Modern Organizational Issues* (London: Whurr, 1998), 99.

26. Richard Maltby (ed.), *Dreams for Sale: Popular Culture in the 20th Century* (London: Harrap, 1989), 19.

27. Melanie Phillips, 'Illiberal Liberalism', in Sarah Dunant (ed.), *The War of the Words: The Political Correctness Debate* (London: Virago, 1994), 47.

28. Glanville Price, 'Romani', in Glanville Price (ed.), *Languages in Britain and Ireland* (Oxford: Blackwell, 2000), 207.

29. See Anthony P. Grant, 'Romani Words in Non-Standard British English and the Development of Angloromani', in Yaron Matras (ed.), *The*

Romani Element in Non-Standard Speech (Wisebaden: Harrassowitz Verlag, 1998).

30. Wierzbicka, *English: Meaning and Culture*, 29, 32, 37, 41, 43, 51–3.
31. This is too large a subject to cover in detail here. A recent and impressive scholarly study is Andrew Goatly, *Washing the Brain – Metaphor and Hidden Ideology* (Amsterdam: John Benjamins, 2007).

Chapter 16: Shabash

1. Steiner, *After Babel*, 61.
2. In the Romance languages, the words for an arm are broadly similar, but a pencil is a *crayon* in French, a *matita* in Italian, and a *lápiz* in Spanish.
3. Urdu and Punjabi are among the languages whose numbers of speakers promise to increase most significantly. If estimates are correct and Pakistan is the world's third most populous country by the middle of this century, Urdu and Punjabi may also be able to lay claim to this status as 'big' languages. But population alone does not guarantee a language's global importance.
4. Ostler, *Empires of the Word*, 7.
5. This statistic comes from Andrew Dalby, *Language in Danger* (London: Allen Lane, 2002). Dalby argues passionately and convincingly that the multiplicity of languages is the very opposite of a nuisance.
6. Nevertheless, a considerable amount of research continues to be written up in other languages, and this research is often overlooked by English-speaking scientists and practitioners.
7. See Tom McArthur, 'English World-Wide in the Twentieth Century', in Mugglestone (ed.), *The Oxford History of English*, 369.
8. See Jeremy Wallach, '"Goodbye My Blind Majesty": Music, Language and Politics in the Indonesian Underground', in Harris M. Berger and Michael Thomas Carroll (eds.), *Global Pop, Local Language* (Jackson: University Press of Mississippi, 2003), 53–86.
9. Jamie Shinhee Lee, 'Language and Identity: Entertainers in South Korean Pop Culture', in Miguel Mantero (ed.), *Identity and Second Language Learning* (Charlotte, NC: Information Age, 2007), 283–303.
10. Quoted in Ferguson, *Empire: How Britain Made the Modern World*, 358.
11. Anderson, *Imagined Communities*, 207.
12. Robert Phillipson, *Linguistic Imperialism* (Oxford: Oxford University Press, 1992), 35–6.
13. David Graddol, *English Next* (London: British Council, 2006), 28.

14. I have taken these examples from Amy Beth Rell and Jason Rothman, 'On the Structure and Discourse Usage of Spanglish', in Mantero (ed.), *Identity and Second Language Learning*, 241–2.

15. Tony Judt, *Postwar: A History of Europe since 1945* (London: Pimlico, 2007), 759.

16. Graddol, *English Next*, 93.

17. See Salah Troudi, 'The Effects of English as a Medium of Instruction', in Adel Jendli, Salah Troudi and Christine Coombe (eds.), *The Power of Language: Perspectives from Arabia* (Dubai: TESOL Arabia, 2007), 6.

18. Susie Dent, *The Language Report*, (Oxford: Oxford University Press, 2003), 20.

19. William Safire, *On Language* (New York: Times Books, 1980), 180.

Bibliography of
Secondary Sources

Abernethy, David B., *The Dynamics of Global Dominance: European Overseas Empires, 1415–1980* (New Haven: Yale University Press, 2000)

Abley, Mark, *Spoken Here: Travels among Threatened Languages* (London: William Heinemann, 2004)

Abrams, Ann Uhry, *The Pilgrims and Pocahontas: Rival Myths of American Origin* (Boulder, Colorado: Westview Press, 1999)

Abulafia, David (ed.), *The Mediterranean in History* (London: Thames and Hudson, 2003)

Ackroyd, Peter, *London: The Biography* (London: Chatto & Windus, 2000)

Adams, J. N., *Bilingualism and the Latin Language* (Cambridge: Cambridge University Press, 2003)

Agius, Dionisius A., and Ian Richard Netton (eds.), *Across the Mediterranean Frontiers: Trade, Politics and Religion, 650–1450* (Turnhout: Brepols, 1997)

Ahmed, Khaled, *The Bridge of Words between East and West* (Lahore: Vanguard, 2001)

Aitchison, Jean, *Language Change: Progress or Decay?* 3rd edn (Cambridge: Cambridge University Press, 2001)

Aitken, A. J., Angus McIntosh and Hermann Palsson (eds.), *Edinburgh Studies in English and Scots* (London: Longman, 1971)

Algeo, John, *British or American English? A Handbook of Word and Grammar Patterns* (Cambridge: Cambridge University Press, 2006)

—— (ed.), *Fifty Years among the New Words: A Dictionary of Neologisms, 1941–1991* (Cambridge: Cambridge University Press, 1991)

Algeo, John, and Thomas Pyles, *The Origins and Development of the English Language*, 5th edn (Boston: Thomson Wadsworth, 2005)

Allen, Rosamund (ed.), *Eastward Bound: Travel and Travellers, 1050–1550* (Manchester: Manchester University Press, 2004)

Ammer, Christine, *Fruitcakes and Couch Potatoes and Other Delicious Expressions* (New York: Plume, 1995)

Anderson, Benedict, *Imagined Communities: Reflections on the Origin and Spread of Nationalism*, rev. edn (London: Verso, 2006)

Anderson, Judith H., *Words That Matter: Linguistic Perception in Renaissance England* (Stanford: Stanford University Press, 1996)

Anttila, Raimon, 'Loanwords and Statistical Measures of Style in the Towneley Plays', *Statistical Methods in Linguistics* 2 (1963), 73–93

Appelbaum, Robert, and John Wood Sweet (eds.), *Envisioning an English Empire: Jamestown and the Making of the North Atlantic World* (Philadelphia: University of Pennsylvania Press, 2005)

Arditi, Jorge, *A Genealogy of Manners: Transformation of Social Relations in France and England from the Fourteenth Century to the Eighteenth Century* (Chicago: University of Chicago Press, 1998)

Ashton, John, *Social Life in the Reign of Queen Anne*, 2 vols. (London: Chatto & Windus, 1882)

Ashtor, Eliyahu, *East–West Trade in the Medieval Mediterranean*, ed. Benjamin Z. Kedar (London: Variorum Reprints, 1986)

Attridge, Steve, *Nationalism, Imperialism and Identity in Late Victorian Culture* (Basingstoke: Palgrave Macmillan, 2003)

Austin, Frances, *The Language of Wordsworth and Coleridge* (Basingstoke: Macmillan, 1989)

Axtell, James, *After Columbus: Essays in the Ethnohistory of Colonial North America* (New York: Oxford University Press, 1988)

Ayto, John, *Dictionary of Word Origins* (New York: Arcade, 1993)

—— *Twentieth Century Words* (Oxford: Oxford University Press, 1999)

Bailey, Richard W., *Images of English: A Cultural History of the Language* (Cambridge: Cambridge University Press, 1991)

—— *Nineteenth-Century English* (Ann Arbor: University of Michigan Press, 1996)

Bailey, Richard W., and Manfred Görlach (eds.), *English as a World Language* (Cambridge: Cambridge University Press, 1984)

Barber, C. L., *The Idea of Honour in the English Drama 1591–1700* (Göteborg: Acta Universitatis Gothoburgensis, 1957)

—— *Early Modern English*, rev. edn (Edinburgh: Edinburgh University Press, 1997)

Barbour, Philip L. (ed.), *The Jamestown Voyages under the First Charter 1606–1609*, 2 vols. (Cambridge: Cambridge University Press, 1969)

Barfield, Owen, *History in English Words* (London: Faber, 1954)

Barker, Ernest (ed.), *The Character of England* (Oxford: Clarendon Press, 1947)

Barker, Stephanie, Stefankai Spoerlein, Tobias Vetter and Wolfgang Viereck, *An Atlas of English Surnames* (Frankfurt am Main: Peter Lang, 2007)

Barnett, Lincoln, *The Treasure of Our Tongue* (London: Secker & Warburg, 1966)

Barnhart, David K., and Allan A. Metcalf, *America in So Many Words: Words That Have Shaped America* (Boston: Houghton Mifflin, 1997)

Barthes, Roland, *Empire of Signs*, trans. Richard Howard (London: Jonathan Cape, 1983)

Bateson, F. W., *English Poetry and the English Language* (Oxford: Clarendon Press, 1934)

Baugh, Albert C., and Thomas Cable, *A History of the English Language*, 5th edn (Upper Saddle River, NJ: Prentice Hall, 2002)

Bauman, Richard, *Let Your Words Be Few: Symbolism of Speaking and Silence among Seventeenth-Century Quakers* (Cambridge: Cambridge University Press, 1983)

Beckett, Katharine Scarfe, *Anglo-Saxon Perceptions of the Islamic World* (Cambridge: Cambridge University Press, 2003)

Beek, M. van, *An Enquiry into Puritan Vocabulary* (Groningen: Wolters-Noordhoff, 1969)

Beja, Morris, and Shari Benstock (eds.), *Coping with Joyce: Essays from the Copenhagen Symposium* (Columbus: Ohio State University Press, 1989)

Benedict, Barbara M., *Curiosity: A Cultural History of Early Modern Inquiry* (Chicago: University of Chicago Press, 2001)

Bennett, Betty T., and Stuart Curran (eds.), *Shelley: Poet and Legislator of the World* (Baltimore: Johns Hopkins University Press, 1996)

Bennett, Tony, Lawrence Grossberg and Meaghan Morris (eds.), *New Keywords: A Revised Vocabulary of Culture and Society* (Oxford: Blackwell, 2005)

Bense, J. F., *Anglo-Dutch Relations from the Earliest Times to the Death of William the Third* (The Hague: Martinus Nijhoff, 1925)

—— *A Dictionary of the Low-Dutch Element in the English Vocabulary* (Oxford: Oxford University Press, 1935)

Bentley, Harold W., *A Dictionary of Spanish Terms in English: With Special Reference to the American Southwest* (New York: Columbia University Press, 1932)

Berg, Maxine, *Luxury and Pleasure in Eighteenth-Century Britain* (Oxford: Oxford University Press, 2005)

Berger, Harris M., and Michael Thomas Carroll (eds.), *Global Pop, Local Language* (Jackson: University Press of Mississippi, 2003)

Birkett, Dea, *Spinsters Abroad: Victorian Lady Explorers* (London: Gollancz, 1991)

Bizup, Joseph, *Manufacturing Culture: Vindications of Early Victorian Industry* (Charlottesville: University of Virginia Press, 2003)

Bjorkman, Erik, *Scandinavian Loan-Words in Middle English* (Halle: Max Niemeyer, 1900)

Black, Jeremy, *Natural and Necessary Enemies: Anglo-French Relations in the Eighteenth Century* (London: Duckworth, 1986)

—— *The British Abroad: The Grand Tour in the Eighteenth Century* (Stroud: Alan Sutton, 1992)

Blake, N. F., *Caxton's Own Prose* (London: André Deutsch, 1973)

—— *The Language of Shakespeare* (Basingstoke: Macmillan, 1989)

—— *A History of the English Language* (Basingstoke: Macmillan, 1996)

Bliss, A. J., *A Dictionary of Foreign Words and Phrases in Current English* (London: Routledge, 1966)

Blondé, Bruno, Peter Stabel, Jon Stobart and Ilja Van Damme (eds.), *Buyers and Sellers: Retail Circuits and Practices in Medieval and Early Modern Europe* (Turnhout: Brepols, 2006)

Bloomer, W. Martin (ed.), *The Contest of Language: Before and Beyond Nationalism* (Notre Dame, Ind.: University of Notre Dame Press, 2005)

Bluestein, Gene, *Anglish–Yinglish: Yiddish in American Life and Literature* (Athens, Ga.: University of Georgia Press, 1989)

Bodmer, Frederick, *The Loom of Language*, ed. Lancelot Hogben (London: Allen & Unwin, 1943)

Boitani, Piero (ed.), *Chaucer and the Italian Trecento* (Cambridge: Cambridge University Press, 1983)

Bolinger, Dwight, and Donald A. Sears, *Aspects of Language*, 3rd edn (New York: Harcourt Brace Jovanovich, 1981)

Bolton, Kingsley, *Chinese Englishes: A Sociolinguistic History* (Cambridge: Cambridge University Press, 2003)

Bolton, W. F., *The Language of 1984* (Oxford: Blackwell, 1984)

Bolton, W. F., and David Crystal (eds.), *The English Language* (London: Penguin, 1993)

Booth, Martin, *Opium: A History* (London: Pocket Books, 1997)

Bosworth, C. E., *Medieval Arabic Culture and Administration* (London: Variorum Reprints, 1982)

Bovill, E. W., *The Golden Trade of the Moors*, 2nd edn (Oxford: Oxford University Press, 1968)

Bowers, Barbara S. (ed.), *The Medieval Hospital and Medical Practice* (Aldershot: Ashgate, 2007)

Boxer, C. R., *The Portuguese Seaborne Empire 1415–1825* (Manchester: Carcanet, 1991)

Bradley, Henry, *The Making of English* (London: Macmillan, 1904)

Bragg, Melvyn, *The Adventure of English* (London: Hodder & Stoughton, 2003)

Braudel, Fernand, *The Mediterranean and the Mediterranean World in the Age of Philip II*, trans. Siân Reynolds, abridged by Richard Ollard (London: HarperCollins, 1992)

—— *A History of Civilizations*, trans. Richard Mayne (London: Penguin, 1995)

Breeze, Andrew, 'Old English *Ealfara*, "Pack-Horse": A Spanish-Arabic Loanword', *Notes and Queries* 38 (1991), 15–17

—— '*Puffin*, A Loanword from Cornish', *Notes and Queries* 52 (2005), 172–3

Bremmer, Jan, and Herman Roodenburg (eds.), *A Cultural History of Gesture* (Cambridge: Polity, 1993)

Brewer, John, *The Pleasures of the Imagination: English Culture in the Eighteenth Century* (London: HarperCollins, 1997)

Brigden, Susan, *New Worlds, Lost Worlds: The Rule of the Tudors 1485–1603* (London: Allen Lane, 2000)

Brotton, Jerry, *Trading Territories: Mapping the Early Modern World* (London: Reaktion Books, 1997)

—— *The Renaissance Bazaar: From the Silk Road to Michelangelo* (Oxford: Oxford University Press, 2002)

Brown, Peter (ed.), *A Companion to Medieval English Literature and Culture* (Oxford: Blackwell, 2007)

Browne, Charles Barrett, *The Contribution of Greek to English* (Nashville: Vanderbilt University Press, 1942)

—— *The Contribution of Latin to English* (Nashville: Vanderbilt University Press, 1946)

Burchfield, Robert, *The English Language* (Oxford: Oxford University Press, 1985)

Burckhardt, Titus, *Moorish Culture in Spain*, trans. Alisa Jaffa and William Stoddart (Louisville, Ky.: Fons Vitae, 1999)

Burgess, Anthony, *A Mouthful of Air* (New York: Morrow, 1992)

Burke, Peter, and Roy Porter (eds.), *The Social History of Language* (Cambridge: Cambridge University Press, 1987)

—— —— *Language, Self, and Society: A Social History of Language* (Cambridge: Polity, 1991)

Burnley, David, *The Language of Chaucer* (Basingstoke: Macmillan, 1989)

—— *The History of the English Language: A Source Book*, 2nd edn (Harlow: Pearson Education, 2000)

Burridge, Kate, *Blooming English* (Cambridge: Cambridge University Press, 2004)

—— *Weeds in the Garden of Words: Further Observations on the Tangled History of the English Language* (Cambridge: Cambridge University Press, 2005)

Buruma, Ian, *Inventing Japan 1853–1964* (London: Weidenfeld & Nicolson, 2003)

Caie, Graham D., Carole Hough and Irené Wotherspoon (eds.), *The Power of Words: Essays in Lexicography, Lexicology and Semantics in Honour of Christian J. Kay* (Amsterdam: Rodopi, 2006)

Cannon, Christopher, *The Making of Chaucer's English: A Study of Words* (Cambridge: Cambridge University Press, 1998)

Cannon, Garland, *A History of the English Language* (New York: Harcourt Brace Jovanovich, 1972)

—— *Historical Change and English Word-Formation* (New York: Peter Lang, 1987)

—— *The Japanese Contributions to the English Language* (Wiesbaden: Harrassowitz Verlag, 1996)

—— 'Turkish and Persian Loans in English Literature', *Neophilologus* 84 (2000), 285–307

Cannon, Garland, and Alan S. Kaye, *The Arabic Contributions to the English Language* (Wiesbaden, Harrassowitz Verlag, 1994)

—— —— *The Persian Contributions to the English Language* (Wiesbaden: Harrassowitz Verlag, 2001)

Cannon, Garland, and Kevin R. Brine (eds.), *Objects of Enquiry: The Life, Contributions, and Influences of Sir William Jones (1746–1794)* (New York: New York University Press, 1995)

Canny, Nicholas, and Anthony Pagden (eds.), *Colonial Identity in the Atlantic World, 1500–1800* (Princeton: Princeton University Press, 1987)

Canup, John, *Out of the Wilderness: The Emergence of an American Identity in Colonial New England* (Middletown, Conn.: Wesleyan University Press, 1990)

Carolino, Pedro, *The New Guide of the Conversation in Portuguese and English* (Peking: privately published, 1869)

Carr, Charles T., *The German Influence on the English Vocabulary* (Oxford: Clarendon Press, 1934)

Cavalli-Sforza, Luigi Luca, *Genes, Peoples, and Languages*, trans. Mark Seielstad (London: Allen Lane, 2000)

Chambers, J. K., *Sociolinguistic Theory: Linguistic Variation and Its Social Significance*, 2nd edn (Oxford: Blackwell, 2003)

Chan, Mimi, and Helen Kwok, *A Study of Lexical Borrowing from Chinese into English with Special Reference to Hong Kong* (Hong Kong: Centre of Asian Studies, University of Hong Kong, 1985)

Chanda, Nayan, *Bound Together: How Traders, Preachers, Adventurers, and Warriors Shaped Globalization* (New Haven: Yale University Press, 2007)

Chang, Raymond, and Margaret Scrogin Chang, *Speaking of Chinese* (New York: W. W. Norton, 2001)

Chantrell, Glynnis (ed.), *The Oxford Dictionary of Word Histories* (Oxford: Oxford University Press, 2002)

Ch'ien, Evelyn Nien-Ming, *Weird English* (Cambridge, Mass.: Harvard University Press, 2004)

Claiborne, Robert, *The Life and Times of the English Language* (London: Bloomsbury, 1990)

Clanchy, M. T., *From Memory to Written Record: England 1066–1307*, 2nd edn (Oxford: Blackwell, 1993)

Clark, G. N., *The Dutch Influence on the English Vocabulary* (Oxford: Clarendon Press, 1935)

Clarke, Mary, and Clement Crisp, *The History of Dance* (London: Orbis, 1981)

Cochrane, Louise, *Adelard of Bath: The First English Scientist* (London: British Museum Press, 1994)

Cohen, Murray, *Sensible Words: Linguistic Practice in England 1640–1785* (Baltimore: Johns Hopkins University Press, 1977)

Cohen, Stephen, *The Language of Power, the Power of Language: The Effects of Ambiguity on Sociopolitical Structures as Illustrated in Shakespeare's Plays* (Cambridge, Mass.: Harvard University Press, 1987)

Colie, Rosalie L., *The Resources of Kind: Genre-Theory in the Renaissance*, ed. Barbara K. Lewalski (Berkeley: University of California Press, 1973)

Colley, Linda, *Britons: Forging the Nation 1707–1837* (New Haven: Yale University Press, 1992)

—— *Captives: Britain, Empire and the World, 1600–1850* (London: Jonathan Cape, 2002)

Collins, David, *Management Fads and Buzzwords: Critical-Practical Perspectives* (London: Routledge, 2000)

Connell, Evan S., *El Dorado and Other Pursuits* (London: Pimlico, 2002)

Conrad, Peter, *Modern Times, Modern Places: Life and Art in the 20th Century* (London: Thames and Hudson, 1998)

Constable, Olivia Remie, *Trade and Traders in Muslim Spain* (Cambridge: Cambridge University Press, 1994)

Corfield, Penelope J. (ed.), *Language, History and Class* (Oxford: Blackwell, 1991)

Corns, Thomas N., *A History of Seventeenth-Century English Literature* (Oxford: Blackwell, 2007)

Craigie, William A., *Northern Words in Modern English* (Oxford: Clarendon Press, 1937)

—— *The Growth of American English* (Oxford: Clarendon Press, 1940)

Crary, Jonathan, *Techniques of the Observer: On Vision and Modernity in the Nineteenth Century* (Cambridge, Mass.: MIT Press, 1990)

Crawford, James (ed.), *Language Loyalties: A Source Book on the Official English Controversy* (Chicago: University of Chicago Press, 1992)

Croft, William, *Explaining Language Change: An Evolutionary Approach* (Harlow: Longman, 2000)

Cronon, William, *Changes in the Land: Indians, Colonists, and the Ecology of New England* (New York: Hill & Wang, 1983)

Crozier, Justin, Cormac McKeown and Elspeth Summers, *I Smirt, You Stooze, They Krump . . .* (Glasgow: Collins, 2006)

Crystal, David, *The Cambridge Encyclopedia of Language*, 2nd edn (Cambridge: Cambridge University Press, 1997)

—— *Language and the Internet* (Cambridge: Cambridge University Press, 2001)

—— *The Cambridge Encyclopedia of the English Language* (Cambridge: Cambridge University Press, 2002)

—— *English as a Global Language*, 2nd edn (Cambridge: Cambridge University Press, 2003)

—— *The Language Revolution* (Cambridge: Polity, 2004)

—— *The Stories of English* (London: Allen Lane, 2004)

—— *How Language Works* (London: Penguin, 2005)

—— *By Hook or by Crook: A Journey in Search of English* (London: HarperPress, 2007)

—— (ed.), *Eric Partridge in His Own Words* (London: André Deutsch, 1980)

Crystal, David, and Ben Crystal, *Shakespeare's Words* (London: Penguin, 2002)

Cunliffe, Barry, *The Ancient Celts* (Oxford: Oxford University Press, 1997)

—— *Facing the Ocean: The Atlantic and Its Peoples 8000 BC–AD 1500* (Oxford: Oxford University Press, 2001)

Curtin, Michael, *Propriety and Position: A Study of Victorian Manners* (New York: Garland, 1987)

Cutler, Charles L., *O Brave New Words! Native American Loanwords in Current English* (Norman: University of Oklahoma Press, 1994)

Dalby, Andrew, *Dictionary of Languages* (London: Bloomsbury, 1998)

—— *Language in Danger* (London: Allen Lane, 2002)

Dalrymple, William, *White Mughals: Love and Betrayal in Eighteenth-Century India* (London: HarperCollins, 2002)

Daryush, A. A., *Persian Words in English* (Oxford: Clarendon Press, 1934)

Daston, Lorraine, and Katharine Park, *Wonders and the Order of Nature 1150–1750* (New York: Zone Books, 1998)

Davenport-Hines, Richard, *The Pursuit of Oblivion: A Social History of Drugs* (London: Weidenfeld & Nicolson, 2001)

Davies, Norman, *The Isles: A History* (London: Macmillan, 1999)

Davis, Ralph, *Aleppo and Devonshire Square: English Traders in the Levant in the Eighteenth Century* (London: Macmillan, 1967)

Dawes, James, *The Language of War: Literature and Culture in the U.S. from the Civil War through World War II* (Cambridge, Mass.: Harvard University Press, 2002)

Deardorff, Neva Ruth, *English Trade in the Baltic during the Reign of Elizabeth* (PhD thesis, University of Pennsylvania, 1911)

Den Otter, A. G., 'Lekker Scrabbling: Discovery and Exploration of Once-Dutch Words in the *Oxford English Dictionary*,' *English Studies* 71 (1990), 261–71

Dent, Susie, *The Language Report* (Oxford: Oxford University Press, 2003)
—— *Fanboys and Overdogs* (Oxford: Oxford University Press, 2005)
—— *Larpers and Shroomers* (Oxford: Oxford University Press, 2005)
—— *The Language Report* (Oxford: Oxford University Press, 2006)

Deroy, Louis, *L'Emprunt linguistique* (Paris: Société d'Edition 'Les Belles Lettres', 1956)

Dessalles, Jean-Louis, *Why We Talk: The Evolutionary Origins of Language*, trans. James Grieve (Oxford: Oxford University Press, 2007)

Deutscher, Guy, *The Unfolding of Language* (London: William Heinemann, 2005)

D'Israeli, Isaac, *Amenities of Literature* (London: Frederick Warne, 1867)

Dixon, R. M. W., *The Languages of Australia* (Cambridge: Cambridge University Press, 1980)

Dolan, Brian, *Exploring European Frontiers: British Travellers in the Age of Enlightenment* (Basingstoke: Macmillan, 2000)

Dowling, Linda, *Language and Decadence in the Victorian Fin de Siècle* (Princeton: Princeton University Press, 1986)

Drysdale, Helena, *Mother Tongues: Travels through Tribal Europe* (London: Picador, 2002)

Duff, Alexander, *New Era of the English Language and English Literature in India* (Edinburgh: John Johnstone, 1837)

Dunant, Sarah (ed.), *The War of the Words: The Political Correctness Debate* (London: Virago, 1994)

Easterling, Heather C., *Parsing the City: Jonson, Middleton, Dekker, and the City Comedy's London as Language* (New York: Routledge, 2007)

Echu, George, and Samuel Gyasi Obeng (eds.), *Africa Meets Europe: Language Contact in West Africa* (New York: Nova Science, 2004)

Ecott, Tim, *Vanilla: Travels in Search of a Luscious Substance* (London: Penguin, 2005)

Edwards, Griffith, *Alcohol: The Ambiguous Molecule* (London: Penguin, 2000)

Eichner, Hans (ed.), *'Romantic' and Its Cognates: The European History of a Word* (Toronto: University of Toronto Press, 1972)

Eisenstein, Elizabeth L., *The Printing Revolution in Early Modern Europe*, 2nd edn (Cambridge: Cambridge University Press, 2005)

Elias, Norbert, *The Civilizing Process*, trans. Edmund Jephcott, rev. edn (Oxford: Blackwell, 2000)

Elliott, J. H., *Empires of the Atlantic World: Britain and Spain in America 1492–1830* (New Haven: Yale University Press, 2006)

Ellis, Markman, *The Coffee-House: A Cultural History* (London: Phoenix, 2005)

Ellis, Steve (ed.), *Chaucer* (Oxford: Oxford University Press, 2005)

Emerson, Ralph Waldo, *English Traits*, ed. Douglas Emory Wilson (Cambridge, Mass.: Harvard University Press, 1994)

Empson, William, *The Structure of Complex Words* (London: Chatto & Windus, 1977)

Enright, D. J. (ed.), *Fair of Speech: The Uses of Euphemism* (Oxford: Oxford University Press, 1985)

Evans, Toshie M., *A Dictionary of Japanese Loanwords* (Westport, Conn.: Greenwood Press, 1997)

Farmer, John S. (ed.), *Americanisms – Old and New* (London: Thomas Poulter, 1889)

Farrington, Anthony, *Trading Places: The East India Company and Asia 1600–1834* (London: British Library, 2002)

Febvre, Lucien, and Henri-Jean Martin, *The Coming of the Book: The Impact of Printing 1450–1800*, trans. David Gerard, ed. Geoffrey Nowell-Smith and David Wootton (London: NLB, 1976)

Fedden, Robin, *English Travellers in the Near East* (London: British Council, 1958)

Fellheimer, Jeannette, 'The Section on Italy in the Elizabethan Translations of Giovanni Botero's *Relationi Universali*', *English Miscellany* 8 (1957), 289–306

Fennell, Barbara A., *A History of English: A Sociolinguistic Approach* (Oxford: Blackwell, 2001)

Ferguson, Niall, *Empire: How Britain Made the Modern World* (London: Allen Lane, 2003)

—— *The War of the World: History's Age of Hatred* (London: Allen Lane, 2006)

Fernández-Armesto, Felipe, *Pathfinders: A Global History of Exploration* (Oxford: Oxford University Press, 2006)

Filppula, Markku, Juhani Klemola and Heli Pitkanen (eds.), *The Celtic Roots of English* (Joensuu: University of Joensuu, Faculty of Humanities, 2002)

Finegan, Edward, and John R. Rickford (eds.), *Language in the USA: Themes for the Twenty-first Century* (Cambridge: Cambridge University Press, 2004)

Finkenstaedt, Thomas, and Dieter Wolff, *Ordered Profusion: Studies in Dictionaries and the English Lexicon* (Heidelberg: Carl Winter, 1973)

Finkenstaedt, Thomas, Ernst Leisi and Dieter Wolff, *A Chronological English Dictionary* (Heidelberg: Carl Winter, 1970)

Finney, Gretchen Ludke, *Musical Backgrounds for English Literature: 1580–1650* (New Brunswick, NJ: Rutgers University Press, 1961)

Fischer, David Hackett, *Albion's Seed: Four British Folkways in America* (Oxford: Oxford University Press, 1989)

Fisher, John H., *The Importance of Chaucer* (Carbondale: Southern Illinois University Press, 1992)

Flavell, Linda and Roger, *The Chronology of Words and Phrases* (London: Kyle Cathie, 1999)

—— *Dictionary of Word Origins* (London: Kyle Cathie, 2004)

Fletcher, Richard, *Moorish Spain* (London: Weidenfeld & Nicolson, 1992)

—— *The Cross and the Crescent: The Dramatic Story of the Earliest Encounters between Christians and Muslims* (London: Penguin, 2004)

Flexner, Stuart Berg, *I Hear America Talking: An Illustrated Treasury of American Words and Phrases* (New York: Van Nostrand Reinhold, 1976)

Foss, Michael, *Undreamed Shores: England's Wasted Empire in America* (London: Harrap, 1974)

Francis, J. H., *From Caxton to Carlyle: A Study of the Development of Language, Composition and Style in English Prose* (Cambridge: Cambridge University Press, 1937)

Francis, Richard, *Judge Sewall's Apology* (London: Fourth Estate, 2005)

Franklin, Michael J. (ed.), *Romantic Representations of British India* (Abingdon: Routledge, 2006)

Freeborn, Dennis, *From Old English to Standard English: A Course Book in Language Variation across Time*, 3rd edn (Basingstoke: Palgrave Macmillan, 2006)

Fulford, Tim, and Peter J. Kitson (gen. eds.), *Travels, Explorations and Empires: Writings from the Era of Imperial Expansion 1770–1835*, 6 vols. (London: Pickering & Chatto, 2001)

Funk, Wilfred, *Word Origins and Their Romantic Stories* (New York: Wilfred Funk, 1950)

Furnham, Adrian, *The Psychology of Managerial Incompetence: A Sceptic's Dictionary of Modern Organizational Issues* (London: Whurr, 1998)

Gabb, Alfred D. F., *1600–1947 Anglo-Indian Legacy*, 2nd edn (York: Quacks, 2000)

Galenson, David W., *Traders, Planters, and Slaves: Market Behaviour in Early English America* (Cambridge: Cambridge University Press, 1986)

Games, Alex, *Balderdash and Piffle* (London: BBC Books, 2006)

Geipel, John, *The Viking Legacy* (Newton Abbot: David & Charles, 1971)

Gharaybeh, Abdul-Karim Mahmud, *English Traders in Syria 1744–1791* (PhD thesis, London University, 1950)

Gilbert, A. J., *Literary Language from Chaucer to Johnson* (London: Macmillan, 1979)

Gilman, Richard, *Decadence: The Strange Life of an Epithet* (London: Secker & Warburg, 1979)

Gilmour, David, *The Ruling Caste: Imperial Lives in the Victorian Raj* (London: John Murray, 2005)

Gimpel, Jean, *The Medieval Machine: The Industrial Revolution of the Middle Ages*, 2nd edn (Aldershot: Wildwood House, 1988)

Glick, Thomas F., *Islamic and Christian Spain in the Early Middle Ages*, 2nd edn (Leiden: Brill, 2005)

Goatly, Andrew, *Washing the Brain – Metaphor and Hidden Ideology* (Amsterdam: John Benjamins, 2007)

Goitein, S. D. (ed.), *Letters of Medieval Jewish Traders* (Princeton: Princeton University Press, 1973)

Gonzalez, Felix Rodriguez (ed.), *Spanish Loanwords in the English Language* (Berlin: Mouton de Gruyter, 1996)

Görlach, Manfred, *New Studies in the History of English* (Heidelberg: Winter, 1995)

—— *English in Nineteenth-Century England: An Introduction* (Cambridge: Cambridge University Press, 1999)

—— *Eighteenth-Century English* (Heidelberg: Winter, 2001)

—— *Explorations in English Historical Linguistics* (Heidelberg: Winter, 2002)

Gorrell, Robert, *What's in a Word?* (Reno: University of Nevada Press, 2001)

Goulding, Christopher, 'Robot: Antedating the Entry in the *Oxford English Dictionary*', *Notes and Queries* 52 (2005), 380–81

Graddol, David, *The Future of English?* (London: British Council, 1997)

—— *English Next* (London: British Council, 2006)

Graddol, David, Dick Leith and Joan Swann (eds.), *English: History, Diversity and Change* (London: Routledge, 1996)

Green, Lisa J., *African American English: A Linguistic Introduction* (Cambridge: Cambridge University Press, 2002)

Greenblatt, Stephen, *Will in the World: How Shakespeare Became Shakespeare* (London: Jonathan Cape, 2004)

—— *Renaissance Self-Fashioning: From More to Shakespeare* (Chicago: University of Chicago Press, 2005)

Greenough, James B., and George L. Kittredge, *Words and Their Ways in English Speech* (New York: Macmillan, 1961)

Griffiths, Jane, *John Skelton and Poetic Authority: Defining the Liberty to Speak* (Oxford: Clarendon Press, 2006)

Grimes, William (ed.), *Eating Your Words* (Oxford: Oxford University Press, 2004)

Groom, Bernard, *A Short History of English Words* (London: Macmillan, 1934)

Gungwu, Wang, *Anglo-Chinese Encounters since 1800* (Cambridge: Cambridge University Press, 2003)

Hackett, Helen, *Virgin Mother, Maiden Queen: Elizabeth I and the Cult of the Virgin Mary* (Basingstoke: Macmillan, 1995)

Hair, P. E. H., and J. D. Alsop, *English Seamen and Traders in Guinea 1553–1565: The New Evidence of Their Wills* (Lampeter: Edwin Mellen, 1992)

Hale, John K., *Milton's Languages* (Cambridge: Cambridge University Press, 1997)

Hankin, Nigel, *Hanklyn-Janklin* (New Delhi: India Research Press, 2003)

Harbus, Antonina, and Russell Poole (eds.), *Verbal Encounters: Anglo-Saxon and Old Norse Studies for Roberta Frank* (Toronto: University of Toronto Press, 2005)

Harper, M. J., *The History of Britain Revealed* (London: Nathan Carmody, 2002)

Harvey, L. P., *Islamic Spain, 1250 to 1500* (Chicago: University of Chicago Press, 1990)

Helgerson, Richard, *Forms of Nationhood: The Elizabethan Writing of England* (Chicago: University of Chicago Press, 1992)

Heller, Louis, Alexander Humez and Malcah Dror, *The Private Lives of English Words* (London: Routledge, 1984)

Henke, James T., *Gutter Life and Language in the Early 'Street' Literature of England* (West Cornwall, Conn.: Locust Hill Press, 1988)

Herndon, Melvin, *Tobacco in Colonial Virginia* (Williamsburg, Va.: Virginia 350th Anniversary Celebration Corporation, 1957)

Herrick, James A., *The Making of the New Spirituality* (Downers Grove, Ill.: InterVarsity Press, 2003)

Hewson, John, *The French Language in Canada* (Munich: LINCOM EUROPA, 2000)

Hickey, Raymond (ed.), *Legacies of Colonial English* (Cambridge: Cambridge University Press, 2004)

Hill, Christopher, *God's Englishman: Oliver Cromwell and the English Revolution* (London: Weidenfeld & Nicolson, 1970)

Hill, Christopher, and Edmund Dell (eds.), *The Good Old Cause: The English Revolution of 1640–1660* (London: Lawrence & Wishart, 1949)

Hill, Geoffrey, *The Enemy's Country: Words, Contexture, and Other Circumstances of Language* (Stanford: Stanford University Press, 1991)

Hilton, Christopher, *Mayflower: The Voyage That Changed the World* (Stroud: Sutton, 2005)

Hine, Thomas, *The Rise and Fall of the American Teenager* (New York: Bard, 1999)

Hobsbawm, Eric, *Age of Extremes: The Short Twentieth Century 1914–1991* (London: Michael Joseph, 1994)

Hoffer, Peter Charles, *Sensory Worlds in Early America* (Baltimore: Johns Hopkins University Press, 2003)

Hogg, Richard (gen. ed.), *The Cambridge History of the English Language*, 6 vols. (Cambridge: Cambridge University Press, 1992–2001)

Hogg, Richard, and David Denison (eds.), *A History of the English Language* (Cambridge: Cambridge University Press, 2006)

Holloway, Joseph E., and Winifred K. Vass, *The African Heritage of American English* (Bloomington: Indiana University Press, 1993)

Holmes, Richard, *Coleridge* (Oxford: Oxford University Press, 1982)

—— *Coleridge: Early Visions* (London: Hodder & Stoughton, 1989)

Hoobler, Dorothy and Thomas, *Captain John Smith: Jamestown and the Birth of the American Dream* (Hoboken, NJ: Wiley 2006)

Hood, John, *Selling the Dream: Why Advertising is Good Business* (Westport, Conn.: Praeger, 2005)

Hope, T. E., 'Loanwords as Cultural and Lexical Symbols', *Archivum Linguisticum* 14 (1962), 111–21

Horobin, Simon, *Chaucer's Language* (Basingstoke: Palgrave Macmillan, 2007)

Horsman, E. A., 'Dryden's French Borrowings', *Review of English Studies* 1 (1950), 346–51

Hourani, Albert, *A History of the Arab Peoples* (London: Faber, 2005)

Housley, Norman, *Contesting the Crusades* (Oxford: Blackwell, 2006)

Howard, Clare, *English Travellers of the Renaissance* (London: John Lane, 1914)

Hudson, Kenneth, *The Jargon of the Professions* (London: Macmillan, 1978)

Hug, Sibylle, *Scandinavian Loanwords and Their Equivalents in Middle English* (Bern: Peter Lang, 1987)

Hughes, Geoffrey, *Words in Time* (Oxford: Blackwell, 1988)

—— *A History of English Words* (Oxford: Blackwell, 1999)

Hughes, Robert, *The Fatal Shore* (London: Collins Harvill, 1987)

Hulme, Hilda M., *Explorations in Shakespeare's Language* (London: Longman, 1962)

Hume, Ivor Noel, *The Virginia Adventure* (Charlottesville: University of Virginia Press, 1997)

Hunt, Tristram, *Building Jerusalem: The Rise and Fall of the Victorian City* (London: Weidenfeld & Nicolson, 2004)

Hyam, Ronald, *Britain's Imperial Century, 1815–1914*, 3rd edn (Basingstoke: Palgrave Macmillan, 2002)

Isaac, I.A., *The Orients: Pioneers of Western Sciences and Civilization* (Balugaon: privately published, 1926)

Isaac, Rhys, *The Transformation of Virginia 1740–1790* (Chapel Hill: University of North Carolina Press, 1982)

Islam, Sirajul, *The Permanent Settlement in Bengal: A Study of Its Operation 1790–1819* (Dacca: Bangla Academy, 1979)

Israel, Jonathan I., *The Dutch Republic: Its Rise, Greatness, and Fall, 1477–1806* (Oxford: Clarendon Press, 1998)

—— (ed.), *The Anglo-Dutch Moment: Essays on the Glorious Revolution and Its World Impact* (Cambridge: Cambridge University Press, 1991)

Jackson, Kenneth, *Language and History in Early Britain* (Dublin: Four Courts Press, 1994)

Jacoby, David, *Trade, Commodities and Shipping in the Medieval Mediterranean* (Aldershot: Variorum, 1997)

James, Lawrence, *The Rise and Fall of the British Empire* (London: Little, Brown, 1994)

—— *Raj: The Making and Unmaking of British India* (London: Little, Brown, 1997)

—— *The Middle Class: A History* (London: Little, Brown, 2006)

Jameson, Fredric, *The Prison-House of Language* (Princeton: Princeton University Press, 1972)

Jardine, Lisa, *Worldly Goods* (London: Macmillan, 1996)

Jendli, Adel, Salah Troudi and Christine Coombe (eds.), *The Power of Language: Perspectives from Arabia* (Dubai: TESOL Arabia, 2007)

Jennings, Francis, *The Invasion of America: Indians, Colonialism and the Cant of Conquest* (Chapel Hill: University of North Carolina Press, 1975)

—— *The Founders of America* (New York: W. W. Norton, 1993)

Jespersen, Otto, *Growth and Structure of the English Language*, 10th edn (Oxford: Blackwell, 1982)

Jones, Richard Foster, *The Triumph of the English Language* (London: Oxford University Press, 1953)

Joos, Martin, *The Five Clocks* (Bloomington: Indiana University Research Centre in Anthropology, Folklore, and Linguistics, 1962)

Judt, Tony, *Postwar: A History of Europe since 1945* (London: Pimlico, 2007)

Kachru, Braj B., *The Alchemy of English* (Oxford: Pergamon, 1986)

Karkov, Catherine E., and Nicholas Howe (eds.), *Conversion and Colonization in Anglo-Saxon England* (Tempe, Ariz.: Arizona Center for Medieval and Renaissance Studies, 2006)

Kastovsky, Dieter, and Arthur Mettinger (eds.), *The History of English in Social Context* (Berlin: Mouton de Gruyter, 2000)

Keay, John, *The Honourable Company: A History of the English East India Company* (London: HarperCollins, 1991)

Kemal, Salim, and Ivan Gaskell (eds.), *The Language of Art History* (Cambridge: Cambridge University Press, 1991)

Kemp, Martin, *The Science of Art* (New Haven: Yale University Press, 1990)

Kennedy, Paul, *The Rise and Fall of the Great Powers* (London: Fontana, 1989)

Keys, David, *Catastrophe: An Investigation into the Origins of the Modern World* (London: Century, 1999)

Kitzes, Adam H., *The Politics of Melancholy from Spenser to Milton* (London: Routledge, 2006)

Klinge, Markus, 'Milton's Balcony in *Areopagitica*, II, 524', *Notes and Queries* 52 (2005), 298–304

Knapp, Peggy A., *Time-Bound Words: Semantic and Social Economies from Chaucer's England to Shakespeare's* (Basingstoke: Macmillan, 2000)

Knoppers, Laura Lunger (ed.), *Puritanism and Its Discontents* (Newark: University of Delaware Press, 2003)

Kochman, Thomas (ed.), *Rappin' and Stylin' Out: Communication in Urban Black America* (Urbana: University of Illinois Press, 1972)

Köprülü, Mehmed Fuad, *The Seljuks of Anatolia: Their History and Culture according to Local Muslim Sources*, trans. and ed. Gary Leiser (Salt Lake City: University of Utah Press, 1992)

Kövecses, Zoltán, *American English: An Introduction* (Peterborough, Ont.: Broadview Press, 2000)

Kurlansky, Mark, *Cod: A Biography of the Fish That Changed the World* (London: Jonathan Cape, 1998)

Kuskin, William (ed.), *Caxton's Trace: Studies in the History of English Printing* (Notre Dame, Ind.: University of Notre Dame Press, 2006)

Labarge, Margaret Wade, *Medieval Travellers: The Rich and Restless* (London: Hamish Hamilton, 1982)

Laird, Charlton, *Language in America* (Englewood Cliffs, NJ: Prentice-Hall, 1970)

Langford, Paul, *A Polite and Commercial People: England 1727–1783* (Oxford: Oxford University Press, 1992)

Lannering, Jan, *Studies in the Prose Style of Joseph Addison* (Uppsala: Appelbergs Boktryckeri, 1951)

Large, J. A., *The Foreign-Language Barrier: Problems in Scientific Communication* (London: André Deutsch, 1983)

Lass, Roger, *The Shape of English: Structure and History* (London: J. M. Dent, 1987)

Law, John E., and Lene Ostermark-Johansen (eds.), *Victorian and Edwardian Responses to the Italian Renaissance* (Aldershot: Ashgate, 2005)

Leech, Geoffrey N., *English in Advertising: A Linguistic Study of Advertising in Great Britain* (London: Longmans, 1966)

Leith, Dick, *A Social History of English*, 2nd edn (London: Routledge, 1997)

Lepore, Jill, *A is for American: Letters and Other Characters in the Newly United States* (New York: Knopf, 2002)

—— 'Noah's Mark: Webster and the Original Dictionary Wars', *New Yorker*, 6 November 2006, 78–87

Lerer, Seth, *Inventing English: A Portable History of the Language* (New York: Columbia University Press, 2007)

—— (ed.), *The Yale Companion to Chaucer* (New Haven: Yale University Press, 2006)

Leur, J. C. van, *Indonesian Trade and Society: Essays in Social and Economic History*, 2nd edn (Bandung: Sumur Bandung, 1960)

Lewis, Bernard, *From Babel to Dragomans: Interpreting the Middle East* (London: Phoenix, 2005)

Lewis, C. S., *Studies in Words*, 2nd edn (Cambridge University Press, 1967)

Lidburg, I. S., *Fashion in Language* (London: privately published, 1906)

Lieberman, Anatoly, *Word Origins . . . and How We Know Them* (Oxford: Oxford University Press, 2005)

Lieberman, Philip, *Eve Spoke: Human Language and Human Evolution* (London: Picador, 1998)

Litzenberg, Karl, *The Victorians and the Vikings: A Bibliographical Essay on Anglo-Norse Literary Relations* (Ann Arbor: University of Michigan Press, 1947)

Longaker, Mark Garrett, *Rhetoric and the Republic: Politics, Civic Discourse, and Education in Early America* (Tuscaloosa: University of Alabama Press, 2007)

Lopez, Robert S., and Irving W. Raymond (eds.), *Medieval Trade in the Mediterranean World: Illustrative Documents* (New York: Columbia University Press, 2001)

Lyovin, Anatole V., *An Introduction to the Languages of the World* (New York: Oxford University Press, 1997)

Macalister, John, 'The Maori Presence in the New Zealand English Lexicon, 1850–2000', *English World-Wide* 27 (2006), 1–24

McArthur, Tom, *Oxford Guide to World English* (Oxford: Oxford University Press, 2003)

—— (ed.), *The Oxford Companion to the English Language* (Oxford: Oxford University Press, 1992)

MacCarthy, Fiona, *Byron: Life and Legend* (London: Faber, 2003)

McCrum, Robert, William Cran, and Robert MacNeil, *The Story of English*, 3rd edn (London: Faber, 2002)

McElderry, Bruce R., 'Archaism and Innovation in Spenser's Poetic Diction', *Publications of the Modern Language Association of America* 47 (1932), 144–70

MacGillivray, H. S., *The Influence of Christianity on the Vocabulary of Old English* (Halle: Max Niemeyer, 1902)

Machan, Tim William, and Charles T. Scott (eds.), *English in Its Social Contexts: Essays in Historical Sociolinguistics* (New York: Oxford University Press, 1992)

Mack, Rosamond E., *Bazaar to Piazza: Islamic Trade and Italian Art, 1300–1600* (Berkeley: University of California Press, 2002)

McKelvy, William R., *The English Cult of Literature: Devoted Readers, 1774–1880* (Charlottesville: University of Virginia Press, 2007)

Mackenzie, Fraser, *Les Relations de l'Angleterre et de la France d'après le vocabulaire*, 2 vols. (Paris: E. Droz, 1939)

McWhorter, John, *The Power of Babel: A Natural History of Language* (London: William Heinemann, 2002)

Mahal, Baljinder K., *The Queen's Hinglish* (Glasgow: Collins, 2006)

Maher, J. Peter, *Creation and Tradition in Language* (Amsterdam: John Benjamins, 1977)

Mair, Christian, *Twentieth-Century English: History, Variation, and Standardization* (Cambridge: Cambridge University Press, 2006)

Mak, Geert, *Amsterdam: A Brief Life of the City*, trans. Philipp Blom (London: Harvill, 1999)

Malamud, Randy, *The Language of Modernism* (Ann Arbor: UMI Research Press, 1989)

Maleska, Eugene T., *A Pleasure in Words*, ed. Hugh Young (London: Hamish Hamilton, 1983)

Maltby, Richard (ed.), *Dreams for Sale: Popular Culture in the 20th Century* (London: Harrap, 1989)

Mancall, Peter C., *Hakluyt's Promise: An Elizabethan's Obsession for an English America* (New Haven: Yale University Press, 2007)

Mandler, Peter, *The English National Character: The History of an Idea from Edmund Burke to Tony Blair* (New Haven: Yale University Press, 2006)

Mantero, Miguel (ed.), *Identity and Second Language Learning* (Charlotte, NC: Information Age, 2007)

Marckwardt, Albert H., *American English*, 2nd ed., rev. J. L. Dillard (Oxford: Oxford University Press, 1980)

Marsh, Joss, *Blasphemy, Culture, and Literature in Nineteenth-Century England* (Chicago: University of Chicago Press, 1998)

Marshall, Jeremy, and Fred McDonald (eds.), *Questions of English* (Oxford: Oxford University Press, 1994)

Massingham, Hugh and Pauline, *The Englishman Abroad* (Gloucester: Alan Sutton, 1984)

Matar, Nabil, *Islam in Britain 1558–1685* (Cambridge: Cambridge University Press, 1998)

—— *Turks, Moors, and Englishmen in the Age of Discovery* (New York: Columbia University Press, 1999)

Matras, Yaron (ed.), *The Romani Element in Non-Standard Speech* (Wisebaden: Harrassowitz Verlag, 1998)

Matthews, Brander, *The Englishing of French Words* (Oxford: Clarendon Press, 1921)

Maurais, Jacques, and Michael A. Morris (eds.), *Languages in a Globalising World* (Cambridge: Cambridge University Press, 2003)

Mellinkoff, David, *The Language of the Law* (Boston: Little, Brown, 1963)

Mencken, H. L., *The American Language*, 4th edn (New York: Knopf, 1963)

Metcalf, Allan, *The World in So Many Words* (Boston: Houghton Mifflin, 1999)

Michaels, Leonard, and Christopher Ricks (eds.), *The State of the Language* (Berkeley: University of California Press, 1980)

Miles, David, *The Tribes of Britain* (London: Phoenix, 2006)

Miller, Lee, *Roanoke: Solving The Mystery of England's Lost Colony* (London: Jonathan Cape, 2000)

Millward, C. M., *A Biography of the English Language*, 2nd edn (Orlando: Harcourt Brace, 1996)

Milton, Giles, *The Riddle and the Knight: In Search of Sir John Mandeville* (London: Alison & Busby, 1996)

—— *Nathaniel's Nutmeg: How One Man's Courage Changed the Course of History* (London: Hodder & Stoughton, 1999)

—— *Big Chief Elizabeth: How England's Adventurers Gambled and Won the New World* (London: Hodder & Stoughton, 2000)

—— *Samurai William: The Adventurer Who Unlocked Japan* (London: Hodder & Stoughton, 2002)

Mitchell, Sally (ed.), *Victorian Britain: An Encyclopedia* (New York: Garland, 1988)

Monmonier, Mark, *From Squaw Tit to Whorehouse Meadow: How Maps Name, Claim, and Inflame* (Chicago: University of Chicago Press, 2006)

Moore, John, *You English Words* (London: Collins, 1961)

Morgan, Marjorie, *National Identities and Travel in Victorian Britain* (Basingstoke: Palgrave, 2001)

Morton, Timothy, *The Poetics of Spice: Romantic Consumerism and the Exotic* (Cambridge: Cambridge University Press, 2000)

Mufwene, Salikoko S., John R. Rickford, Guy Bailey and John Baugh (eds.), *African-American English: Structure, History, and Use* (London: Routledge, 1998)

Mugglestone, Lynda, *Lost for Words: The Hidden History of the Oxford English Dictionary* (New Haven: Yale University Press, 2005)

—— (ed.), *The Oxford History of English* (Oxford: Oxford University Press, 2006)

Mullan, John, *Sentiment and Sociability: The Language of Feeling in the Eighteenth Century* (Oxford: Clarendon Press, 1990)

Nash, Walter, *Jargon: Its Uses and Abuses* (Oxford: Blackwell, 1993)

Needham, Joseph, *The Grand Titration: Science and Society in East and West* (London: Allen & Unwin, 1969)

Nettle, Daniel, *Linguistic Diversity* (Oxford: Oxford University Press, 1999)

Nicholl, Charles, *The Creature in the Map* (New York: Morrow, 1995)

Nichols, Pierrepont H., 'Chaucer's Influence on the Aureate Terms of the Scottish Chaucerians', *Publications of the Modern Language Association of America* 47 (1932), 516–22

Nicolson, Adam, *Power and Glory: Jacobean England and the Making of the King James Bible* (London: HarperCollins, 2003)

Nielsen, Hans F., and Lene Schosler (eds.), *The Origins and Development of Emigrant Languages* (Odense: Odense University Press, 1996)

Ogée, Frédéric (ed.), *'Better in France?' The Circulation of Ideas across the Channel in the Eighteenth Century* (Lewisburg, Pa.: Bucknell University Press, 2005)

Olsen, K. E., A. Harbus and T. Hofstra (eds.), *Germanic Texts and Latin Models: Medieval Reconstructions* (Leuven: Peeters, 2001)

Onions, C. T. (ed.), *The Oxford Dictionary of Etymology* (Oxford: Clarendon Press, 1966)

Oropeza, Ruben, *Between Puffs: A History of Tobacco* (Orlando, Fla.: Rivercross, 2005)

Orr, John, *The Impact of French upon English* (Oxford: Clarendon Press, 1948)

Osborne, Edna, *Oriental Diction and Theme in English Verse, 1740–1840* (Lawrence: University of Kansas, 1916)

Ostler, Nicholas, *Empires of the Word: A Language History of the World* (London: HarperCollins, 2005)

Oueijan, Naji B., *A Compendium of Eastern Elements in Byron's Oriental Tales* (New York: Peter Lang, 1999)

Pagden, Anthony, *Peoples and Empires* (London: Weidenfeld & Nicolson, 2001)

Page, Norman (ed.), *The Language of Literature* (Basingstoke: Macmillan, 1984)

Pakenham, Thomas, *The Scramble for Africa* (London: Weidenfeld & Nicolson, 1991)

Parry, Albert, 'On "Aesopian" Language and Borrowings from Russian', *American Speech* 25 (1950), 190–96

Partridge, Eric, *Slang: Today and Yesterday* (London: Routledge, 1933)

—— *Words at War, Words at Peace* (London: Frederick Muller, 1948)

Paxman, Jeremy, *The English: A Portrait of a People* (London: Michael Joseph, 1998)

Pei, Mario, *The Story of the English Language* (London: Allen & Unwin, 1968)

Pennanen, Esko V., *On The Introduction of French Loan-Words into English* (Tampere: Tampereen Yliopisto, 1971)

Pennycook, Alastair, *Global English and Transcultural Flows* (Abingdon: Routledge, 2007)

Perloff, Marjorie, *Differentials: Poetry, Poetics, Pedagogy* (Tuscaloosa: University of Alabama Press, 2004)

Perreault, Melanie, *Early English Encounters in Russia, West Africa, and the Americas, 1530–1614* (Lampeter: Edwin Mellen, 2004)

Pfeffer, J. Alan, 'German Political Loanwords in English', *Germanic Notes and Reviews* 30 (1999), 153–63

Phillips, K. C., *Language and Class in Victorian England* (Oxford: Blackwell, 1984)

Phillipson, Robert, *Linguistic Imperialism* (Oxford: Oxford University Press, 1992)

Pinnavaia, Laura, *The Italian Borrowings in the Oxford English Dictionary* (Rome: Bulzoni, 2001)

Pons-Sanz, Sara M., *Norse-Derived Vocabulary in Late Old English Texts* (Odense: University Press of Southern Denmark, 2007)

Poole, Steven, *Unspeak* (London: Abacus, 2007)

Power, Eileen, and M. M. Postan (eds.), *Studies in English Trade in the Fifteenth Century* (London: Routledge, 1933)

Prasad, Ram Chandra, *Early English Travellers in India* (Delhi: Motilal Banarsidass, 1980)

Praz, Mario, *The Romantic Agony*, 2nd edn (London: Oxford University Press, 1951)

—— *The Flaming Heart* (Garden City, NY: Doubleday, 1958)

Price, Glanville, *The Languages of Britain* (London: Edward Arnold, 1984)

—— (ed.), *Languages in Britain and Ireland* (Oxford: Blackwell, 2000)

Price, H. T., *Foreign Influences on Middle English* (Ann Arbor: University of Michigan Press, 1947)

Prins, A. A., *French Influence in English Phrasing* (Leiden: Universitaire Pers Leiden, 1952)

Quinion, Michael, *Gallimaufry: A Hodgepodge of Our Vanishing Vocabulary* (Oxford: Oxford University Press, 2006)

Quinn, David Beers (ed.), *The Roanoke Voyages 1584–1590*, 2 vols. (London: Hakluyt Society, 1955)

Rawson, Hugh, *A Dictionary of Euphemisms and Other Doubletalk* (London: Macdonald, 1981)

Redford, Bruce, *The Converse of the Pen: Acts of Intimacy in the Eighteenth-Century Familiar Letter* (Chicago: University of Chicago Press, 1986)

Rees, Joan, *Samuel Daniel: A Critical and Biographical Study* (Liverpool: Liverpool University Press, 1964)

Regenos, Graydon W., 'Latin Words in Current English', *Classical Journal* 48 (1952), 85–108

Restall, Matthew, *Seven Myths of the Spanish Conquest* (Oxford: Oxford University Press, 2003)

Riesman, David, *The Lonely Crowd: A Study of the Changing American Character* (New Haven: Yale University Press, 1950)

Roberts, Jane, and Janet L. Nelson (eds.), *Alfred the Wise: Studies in Honour of Janet Bately on the Occasion of Her Sixty-fifth Birthday* (Cambridge: D. S. Brewer, 1997)

Roesdahl, Else, *The Vikings*, trans. Susan M. Margeson and Kirsten Williams, 2nd edn (London: Penguin, 1998)

Romaine, Suzanne, *Bilingualism*, 2nd edn (Oxford: Blackwell, 1995)

Ross, Alan S. C., *Etymology* (London: André Deutsch, 1958)

Rosten, Leo, *Hooray for Yiddish!* (London: Elm Tree Books, 1983)

Roth, Cecil, *A History of the Jews in England*, 3rd edn (Oxford: Clarendon Press, 1964)

Rothwell, W., 'The Missing Link in English Etymology: Anglo-French', *Medium Aevum* 60 (1991), 173–96

—— 'The Legacy of Anglo-French: *faux amis* in French and English', *Zeitschrift für romanische Philologie* 109 (1993), 16–46

—— 'Arrivals and Departures: The Adoption of French Terminology into Middle English', *English Studies* 79 (1998), 144–65

—— 'Sugar and Spice and All Things Nice: From Oriental Bazar to English Cloister in Anglo-French', *Modern Language Review* 94 (1999), 647–59

Rowan, David, *A Glossary for the 90s* (London: Prion, 1998)

Safire, William, *On Language* (New York: Times Books, 1980)

Said, Edward, *Culture and Imperialism* (London: Chatto & Windus, 1993)

—— *Orientalism* (London: Penguin, 2003)

St George, Andrew, *The Descent of Manners: Etiquette, Rules and the Victorians* (London: Chatto & Windus, 1993)

Salaman, Redcliffe N., *The History and Social Influence of the Potato*, ed. J. G. Hawkes (Cambridge: Cambridge University Press, 1985)

Sale, Kirkpatrick, *The Conquest of Paradise: Christopher Columbus and the Columbian Legacy* (London: Hodder & Stoughton, 1991)

Salmon, Vivian, *Language and Society in Early Modern England* (Amsterdam: John Benjamins, 1996)

Salzman, L. F., *English Trade in the Middle Ages* (Oxford: Clarendon Press, 1931)

Sandbrook, Dominic, *Never Had It So Good: A History of Britain from Suez to the Beatles* (London: Little, Brown, 2005)

—— *White Heat: A History of Britain in the Swinging Sixties* (London: Little, Brown, 2006)

Sassoon, Donald, *The Culture of the Europeans from 1800 to the Present* (London: HarperCollins, 2006)

Sauer, Hans, and Renate Bauer (eds.), *Beowulf and Beyond* (Frankfurt am Main: Peter Lang, 2007)

Sawyer, Peter, *Scandinavians and the English in the Viking Age* (Cambridge: University of Cambridge, Department of Anglo-Saxon, Norse, and Celtic, 1995)

Schaefer, Ursula (ed.), *The Beginnings of Standardization: Language and Culture in Fourteenth-Century England* (Frankfurt am Main: Peter Lang, 2006)

Schama, Simon, *The Embarrassment of Riches: An Interpretation of Dutch Culture in the Golden Age* (London: Collins, 1987)

Schlauch, Margaret, *The Gift of Tongues* (London: Allen & Unwin, 1943)

Scott, Jonathan, *England's Troubles: Seventeenth-Century English Political Instability in European Context* (Cambridge: Cambridge University Press, 2000)

Sen, Amartya, *The Argumentative Indian: Writings on Indian Culture, History and Identity* (London: Allen Lane, 2005)

Serjeantson, Mary S., *A History of Foreign Words in English* (London: Kegan Paul, Trench, Trubner & Co., 1935)

Setright, L. J. K., *Drive On! A Social History of the Motor Car* (London: Granta, 2003)

Shapiro, James, *1599: A Year in the Life of William Shakespeare* (London: Faber, 2005)

Sheard, J. A., *The Words We Use* (London: André Deutsch, 1954)

Sinha, S. P., *English in India: A Historical Study with Particular Reference to English Education in India* (Patna: Janaki Prakashan, 1978)

Smit, Ute, Stefan Dollinger, Julia Hüttner, Gunther Kaltenböck and Ursula Lutzky (eds.), *Tracing English through Time* (Vienna: Braumüller, 2007)

Smith, Bruce R., *The Acoustic World of Early Modern England* (Chicago: University of Chicago Press, 1999)

Smith, G. Gregory (ed.), *Elizabethan Critical Essays*, 2 vols. (Oxford: Clarendon Press, 1904)

Smith, Jeremy, *An Historical Study of English: Function, Form and Change* (London: Routledge, 1996)

Smith, Logan Pearsall, *Words and Idioms: Studies in the English Language* (London: Constable, 1925)

—— *The English Language*, 3rd edn (Oxford: Oxford University Press, 1966)

Smock, John C., *The Greek Element in English Words*, ed. Percy W. Long (New York: Macmillan, 1931)

Southern, R. W., *Western Views of Islam in the Middle Ages* (Cambridge, Mass.: Harvard University Press, 1962)

Spadafora, David, *The Idea of Progress in Eighteenth-Century Britain* (New Haven: Yale University Press, 1990)

Spicer, Edward H., *Cycles of Conquest: The Impact of Spain, Mexico, and the United States on the Indians of the Southwest, 1533–1960* (Tucson: University of Arizona Press, 1962)

Stanley, K. P., *Slavonic Loanwords in English, Celtic and Pre-Classical Greek* (Oxford: privately published, 1985)

Stearns, Peter N., *Consumerism in World History*, 2nd edn (Abingdon: Routledge, 2006)

Steiner, George, *Language and Silence* (London: Faber, 1985)

—— *After Babel: Aspects of Language and Translation*, 3rd edn (Oxford: Oxford University Press, 1998)

Steinmetz, Sol, *Yiddish and English: The Story of Yiddish in America*, 2nd edn (Tuscaloosa: University of Alabama Press, 2001)

Stewart, Larry, *The Rise of Public Science: Rhetoric, Technology, and Natural Philosophy in Newtonian Britain, 1660–1750* (Cambridge: Cambridge University Press, 1992)

Stockwell, Robert, and Donka Minkova, *English Words: History and Structure* (Cambridge: Cambridge University Press, 2001)

Stoye, John, *English Travellers Abroad 1604–1667*, rev. edn (New Haven: Yale University Press, 1989)

Strang, Barbara M. H., *A History of English* (London: Routledge, 1989)

Strohm, Reinhard (ed.), *The Eighteenth-Century Diaspora of Italian Music and Musicians* (Turnhout: Brepols, 2001)

Strong, Roy, *Gloriana: The Portraits of Queen Elizabeth I* (London: Thames and Hudson, 1987)

—— *Feast: A History of Grand Eating* (London: Jonathan Cape, 2002)

Stubbs, Michael, 'German Loanwords and Cultural Stereotypes', *English Today* 14 (1998), 19–26

Sweet, Henry, *A History of English Sounds* (Oxford: Clarendon Press, 1888)

Tadié, Alexis, *Sterne's Whimsical Theatres of Language* (Aldershot: Ashgate, 2003)

Taha, Abdulwahid Dhanun, *The Muslim Conquest and Settlement of North Africa and Spain* (London: Routledge, 1989)

Tannen, Deborah, *Conversational Style: Analyzing Talk among Friends*, 2nd edn (New York: Oxford University Press, 2005)

Taylor, Charles, *Sources of the Self: The Making of the Modern Identity* (Cambridge: Cambridge University Press, 1989)

Taylor, Walt, *Arabic Words in English* (Oxford: Clarendon Press, 1933)

Tazón Salces, Juan E., and Isabel Carrera Suárez (eds.), *Post/Imperial Encounters: Anglo-Hispanic Cultural Relations* (Amsterdam: Rodopi, 2005)

Terry, Richard (ed.), *James Thomson: Essays for the Tercentenary* (Liverpool: Liverpool University Press, 2000)

Thiong'o, Ngugi wa, *Decolonising the Mind: The Politics of Language in African Literature* (London: James Currey, 1986)

Thomas, Hugh, *The Slave Trade: The History of the Atlantic Slave Trade: 1440–1870* (London: Picador, 1997)

—— *Rivers of Gold: The Rise of the Spanish Empire* (London: Weidenfeld & Nicolson, 2003)

Thomas, Keith, *Religion and the Decline of Magic* (London: Weidenfeld & Nicolson, 1971)

Thomason, Sarah G., *Language Contact* (Edinburgh: Edinburgh University Press, 2001)

—— (ed.), *Contact Languages: A Wider Perspective* (Amsterdam: John Benjamins, 1997)

Thomason, Sarah G., and Terrence Kaufman, *Language Contact, Creolization, and Genetic Linguistics* (Berkeley: University of California Press, 1988)

Thompson, C. J. S., *The Quacks of Old London* (London: Brentano, 1928)

Thorne, Tony, *Shoot the Puppy: A Survival Guide to the Curious Jargon of Modern Life* (London: Penguin, 2006)

Thumboo, Edwin (ed.), *The Three Circles of English: Language Specialists Talk about the English Language* (Singapore: UniPress, 2001)

Toomer, G. J., *Eastern Wisedome and Learning: The Study of Arabic in Seventeenth-Century England* (Oxford: Clarendon Press, 1996)

Traugott, Elizabeth Closs, *A History of English Syntax* (New York: Holt, Rinehart and Winston, 1972)

Trudgill, Peter, *Sociolinguistics* (London: Penguin, 2000)

Tsuchihashi, Shoko, 'History of Japanese Loanwords in English', in Alan K. Melby (ed.), *The Twenty-Third LACUS Forum 1996* (Chapel Hill, NC:

The Linguistic Association of Canada and the United States, 1997), 683–92

Tsuzaki, Stanley M., and Samuel H. Elbert, 'Hawaiian Loanwords in English', *General Linguistics* 9 (1969), 22–40

Tucker, Susie I., *Protean Shape: A Study in Eighteenth-Century Vocabulary and Usage* (London: Athlone, 1967)

—— (ed.), *English Examined* (Cambridge: Cambridge University Press, 1961)

Tulloch, Alexander, *Word Routes: Journeys through Etymology* (London: Peter Owen, 2005)

Tulloch, Graham, *The Language of Walter Scott* (London: André Deutsch, 1980)

Turner, Jack, *Spice: The History of a Temptation* (London: HarperCollins, 2004)

Turville-Petre, Thorlac, *England the Nation: Language, Literature, and National Identity, 1290–1340* (Oxford: Clarendon Press, 1996)

Tyerman, Christopher, *God's War: A New History of the Crusades* (London: Allen Lane, 2006)

Ungerer, Gustav, *Anglo-Spanish Relations in Tudor Literature* (Madrid: Clavileño, 1956)

Vallins, G. H., *The Making and Meaning of Words* (London: A. & C. Black, 1949)

Veale, Elspeth M., *The English Fur Trade in the Later Middle Ages*, 2nd edn (London: London Record Society, 2003)

Versteegh, Kees, *The Arabic Language* (Edinburgh: Edinburgh University Press, 2001)

Vickers, Brian, *In Defence of Rhetoric* (Oxford: Clarendon Press, 1989)

—— (ed.), *English Renaissance Literary Criticism* (Oxford: Clarendon Press, 1999)

Vickers, Brian, and Nancy S. Struever, *Rhetoric and the Pursuit of Truth: Language Change in the Seventeenth and Eighteenth Centuries* (Los Angeles: William Andrews Clark Memorial Library, 1985)

Wardhaugh, Ronald, *Languages in Competition: Dominance, Diversity, and Decline* (Oxford: Blackwell, 1987)

Wasserstein, David, *The Rise and Fall of the Party-Kings: Politics and Society in Islamic Spain 1002–1086* (Princeton: Princeton University Press, 1985)

Watt, W. Montgomery, *A History of Islamic Spain* (Edinburgh: Edinburgh University Press, 1965)

Weaver, Mike (ed.), *British Photography in the Nineteenth Century: The Fine Art Tradition* (Cambridge: Cambridge University Press, 1989)

Webby, Elizabeth (ed.), *Colonial Voices: Letters, Diaries, Journalism and Other Accounts of Nineteenth-Century Australia* (St Lucia: University of Queensland Press, 1989)

Webster, Jason, *Andalus: Unlocking the Secrets of Moorish Spain* (London: Doubleday, 2004)

Weekley, Ernest, *The Romance of Words* (London: John Murray, 1912)

Weinreich, Uriel, *Languages in Contact: Findings and Problems* (The Hague: Mouton, 1966)

Wells, H. G., *A Short History of the World* (London: Collins, 1934)

Weston, Stephen, *Remains of Arabic in the Spanish and Portuguese Languages* (London: Payne & Clark, 1810)

White, Richard, *The Middle Ground: Indians, Empires, and Republics in the Great Lakes Region, 1650–1815* (Cambridge: Cambridge University Press, 1991)

Wierzbicka, Anna, *English: Meaning and Culture* (Oxford: Oxford University Press, 2006)

Williams, Raymond, *Keywords: A Vocabulary of Culture and Society* (London: Fontana, 1988)

Winchester, Simon, *The Meaning of Everything: The Story of the Oxford English Dictionary* (Oxford: Oxford University Press, 2003)

Wogan-Browne, Jocelyn, Nicholas Watson, Andrew Taylor and Ruth Evans (eds.), *The Idea of the Vernacular: An Anthology of Middle English Literary Theory, 1280–1520* (Exeter: University of Exeter Press, 1999)

Wolfram, Walt, and Ben Ward (eds.), *American Voices: How Dialects Differ from Coast to Coast* (Oxford: Blackwell, 2006)

Wood, Frederick T., *An Outline History of the English Language*, 2nd edn (London: Macmillan, 1969)

Wright, J. Leitch, *Anglo-Spanish Rivalry in North America* (Athens, Ga.: University of Georgia Press, 1971)

Wright, Laura (ed.), *The Development of Standard English 1300–1800* (Cambridge: Cambridge University Press, 2000)

Yule, Henry, and A. C. Burnell, *Hobson-Jobson: Being A Glossary of Anglo-Indian Colloquial Words and Phrases, and of Kindred Terms* (London: John Murray, 1886)

General Index

Abbasid caliphs, 65, 72
'Abd al-Rahman, 65
'Abd al-Rahman III, 66
Abenaki languages, 151, 157–8
Aboriginals (Australia), 221–2
Abraham the Patriarch, 64
Acadia, 142
Acton, Eliza: *Modern Cookery for Private Families*, 291
Adair, James: *The History of the American Indians*, 251
Adams, Douglas: *The Hitch-Hiker's Guide to the Galaxy*, 343
Adams, John, 249–50
Adams, John Quincy, 250
Adams, William, 166
Addison, Joseph, 203, 206; *Remarks on Several Parts of Italy*, 215
Adelard of Bath, 68
adjectives: absorbed, 44
advertising, 317–18
Aelfric of Eynsham, 50
Africa: competition for colonies and exploitation, 299–300; travel in, 220; words from, 300–1
African languages, 301–2; in USA, 302–5
Afrikaans language, 223
Afro-Asiatic languages, 8
Aguilar, Jerónimo de, 100
Albuquerque, Afonso de, 226
Alcatraz (island, San Francisco Bay), 53
alchemy, 68
Alcock, Sir Rutherford: *The Capital of the Tycoon*, 169
Alford, Henry: *A Plea for the Queen's English*, 279, 283
Alfred, King of the West Saxons, 30–1, 144

Algonquian languages, 139, 148, 154, 157–8
Allen, Grant: *The European Tour*, 284
Allen, Woody, 259–60
Alsatians (dogs), 311
Altaic languages, 8
Amadas, Philip, 146
America (New World): culture clash, 153–5, 161, 164; English-Spanish rivalry in, 103, 141–3, 146; European exploration, trade and settlement, 98–101, 141–56, 159–61, 194, 231; Indians, 144, 153–5, 159–60, 163–4, 255; land problem, 247–8; native languages, 104–5, 139–41, 156–8, 160; pidgin English in, 162; polyglot languages, 163; products from, 139–40; resistance to British sovereignty, 247–9; Spanish place names, 142; wins independence from Britain, 241, 249; *see also* United States of America
American Civil War (1861–5), 262
American Philological Society, 249–50
American Speech (journal), 322
Ancren Riwle, 42, 76
Anderson, Benedict, 208; *Imagined Communities*, 338
Anglo-Norman dialect and society, 37–40, 42–3
Anglo-Saxon Chronicle, 27, 36
Anglo-Saxon language, 31, 34, 50–1, 110, 275–6
Anglo-Saxons: invade and settle in England, 24–5; words, 21–2
Ansgot of Burwell, 69
Antigua, 106
Apollinaire, Guillaume, 313
Arabian Nights, The, 219

Index of Words and Terms

The words and terms listed are those mentioned or defined in the text